William Chambers

The Scottish Church From the Earliest Times to 1881

to which is prefixed an historical sketch of St. Giles' Cathedral

William Chambers

The Scottish Church From the Earliest Times to 1881
to which is prefixed an historical sketch of St. Giles' Cathedral

ISBN/EAN: 9783337237455

Printed in Europe, USA, Canada, Australia, Japan

Cover: Foto ©Lupo / pixelio.de

More available books at **www.hansebooks.com**

ST GILES' CATHEDRAL CHURCH.—FROM THE WEST.
From *Old and New Edinburgh*; by permission of Messrs Cassell, Petter, & Galpin.

ST GILES' LECTURES

FIRST SERIES

THE SCOTTISH CHURCH

FROM THE EARLIEST TIMES TO 1881

TO WHICH IS PREFIXED AN

HISTORICAL SKETCH OF ST GILES' CATHEDRAL

BY W. CHAMBERS, LL.D.

W. & R. CHAMBERS
EDINBURGH AND LONDON
1881

Edinburgh:
Printed by W. & R. Chambers.

PREFATORY NOTE.

THE following Lectures were delivered in St Giles' Cathedral, Edinburgh, on the afternoons of Sundays in 1880-81, at an hour when there is usually no service in the church. They were also delivered in the Park Church, Glasgow. They were largely attended, and are now published in a volume, in the hope that they may prove interesting to many who had not the opportunity of hearing them. The Committee by whom the arrangements in connection with the course were made, desire to record their obligations to the Lecturers for their services, and in particular to Dr William Chambers for so appropriately prefixing to this volume his historical account of St Giles'. It is right also to state here that each Lecturer is only responsible for what is contained in his own Lecture.

St Giles', Edinburgh,
   May 1881.

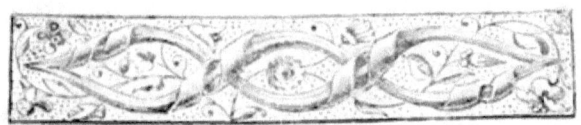

CONTENTS.

                                          PAGE

HISTORY OF ST GILES' CATHEDRAL CHURCH.
        By W. CHAMBERS, LL.D.................................ix

LECTURE   I.—Heathen Scotland to the Introduction of Christianity.
        By the Rev. JAMES CAMERON LEES, D.D., St Giles' Cathedral (High Kirk), Edinburgh............1

LECTURE   II.—Early Christian Scotland, 400 to 1093 A.D.
        By the Rev. A. K. H. BOYD, D.D., First Minister of St Andrews......................................33

LECTURE   III.—Mediæval Scotland, 1093 to 1513 A.D.
        By the Rev. JAMES CAMPBELL, D.D., Minister of Balmerino.......................................65

LECTURE   IV.—Pre-Reformation Scotland, 1513 to 1559 A.D.
        By the Rev. ALEXANDER F. MITCHELL, D.D., Professor of Ecclesiastical History in the University of St Andrews................................97

LECTURE   V.—The Reformation, 1559 to 1572 A.D.
        By the Rev. DONALD MACLEOD, D.D., Minister of the Park Church, Glasgow; and one of Her Majesty's Chaplains........................129

LECTURE   VI.—Episcopacy, Presbytery, and Puritanism in Scotland, 1572 to 1660 A.D.
        By the Rev. JOHN CUNNINGHAM, D.D., Minister of Crieff.................................161

LECTURE   VII.—The Covenant, 1660 to 1690 A.D.
        By the Rev. ROBERT FLINT, D.D., LL.D., Professor of Divinity in the University of Edinburgh..193

Contents.

PAGE

LECTURE VIII.—The Revolution Settlement, 1690 to 1707 A.D.
By the Rev. ROBERT HERBERT STORY, D.D., Minister of Rosneath..................225

LECTURE IX.—The Church of the Eighteenth Century, 1707 to 1800 A.D.
By the Very Rev. JOHN TULLOCH, D.D., LL.D., Principal of St Mary's College, St Andrews, and one of Her Majesty's Chaplains..................257

LECTURE X.—The Church of the Nineteenth Century to 1843.
By the Rev. A. H. CHARTERIS, D.D., Professor of Biblical Criticism in the University of Edinburgh; one of Her Majesty's Chaplains............289

LECTURE XI.—The Church from 1843 to 1881 A.D.
By the Rev. ARCHIBALD SCOTT, D.D., Minister of St George's Parish, Edinburgh....................321

LECTURE XII.—The Church of the Present Day: How far an outgrowth from the past, and an expression of the religious thought and life of Scotland.
By the Rev. JAMES MACGREGOR, D.D., Senior Minister of St Cuthbert's Parish, Edinburgh.......353

HISTORY

OF

ST GILES' CATHEDRAL CHURCH.

BY W. CHAMBERS, LL.D.

ST GILES' CATHEDRAL CHURCH, in which certain noted Lectures on the History of the Scottish Church have recently been delivered, is the original parish church of Edinburgh. Its history can be satisfactorily traced to the early part of the twelfth century, when it superseded a church of much older date. Occupying a prominent central situation on the south side of High Street, its lofty and beautiful spire is seen from a great distance. In the course of time St Giles' has undergone various changes as regards extent and style of architecture. Externally, it seems a modern Gothic structure, with choir, nave, and transepts; but it is in reality old, of various eras, shrouded in an indifferent and comparatively recent casing. No ecclesiastical edifice in Scotland has passed through so many vicissitudes, or has been so cruelly maltreated, and yet has so tenaciously survived as an interesting memorial of the past. Identified with many stirring events in Scottish history, St Giles' may claim a national character, while it invites attention as a relic of art from the twelfth to the fifteenth century. The present narrative aspires to be only a brief historical sketch of this venerable edifice, along with some account of the effort lately made towards its Restoration.

As early as 854, there was a church in Edinburgh included in the list of ecclesiastical establishments belonging to the Bishopric of Lindisfarne, or Holy Island; for at that time Lothian, in which Edinburgh is situated, formed a portion of the province of Northumbria. In 1020, Earl Eadulf ceded this part of his territory to Malcolm II., king of Scotland. Whether the church in Edinburgh was at first dedicated to St Giles, is uncertain. It might have been so, for St Giles lived in the sixth century. A word may be said regarding this personage.

St Giles, or Sanctus Egidius, as he is termed in Latin, was a renowned mediæval saint, of whom there are numerous legends. He is said to have been a native of Athens in Greece, and of royal lineage. From Greece he migrated to the south of France, and there in the neighbourhood of Nimes, retired to a cave to spend his life in devotion as a hermit. The only companion of his solitude was a hind, on the milk of which animal he partly subsisted. One day, this favourite was pursued by dogs and hunters, and fled to him for protection, which it readily received. Artists have usually painted St Giles in the garb of a monk, with a hind pierced by an arrow, either in his arms or at his feet. Lucas van Leyden, a Dutch painter (1494-1533), represents St Giles with an arrow piercing his hand while he is sheltering the hind; as shewn in the adjoining wood-cut. St Giles died in 541.

St Giles.

Numerous churches and other ecclesiastical establishments, also hospitals, were founded in his honour. In England alone there were a hundred and forty-six churches dedicated to St Giles. His fame having reached Edinburgh, he was adopted as the patron saint of the church, and a hind figures as one of the supporters in the city arms. For further particulars concerning 'Sanct Geill and his Hynde' we may refer to the late Mrs Jameson's tasteful work, *Sacred and Legendary Art*, 2 vols. 1857.

A new church was erected by Alexander I. about 1120. It consisted of a choir and nave, with small side aisles and central tower, built in a massive style of the early Norman period. From all that can be learned, it covered less space than is occupied by the present edifice. It might be described as a substantial parish church, bordered by the parish burying-ground on the south, the site of which ground is now occupied by the present Parliament Square. To this St Giles' Church there are various references in old charters and other records. It is mentioned in an Act of the reign of Robert the Bruce. The circumstance of the Castle of Edinburgh having been selected as a residence by David I., is understood to have furthered the endowment and decoration of St Giles'. In 1359, David II., by a charter under the great seal, 'confirmed to the chaplain officiating at the altar of St Katherine's Chapel, in the parish church of St Giles, all the lands of Upper Merchiston, the gift of Roger Hog, burgess of Edinburgh.'

The church at this early period had for its chief clergyman an official bearing the title of Vicar of St Giles, who possessed an interest in a farm called St Giles' Grange, or more familiarly Sant Geilies Grange, situated about a mile southwards, and which has communicated the name of The Grange to a pleasant suburb in this quarter. 'Under the date of 1243,' says Dr Laing, 'we find the name of a Perpetual Vicar of the Church of St Giles, Edinburgh; this circumstance, along with the earlier reference to its Grange, suggests that the church must have been attached to some religious house, and like the

Priory of Coldingham, it might for a time have remained subordinate to Lindisfarne.'[1]

St Giles' Church was destined to suffer an unexpected disaster, consequent on the unhappy wars between England and Scotland in the fourteenth century. Richard II., in retaliation for alleged wrongs, invaded Scotland with an English army in 1385. He laid waste the country, took possession of Edinburgh, and after an occupation of five days, committed the city to the flames. St Giles' Church perished in the conflagration. All that remained of the building were the entrance porch, a part of the choir and nave, with the heavier portions that formed the base of the spire.

Rallying after this grievous calamity, the town was rebuilt, and the civic authorities made a strenuous effort to reconstruct St Giles'. They entered into a contract for the building of 'five chapels' in St Giles', with pillars and vaulted roofs, covered with stone, and lighted with windows. The contract was dated 29th November 1387, in the reign of Robert II., and we may assume that the alteration was completed early in the fifteenth century. The part so executed was on the south-west of the nave. The style of art was lighter and more ornamental than that which had been destroyed. Afterwards, some side aisles were added through the munificence of pious individuals. These new parts are the fifteenth-century style of art, as will be afterwards more particularly described.

On entering the building by the doorway from the High Street, the visitor immediately ascends a flight of steps into the spacious lobby constructed out of the transept, and turning

---

[1] *The Charters of the Collegiate Church of St Giles, Edinburgh*, edited by the late Dr David Laing. Forming one of the Bannatyne Club books, presented by Sir George Clerk, Baronet, of Penicuick, and Alexander Maconochie Welwood of Meadowbank and Garvock, Esq., the work is remarkable as a monument of Dr Laing's literary industry and antiquarian knowledge.

to the left, enters the choir on the east. Here, he will have a good opportunity of observing the diversity in the architecture. The pillars first reached are of a plain style, octagonal in shape, with capitals to correspond. They bear no heraldic devices. These were the original pillars of 1120, which survived the fire of 1385. In the course of the repairs recently completed, when the colouring and dirt of centuries had been removed, the marks of fire were seen on these sturdy Norman pillars, now seven hundred years old, and seemingly indestructible.

In the north wall, under the second window from the east, there is a plain arched recess, the lower part being level like a shelf. An opinion has been entertained that the recess had formed part of a monument to Napier of Merchiston, inventor of logarithms. This opinion is untenable. Napier died in 1617, whereas the recess has been in the wall since the fifteenth century. The recess is the relic of a mural tomb or shrine; the level part having most likely been appropriated to a recumbent figure. Originally, the label moulding on the outer edge of the arch had been fringed with finely-carved crockets representing bunches of oak leaves, but these decorations were cut away at some unknown period, to suit the plastering of the wall! The marks of the crockets have been traced. This arched recess has been copied in forming a similar one on the outer side of the wall in 1829, which contains a tablet evidently removed from a monument of the Napier family. The tablet is no doubt that which marked the burial-place of the family on the south side of the church.

Passing beyond the old pillars, and approaching the great east window, we find two arches, one on each side, resting on pillars of an ornate fifteenth-century style. These pillars have bases of foliated sculpture, fluted shafts, and elaborately ornamented capitals. Two similar pillars are half sunk in the eastern gable. The date of these four pillars with their lofty arches is determined by their heraldic devices, more particularly the devices on the first pillar on the north, usually called the

St Giles' Cathedral Church.

King's Pillar. This pillar bears four distinct shields, which have reference to James II., king of Scotland, and his queen, Mary of Gueldres, to whom he was married in 1449. These two had a son, James, who was born in 1453. There is reason to believe that the shield facing the east, which we indicate as No. 1, was carved and set up in honour of that infant prince. It shews the Scottish lion, rampant, within a double tressure, with a label of three points, denoting an heir or prince. The shield No. 2, facing the north, impaled, and incomplete at the top, is that of the queen, Mary of Gueldres. The shield No. 3, facing the west, which has the lion, with a double tressure, also incomplete, is that of the king, James II. The shield No. 4, facing the south, has three fleurs-de-lis for France, with which country Scotland had intimate relations.

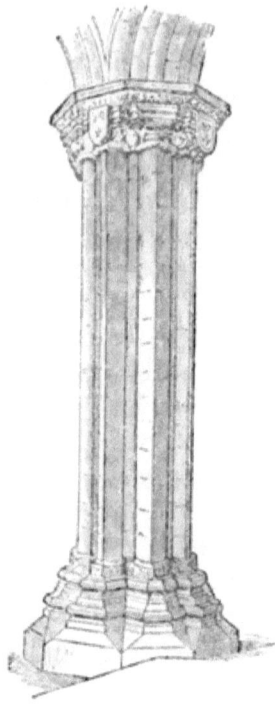

King's Pillar.

No. 1.

No. 2.

No. 3.

St Giles' Cathedral Church.

These royal shields, silent and unobtrusive, and which have happily weathered the civil and religious broils of four centuries, tell a tale of mingled joy and sorrow—the birth of an heir to the throne, the death of the king, shortly followed by the death of the heart-broken queen-mother. The happiness of James II. and his queen, Mary of Gueldres, was of short duration. James, who had been a kind patron of Edinburgh, was brought to it a lifeless corpse from Roxburgh, where he had been killed by the bursting of a cannon, 1460. Mary of Gueldres, his pious widow, a patroness of art, and foundress of the Trinity College Church, survived him only three years. Their son, the boy prince, who on the death of his father became James III., was murdered 1488. All things considered, we are inclined to think that the date of the pillar must be set down as 1460, the imperfection in the upper part of the king and queen's shields almost pointing to the tragical event of that year. The work of reconstructing the choir went on, however, for a number of years afterwards.

No. 4.

On the half-pillar on the north side of the great eastern window, there is a shield, No. 5, with three cranes gorged; such being the arms of Thomas Cranstoun, a burgess and chief magistrate of Edinburgh in 1439, and again in 1454, and who most likely had taken an active part in promoting the reconstruction of the church—the city improver of his day.

No. 5.

We now proceed to the pillar immediately opposite, on the south side of the choir. Here there are four shields, which we shall speak of separately. Shield No. 6, facing the east, bears the heads of three unicorns. Such were the Preston arms, set up in honour of William Preston of Gorton, to whom we shall immediately refer as an esteemed benefactor of the church. Shield No. 7, facing the north, bears three otter heads, being the arms of the family of Otterburn. The person specially

honoured was probably Nicholas de Otterburn, as he is styled in old writs, a learned official, much employed in public affairs, and who was Vicar of Edinburgh in 1455. He had a nephew,

John de Otterburn, who founded commemorative services in St Giles'. Shield No. 8, facing the west, bears the arms of Kennedy, being a chevron between three crosses crossleted. This is a finely executed shield, with a double tressure, and refers to a person of distinction. We have no doubt it was placed in honour of Lord James Kennedy, a grandson of Robert III., and Bishop of St Andrews, who rendered valuable assistance to the state on the sudden death of James II., and superintended the education of James III. He was designated by Mary of Gueldres, 'our dearest cousin,' and is remembered as one of the greatest men of his time—great from being a man of learning and peaceful counsels. No. 9, facing the south, is a plain shield, with a castle, the central figure in the city arms.

On the half-pillar next the great window on the south, is seen a shield, No. 10, bearing the arms of Napier of Merchiston, who was Lord Provost of Edinburgh in 1457. The shield, styled the Lennox shield, has a saltire, engrailed, cantoned with four rosettes, which the family of Napier assumed before the middle of the fifteenth century.

No. 10.

There are three other renderings of the city arms in the choir, but only one of them requires notice. It is a square carving in stone over the doorway to the small vestry, on the left on entering the church. As shewn in the accompanying wood-cut, an angel is represented holding a shield, No. 11, on which a castle is emblazoned. This we consider to be a very old rendering, as early as the twelfth or thirteenth century. The ornamental bordering is of unusual elegance. The existence of the stone was unknown until the recent Restoration of the choir, when by the removal of a stair, the doorway with its characteristic mouldings was disclosed.

No. 11.

Besides the extension of the choir eastwards about 1460, the walls surmounting the older pillars were raised and improved. Part of the original groining which sprang from the capitals of the pillars still remains, partially chiselled away. The clerestory groining is remarkable for its rich variety of bosses. On one of the bosses is seen the monogram i h s. Around another bosse is the following legend: Ave. gra. pla. Dus. tecu; such being an abbreviation of the words, *Ave Maria, gratia plena,*

dominus tecum (Hail Mary, full of mercy, the Lord be with thee). We present a wood-engraving of this remarkable bosse, which escaped erasure at the Reformation seemingly on account of its great height from the ground. It is to be viewed as an antiquarian curiosity. In the centre of some other bosses is an orifice from which had depended a chain or cord sustaining a lamp. One of these lamps had hung immediately in front of the high-altar. It is learned that the high-altar of the early church of 1120 was not shifted on the reconstruction of the choir. It remained in its original place, and there was an altar of lesser importance placed behind it, under the great eastern window.

The part of the choir between the southern row of pillars and the south wall was originally known as the Lady Aisle. Of this aisle Dr Laing says: 'In the charter dated 11th January 1454–5, it is narrated that William Preston of Gourton, then deceased, and interred in the Lady Aisle, had with diligent labour and great expense, and aided by a high and mighty prince, the king of France, and many other Lords of France, succeeded in obtaining possession of the arm-bone of St Giles; and this inestimable relique had been freely bequeathed by him "to oure mothir kirk of Sant Gell of Edynburgh withouten any condicion." The Provost, Bailies, and community of Edinburgh, deeply impressed with the importance of such an acquisition, voluntarily undertook to commence within one year, and to complete in the space of six or seven years, an aisle "furth fra our Lady Isle, where the said William lyis," to erect there his monument with a brass tablet, with his arms and an inscription, specifying his having brought that relique to Scotland; his arms also to be put in hewn stone in three other parts of the aisle; also an altar, and to endow a chaplain to sing for him from that time forth, and granting to his nearest relations the privilege of carrying the relique in all public processions.'

Such is the account given of William Preston of Gorton, whose arms, as above mentioned, consist of three heads of unicorns. The obligations in the charter were faithfully carried out. An aisle was constructed on the south, outside the Lady Aisle. For the purpose of bringing it into connection with the church, the wall, in which there were three windows, was removed; and instead of the windows, three arches were formed, with pillars corresponding to the fifteenth-century arches and pillars in the choir. A window was placed in the east end of the Preston Aisle, and three windows along its south side. The west end of the aisle opened into the south transept. The Preston Aisle was fifty-nine feet in length by twenty-four feet in breadth, by which addition the choir was considerably enlarged, while the architectural effect, enhanced by a vista of pillars, was materially improved. In the charter, a monument to Preston with a brass tablet is spoken of. It has long since disappeared.

About the time of the erection of the Preston Aisle, the ecclesiastical organisation of St Giles' underwent an important change. In 1466, a charter of James III., who was still a boy of thirteen years of age, converted the parish church of St Giles' into a collegiate foundation, with a chapter to consist of a Provost, Curate, sixteen Prebendaries, a Minister of the Choir, four Choristers, a Sacristan, and a Beadle; all of whom were exclusive of chaplains ministering at thirty-six altars throughout the establishment. Altogether, the number of ecclesiastics would not be less than a hundred, supported by particular endowments drawn from certain lands, oblations at the altars, and by donations of food and other articles. In the transition from the parochial to the collegiate organisation,

St Giles' Cathedral Church.

William Forbes, Perpetual Vicar, was advanced to the Provostship of the new foundation. At his decease he was succeeded by Gawin Douglas, third son of Archibald, fifth Earl of Angus, and who with poetical tastes did good service to Scottish literature, which was still in its infancy. His longest poem was the 'Palace of Honour,' an apologue addressed to James IV. The most remarkable of his productions was a translation of Virgil's *Æneid* into Scottish verse, being the first version of a Latin classic into any British tongue. Gawin Douglas was promoted to be Bishop of Dunkeld, and died in 1522.

From his literary attainments, as well as from his social position while Provost of St Giles', and as being a son of the Earl of Angus who was Lord Provost of Edinburgh, we are to imagine Gawin Douglas as a favourite guest at Holyrood, where James IV. held court with his queen, Margaret, both of whom were encouragers of learning and the useful arts. The art of printing had been introduced by Caxton into England about 1477; but it was unknown in Scotland until it was introduced by Walter Chepman and Andrew Myllar, under the auspices of James IV. and his Queen, in 1507. The types, apparatus, and workmen appear to have been brought from France. Chepman was the moneyed man in the concern, and from all we can learn, he was a person of extraordinary energy. The first work attempted was a collection of ancient ballads, forming a thin quarto volume in black-letter, which appeared in 1508. A fac-simile was reprinted in 1827, under the indefatigable editorship of Dr Laing; but copies of it are exceedingly scarce. Myllar finally gave up the printing profession, which continued to be carried on with success by Chepman, in an establishment at the head of Blackfriars Wynd, High Street. Walter Chepman became a wealthy and respected citizen, and with other properties, acquired the estate of Ewerland, near Cramond.

The wealth, piety, and munificence of Walter Chepman, the Scottish Caxton, were manifested in various endowments con-

St Giles' Cathedral Church.

nected with St Giles'. On the 21st August 1513, he founded a chapel, or aisle, in honour of his royal patron and kind friend, James IV., the Queen Margaret, and their offspring. In less than a month, James perished at Flodden, 9th of September 1513. This unfortunate event did not stop the completion of the aisle. It projected southwards from the Preston Aisle, one of the windows of which was appropriated to form the entrance, and was immediately east of the south transept, of which exteriorly it seemed an enlargement. This handsome aisle became a family chapel and place of burial. Walter Chepman died in 1532, and here in the vault below he was buried.

The disturbances consequent on the change of religious sentiment in Scotland, began to break out in Edinburgh in 1556, and came to a head in 1558, when a procession of clergy on the anniversary of St Giles, 1st September, was riotously dispersed by the populace. An effigy of the saint was torn in pieces; and soon afterwards, in the national convulsion, the clerical community of this ancient church disappear, while their means of livelihood are confiscated. As concerns the deplenishing of the church, the civic authorities interfered. By the help of sailors from Leith, with ropes and ladders, the altars were taken down, and cleared out. All the gold, silver, and other valuables were carefully catalogued and secured, as may be seen from existing town records. After being stripped of its silver mountings, the arm-bone of St Giles, which about a hundred years previously had been thought so very precious, was, as is alleged, thrown into the adjacent burying-ground. It was a clean sweep. Excepting perhaps a pulpit or a reading-desk, and a few benches, nothing was left in the old edifice.

Under the settlement of affairs at the Reformation, 1560, the collegiate character of St Giles' Church disappeared, and it resumed its original condition of a parish church. John Knox was constituted pastor, with a suitable stipend from the city funds. In starting afresh after the recent clearing out, the church must have presented an empty, desolate appearance. At that period there were no fixed pews. The seats were chairs or wooden stools, provided chiefly by worshippers for their own accommodation. The bulk of the people stood, and they would gladly stand for hours listening to their favourite preacher. John Knox often preached, it is said, to three thousand persons. The work he went through was immense. He preached twice on Sunday, and three times every other day of the week, besides attending to other clerical duties. His only assistant was a 'Reader.' The choir of the church with its extensions on the south we have referred to, formed the place of assemblage; but the voice of the preacher rang through the nave and far withdrawing aisles, which were left open, and formed a convenient lounge for the citizens. That is the picture we are to form of the interior of St Giles' Church immediately after the Reformation.

Knox occupied a conspicuous position when acting as chaplain at the funeral of the 'Good Regent,' James Stewart, Earl of Murray, who was assassinated at Linlithgow, 23d January 1569-70. The occasion is memorable in the history of St Giles'. 'Upon Tuesday, the 14th of February,' says M'Crie, 'the Regent's corpse was brought from the palace of Holyrood, and interred in the south aisle of the collegiate Church of St Giles'. Before the funeral, Knox preached a sermon on these words: "Blessed are the dead who die in the Lord." Three thousand persons were dissolved in tears before him while he described the Regent's virtues and bewailed his loss. Buchanan paid his tribute to the memory of the deceased by writing the inscription placed on his monument with that impressive simplicity and brevity which are dictated by genuine grief.'

The death of Murray led to a keen contest as to who should be Regent. The choice fell on the Earl of Lennox, paternal grandfather of the young king, James VI. This gave offence to Sir William Kirkaldy of Grange, who had hitherto belonged to the king's party, and as such was Governor of Edinburgh

St Giles' Cathedral Church.

Castle. He now changed sides, went over to the party of the exiled Mary Queen of Scots, and commenced a fierce civil war, in which he fortified Edinburgh, and on the 28th March 1571, placed a military force on the roof and steeple of St Giles' Church, to keep the citizens in awe. The craftsmen of the city, however, were not easily daunted. They broke into the church, and to bring matters to a crisis, proposed to pull down the pillars which sustained the roof. Alarmed for their safety, Kirkaldy's men, on the 4th June, began to make holes in the vaulted ceiling, from which they fired down with muskets on the crowd of assailants. Calderwood, the church historian, says they 'made the vaute like a riddle to shoot through;' which gives us an impressive idea of this warlike strife inside a church. Kirkaldy withdrew his forces in July 1572. Under the merciless Regency of Morton, he was hanged at the Cross of Edinburgh, 3d August 1573.

The roof of the church being duly repaired after the late hostile visitation, things went on in their usual quiet way. But St Giles' was destined to suffer infinitely more damage than anything that had been done to it by the operations of Kirkaldy of Grange—damage that has taken three centuries to remedy, and is not remedied yet. Previous to the death of Knox, the magistrates and council began to section the church of St Giles' into separate divisions. This proceeding was commenced within ten years after the Reformation. The first division we hear of was for the Tolbooth Church, situated at the south-west corner of the edifice. 'On Sunday, 21st September 1572,' says M'Crie, 'Knox began to preach in the Tolbooth Church, which had been fitted up for him.' On Sunday, 9th November following, he preached in the same place at the installation of Lawson, his colleague and successor. 'After the sermon,' adds M'Crie, 'he removed with the audience to the larger church,' that is, to the choir, which luckily escaped sectionising. This was John Knox's last sermon. On quitting the church leaning feebly on his staff, he was attended down the street to his house by his audience, to take the last look of their pastor. He died on the 24th November, and was buried in the churchyard of St Giles'. The spot cannot now be identified. It is near to the equestrian statue of Charles II. in the Parliament Square.

In May 1590, James VI. and his young queen, Anne of Denmark, ceremoniously visited St Giles' Church, when there were thanksgivings for their marriage and safe arrival in Scotland. The choir, which was fitted up for the occasion, henceforth became a place of public worship for the king and queen, and from this time we begin to hear of a royal pew, or 'loft,' with seats for the officers of state, the judges, and the magistrates of the city. James sometimes went to St Giles' for the purpose of delivering public orations; he did so on Sunday, 3d April 1603, to bid farewell to the citizens on his departure to take possession of the throne of England.

We now arrive at the important events in the history of St Giles', consequent on the introduction of Episcopacy into Scotland by James VI., and his successor, Charles I., in the early part of the seventeenth century. Hitherto, Edinburgh and the adjacent district of country had ecclesiastically pertained to the diocese of St Andrews. Charles I. now resolved to form Edinburgh into a bishopric, by royal charter, and to constitute St Giles' the cathedral of the new diocese. The proceedings of Charles on this occasion are faithfully detailed by Maitland in his valuable *History of Edinburgh* (1 vol. folio 1754). The facts of the historian are drawn from city records, and are narrated as follows:

'King Charles I., by his Charter of the 29th September, *anno* 1633, having founded a Bishopric in Edinburgh, appointed for its Diocess all Parts besouth the Frith of Forth, belonging to the Arch-bishopric of St Andrews, in the County of Edinburgh, Constabulary of Haddington, and Shires of Linlithgow, Stirling, and Berwick, and Bailiwick of Lauderdale; with all the Rights, Powers and Privileges of a distinct Bishopric or

Diocess, in as full and ample a Manner as any other Bishopric in Scotland; and appointed St Giles's Church in Edinburgh for its Cathedral; with all the Rights, Liberties and Immunities belonging to a Cathedral Church, and this new Erection to be denominated the Bishopric and Diocess of Edinburgh; to have and injoy all the Honours, Dignities, Privileges, Authorities and Jurisdictions, with all the Liberties and Immunities injoyed or possessed by any Diocesan or Bishop within Scotland, and to be a Suffragan to the Arch-bishop of St Andrews.

'And the Bishop to have Precedence of all other Scottish Suffragans in Parliament, Councils and publick Conventions, immediately after the Archbishop of Glasgow. And, for the good Government of this new Bishopric, by the Charter of Foundation, it was to consist of a Bishop, a Dean, and twelve Prebendaries, to whom and their Successors the King granted the Churches of St Giles, Grayfriars, Trinity College, and that of the South-east Parish in Edinburgh, with those of Holyroodhouse, Dalkeith, Dunbar, Haddington and Tranent in the County of East Lothian; Liberton in Mid-Lothian; Falkirk in Linlithgowshire; and that of the Town of Stirling in Stirlingshire, with their appurtenancies; with a Power to the Bishop to have a Seal like other Bishops, to transact his Affairs with; besides, another Seal for him and the Chapter, for transacting the Business of the Chapter, to be called the Seal of the Chapter of the Bishopric of Edinburgh: And to prepare St Giles's Church for the Reception of the new Establishment, the King sent a Letter to the Common Council of Edinburgh; of which the following is a Copy:

"CHARLES R.

"Trustie and weill belovit we greit you weill.

"Wheras of oure Princelie Motive and Zeale for the Advancement and Government of the Churche of that oure Kingdome, we have, by the Advice of the chiefest of oure Clergie, thairof, erected at our Chairges, a Bishopric of new, to be callit the Bishopric of Edinburgh, whairby none of your

St Giles' Cathedral Church.

Priviledges or Liberties ar anie wayes to be infringed, but rather preservit and increased: And wheras to that Purpose, it is verie expedient, that Saint Geille's Church (designed by us to be the Cathedral Churche of that Bishopric) be ordered, as is decent and fitt for a Churche of that Eminencie, and according to the first Intentioun of the Erectors and Founders thairof; which was to be keiped conforme to the Largeness and Conspecuitie of the Foundatioun and Fabrick: and not to be indirectlie parcelled and disjoinit by Wallis and Partitiounes, as now it is, without anie Warrant from anie of oure Royall Predecessoures.

"Oure Pleasure is, that with all Diligence, you caus raze to the Ground the East-wall of the said Churche; and sick-lyke, that you caus raze to the Ground the Wester-wall therin, betwixt this and Lambas insewing; at or before which Tyme, we require you to caus finish the new Tolbuith, to the effect it may be for the Use of oure Churche and uther Judicatories and Commissiounes, as the Tyme and Occasioun shall require. We bid you fairweill, from oure Court at Whitehall, the 11th October 1633."

'In the year 1636, the Town Council, on the tenth Day of February, ordered one of the Bailiffs, and one of the Clerks of Edinburgh, to desire James Hanna, the Dean of St Giles's Church, to repair to Durham in the Northern Part of England, to take a Draught of the Choir of the Cathedral Church in that City, in order to fit up and beautify the Inside of the Choir of St Giles's Church after the same Manner.'

'Surely,' continues Maitland, 'never was the Church Hierarchy by a Bishop of so short Duration, as this of Edinburgh; for it was erected in the year 1633, and subverted *anno* 1639, by the Abolishment of Episcopacy in Scotland, both by the Parliament and General Assembly.'

The change in the ecclesiastical organisation of the country might in time have been accepted and tolerated but for the indiscreet zeal of Charles I., who, by an imperious command, ordered the English Service-book to be read in every parish church. This brought matters to a crisis. The day on which the Book of Common Prayer was first attempted to be read in the Church of St Giles', was Sunday, the 23d of July 1637. The officiating clergyman was the dean, Mr James Hanna; and on his intimating that the collect for the day was that of the seventh Sunday after Trinity, a popular outbreak took place, and a strenuous female, uttering some violent reproaches, threw the stool on which she had been seated at the dean's head. The bishop from the pulpit endeavoured to calm the uproar which ensued, but in vain. The magistrates also made efforts to allay the disturbance, but failed to do so; and they were obliged to clear out the multitude by main force. The uproar of course arose from dislike to the Anglican liturgical service, which differed from the Book of Common Order hitherto in use in St Giles', as indeed throughout the country generally since the time of John Knox. There seems to have been a notion among the rioters that Popery was about to be introduced along with the Anglican service, and hence the intensity of the excitement. As regards the Collect for the day which had been intimated by Dean Hanna, there is nothing in it to give offence to any one.[1]

The scene of this extraordinary tumult was in the south transept, or the middle church, as some historians call it; the choir, at the time, being in course of preparation for the cathedral service. The spot on which Dean Hanna was assailed was, as nearly as can be defined, near the base of the stone arch on the left on entering the transept from the Preston Aisle. Consequent on the tumult and the circumstances that ensued, St Giles' ceased to have the status of a

[1] The collect is as follows: 'Lord of all power and might, who art the author and giver of all good things, graft in our hearts the love of Thy name, increase in us true religion, nourish us with all goodness, and of Thy great mercy keep us in the same; through Jesus Christ our Lord. Amen.'

cathedral; but this was resumed on the establishment of Episcopacy in 1662. It remained so until the Revolution of 1688, when Alexander Rose, the last of the race of prelates, was ejected. The building is still popularly designated St Giles' Cathedral, or St Giles' Cathedral Church. As is seen by our quotation from Maitland, Charles I. commanded the removal of the cross partition walls in St Giles', in order to adapt it as a cathedral—which was in effect a kind of restoration. On the resumption of Presbytery in 1639, the walls were speedily re-erected, and the building relapsed into the unsightly condition it has retained until our times.

Spottiswood, in his *History of the Church and State of Scotland* (1655), gives the following list of the bishops of Edinburgh until his time:

'The first Bishop of Edinburgh was William Forbes, Doctour of Divinity, one of the Preachers in Edinburgh (before, Principal of the Marischal Colledge of Aberdene), a very worthy Person. His Works shew him to have been a man of vast Learning and sound Judgment. He sate but a little while, and died at Edinburgh about the year 1634.

'Upon his death, David Lindsay, Bishop of Briechen, was translated to Edinburgh. The Fury of the rude Multitude fell heavy upon this Bishop, even to the manifest danger and hazard of his Life, upon the first reading of the Book of Common Prayer in Edinburgh, July 1637. He was thrust out, with the rest of the Bishops, by the Covenanters, 1638.

'George Wishart, Doctour of Divinity, was, upon the Restitution of the Hierarchy, *anno* 1662, promoted to the Bishopric of Edinburgh. This worthy man was, 1638, Preacher at Leith, and for his Loyalty had very hard measure from the Covenanters, being thrice plundered of all that he had, and thrice imprisoned. But being delivered from thence, he went beyond Sea with the Marquess of Montrose, 1646.[1] He died at

---

[1] Wishart was a man of considerable erudition. He wrote a memoir of Montrose in Latin, which has been translated into English.

St Giles' Cathedral Church.

Edinburgh, *anno* 1670. Upon his death, Alexander Young, Archdeacon of Saint Andrews, was preferred to the Bishopric of Edinburgh.'

To proceed with our account of the Cathedral Church. It has been stated that the ancient entrance porch was among the parts spared at the conflagration of 1385. This porch was on the north side of the building, and was connected with the nave, so as to form a convenient entrance from the public thoroughfare. The arch, rounded in form, was of an ornate Norman style. The archivolt in several divisions exhibited figures of animals and grotesque heads, along with crenellated and chevron mouldings. By an act of barbarism, this ancient arch, a precious relic of the twelfth century, was taken down and utterly destroyed in the course of some repairs on the building in 1797 or 1798. Fortunately, before its removal, a representation of it was taken by an artist, of which an engraved copy appears as a frontispiece to Dr Laing's laborious work on St Giles'.

Besides the choir, which formed the parish church, there was at first only the Tolbooth Church, as a subordinate place of worship in St Giles'. It derived its name from including a portion of the Tolbooth, or Town-House of Edinburgh; the original meaning of the word Tolbooth being a place for receiving rents or duties imposed by the civic authority. Even before it became a church, this part of St Giles', along with a portion of the nave, had been used for meetings of Parliament. In the upper part of an adjoining building now removed were the Justiciary Court-room, and the Council Chamber for the city, connected with which was the Town Clerk's office. The Tolbooth Church, it must be understood, had no connection with the tall dark building in High Street, latterly known as the Tolbooth, or common prison, which was removed within our recollection.

In the palmiest of its pre-Reformation days, St Giles' had from these circumstances a certain dash of secularism. It was in some sort a public Exchange. From the want of a place of resort for men of business, the church offered a means of meeting to persons who had to enter into or discharge contracts, to pay accounts, and so forth; for which miscellaneous purposes the high-altar of St Giles', or some other altar in the church, was a stipulated place of meeting. In such acts of desecration, one is in a small way reminded of the practices which were so objectionable in the Temple of Jerusalem.

After the clearance at the Reformation, St Giles' was still haunted for business transactions. The south transept became the favourite resort; and when the Earl of Murray's monumental tomb was set up, it answered as well as the old high-altar at which to make bargains or to discharge obligations. From a popular belief that Duke Humphry of Gloucester, youngest son of Henry IV., was buried in Old St Paul's, there arose the jocularity that persons who strolled about in St Paul's for want of a dinner, were said to dine with Duke Humphry. A similar pleasantry prevailed concerning the tomb of the Earl of Murray. Sempill, a Scottish poet, refers in verse to the spot as a convenient lounge for impecunious and hungry idlers. One of them with sad internal commotion pathetically says:

> 'I dined with saints and gentlemen,
> Ev'n sweet Saint Giles and the Earl of Murray.'

Long before the Reformation, St Giles' had been freely used as a place of interment. In most cases the interments were in graves below the floor, as was not unusual in old edifices of this kind, and is still in a limited way the case in Westminster Abbey. Persons of distinction were entombed in one or more vaults in the southern aisles. Here the Earl of Murray, as above related, was interred in 1569-70; his representative is the present Earl of Moray. The next individual of note laid in this quarter was John Stewart, fourth Earl of Athole, Lord High Chancellor of Scotland, who died in 1579. His title was conferred on John Murray, Earl of Tullibardine, who married his grand-daughter. The representative of the family is now the Duke of Athole. A third distinguished person entombed near the spot was John Graham, third Earl of Montrose, High Treasurer, and afterwards Lord High Chancellor. On the accession of James VI. to the throne of England, he was appointed Viceroy in Scotland, presided at the parliament at Perth, 1606, and died in 1608.

The grandson of this last-mentioned personage was James Graham, fifth Earl, created Marquis of Montrose, who distinguished himself as a military commander in the cause of Royalty during the Civil War. Montrose's history is well known. Captured and brought into Edinburgh, he was condemned, and executed 21st May 1650. His body was dismembered. His limbs were sent to different parts of Scotland, his head was stuck on a pike on the Tolbooth or common prison, while his body was buried in the Boroughmuir under the gallows. Here, two days afterwards, some adventurous spirits in the cavalier interest contrived to take away the heart of Montrose, and convey it to Margaret, Lady Napier, wife of Alexander, first Baron Napier of Merchiston, and daughter of John, fourth Earl of Montrose. The heart of the great hero being duly embalmed, was inclosed in a gold casket for careful preservation. There is a portrait of Lady Napier with this interesting object by her side. It was the destiny of the casket to undergo a number of romantic adventures at home and abroad, which we have not space to relate. Ultimately, when in the custody of a person in France, it disappeared during the revolutionary troubles, and has not since been heard of.

After the Restoration, the scattered remains of Montrose were collected with tokens of respect, and deposited in the Abbey of Holyrood. Thence they were brought by a solemn funeral procession, at which the magistrates of Edinburgh assisted, and entombed in St Giles', 14th May 1661. The ordinary belief is that his tomb was in the vault underneath the aisle of Walter Chepman. Mark Napier, in his Memoirs of Montrose, states that he was interred in the vault of his grandfather, the Viceroy of Scotland. Our own opinion coincides with the ordinary belief, that Montrose was buried in the vault beneath Chepman's Aisle, where possibly his grandfather had been previously interred. The descendant and representative of the great Marquis is the present Duke of Montrose. The burial of persons of note in St Giles' did not cease till past the middle of the eighteenth century.

In process of time, as Edinburgh grew in population, more parish churches were required. The proper course would have been to build new churches within the parishes to which they nominally pertained. Instead of this, a plan was adopted of utilising St Giles', by cutting it up into sections, and calling each section a parish church. Hence, the grouping of churches for different congregations in this unfortunate building. A number of offices for secular affairs got edged out, and the general condition of the building was more spiritualised, though in a manner not a little repugnant to the senses. At the middle of the eighteenth century, the list of churches in the edifice stood as follows. The Choir or High Church in the east. The Tolbooth Church in the south-west. The Old Church in the middle and part of the south side. The Little Kirk, or Haddo's Hole, in the north-west. Such name was familiarly given to it in consequence of an apartment above it having served as a prison to Sir John Gordon of Haddo in 1644, previous to his trial and execution. The allocation into these several places of worship left two portions of the building undisposed of. These were the Preston Aisle, which was used for meetings of various kinds; and the dark central space under the spire with the north transept. This last-mentioned portion was finally fitted up as the Police Office. We remember St Giles' in this condition in 1818.

If neither comfortable nor pleasing to the eye, the various churches grouped in St Giles', possessed in former times an amusing difference of character. 'The High Church,' says the author of the *Traditions of Edinburgh*, 'had a sort of dignified aristocratic character, approaching somewhat to prelacy, and was frequented only by sound church-and-state men, who did not care so much for the sermon, as for the gratification of sitting in the same place with His Majesty's Lords of Council and Session, and the magistrates of Edinburgh, and who desired to be thought men of sufficient liberality and taste to appreciate the prelections of Blair. The Old Church, in the centre of the whole, was frequented by people who wished to have a sermon of good divinity, about three-quarters of an hour long, and who did not care for the darkness and dreariness of their temple. The Tolbooth Church was the peculiar resort of a set of rigid Calvinists from the Lawnmarket and head of the Bow, termed the Towbuith Whigs, who loved nothing but extempore evangelical sermons, and would have considered it sufficient to bring the house down about their ears, if the precentor had ceased, for one verse, the old hillside fashion of reciting the lines of the psalm before singing them. Dr Webster was long one of the clergymen of this church, and deservedly admired as a pulpit orator.'

As a type of the places of worship inconveniently crammed within the nave and aisles of St Giles' a hundred years ago, the Tolbooth Church became a subject for the satirical pencil of Kay, a notable Edinburgh caricaturist. His sketch is entitled 'A Sleepy Congregation.' The idea is conveyed of a church of limited dimensions, with a gallery, crowded in all its parts without an inch of free space, for even the passages were provided with benches, which were let down on hinges for sitters as soon as the clergyman entered the pulpit. Two of the heavy stone pillars that were never designed for a church of this kind, stood inconveniently among the seats. One of them was so directly in front of the preacher, as to cause some difficulty in managing the voice.

Mr W. Browne, who is a surviving member of the congregation as it existed in the early years of the present century, has written *Notes and Recollections of the Tolbooth Church*, printed for private circulation, in which is given an amusing account of the state of affairs. We have space for only one particular. 'The walls were dingy in colour, and seemed to have dust resting on every available place. On one occasion, when either Mr Whitefield or Mr Simeon preached, he noticed a large cobweb which had been placed at a height above the reach of ordinary besoms, and remarked: "That is the very cobweb which I saw when I was last here"—so many years ago.'

What will strike every one with surprise is, that throughout the eighteenth and the early years of the present century there should have been such a general acquiescence in the odious internal condition of St Giles' Church. Arnot, the historian of Edinburgh, who wrote in 1779, and gives a list of the congregations which then confusedly nestled in the building, and must have suffered from the mass of decaying mortality beneath their feet, has not a word of remonstrance on the subject. There were accomplished men of letters in Edinburgh at a still later period who are now reckoned among national luminaries. Not one of them, as far as we know, imagined there was anything wrong in the unseemly state of St Giles'. They complacently saw before their eyes an edifice abounding in some of the finest specimens of fifteenth-century architecture degraded into a collection of wretchedly fetid caverns. Lord Cockburn, in his *Memorials*, makes some remarks on the total want of taste which prevailed at this period. Speaking of St Giles', he says: 'It might have been painted scarlet without any one objecting.' But the same dearth of taste as regards ecclesiastical structures and the comfort of congregations prevailed almost everywhere until very recent times.

Before it was despoiled, 1558-60, the vast interior of this grand old building, with its many pillars and groined roof, must have presented an appearance resembling that of a spacious English cathedral of the olden class. The policy of cutting up and apportioning this handsome structure, on which so much architectural taste had been lavished, is inexcusable. The transformation was effected in a manner altogether tasteless. No care was taken to preserve the finer parts of the architecture. Rows of fluted pillars sustaining lofty arches were merged in the rough walls which were erected lengthwise and crosswise to form the several compartments. The foliated bases and capitals of pillars were hacked without mercy to bring them within the required line. Characteristic heads carved among the foliage were knocked off with hammers, and are found buried in rubbish beneath the floor. The erection of galleries in all the churches caused further dilapidation, as cavities for beams to sustain these galleries were dug in the sides of several pillars.

Under the authority of successive acts of Parliament, the municipality of Edinburgh was extended, and churches for new parochial divisions were erected in various places at considerable cost to the civic corporation. Nevertheless, St Giles' remained in the condition now described until the first quarter of the nineteenth century. There were still four churches and a Police Office under one roof. In 1817, by the removal of small shops or 'krames,' which had long existed within the niches of the ancient building, the exterior had a very ragged appearance. Public sentiment was roused. Something must be done to renovate St Giles'. For several years the subject received the consideration of the Town Council, and a plan for remodelling the church, by Mr Burn, architect, was at length adopted. The cost was to be about £20,000, towards which sum government contributed £12,600. Dr Laing gives a ground-plan of St Giles', before it was touched by Mr Burn; but by a singular mistake of the artist in framing the scale of feet, the building is represented as being about two hundred and fifty feet long. Its true measurement was a hundred and ninety-six feet in length within the walls, by a hundred and thirty feet wide at the transepts. The ground-plan we subsequently offer shews its present dimensions and character.

Burn commenced his operations in 1829, and the work was finished in 1833. On the south-west, two of the 'five chapels' or aisles, contracted for in 1387, were removed, in order to widen the entrance to the Parliament Square from the west, while other alterations were made in this part of the building. On the north side of the nave, two chapels were removed. One of these, which adjoined the transept, says Daniel Wilson, in his interesting *Memorials of Edinburgh*, 'was the only portion of the church in which any of the coloured glass remained, with which, doubtless, most of its windows were anciently filled. Its chief ornament consisted of an elephant, very well executed; underneath which were the crown and hammer, the armorial bearings of the Incorporation of Hammermen, inclosed within a wreath. From these insignia, we may infer that this was St Elois' Chapel, at the altar of which, according to the traditions of the burgh, the craftsmen of Edinburgh, who had followed Allan, Lord High Steward of Scotland, to the Holy Land, and aided in the recovery of the Holy Sepulchre from the Infidels, dedicated the famous *Blue Blanket*, or Banner of the Holy Ghost.'

Burn changed the entire exterior aspect of St Giles', the spire alone excepted. Picturesque roofs and pinnacles disappeared. The whole fabric was new cased in a bald style of art. As concerns the interior, the sectioning into parts was only modified. The choir remained as before. The southern section of the building was fitted up for meetings of the General Assembly; but this appropriation not being found satisfactory, the Old Church in a few years afterwards was here located. The best thing done was the expulsion of the Police Office. For it, was substituted a capacious lobby, common to the several congregations, who all entered by one outer door in the north transept. There was an alteration of names. The Tolbooth Church and Haddo's Hole statutorily vanish. The nave is occupied by the New North Church, now designated West St Giles'. It is much to be deplored that, in the course of this remodelling, the fine old monument of the Earl of Murray, which had once been a place of resort, and was otherwise interesting, was destroyed. 'It might have been thought,' says Dr Laing, 'that such a monument would have escaped any sacrilegious hand; but to the disgrace of our civic authorities, it was allowed to be demolished, and the brass tablet, containing engraved figures of Justice and Faith, with an inscription written by Buchanan, was removed.' The brass tablet, however, was not lost. As after described, it is to be seen on the modern monument of the Earl of Murray.

So much for Mr Burn's improvements on St Giles'. By some, they are thought to have made matters worse rather than better. We are certainly left to lament that from whatever cause, he took away or mutilated much that can never be replaced.

As regards the spire of St Giles', it dates from the twelfth century, in which, as has been stated, the church was built. Of this antiquity, there is sufficient evidence in the massive substructure of octagonal pillars resembling those in the choir. Injured by the fire in 1385, the spire participated in the renovations that took place in the fifteenth century. It is known to have been repaired without detriment to its original character in 1648. And so it remains till the present day. As will be seen from our frontispiece, it is a handsome square structure, terminating in decorated arches and pinnacles, producing the appearance of an imperial crown, and rising to a height of one hundred and sixty-one feet. Billings, in his pictorial work on the Baronial and Ecclesiastical Antiquities of Scotland, observes that of all the Scottish instances of this species of structure, the spire of St Giles' 'is at once the richest and the finest.' As far as we are aware, there is nothing to compare to it in point of effect in modern ecclesiastical architecture.

St Giles' Cathedral Church.

The bells in St Giles' formed an important part of the ancient establishment, but nowhere do we find any accurate description of their number and character. There was, it seems, a bell called the St Mary Bell, which was sold with certain church furnishings in 1563. There still remained the 'great bell of St Giles',' as it was called, which dated from 1460. This bell is spoken of by historians and poets as being that which was rung on special occasions, such as summoning the inhabitants to assemble in military array for defence of the city after the battle of Flodden. In one of Dunbar's satirical poems, a dwarfish personage is introduced saying to the citizens of Edinburgh:

> 'I come among you hier to dwell:
> Fra sound of Sanct Gelis' bell
> Nevir think I to flie.'

Referring to this famous old bell, Dr Laing says it 'was cast in Flanders, and is described as having the arms of Guelderland upon different parts of it, together with figures of the Virgin and Child, and other devices, and had the following Latin inscription: "HONORABILES VIRI BURGENSES VILLAE DE EDINBURGH, IN SCOTIA, HANC CAMPANUM, FIERI FECERUNT ANNO DNI: M.CCCC.LVV. [1460]. JOHS ET WILHELMUS HOERHEN ME FECERUNT; IPSAMQUE CAMPANUM GYELIS VOCARI VOLUERUNT. DEFUNCTOS PLANGO: VIVOS VOCO: FULMINA FRANGO." *Translation*—"The honourable men, burgesses of the City of Edinburgh in Scotland, caused this bell to be made in the year of our Lord one thousand four hundred and sixty. Johannes and Wilhelm Hoerhen made me. And they determined that I should be called Giles's bell. I mourn the dead: I summon the living: I disperse the thunder."'

The latter part of the inscription reminds us of ancient usages and beliefs. 'I mourn the dead:' This refers to the solemn sounds of the passing-bell on the occasion of a death. 'I summon the living:' This signifies the call to church, or to arms. 'I disperse the thunder:' Here is a testimony to the old superstitious belief that thunder could be dispersed by making loud noises with bells. A similar inscription is found on many old church bells of large dimension. It would seem that the strange notion that bells are efficacious in dispelling storms is by no means extinct. In 1852, the Bishop of Malta ordered the church bells to be rung for an hour to allay a gale! The old great bell in St Giles' unfortunately suffered a fracture, and had to be recast, thereby obliterating the inscription. Its modern representative was founded by C. & G. Mears, London, in 1844. It measures four feet six inches and a half in diameter across the mouth, and three feet four inches in height. It is this bell on which the hours are struck, and which is rung for public worship. Near it are two lesser bells, or chimes, for striking the quarters, respectively dated 1700 and 1728.

Situated in a dark corner, which is inapproachable without the light of a lantern, we find an old bell, indeed the only genuine old bell in St Giles', one that has survived from pre-Reformation times. Although complete in its machinery for suspension and ringing, it can no longer ring, for by some accident it has lost its clapper, and there it hangs mute, unnoticed, covered with the dust of ages, a waif wrecked on the stream of time. Shapely in appearance, it measures seventeen and a half inches in diameter, and thirteen and a half inches high. According to tradition, it is the original Vesper Bell of St Giles'; though possibly, judging from the pious inscription it bears, it may have been the Ave or Pardon Bell tolled before and after divine service, to call the worshippers to a preparatory prayer

Vesper Bell.

to the Virgin before engaging in the solemnity, and an invocation for pardon at its close. The following is the inscription in black-letter capitals: 'O MATER DEI, MEMENTO MEI : ANNO D.M.IIII.' *Translation*—'O Mother of God, Remember me, 1504.' This unfortunate bell, a curious archæological relic, might be rung as of old were it provided with a new clapper. Perhaps the present notice will lead to its resuscitation for some useful purpose.

Besides these bells, there are twenty-three small music-bells, and a set of eight chime-bells; making the entire number of thirty-five bells in St. Giles'. The music-bells are fitted on a frame in the open or upper part of the spire, and played by hand. These music-bells, which date from 1698, were until lately played daily by a lady of advanced age, and are by no means in a good condition. A thorough repair is requisite. The eight chime-bells were erected so lately as 1858. From the imperfect nature of the mechanism and the unsuitableness of the place where they are situated, they are not played.

FIRST RESTORATION—THE CHOIR.

When the present writer had the honour of being Lord Provost of Edinburgh, 1865–69, he had often occasion to attend public worship officially with the other magistrates and members of the Town Council. The place of assemblage was the choir, or High Church, in the front of a gallery on the north side, having the King's Pillar on the right, and the half-pillar with the Cranston arms on the left. In the corresponding gallery on the south were the seats for the judges of the Supreme Court of Scotland. Intermediately, in front of the great east window, was a huge dark pulpit, with a lofty sounding-board; such being the pulpit from which Hugh Blair delivered his admired sermons a hundred years ago. At the west end of the church was the gallery with the Royal pew. It was a homely structure, consisting of a light blue-painted canopy, supported by four wooden posts, over a few tawdry arm-chairs. The technical name of this kind of structure is a baldachino. No one could look at it without being reminded of a four-post bed. Here George IV. was seated when he attended church on his visit to Edinburgh, 1822; and here for two Sundays every year sat the Lord High Commissioner to the General Assembly. The whole seating of the church was of plain deal. A cram of old-fashioned pews from floor to ceiling. There was a distressing mustiness in the atmosphere, which ventilation failed to remedy, for the ground was saturated with human remains, which ought long since to have been removed as dangerous to the health of the congregation.

There and then, when seated in that elevated gallery close to the carved shields of the boy-prince James and his mother the inestimable Mary of Gueldres, we conceived the idea of attempting a restoration of the building, and producing a church in which the people of Edinburgh might feel some pride—a shrine fitting for the devotional exercises of Royalty. It would cost some trouble. But what good thing is ever done without trouble? There would be no harm in trying. Shortly afterwards, we called a meeting to take the matter into consideration, 1st November 1867. The scheme was generally approved; but difficulties interposed, and it was laid aside until 1871, when with recovered health and more leisure, it could be prosecuted with a better chance of success. At a public meeting, a Restoration Committee was appointed, with the present writer as Chairman. The object of the Committee was eventually to restore as far as practicable the whole interior of St Giles', but to effect this step by step as circumstances permitted, and to confine operations in the first place to the choir. The idea of thoroughly restoring an edifice so damaged by alterations was hopeless. But much might be done. The intervening walls could be taken down. The pillars might be mended. With patience, the outlay of money, and the concurrence of the civic and ecclesiastical authorities, the building could probably be brought back to something like what it had been in long-past times.

The efforts to gather subscriptions for the object in view were at first as successful as could be expected. Her Majesty the Queen headed the list with a subscription of £200. The

Pulpit.

Town Council of Edinburgh, the Royal College of Surgeons, the Societies of High Constables of Edinburgh and Holyrood, and the Society of Writers to the Signet, were among the public bodies who subscribed liberally. Nobility and gentry of all denominations contributed to facilitate an object which was felt to be national in its character. In June 1872, when the amount of subscriptions had reached £2000, the Committee, with consent of the authorities concerned, felt warranted in commencing the work. The galleries which disfigured the building were wholly removed, thereby developing the fine old pillars, which were mended with stone to resemble the original. The baldachino and the furniture of the Royal pew were taken away as crown property. All the pews and the pulpit were removed. When everything was gone, the floor was trenched

Royal Pew.

throughout to a depth of several feet. No vaults were discovered, but there was an immense quantity of human remains, which were taken away in hearses and decently buried in a churchyard. A number of large grave-stones were removed that had served as pavement, on which the professional devices of craftsmen were rudely carved. These slabs were put at the disposal of a corporate body representing the craftsmen of Edinburgh. As a final act, the walls and groined roof of the choir were cleaned, and rendered pleasing to the eye.

St Giles' Cathedral Church.

Under direction of Mr W. Hay, architect, the process of renewal according to a style of art appropriate to the character of the building, was now commenced. The passages were laid with Minton tiles bearing antique Scottish devices. A pulpit of Caen stone exquisitely carved by Mr John Rhind, an Edinburgh sculptor, was placed against the pillar on the south side nearest the east window. All the seatings were of oak. The seats for the magistrates and for the judges bore appropriate carvings. The Royal pew at the west end, raised above the general level, was a highly ornamental structure, with suitable devices. The cost of the Government pews, including the Royal pew, and pews for the judges, alone cost the sum of £1586, towards which the Treasury made a grant of £500. Altogether the cost of restoring the choir, as now described, including the expense of heating by hot-water pipes, amounted to £4490. The subscriptions actually realised fell short of that sum to the extent of £650, which deficiency was made good by the Chairman and several members of Committee. Thus the transaction was closed. Throughout the whole affair, the Committee owed much to the valuable services of Mr Lindsay Mackersy, W.S., Honorary Secretary.

According to appointment, the choir, in its renovated form, was opened for public worship on Sunday, 9th March 1873. From the interest taken in the alterations, the church was crowded. At the morning and afternoon services, the judges, magistrates, and various public bodies attended in official costume, the spectacle being peculiarly effective. Latterly, under the incumbency of the Rev. Dr J. Cameron Lees, the church in its improved form has become one of the most attractive in Edinburgh.

SECOND RESTORATION—SOUTHERN AISLES.

The choir in its restored state was still disfigured by three arches, with blocked-up windows, forming the partition of separation from the Preston Aisle on the south. To render the restoration of the choir complete, it was obvious that there must be a second step in the alterations which should embrace the Preston Aisle and other aisles on the south. These southern aisles, as already mentioned, had been used as the Old Church, with windows overlooking the Parliament Square. By an Act of Parliament, 1870, the Old Church parish was dropped out of the statutory parochial divisions. The church was occupied for a time on a temporary footing, and at length disused. Such was the state of matters in 1878, and an opportunity was afforded of clearing out and restoring this portion of the building. Plans prepared by Mr W. Hay were submitted to the Ecclesiastical Commissioners and the Magistrates and Council, and received their approval, but only under a guarantee given by the present writer that he would be responsible for the expense of the undertaking. In giving this guarantee, we resolved to relieve the Restoration Committee of any further trouble and responsibility, and to proceed entirely on our own judgment and at our own cost.

In February 1879, this second restoration was begun by removing the galleries and pews, taking down partitions and staircases, lifting the floor, and opening up the aisles. By the lifting of the floor, a hideous scene of decaying mortal remains was disclosed, as afterwards referred to. In the soil of the Preston Aisle, about a foot below the surface, was found a leaden coffin, bearing the inscription, 'Brigadier Richart Cunyngham, Died 26th Nov. 1697, Ætat 47.' The Brigadier had probably been a connection of the Dick-Cunynghams, baronets, of Prestonfield. The coffin was in an imperfect condition, and has been left undisturbed.

After a general clearance, the first operations were directed to the aisle founded by Chepman. This once elegant aisle was in a revolting condition. The arch between it and the Preston Aisle had been built up. It was divided into three floors. The lower floor was degraded into a coal-cellar; in the middle floor was placed a tall iron stove for heating by means of flues; and the upper floor formed an apartment, with a fireplace and other accessories. The floors were taken down, and the whole interior cleared out. It was expected that the remains of Montrose would be found in the coal-cellar; but nothing of the kind was discovered.

When the thick wall that blocked up Chepman's Aisle was removed, the fluted jambs sustaining the arch were found to be much shattered. About twelve feet of the jambs on each side had been cut away. A chimney had been run right through the key-stone of the arch. The whole was repaired by inserting fresh hewn stone to resemble the original. The result has been a handsome arch in the style of the fifteenth century. The lath and plaster which had been stuck on the walls of the aisle were wholly removed, and the original character of the stone-work was developed. A floor supported on brick arches over a vault completed the restoration.

Chepman's Arms.

Emblem of St John.

In the process of cleaning the groined roof of the aisle, which was begrimed with dirt and coatings of whitewash, a finely carved bosse was discovered, bearing the arms of Walter Chepman impaled with those of his first wife, who had belonged to the family of Kerkettill. The joint arms are on a shield held up by an angel. A corbel which terminated the groining of the roof on the west side bore a pious symbolic carving. It represents an eagle, the emblem of St John the Evangelist; the eagle, in sacred and legendary art, being the symbol of the highest inspiration, because St John soared upwards to the contemplation of the divine nature of the Saviour. Close to the eagle is a scroll legend in black-letter, *In principio*, being the two words with which the gospel of St John in the Latin Vulgate begins—*In principio erat Verbum*: 'In the beginning was the Word.' According to the charter of endowment, Chepman dedicated the altar in his chapel to St John, whom he had probably adopted as his patron saint. The disclosing of these old carvings adds to the archæological interest in St Giles'.

It has been thought that as something is due to Chepman for his service to literature, it would only be becoming to set up a tablet with a suitable inscription to his memory. A brass tablet accordingly is now placed in his aisle, bearing the following inscription: 'TO THE MEMORY OF WALTER CHEPMAN, DESIGNATED THE SCOTTISH CAXTON, WHO UNDER THE AUSPICES OF JAMES IV. AND HIS QUEEN MARGARET, INTRODUCED THE ART OF PRINTING INTO SCOTLAND 1507; FOUNDED THIS AISLE IN HONOUR OF THE KING AND QUEEN AND THEIR FAMILY 1513; AND DIED IN 1532; THIS TABLET IS GRATEFULLY INSCRIBED BY WILLIAM CHAMBERS, LL.D., 1879.'

As a final improvement, the floor of the Chepman Aisle was laid with encaustic tiles with suitable devices; while its entrance was closed by a fanciful grille in hammered iron after the antique, with a gate. This tasteful work of art was executed by Skidmore of Coventry.

The work on the Preston Aisle was the heaviest and lengthiest part of the second restoration, for the aisle, which abounds in artistic beauty, was in a sadly deteriorated condition. The finest carvings had been recklessly broken. The groined roof, on which immense labour had been expended by the artificers employed by the magistrates of Edinburgh, in the fifteenth century, was so thickly covered with whitewash as to have no appearance of stone-work. The first thing done was to clear the groined roof of its odious coatings. Months were occupied on these repairs; the result being that the roof of the Preston Aisle, as now developed, perhaps excels in beauty of groining anything of the kind in Great Britain, or in the world. When the roof was finished, repairs were made on the pillars which stand in a row betwixt the aisle and the choir. These pillars had been seriously damaged by the insertion of beams and otherwise. In some instances, the bases and the ornamental capitals, with portions of the shafts, had to be replaced. The wall part of the aisle was also repaired in a manner as nearly as possible to resemble the original. A small arched recess or shrine, which possibly had some connection with the altar set up to commemorate Preston's munificence, was opened up in a creditable style of art. It is not improbable that the recess had been used as the shrine for the arm-bone of St Giles. Last of all, the floor was laid with encaustic tiles; and the aisle, fitted up with ornamental oak pews, now affords accommodation for eighty sitters in addition to those in the choir. The visitor is invited to look upon the Preston Aisle as a wonderfully fine specimen of fifteenth-century art. It is the gem of St Giles'.

In several parts of the Preston Aisle will be seen the arms of Preston, three unicorns' heads, formerly referred to. On one of the bosses on the groined ceiling is a shield bearing the arms of Sir Patrick Hepburn of Hales, a trusted statesman, who was created a peer with the title of Lord Hales, 1456. His grandson, Patrick, third Lord Hales, was created Earl of Bothwell by James IV. His great-grandson was the infamous Earl of Bothwell in the reign of Mary Queen of Scots. The arms on the shield consist of two chevrons, each shewing two lions plucking at a rose.

Before quitting the Preston Aisle, visitors will observe a baptismal font in Caen stone, executed by Mr Rhind, an Edinburgh sculptor, on the model of Thorwaldsen's famous work at Copenhagen. It represents an angel wreathed with flowers, kneeling on one knee, holding a large shell, intended to contain the water for baptism. The font, which has been

Baptismal Font.

presented to the church through the munificence of a friend of the Rev. Dr J. C. Lees, is at present placed in the Chepman Aisle.

In repairing the Preston Aisle, it was found necessary to build up the huge doorway in the eastern gable which had been introduced by Mr Burn; on which account, some alterations will require to be executed in this quarter on the exterior of the building. This will form one of the closing acts in the work of restoration.

Previous to the repairs being executed, the spacious stone arch which spans the west end of the Preston Aisle and divides it from the south transept, was, as a result of Mr Burn's proceedings, found to be fancifully clothed in stucco. This stucco coating, which was wholly out of place, was removed, and the simple beauty of the original stone arch has been brought into view. Meanwhile, until the restorations are completed, the arch is closed by a wooden screen, the door in which admits to the south transept and aisles.

The work of restoring the south transept and adjoining aisles on the west, involved some excavations by which it was hoped a discovery would be made of certain burial vaults that were believed to be in this part of the building. A search for these vaults took place on the 10th April 1879. Only one vault was discovered. It was that in which the Regent Murray was entombed, 1569-70. It was situated close to the west wall of the transept. The vault measured about sixteen feet in length from north to south, and was little more than three feet in width. The search was to a certain extent disappointing. No coffin of any kind could be found containing the remains of the illustrious Regent. Three leaden coffins were discovered in a bad condition. The most perfect of these coffins, as seen by the arms and inscriptions, contained the remains of Alexander, fourth Earl of Galloway, born 1670, died 1690. The other two leaden coffins bore neither arms nor inscriptions, and seemed to pertain to persons of a slight figure. It was the opinion of a medical authority present that the remains in one of the coffins were those of a young man; and that the remains in the other were those of a female of middle age. Near these leaden coffins was found a leaden plate, bearing the engraved inscription, 'Francis Steuart, Esq., died at Rheims in France, 7th Octr. 1768, Aged 22.' The plate had probably been on a wooden coffin that lay in fragments, and in which the leaden coffin had been placed. The Francis Steuart referred to was a son of the Hon. Francis Steuart of Pittendriech, third son of Francis, sixth Earl of Moray.

The burial vault of the Regent, as we learn by a notice in the Edinburgh newspapers, under date January 23, 1830, had been disturbed by the alterations then going on, and this may account for the absence of any coffin recognisable as that pertaining to the Regent. To all appearance, a coffin of some kind had been emptied of its contents, which now lay as a confused heap of bones. A skull picked up from the heap was viewed with much respect. Massive, and with craniological indications of mental superiority, it was believed to be that of the Regent Murray. Such, at least, was our own belief, and that of one or two other persons present. The skull was carefully replaced in the heap of bones alongside the leaden coffins, and to prevent intrusion, the vault was immediately built up.

Attempts to find other burial vaults during the excavations of 1879 proved unsuccessful. On lifting the pavement of the crypt eastward from the Regent's tomb, within the compass of the south transept, there were seen two inclosures formed by dwarf walls that might at one time have been vaults. They were found to contain rubbish, with which a few bones of no significance were mingled. The inclosure farthest to the east was probably the vault in which the body of John, fourth Earl of Athole, was entombed, 1579.

Descending by a few steps to the vault underneath the Chepman Aisle, a rigorous search was now made for the remains of the Marquis of Montrose, which had undoubtedly been entombed here in 1661. No coffin nor any fragment of coffin could be discovered. Only some small pieces of bones were picked up from the soil. These we placed in a small box, and reverently deposited it on the spot where the remains of the Marquis had been ceremoniously interred. The floor of the vault was then laid with pavement, in which was inserted a marble tablet with the inscription, 'MONTROSE, 1661.'

The trenchings and the excavations that took place over the floor of the southern aisles need not be particularly described. The quantity of bones dug up was immense, the whole probably amounting to five tons in weight. After examination, the whole were placed in boxes, and removed to Greyfriars Churchyard for interment. It was unsatisfactory to be driven to the conclusion, that the vaults in which a number of distinguished personages were entombed, had been rifled of the leaden coffins with their contents in the course of alterations on this part of the building, 1829 to 1833, at which time the ancient and historical tomb of the Earl of Murray was destroyed. The strange disappearance of the remains of illustrious dead from the spot in which by history and tradition they are said to have been placed, raises a painful reflection regarding the indifference to matters of this kind so lately as half a century ago. Only in 1879 did the disappearance of the remains become known.

In the general work of restoration a commencement was made by repairing the walls of that part of the transept which projects like a recess southwards. The walls were in an exceedingly bad condition, and to render them at all seemly, portions were renewed with hewn stone. The floor, raised two steps to give head-room in the crypt beneath, was laid with encaustic tiles. A spacious stone arch, the fellow of that adjoining the Preston Aisle, was stripped of its coating of stucco, and by sundry mendings brought back to its original condition.

The south transept, as now cleared out and embellished, forms a recess of about twenty feet square. How it is to be ultimately appropriated we know not. The design we permitted ourselves to entertain was that it might perhaps be adopted as the place of ceremonial assemblage by the Knights of the ancient and noble Order of the Thistle, and where their banners may be suitably displayed; for since the Chapel Royal of Holyrood fell into ruin, they have possessed no place of installation, or where their banners could be shewn.

In the course of his operations, Mr Burn had made very considerable havoc with the southern aisles. As already mentioned, he had taken away two of these aisles with the view of improving the access to the Parliament Square, and he reduced a remaining aisle to half its dimensions. This reduced aisle he transformed into a staircase in connection with certain galleries of modern construction. The aisle in its original state contained an ancient tomb, so called in Dr Laing's plan of the building; and to accommodate this relic of art, he removed it eastwards into the wall of the staircase. Obviously, anything like a restoration of this part of St Giles' was impossible. The site of the missing aisles was part of the public street. All that could be attempted was to bring this portion of the building into harmony with the Preston 'Aisle, the south transept, and other restored parts of the structure. The diminished aisle with its flight of stairs was cleared out. The wall that inclosed it was taken down, and the open space on its north side was arched with stone;

Mural Tomb or Shrine.

so that when completed, there was a distinct new aisle as a recess on the south, and which is now entitled the Moray Aisle.

This Moray Aisle, forming an acquisition to the church, has

been enriched in various ways. In the first place, the mural tomb already spoken of was removed from its mean and obscure position, and so elevated on the wall beneath the window as to be in front of the spectator. The tomb is in reality a shrine dedicated to the Passion of Christ, and the wonder is how it escaped the wrath of the iconoclasts in 1558. Like the similar but less ornamental relic of art in the choir, it consists of a Gothic arch over a level slab, on which possibly there had been a recumbent figure. The emblematic carvings are profuse and minute. They embody

Old Tablet, Earl of Moray's Tomb.

representations of the crown of thorns, the scourge, the nails, the sponge, and other symbols of the Passion. In the removal of the shrine, much care was taken to preserve the delicate carvings, and accordingly this beautiful work of art may be said to be very much what it was in the early part of the sixteenth century.

Allusion has been made to a modern monument of the Regent Murray. It stood on the west side of the south transept. Its site, on examination, having been found to be insecure, it was removed to the west side of the Moray Aisle, which was in all respects more appropriate. The monument is a wall structure of Caen stone, erected by the late John, twelfth Earl of Moray, 1864. Near the top is placed the old brass tablet, which, besides the arms of the Regent, with the motto, SALUS PER CHRISTUM (Salvation through Christ), bears on one side an emblematic figure of Faith or Piety, with the words, PIETAS SINE VINDICE LUGET (Piety mourns without defence); on the other side a figure of Justice, with the words, JUS EXARMATUM EST (Justice has been disarmed). Date beneath, '23 JANUARII 1569,' followed by Buchanan's admired Latin inscription: 'JACOBO STOVARTO MORAVIÆ COMITI SCOTIÆ PROREGI VIRO ÆTATIS SUÆ LONGE OPTIMO AB INIMICIS OMNIS MEMORIÆ DETERRIMIS EX INSIDIIS EXTINCTO CEU PATRI COMMUNI PATRIA MŒRENS POSUIT.' Translation: 'To James Stewart, Earl of Moray, Regent of Scotland, a man by far the noblest of his time, barbarously slain by enemies, the vilest in history; his country mourning has raised this monument as to a common father.'

Adorned with this modern monument, the Moray Aisle has been further enriched by filling the window with stained glass, representing an important historical circumstance, the assassination of the Regent, and the impressive scene at his interment in St Giles', with John Knox preaching the funeral sermon. At the base of the window there is the inscription: 'In memory of the Regent Murray; presented by George Stuart, fourteenth Earl of Moray, 1881.'

Closed in by a hammered iron grille by Skidmore of Coventry, and laid with encaustic tiles, the Moray Aisle may be considered the vestibule to the crypt and vaults already mentioned. The crypt, gained by a flight of steps and doorway, is lighted by small Gothic windows to the south.

The work on the south aisles generally was completed by mending the walls with hewn stone, and by laying pavement in small squares. A new doorway, designed principally as an entrance to the Judges of the Court of Session, but to be used also as a door of exit, was constructed in the western gable. The jambs and lintel of the doorway are in the fifteenth-century style of Gothic art. The carvings over the door embrace a royal Scottish shield bearing a lion rampant, environed by the inscription: 'ROBERTUS SECUNDUS REX SCOTORUM, 1387,' such being the date of construction of the southern aisles by the community of Edinburgh.

One of the objects aimed at by the restoration of the building has been to give an opportunity for the erection of monuments to distinguished Scotchmen of past and future times. Wherefore, St Giles', in a sense, might be viewed as the Westminster Abbey of Scotland. In furtherance of this idea the wall of the south aisles underneath the two windows has been prepared and set aside for marble tablets commemorative of eminent Scottish poets, beginning with the royal poet James I., author of *Peebles to the Play*, Sir David Lindsay of the Mount, and others. When the nave is opened up, portions of the walls will be appropriated to monuments for distinguished historians, statesmen, divines, lawyers, soldiers, scientific discoverers, &c.

The restoration of the southern aisles was concluded, so far as practicable, early in 1880. From first to last the work of alteration had gone on very quietly, but not unnoticed. Great numbers of visitors flocked to the building to see what had been effected, and we are glad to say that, including observations by the press, the feelings expressed were those of general approval. No prejudice had been roused. There were no objections on the score of removing galleries prized by traditions and recollections. A building that had for the last three hundred years been unsightly and repulsive, was now seen to possess claims to artistic beauty, and to have become an object of considerable attraction. Conducted purely on the grounds of restoring a grand, old, historical monument, our operations, happily, did not incur anything like the hostile criticism that might have ensued had they been promoted for denominational purposes.

Pleasing as the results may be, we have never disguised the fact that the operations did not come up to what is called a thorough restoration. Clearly, in the circumstances, such could not have been attempted. We had no authority to deal with the exterior of the building, nor to restore the ancient entrance porches. Mr Burn, as already shewn, had removed much that could not be brought back. Besides, in executing the restorations in the choir, the Committee in charge of the works were embarrassed by a short-coming of funds. At the same time, let it be understood that there has not on any occasion been a pedantic attempt to imitate what was old without sufficient grounds for doing so. The restoration of ancient structures must be accepted under reasonable qualifications. Modern science and art, if only for sanitary reasons, must be taken into account. Accordingly, in all that concerns ventilation, heating, and artificial lighting, the restored St Giles' will be found immensely in advance of its prototype of the fifteenth century. For example, in the matter of artificial lighting, we could not have left the congregation to depend on candles and oil-lamps according to the fashion of by-gone ages. Nor could we have neglected artificial lighting altogether, as has been the case with certain restored ecclesiastical buildings; for that would have been to render the church valueless for public worship in the evening, and on Sunday afternoons during the winter. A compromise in the sentiment of restoration was therefore indispensable. The whole church is lighted with gas by means of brass standards from the floor, with ornamentation after the antique, the effect being very satisfactory.

St Giles' Cathedral Church.

THIRD RESTORATIONS—THE NAVE.

When the restoration of the southern aisles was completed to the extent described, there still remained to be put in decent order the whole of the nave, the Albany Aisle, with other aisles on the north side of the building, and the whole of the transepts except the portion on the south. Such will be the third step in the restoration of St Giles'. And to give an idea of its extent, we refer to the following wood-engraving, which represents a ground-plan of the building as it now exists.

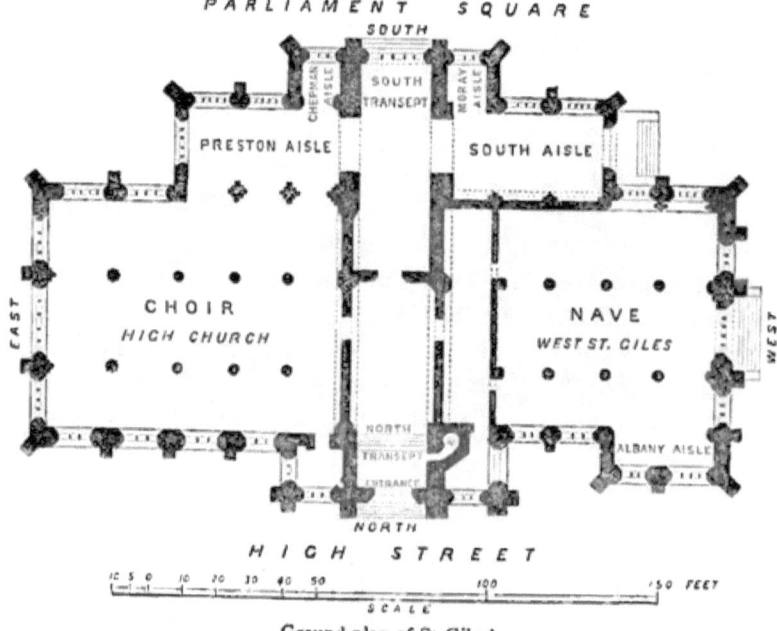

Ground-plan of St Giles'.

From this plan it appears that the whole edifice measures a hundred and ninety-six feet in length within the walls, by a hundred and twenty-five feet across at the transepts. The nave may be spoken of as about a hundred and twenty feet square in measurement. To effect a restoration of the nave and parts adjoining will involve some heavy work, with a number of delicate details connected with the arches and pillars. Certain stone and lime walls which block up arches will need to be removed in order to open up the entire structure from end to end and from side to side, and thus, if possible, to bring back the interior of St Giles' to that architectural state it possessed

Albany Aisle.

previous to the Reformation. The bulky partition walls here alluded to are principally those which had been removed by command of Charles I. on the institution of the bishopric of Edinburgh in 1633, but which were re-erected on the resumption of Presbytery in 1639.

St Giles' Cathedral Church.

One of the contemplated improvements is the opening up of the western doorway of the nave (at present shut up), and constituting it the principal entrance to the entire cathedral church. Some characteristic architectural ornaments will be executed over this the great doorway, to express the date of the building, 1120, in the reign of Alexander I., king of Scots; for strange to say, if any such date was ever sculptured on the walls of St Giles', it has long since been obliterated.

Among the lesser but essential improvements will be the restoration of the stone arches and pillars in the nave and its aisles. The painted stucco ornaments which form the capitals of the pillars will be replaced by carved ornaments in stone. A special satisfaction will be experienced in restoring the Albany Aisle to its original artistic beauty. This interesting aisle, hitherto shrouded from observation, occupies the north-west corner of the nave, and causes a projection into High Street.

In the centre of this beautiful aisle stands a light and graceful pillar, which sustains a groined roof all around. The aisle takes its name from Robert, Duke of Albany, the second son of King Robert II., who, having been intrusted with the custody of his nephew, David, Duke of Rothesay, cruelly starved him to death in a dungeon in the castle of Falkland, 1402. Though escaping punishment for this atrocious act, Albany and his prime associate, Archibald, fourth Earl of Douglas, seem to have been haunted with a consciousness of guilt. According to the practice of the period, they are said to have built the Albany Aisle in St Giles' as a chapel expiatory of their crime. The capital of the pillar in the centre of the aisle bears two shields. One of these bears the Albany arms, in which the Scottish lion is quartered with the fess chequé of the Stewarts. The other shield has the heart and other armorial bearings of the Earl of Douglas. This remarkably fine pillar, surviving as a memento of a terrible tragedy in Scottish history, and of the remorse which it occasioned, has for ages been almost buried and lost amidst the gallery and seating of the church.

The steps taken towards proceeding with these concluding restorations may now be adverted to. The nave being occupied as a church by the congregation of West St Giles', nothing could be done in the way of alteration until another church was provided. This was a matter in which we could not possibly interfere; the solution of the difficulty lay with the public authorities, whom we addressed on the subject. Early in 1879, while still engaged in restoring the southern aisles, we made an offer to the Town Council and Magistrates, and to the Edinburgh Ecclesiastical Commissioners, to restore the whole of this ancient, historical building at our own expense, provided we were put in possession of the nave not later than Whitsunday 1880. The offer was entertained by the citizens, and steps were taken to secure its acceptance.

The first thing done was to procure an Act of Parliament to sanction the removal of the West St Giles' Congregation. By this Act, obtained in August 1879, and which received the approval and support of government, it was stipulated that upon payment of £10,500, the West St Giles' Congregation should be bound within a year to vacate the building and provide a new church for themselves. Thereafter a Committee, under the auspices of the Lord Provost, Magistrates, and Council, was formed to collect subscriptions for the purpose of fulfilling the condition of the Act of Parliament.

As the proposed restoration was national and unsectarian in its object, the Committee was composed of gentlemen of different religious denominations, and through their instrumentality, as at Whitsunday 1880, contributions to the amount of about £5200 were received or promised. There being, however, still a large deficiency, we, on being applied to, were induced to extend the time for collection for one year—namely, till Whitsunday 1881—but only on condition that if the full sum

St Giles' Cathedral Church.

required should not be then collected, our offer was to be withdrawn, and was not to be renewed. Along with this offer a proviso was made which it is necessary to explain.

There being no official authorities in the form of a dean and chapter who could regulate various matters connected with St Giles' in its complete state, we made a stipulation to the following effect—That to facilitate arrangements for the erection of monuments to distinguished Scotchmen in St Giles', to regulate the introduction of coloured-glass windows, and for managing the interior of the building after the restoration, the Town Council would be expected to concur in appointing a committee of management, which we had formerly specified for these special purposes.

It would be needless to recount the various steps taken, some of them under difficulties, to gather subscriptions sufficient to complete the required sum of £10,500. It is enough to say, that the Magistrates and Council, assisted by Mr Robert Adam, City Chamberlain, made a decisive effort for the purpose in February 1881, and were materially aided by an auxiliary Committee composed of leading members of the Church of Scotland, headed by the Right Hon. Lord Justice-General. These united efforts were so successful that there can be no doubt the entire sum required will be obtained by the appointed date, Whitsunday 1881. As regards the stipulation above hinted at, it has been amply secured by the united consent of the Magistrates and Council, the Kirk Session of the High Church, and the Ecclesiastical Commissioners. All that remains to be done is to pay the money; after which it will be a mere matter of adjustment when the West St Giles' Congregation will remove, and the work of restoring the nave be allowed to proceed. One thing is certain: when the keys of this part of the building are put into our hands, not an hour will be lost in commencing this important undertaking. And may God grant us life and health to carry it to a successful issue.

W. C.

St Giles' Cathedral Church.

POSTSCRIPT.—As preparatory to the required restorations in the nave and transepts, Messrs Hay and Henderson, architects, have made a thorough survey of St Giles', embracing measurements of every part, with the view of making a set of plans, elevations, and sections of the whole fabric. By this means specifications will be drawn up of what is intended to be done, or what may be properly attempted. Such specifications will be submitted to the public authorities.

NOTE.

THE MEMORIAL WINDOWS IN ST GILES'.

St Giles' is known to have possessed at least some coloured-glass windows previous to the Reformation, but they had long since disappeared; and their re-introduction required a new and special effort. The windows throughout the Church are uniform in style and character. They may be described as a blending of the perpendicular and flamboyant styles of Gothic art, with cross bars or transoms dividing the windows into upper and lower lights. They are therefore well adapted for admitting illustrations of different subjects, or of a subject in several parts. On the occasion of restoring the choir, the introduction of stained glass received the attention of a special Committee. The design entertained was that all the windows in the choir should refer exclusively to events in the history of Our Lord. This plan has accordingly been carried out, by the gifts of private individuals. The subject of each window was prescribed. No heraldic or extraneous devices were allowed to be introduced. But the donors were permitted to place a memorial inscription of a single line at the foot of their respective windows. The result has been entirely satisfactory.

The following is a list of the Memorial Windows in the choir. They were executed by James Ballantine and Son, under the honorary supervision of R. Herdman, R.S.A.

First Window.—The Nativity, and Holy Family; the Presentation in the Temple; The Flight into Egypt; Disputation with the Doctors.—In memory of James Monteith, merchant, Calcutta, died 1872. Erected by his brother, Duncan Monteith, 1874.

St Giles' Cathedral Church.

Second Window.—The Baptism of Our Lord; the Calling of the Apostles; First Miracle at Cana; Healing the Sick.—In memory of James Richardson, merchant, Edinburgh, died 1868. Erected by his widow and children, 1875.

Third Window.—Christ blessing little Children; Stilling of the Tempest; Healing of the Blind; Raising of Lazarus.—In memory of Dean of Guild Lorimer, who perished when rendering help at a fire in 1865. Erected by his widow and family.

Fourth Window.—Christ's Entry into Jerusalem; Christ purging the Temple; Christ commending the poor Widow at the Treasury; Christ preaching daily in the Temple.—In memory of Robert Stevenson, Engineer to the Northern Light-houses, died 1850. Erected by his sons, 1875.

Fifth Window (East gable).—The Last Supper; Christ's Agony in the Garden; Betrayal; Bearing the Cross.—Gift of William Law, Lord Provost of Edinburgh, 1869 to 1872.

Sixth Window (Great East Window).—The Crucifixion, with numerous figures; Ascension, with eleven apostles grouped.—Presented by the Right Hon. Sir James Falshaw, Baronet, Lord Provost of Edinburgh, 1872 to 1877.

Seventh Window.—Angels announcing the Resurrection to the Marys at the Sepulchre; the Appearance of Our Lord to Mary Magdalene, to St Thomas and the Disciples.—In memory of Robert Smith, S.S.C., died 1875. Erected by his relatives and friends.

Eighth Window, being first in south wall.—Parable of Good Samaritan; Parable of Prodigal Son.—In memory of James Webster, S.S.C., died 1879.

Ninth Window.—Parables of the Ten Virgins, and of the Talents.—In memory of Alexander Clapperton, merchant, Edinburgh, died 1849, and Anne Hume, his wife, died 1873. Erected by their sons, John and Alexander Clapperton, 1876.

THE CLERESTORY WINDOWS IN CHOIR.

These windows are appropriated to the arms of the Craftsmen of Edinburgh. Those of the Wrights and Masons, Painters and Glaziers, Baxters, and the High Constables, are already put up.

Window in the MORAY AISLE representing the assassination of the Earl of Murray, and the preaching of his funeral sermon by John Knox.—Presented by the present Earl of Moray. This admired window has also been executed by James Ballantine and Son.

ST GILES' LECTURES.

FIRST SERIES—THE SCOTTISH CHURCH.

LECTURE I.

HEATHEN SCOTLAND TO THE INTRODUCTION OF CHRISTIANITY.

By the Rev. JAMES CAMERON LEES, D.D., St Giles' Cathedral (High Kirk), Edinburgh.

IT has, as some of you know, been proposed to have a series of Lectures upon Scottish ecclesiastical history from the earliest times down to the present day, to be given by various well-known ministers in this ancient church. It is to be hoped that this course will be both interesting and instructive. The lectures are delivered here without infringing upon our ordinary hours of public worship, and will I believe be thoroughly in accordance with the spirit of the day of rest and prayer. Nothing surely can have a more religious tendency, and be more calculated to awaken in the mind sentiments truly religious than to trace the progress of Christianity in our land from the barbarism of the prehistoric age, to the light and civilisation of the present day; from where it triumphed over heathen temples and overthrew the shrines of heathen gods, to its influence in our own time, and its power as a chief factor in the civilisation of the nineteenth century. We all know how deeply interesting is the book of Acts, which tells of the commencement of the Christian church, and its conflict with Roman, Greek, and other religions. Every account of its progress since that time is a sequel to that book, and shews us how the river of whose rise that book tells has flowed onward, like the stream described by Ezekiel, making waste places glad, and changing desolation and barrenness into fertility. The history of the church in Scotland, like that of the civil history of this same country, is full of romance, of stirring scenes, and of most picturesque and weird effects. These will doubtless be dwelt upon in turn; but what the devout mind will see and reverently admire is, that amid many changes and overturnings there has been a steady progress on the whole, and evidence of an overruling power causing all things to work together for good. To be able to recognise this, it is necessary to take a view, not of one portion, but of the whole history of our country's faith, to review the causes that have been at work for generations—to trace them in their operation from age to age down to the present hour. All know that Scotchmen have been made in great measure what they are by their national religion; its story, too little known, ought therefore to prove attractive. That it will be so in the hands of those who tell it I cannot doubt. It could not be told in a more suitable place than in this church, with which so many historic associations are connected.

I have been honoured by those who have instituted this course by being asked to give the introductory lecture. It seems to me that I can best discharge this duty by bringing before you, so far as can be ascertained, the state of Scotland at the advent of Christianity, when those influences, of which subsequent lectures will give a full account, first began to tell on our country, and which, reaching down to the present day, have created and moulded our national and religious life.

The materials for forming an estimate of the state of pre-

Christian Scotland are of the very scantiest character. Few monuments of those dark ages which preceded the coming to our land of Christian teachers have come down to us. There is almost nothing in the discoveries or treasures of archæology; neither temple nor sacrificial knife nor altar, from which we can glean an idea of what the religion of our Scottish forefathers was. The little that we can learn is chiefly from Christian historians, who describe the conflict of their religion with heathendom, and who incidentally tell somewhat of those rites and superstitions from which the first converts to the new faith were delivered. But as these historians wrote after Christianity had obtained a firm hold upon the country and people, it is difficult to say how much of what they relate may be relied upon. St Patrick, St Columba, St Cuthbert, are Christian heroes whose lives are glorified with a halo of miracle and romance. It is not easy to discriminate between what is legend and what is fact in the story of their words and deeds. Some slight knowledge of Christianity had apparently been previously imparted through the Roman occupation, and also through the preaching of St Ninian.

When Christianity first made itself felt as a permanent power in these lands, the country we now call Scotland was divided into four kingdoms. To the north of the line of the Forth and Clyde lay the kingdoms of the Scots and Picts, separated from one another by a mountain chain called by the old writers, Dorsum Britanniæ or Drumalban. The kingdom of the Scots comprehended generally what are now called the counties of Argyll and Bute and Arran. That of the Picts, those of Orkney and Shetland, Caithness, Sutherland, Ross, Inverness, Perth, and Fife. The part of Scotland to the south of the line of the Forth and Clyde was divided between two other kingdoms—those of the Britons of Strathclyde, and the Saxons of Northumbria. The territory of the Britons extended southwards from the Clyde to the river Derwent in Cumberland. It comprehended part of Cumberland and Westmoreland, and the counties of Dumfries, Lanark, Ayr, Renfrew, and Peebles. To the east of this kingdom was that of the Saxons or Angles, which included Northumberland, Berwick, Roxburgh, East-Lothian, and perhaps Mid-Lothian, where then, as now, there stood the strong fortified position that still bears the name of the Saxon King Edwin—Edwinsbruch. Galloway was occupied by a colony of Picts.[1]

The Scots were the descendants of a colony of Irish who in the fifth century had settled along the western coast of Scotland, and who were in close connection with their mother-country of Ireland. The Picts were the ancient Caledonians, that fierce people of whom we have an account from the Roman historians—men of red hair and large limbs, who had no walled cities, who lived by pasturage and the chase, who fought in chariots and painted their bodies with pictures of wild animals, and who could stand for days immersed in the waters of their marshes.[2] The Britons were the native Celtic race, who had been colonised by the Romans, and who called themselves Roman citizens. They had received some knowledge of Christianity at a very early period; but apparently after the withdrawal of the Romans they relapsed into Paganism.[3] The Saxons were the Teutons from Hanover and Friesland, who had made a settlement on the eastern coast, and who were continually trenching on the territory of their neighbours.

The language of the Scots, and probably also of the Picts,[4] was that which is now known as the Gaelic. That of the Britons still lingers in Wales. That of the Saxons or Angles is

---

[1] The four old kingdoms are referred to by more than one early historian. In a poem relating to the labours of St Columba, it is said:

> 'The people of Alba to the Ictian Sea,
> The Gaedhil cruithneans, Saxons, Saxo-Brits.
> Best of men was the man who went [to them].'

See also Bede, c. 14.

[2] Dion Cassius.   [3] Skene's *Celtic Scotland*, vol. i., p. 157.

[4] Mr Skene seems to have shewn this conclusively.

represented by the English tongue. Each of these kingdoms had its capital—a fortress of great strength, the seat of government, where the king resided. The capital of the Scots was at Dunadd, a rocky eminence near the Crinan Canal. That of the Picts, at the commencement of the Christian period, was near the mouth of the river Ness—probably the height called Craig Patrick, near the modern town of Inverness.[1] The capital of the Britons was at Alcluith or Dumbarton, and that of the Saxons at Bamburgh on the Northumbrian shore.

Between these races there was continual warfare. Like all barbarians, they delighted in the chase and martial achievements. Their annals, such as they are, are the record of petty feuds. The northern Caledonians hunted the deer, the boar, and the wolf. They navigated lake and sea in canoes made out of a hollow tree, such as are still occasionally dug up out of the morasses; or in boats made of wicker-work covered with the skins of animals, like those that are still used in some parts of the west of Ireland. They had advanced a certain stage in civilisation. They had emerged from the stone and bronze age, were conversant with the use of metals, and the Britons at least had local government in a more or less organised form. Probably the nearest resemblance to the northern Scot may be found in an African tribe of the present day, with its scattered villages and head township strongly fortified, where the king resides.

The religion of the two northern kingdoms, those of the Picts and the Scots, seems to have been very much the same in its character. We can only form an idea of what it was from the history of the early Christian missionaries. Holding a high place among both Scots and Picts, was a class of men called Druids. They are mentioned frequently in the lives of St Columba and St Patrick; and in the ancient Celtic manuscripts

---

[1] See Adamnan's account of St Columba's visit to King Brude.

which have come down to us from Irish sources, Druids appear to have held a distinct position in connection with the religious life of the people such as it was. They resided at the residence of kings, and they exercised great power in national affairs. An order of priests bearing this name inhabiting Gaul and Southern Britain has been described by the Roman historians with considerable minuteness. These Druids, according to them, presided at sacrifices; they were instructors of the young, and were judges in all matters of controversy. They took no part in war, nor were liable to pay taxes. They made use of the Greek letters in writing. They inculcated the immortality of the soul and its transmigration into different bodies. They taught the youths astronomy, and 'much about the nature of things and the immortal gods.' They used rites of augury from the slaughter of a human victim, and dwelt in dense groves in remote places. They taught in caves or hidden forests, and they burned or buried with the dead what was most prized by them when living. They considered the oak as the emblem of the Almighty, and the misletoe was regarded with peculiar veneration. It was detached from the parent tree by a golden knife, and carried home with imposing ceremony. Cæsar and also Pliny have a good deal to say of these mysterious persons the Druids, and they still furnish material for much antiquarian and historic controversy. Into such controversy we cannot of course enter. All that we have to say is, there is no trace of any such organised priesthood existing in Northern Britain as the Roman historians describe.

Whatever may be the degree of belief put in the legends respecting the character and even the designation of the Druids—supposing we go the length of saying there were never any such persons—we are confronted with certain tangible memorials existing to this day of a religious or ceremonial observance unrecorded in history. There they are, and as rational beings we are invited to account for them. Most probably, as we venture to think, these memorials are the significant relics of a system of pagan worship which vanished on the introduction of Christianity. We allude in a special manner to those mysterious circles and groups of stones of different dimensions, and varied in their mechanical preparation, that are found in the British Islands and in France, the Gaul of the Romans. The grandest and most remarkable of these memorials is the well-known Stonehenge in Wiltshire. Two others, less imposing, but equally suggestive, are the standing-stones of Stennis in Orkney, and of Callernish in the island of Lewis. Differing as these circles do in some respects, they are clearly all of one character. They have had the same meaning. They belong to a people possessing a similarity in superstitious or symbolic observance.

We are aware that the custom of fixing large stones in an upright posture in the ground commemorative of men or important events is of prodigious antiquity in almost all nations. Besides being found in Britain and continental Europe, these monoliths are seen in Assyria, Persia, India, and Mexico. Such memorials receive notice in the Old Testament. We read in Judges, ix. 6, of Abimelech being made king 'by the pillar which was in Shechem;' and in 2 Kings, xi. 14, of Joash, when he was anointed king, standing 'by a pillar, as the manner was.' A like usage prevailed in ancient Britain when the king or chief was elected. At Carnac in Brittany there is a surprisingly large number of upright stones, not in circles, but in straight lines, with a curved row at one end, while all around are seen barrows and cromlechs. The whole had evidently been connected with sepulchral, judicial, or other solemnities. In Norway and the north-east of Scotland exist many rudely sculptured stones which had been set up in a remote period of paganism, but some of which had received carvings of Christian symbols, such as the cross, after the diffusion of Christianity.

Let us not despise these rude testimonies, obscure though they be, and of no recognisable value, according to ordinary notions. There is something to touch the feelings in observing these sculptured records of an extremely ancient heathenism. There is, indeed, always matter for elevating emotion in contemplating objects of human art which carry us back to the far-reaching past, into what might be called the infancy of mankind. Uncouth as they are, there is a sentiment of good in these old stones. We can at least say that at first sight of the gigantic monoliths of Stonehenge, we experienced feelings of awe akin to those which usually occur on coming in presence of the Pyramids. We saw before us the relics of a huge work of art, excelling all similar constructions in Britain, and the age of which could not reasonably be deemed less than three thousand years, a stretch of time that takes us back to the era of Moses, the venerated lawgiver of Israel. Nor, in looking at Stonehenge, standing as it does in melancholy solitude, were our emotions of a less solemnising nature by knowing that we were within a few miles of that noble Christian fane, Salisbury Cathedral, with its lofty and exquisitely tapering spire piercing the skies, reminding us of an eminent Scotsman and church dignitary, Bishop Gilbert Burnet, the historian of the Reformation, and the eloquent advocate of civil and religious liberty.

Reverting to those shadowy persons, the Druids, it is alleged that one of them of considerable celebrity named Broichan, resided at the court of the Pictish King Brude, and that the Highland apostle St Columba had with him more than one trial of strength, which has been duly recorded. 'On a certain day,' says the biographer of Columba, 'Broichan, while conversing with the saint, said to him : " Tell me, Columba, when dost thou propose to sail?" The saint replied : " I intend to begin my voyage after three days, if God permits me and preserves my life." Broichan said : " On the contrary, thou shalt not be able, for I can make the winds unfavourable to thy voyage, and cause a great darkness to envelop you in its shade." That same day, the saint, accompanied with a number of his followers, went to the long lake of the river Nesa (Loch

Ness), as he had determined. Then the Druids began to exult, seeing that it had become very dark, and that the wind was very violent and contrary. Our Columba called on Christ the Lord, and embarked in his small boat; and while his sailors hesitated, he the more confidently ordered them to raise the sails against the wind. No sooner was this order executed, while the whole crowd was looking on, than the vessel ran against the wind with extraordinary speed.'[1] This is one instance in which the magical pretensions of the Druids have been specified. It is not the only one: the Christian teachers seem constantly to have been in conflict with them, and are represented as triumphing over their black art by means of the miraculous powers they are supposed to have possessed. 'A few days after his conversion,'[2] says the writer we have already quoted, 'a son of a householder was attacked with a dangerous illness, and brought to the very borders of life and death. When the Druids saw him in a dying state, they began with great bitterness to upbraid his parents, and to extol their own gods as more powerful than the God of the Christians, and thus to despise God, as if he were weaker than their gods. When all this was told to the blessed man (Columba), he turned with zeal for God, and proceeded to the house of the friendly peasant.' The saint, of course, triumphs over the Druids, and raises the boy who had died to life again.

Among the Irish Scots, St Patrick had conflicts of a similar nature, in which he also came off victorious. A Druid pours poison into the cup of St Patrick, who blesses the cup, and the fluid it contains congeals. He inverts it, and the poisonous drops fall out. The Druid then by his incantations covers the plain with snow, but admits his inability to remove the enchantment till the same hour on the morrow; Patrick blesses the plain, and the snow disappears. The Druid brings on a thick darkness, but is unable to remove it. Patrick prays, straight-

---

[1] *Life of St Columba*, by Adamnan, Book II., chap. xxxv.
[2] *Ibid.*, Book II., chap. xxxiii.

way the darkness vanishes, and the sun begins to shine.[1] In an ancient Irish manuscript,[2] these magicians are represented as drying up by their spells and incantations all the rivers, lakes, and springs of a district. A great Druid shoots an arrow into the air, and a fountain bursts forth where the arrow falls. Many allusions are found in these old manuscripts to the necromancy of the Druids, and to their different spells and incantations. A favourite method of divination with them was by sneezing,[3] or by the song of a bird perched on a tree. In an old poem attributed to St Columba, these and other similar practices are referred to and abjured. 'Our fate,' sings the poet, 'depends not on sneezing:

> Nor on a bird perched on a twig,
> Nor on the root of a knotted tree,
> Nor on the noise of clapping hands.
> Better is He in whom we trust—
> The Father, the One and the Son.'[4]

And in another verse of the same poem, he says:

> 'I adore not the noise of birds,
> Nor sneezing, nor lots in this world,
> Nor a son, nor chance, nor woman—
> My Druid is Christ, the Son of God.'[5]

In another poem, in the form of a prayer, the same saint alludes to the magical arts of his adversaries. He recognises their power over the elements of nature, and exclaims:

> 'My Druid—may he be on my side!—
> Is the Son of God, and truth with purity.'[6]

---

[1] Todd's *Life of St Patrick*, p. 452.
[2] Professor Occury's *Lectures*, p. 271.
[3] Both among the Greeks and Romans, sneezing was used for the same purpose. In the middle ages, this method of divination was denounced by ecclesiastical councils.
[4] Todd's *Life of St Patrick*, p. 122.   [5] *Ibid.*, p. 132.   [6] *Ibid.*, p. 120.

These notices are probably sufficient to shew what was the character of Druidism among the Celts. It was a system of necromancy like that which has ever been inseparably connected with heathenism [1]—a belief in men who can bring storms, and bewitch fields, and bring down rain—a belief in oracles and divinations and charms. Belief in such men has always accompanied the lowest forms of religious faith.

The religion of the northern kingdoms of the Picts and Scots, of which the Druids were the ministers, was in itself, as might be expected from what we have said, of a very debased and grovelling kind. It seems to have been mainly a kind of fetichism, an adoration of natural objects and of the powers of the external world—the rocks, the wind, the thunder; and if the people rose in thought above what came within the knowledge of the senses, it was only to people the material world with demons and malignant spirits, to whom all phenomena were attributed, and whose aid was to be sought, or whose wrath was to be averted, by means of charms and magical spells. Among the pagan Scots, pillar stones were objects of worship,[2] and were either overthrown, or consecrated with the sign of the cross, by the early Christian teachers. On a great plain in Ireland stood, it is said, a great stone idol, called *Cenn Cruaich*, ornamented with gold and silver, with twelve other idols around it, ornamented with brass, which were worshipped by the natives, and which St Patrick cast down by simply raising his pastoral staff.[3] In a poetic life of the same saint, it is said that

> 'He preached three-score years
> The cross of Christ to the Tuatha of Feni;
> On the Tuatha of Erin there was darkness.
> The Tuatha adored the Sidhe.'[4]

---

[1] *Conflict of Christianity*, by Gerhard Uhlhorn, Book II., chap. iii.
[2] Todd's *Life of St Patrick*, p. 127.
[3] Professor Occury's *Lectures*, p. 539; Todd's *Life of St Patrick*, p. 127.
[4] *The Celts*, by Rev. G. R. M'Lear, p. 23.

The *sidhe* were spirits who were supposed to haunt nature, and to dwell underground, and a belief in their dread power remained long after Christianity had obtained firm hold on Scotland, and lingers in some parts of our country to the present day.[1] St Columba seems to have had full belief in the existence of these demons, which were believed to have their usual dwelling-place in fountains and green hillocks, and delighted in exorcising them. 'While[2] the blessed man was stopping,' says his biographer, 'for some days in the province of the Picts, he heard that there was a fountain famous among this heathen people, which foolish men, having their senses blinded of the devil, worshipped as a god. For those who drank this fountain, or purposely washed their hands or feet in it, were allowed by God to be struck by demoniacal art, and went home either leprous or purblind, or at least suffering from weakness or other kinds of infirmity. By all these things the pagans were seduced, and paid divine honours to the fountain. Having ascertained this, the saint one day went up to the fountain fearlessly; and on seeing this, the Druids, whom he had often sent away vanquished and confounded, were greatly rejoiced, thinking that, like others, he would suffer from the touch of that baneful water.' The saint then blessed the fountain, 'and from that day the demons departed from the water; and not only was it not allowed to injure any one, but even many diseases amongst the people were cured by this same fountain after it had been blessed and washed in by the saint.' At another time, when the saint began to pray, he beheld 'a very black host of demons fighting against him with iron darts;' and in an ancient life of St Patrick, mention is made of his meeting with nine Druids clad in white garments with a magical host.[3] These invisible spirits pervaded the elements of nature

---

[1] See a curious book on the underground people, by Mr Kirke, minister of Balquhidder.

[2] Adamnan's *Life of St Columba*, p. 45.

[3] Betham, *Ant. Res.*, II., Ap., p. xxxi.

—the clouds, the waters, the earth, the trees. One of the legendary kings of Ireland is stated to have received as pledges from the nation, 'sun, moon, and every power which is in heaven and in earth,' that the sovereignty should always remain in his own race; and in a striking poem, said to be by St Patrick, there are signs that even he had not altogether shaken himself free from a sense of the mysterious power of the elements of nature. He realised it very vividly. He says:

> 'I bind to myself to-day
> The power of Heaven,
> The light of the Sun,
> The whiteness of the Snow,
> The force of Fire,
> The flashing of Lightning,
> The velocity of Wind,
> The depth of the Sea,
> The stability of the Earth,
> The hardness of Rocks.'

He invokes these with Christian powers, such as the power of Christ's incarnation, crucifixion, and resurrection, to defend him from the magical and evil influences by which he believed himself surrounded.

> 'I have set around me all these powers,
> Against every hostile savage power
> Directed against my body and my soul;
> Against the incantations of false prophets;
> Against the black laws of heathenism;
> Against the false laws of heresy;
> Against the deceits of idolatry;
> Against the spells of women and smiths and Druids;
> Against all knowledge which blinds the soul of man.'

The same saint is described as having an interview with the daughters of the Irish king, who supposed him and his companions to be *Duine Sidhe*[1]—gods of the earth. Then the following questions are put by one of the princes to the evangelist—and they shew traces of the nature-worship of the inquirer:

> 'Who is God?
> And where is God?
> And what is God? . . .
> Is He in heaven or in earth?
> In the sea?
> In rivers?
> In mountainous places?
> In valleys?
> Declare unto us the knowledge of Him.'

The Scots and the Picts were in that low religious condition in which Nature and her powers are objects of dread. Their religion was one of fear. It was a fetichism, and can scarcely be called anything more. Polytheism or Monotheism it was not, for they seemed to have had no idea of higher powers than these spirits of evil, governing and controlling all visible things. 'They knew not God.'

The religion of the Britons of Strathclyde was not very different from that of the northern kingdoms which we have described; any Christianity they had been taught had vanished. They were as heathen as their neighbours, and followed the customs of their forefathers. They gave a high place in their society to the bards or poets, some of whose effusions have come down to us, and like the Picts and Scots seem to have venerated natural objects, grafting on their own original paganism some of the superstitions of their Saxon neighbours. In the account given of the preaching at Hoddam, in Dumfriesshire, of Kentigern, who finally converted the Britons to Christianity, there is a reference made to their religious practices,

---

[1] Todd's *St Patrick.*

which is suggestive enough. That teacher shewed them 'that idols were dumb, the vain inventions of men, fitter for the fire than for worship. He shewed that the elements, in which they believed as deities, were creatures and formations adapted by the disposition of their Maker to the use, help, and assistance of men. But Woden, whom they, and especially the Angles, believed to be the chief deity from whom they derived their origin, and to whom the fourth day of the week is dedicated, he asserted with probability to have been a mortal man, king of the Saxons, by faith a pagan, from whom they and many nations have their descent.'[1] From this extract we can glean an idea of what was the religious condition of the inhabitants of the British kingdom.

Such is a slight sketch of the paganism of the three Celtic kingdoms—those of the Picts, Scots, and Britons. Many traces of this paganism survive to the present day. In the belief in fairies, in charms, in witchcraft, that still lingers in many parts of Scotland, we have the remains of the old Celtic heathenism; and any one who is familiar with what is called folk-lore will find abundant evidence of old druidical superstitions still existing in the midst of our present civilisation. Many of these superstitions were treated not a little kindly by the Christian teachers, and perhaps on this account have survived. Pillar stones had engraven on them the sign of the cross, and became objects of Christian veneration.[2] Fountains were blessed and became holy wells. Demonology was fully recognised and exorcism practised. Heathen festivals were converted into Christian holidays. Few who observe May-day and All-hallow E'en know that these were festive days before even the name of Christ was heard in this land; and the very ceremonies by which they are still observed have their origin in far-away pagan times. It was

---

[1] Jocelyn, *Vit. S. Kin.*, chap. xxxii., quoted by Skene.
[2] Todd's *Life of St Patrick*, p. 500.

an advice given by one of the popes to British missionaries[1] that they should disturb as little as necessary pagan practices. 'The temples, cleansed with holy water, were to be hallowed for Christian worship; and heathen festivals, instead of being rudely abolished, might be devoted to the celebration of the festival of the saints;' for, as he argues, 'you cannot cut off everything at once from rude natures—he who would climb a height must ascend step by step, and not by leaps and bounds.' It is on this principle, so clearly laid down by high authority, that the Christian teachers of Scotland seem to have acted, and hence the existence in our own time of many traces of that paganism against which they contended.

When we turn from Celtic to Saxon heathenism, and come from the mountains of the north, and the regions of the west, to the kingdom of Northumbria and the eastern Lowlands of Scotland, we feel that we are upon sure ground; for the religion of the Teuton or Saxon was well defined, and we have ample information as to its character. It prevailed over a great part of Europe. It was a polytheism; for it had a system of recognised deities, and it also had a cosmogony, or theory of creation, and a doctrine of a future state peculiarly its own.[2] Let us glance at some of the main features that distinguished it.

The greatest of the Saxon gods was Odin, or Woden, whose name is given to the fourth day of the week—Wednesday, or Wodensday. To him warriors were dedicated; and when they went to battle, they vowed to give him a certain number of souls. He was the supreme deity. The next among the gods was Thor, after whom the fifth day of the week is called Thursday, or Thorsday. He was the thundering god—powerful

---

[1] Bede, *H. E.*, i. 30.
[2] This sketch of Saxon heathenism is chiefly founded on the following authorities: *Ten Great Religions*, by F. Clark; Kemble's *Saxons in England*; Mallet's *Northern Antiquities*; *The English*, by the Rev. G. F. M'Lear; and Dasent's *Burnt Njal*.

over the elements, guiding the storms, sending rain. He carried a hammer or club which, as often as he hurled it from him, came back to his hand again. Tiew, whose name the third day of the week bears, was the giver of victory, the god of battle. Frea was the god of fertility, of the life-giving sunshine, of fruitfulness and peace. Balder was the god of light and grace, of splendour, manly excellence, and beauty. The goddess Friege was the wife of Woden, and gave the name to the sixth day of the week. And lastly, there was Saetere, of whom we know little more than that he gave his name to the seventh day.

Inferior to these, there were other gods and goddesses too numerous to mention, and in addition a plentiful supply of demons or evil spirits who wrought woe to the human race, and whose machinations were unending. The chief of these was Loki, who bore a fearful character as 'the calumniator of the gods, the grand contriver of deceit and fraud, the reproach of gods and men,' beautiful in figure, and surpassing all mortals in his powers of craftiness. 'Three monsters owe their birth to him—the wolf Fenris, the serpent Midgard, and Hela or Death. All three are enemies to the gods, who after various struggles have chained this wolf till the last day, when he shall break loose and devour the sun. The serpent hath been cast into the sea, where he shall remain till he shall be conquered by the god Thor; and Hela or Death has been banished into the lower regions, where she has the government of nine worlds, into which she distributes those sent to her. Here she possesses a habitation protected by exceedingly high walls and strongly barred gates. Hunger is her table, starvation her knife, delay her man, slowness her maid, precipice her threshold, care her bed, and burning anguish forms the hangings of her apartments.'

The life and transactions of the various deities are very particularly chronicled. In their manner of life they are thoroughly human. Their court is kept under 'a great ash-tree, where they distribute justice. Its branches cover the face of the earth. Its top reaches to the highest heaven. It is supported by three vast roots, one of which extends to the ninth world. An eagle whose piercing eye discerns all things, perches upon the branches; a squirrel is constantly running up and down it to bring news, while a parcel of serpents fastened to the trunk endeavour to destroy it. From one of the roots runs a fountain where wisdom lies concealed. From a neighbouring spring (the fountain of past things) three virgins are continually drawing a precious water with which they water the ash-tree. These three virgins always keep under the ash, and it is they who dispense the days and ages of men. Every man has a destiny appropriated to himself, who determines the duration and events of his life; but the three destinies of more special note are Urd[1] (the past), Werande (the present), and Sculde (the future).'

The account of the creation of all things was of the same definite yet imaginative character, and it is instructive to compare it with the Scripture and other cosmogonies. 'In the day-spring of the ages there was neither sea nor shore, nor refreshing breezes. There was neither earth below nor heaven above to be distinguished. The whole was only one vast abyss without herb and without seeds. The sun had then no palace, the stars knew not their dwelling-places, the moon was ignorant of her power. After this there was a luminous, burning, flaming world towards the south; and from this world flowed out incessantly into the abyss that lay towards the north, torrents of sparkling fire, which, in proportion as they removed far away from their source, congealed in their falling into the abyss, and so filled it with snow and ice. From the icy vapours, melted into warm living drops by a wind from the south, came the giant Ymir. From him came a race of wicked giants. Then arose in a mysterious manner Bor, the father of three

---

[1] Hence the word *weird*.

sons—Odin, Vili, and Ve. The sons of Bor slew the giant Ymir, and the blood ran with such abundance from his wounds that it caused a general inundation, wherein perished all the giants except one who, saving himself in a bark, escaped with all his family. Then a new world was formed. The sons of Bor dragged the body of the giant into the abyss, and of it made the earth; the sea and the rivers were composed of his blood; the earth of his flesh; the great mountains of his bones; the rocks of his teeth and of splinters of his broken bones. They made of his skull the vault of heaven, which is supported by four dwarfs named South, North, East, and West. They fixed there tapers to enlighten it. The days were distinguished; the nights were numbered. They made the earth round, and surrounded it with the deep ocean. One day, as the sons of Bor were taking a walk, they found two pieces of wood floating on the water; these they took and out of them made a man and a woman. The eldest of the gods gave them life and souls; the second, motion and knowledge; the third, the gift of speech, hearing, and raiment. From this man and woman, named Askus and Embla, is descended the race of man who now inhabit the earth.'

Such is the account of creation which the Teutons believed. It resembles the Greek story of the origin of the gods, and in its idea of the origin of all things from nebulous vapours and heat, it reminds us of some of those scientific theories which are frequently set forth at the present day. Not less striking than their cosmogony, was their theory of another world. It is as materialistic as can well be conceived, but at the same time most characteristic of the race that held it. 'The realm of Hel was cold, cheerless, and shadowy. No simulated war was there from which warriors desisted with renovated strength and glory. No capacious quaichs of mead or cups of life-giving wine: chill and ice, frost and darkness, shadowy realms without a sun, without song or wine or feast.' While Hel was of this gloomy character, the heaven of the

Saxon, Wacheal or Valhalla, was very different. 'The heroes who are received into the palace of Odin have every day pleasures among themselves, of passing in review, ranging themselves in order of battle, of cutting one another to pieces; but as soon as the hour of repast arrives, they return all safe to the hall of Woden, and fall to eating and drinking. Though the number of them cannot be counted, the flesh of the boar *Serimner* is sufficient for them all; every day it is served up at table, and every day it is renewed entire. Their beverage is beer and mead; one single goat, whose milk is mead, furnishes enough to intoxicate the heroes. Their cups are the skulls of the enemies they have slain.' It is evident how strongly this conception of the future takes its colour from the whole existence, temperament, and history of the warlike race who believed in it. It was the shadow projected by their life.

The legends of their gods would occupy, and indeed do occupy volumes. They were not, like the classic deities, dwelling in unbending dignity on Mount Olympus; but roamed to and fro, and were as much given to adventure as their worshippers on earth. We will give only one of these legends as a specimen of many. It is supposed to be, like them all, parabolic—to have a deep moral and spiritual meaning—to set forth the 'struggles of the soul against the inexorable laws of nature, freedom against fate, the spirit with the flesh, mind with matter, human hope with change, disappointment, loss.' Thor goes to visit his enemies the giants of cold and darkness. The king of the city where they dwell inquired what great feat Thor and his companions could perform. 'One professed to be a great eater, on which the king summoned one of his servants, called Logi, and placed between them a trough filled with meat. Thor's companion ate his share, but Logi ate meat and bones too, and the trough into the bargain, and was considered to have conquered. Thor's other companion was a great runner, and was set to run with a young man called Hugi, who so outstripped him that he reached the goal before the other had gone half-way. Then Thor was asked what he could do himself. He said he would engage in a drinking-match, and was presented with a large horn, and requested to empty it at a single draught, which he expected easily to do; but on looking, the liquor appeared hardly diminished. The second time he tried, and lowered it slightly; a third time, and it was sunk only half an inch. Then he was brought to try a new feat. He was asked to lift a cat from the ground, and ignominiously failed. Lastly he wrestled with an old toothless woman, and lost his footing. Afterwards the discomfiture of Thor was thus explained. The triumphant eater was fire itself, the devourer of all things, disguised as a man. The successful runner was thought, whose fleet step none can outstrip. The horn out of which he tried to drink was the ocean, which was lowered a few inches by his tremendous draughts. The cat was the great Midgard serpent which goes round the world, and Thor had actually pulled the world a little way out of its place; and the old woman was old age, with whom the strongest will wrestle in vain.'

In legends like these, through which ran a thread of moral meaning, the Saxon delighted. They were the reflection of the qualities that distinguished him, and the outcome of his own daily life in its struggle with the severities of a northern clime. His worship corresponded to his mythology. Temples of the gods abounded. Plentiful sacrifices of animals were offered to them, and human sacrifices were not spared on occasions of importance. 'Near every gathering-place of a tribe stood the stone of sacrifice, on which the necks of the victims were crushed and broken; and the holy pool, in which another kind of human sacrifices were sunk.'[1] There were great feasts, religious in their character, which were frequently held. At these the people gathered round smoking caldrons, in which the animals that had been sacrificed were boiled, and all in turn partook. The feasts ended with much

---

[1] Dasent, *Burnt Njal*, xxxviii.

drinking, and cups were solemnly drained in honour of the gods. 'The first bowl, for victory and strength, was drained to Woden; the second to Freye, for peace and good harvests.' All the other gods were remembered in the same way, and the last bowl was drunk to the memory of the dead. The superstitions which clustered round the Teutonic religion were more numerous than we can even mention; and in the laws of Christian times, which denounce them, we have them tabulated with great minuteness. They were of the most grovelling kind.[1] Magic was common. Well-worship, divinations, enchantments, spells[2] of all kinds are continually mentioned; and in many particulars they resemble the practices to which we have referred as connected with Celtic paganism.

This is an account, necessarily slight, of the state of heathen Scotland in its various parts previous to the advent of Christianity. The heathenism that prevailed was of the darkest kind, and in its best form can hardly be called higher in character than that which exists to-day in China or any other missionary field: but little impulse could come from it to civilisation and progress, hardly any to morality. It seems strange indeed to think that little more than a thousand years ago Scotland was peopled with idolaters, and the greater part of it with idolaters of the most benighted description—that amid the hills and valleys and islands of the north, there dwelt 'savage tribes and roving barbarians,' fierce as the New Zealander, cunning as the Red Indian, degraded in their belief as the Zulu—that here, in the capital of Scotland, perhaps on the site of this ancient Christian church where we now worship, there may have stood a temple to Woden or Thor, and have been witnessed the orgy of an idol's feast,

---

[1] See Kemble's *Saxons*, vol. i., appendix, where many of these notices are given.

[2] Such as sticking pins into a clay figure, which was supposed to injure the person represented.

or the horrors of human sacrifice. It is difficult to realise this; to place ourselves even in thought in these dark ages; to pass even in imagination from the light of our Christianity and civilisation under the veritable 'shadow of death' that rested upon our land. Students of comparative theology know how in the heart of many of the old religions there lay a hope of a good time coming to the race; and the 'unconscious prophecies of heathenism,' telling of a great conqueror to come, have been often referred to.[1] Whether these were mere dim longings for something better, that took shape in words, or whether they were the echoes of the Jewish prophecies which had reached distant lands, it is impossible to determine. When we read in Zoroaster that 'Osideberga will manifest himself to the inhabitants of the world, promote religiousness, destroy iniquity, and restore the ancient order of things. In his time rest and peace shall prevail, dissensions cease, and all grievances be done away'—Or in the works of Confucius, 'that a great and holy one shall appear in the latter days, to whom nations look forward as fading flowers thirst for rain'—When we hear Plutarch saying that 'the god of the lower world will eventually be utterly deprived of his power, and then men be happy, and will no longer stand in need of nourishment, or throw a shadow'—Or Virgil, as he tells how a child was to come from heaven, a dear offspring of the gods, Jove's great descendant, and the golden age was to arise over the whole world'—we feel as if we were listening to an echo of the sublime strains of Isaiah. 'Unconscious prophecies,' like those of other religions, were not wanting in Scottish paganism: the early Christian missionaries to the Picts and Scots appeal to such prophecies existing among these peoples. There were sages, one of them tells us distinctly, before their own coming, 'who had fore-

---

[1] *Christianity confirmed by Jewish and Heathen Testimony*, by T. Stevenson (Edinburgh: David Douglas); an interesting work. Also Walsh, *Donellan Lectures*, p. 213.

told the bright word of blessing that would come to the land of the letter; for it was the Holy Spirit that spoke and prophesied through the mouths of just men, as he had prophesied through the mouths of the chief prophets and fathers in the patriarchal law; for the law of nature had prevailed where the written law did not reach.[1] In the religion of the Saxons, there is a very marked and distinct announcement of a great deliverer who was to restore all things, and harmonise those discordant elements which were ever present to the Teutonic mind, and close for ever that warfare which he saw prevailing on every side around him. The central idea of his curious belief was the struggle of the soul against natural obstacles—the conflict of life with death, of freedom with fate, of choice with necessity, of good with evil. The gods of the Teuton were always at war. His religion was a dualism in which sunshine, summer, and growth were waging perpetual battle with storm, snow, winter, ocean, and terrestrial fire.'[2] This conflict was to grow more intense as the ages succeeded each other, and at last to end in harmony. The poetry in which this is expressed is of a lofty character.[3]

> 'Brothers slay brothers;
> Sisters' children
> Shed each other's blood;
> Hard is the world;
> Sensual sin grows huge.
>
> There are sword ages,
> Earth cleaving cold;
> Storm ages, murder ages,
> Till the world falls dead,

---

[1] *The Senchus Mor*, vol. i., p. 27.
[2] Clark's *Ten Great Religions*.
[3] Clark's *Ten Religions*, p. 366; Kemble's *Saxons in England*, p. 410; Brace, *Travels in Norway and Sweden*.

>   And men no longer spare
>   Or pity one another.
>
>   Black wanes the sun;
>   In waves the earth shall sink;
>   From heaven shall fall
>   The friendly stars;
>   Round the tree
>   Red fire shall rustle;
>   High heat play
>   Against the heaven.'

But when all the powers of evil are conquered, a better state shall arise:

>   '" In Gimle" the lofty;
>   Then shall the hosts
>   Of the virtuous dwell,
>   And through all ages
>   Feast of deep gladness.
>
>   Then unsown
>   The swath shall flourish,
>   Back come Baldr.'

Then shall descend the mighty one from above—He who ruleth over all, whose name man dares not to utter.

>   Then one is born
>   Higher than all.
>   He becomes strong
>   With the strengths of the earth;
>   The mightiest King
>   Men call him;
>   Fast knit in peace
>   With all powers.

> Then comes another
> Yet more mighty;
> But him I dare not
> Venture to name,
> Than to where Odin
> To meet the wolf goes.'

With mysterious and weird prophecies like these, familiar to them, sung by their bards, repeated by their priests, our forefathers found themselves face to face with Christianity and its message of hope.

It does not fall within my province to tell how that message was received, or what change its reception wrought on the personal and national life of the inhabitants of Scotland. This much I may say, without trenching on the ground of those who are to follow me, that Christianity took up and consolidated the national characteristics of our forefathers. Among the Celts it enlisted the spirit of clanship in the service of Christianity. Among the Saxons it allied itself 'with what was dearest and what was highest—with their homes, their assemblies, their crowns, their graves.'[1] It fused the different races—Picts, Scots, Britons, Saxons—into one great strong people through the idea of a spiritual society which it inculcated and held up before them, the purest, perhaps, which ever drew men together.[2] They seem to have embraced Christianity with wonderful facility when it was presented to them, and, though there were occasional relapses into paganism, and some heathen practices were tenaciously retained, the converts appear to have adhered with wonderful constancy to the rites and worship of the new faith. Their teachers were gentle with them, tender to their superstitions, and forbearing with native usages of which they might not altogether approve. Many notices have come down

---

[1] *Influences of Christianity on National Character*, by R. W. Church.
[2] Guizot, Lecture xii., p. 230.

to us illustrative on the one hand of the way in which the new religion approached them, and of the manner in which they embraced it. Of these we may give two instances—one from Celtic, the other from Saxon sources. They are voices from out of the heart of the old paganism of Scotland, that touching in their character. In an ancient Gaelic poem the heathen poet Oisin is represented as holding a dialogue with the first Christian teacher of the Scots—St Patrick. This poem is found in many forms in Irish and Gaelic manuscripts, and though it may not be of much historic value, it must, I think, be regarded as a last voice of Celtic heathenism. The old bard rejoices in the worship of nature, and records the prowess of his heroic forefathers; the missionary tells of the power of God beyond all visible things, and speaks in dogmatic terms of the future state.[1]

'Patrick of the solemn psalms,' begins the old pagan, 'how great your love for God must be, since you do not close your book and listen to the voice of the blackbird! Sweet blackbird high on yon bending bough, how soothing is your song! Although you never heard mass said by priests, how delightfully you whistle.' He then goes on to tell of the music of his warlike ancestor, Fionn: 'He played melodiously with the harp, while I am here in grief with the clergy;' and then he sings in heroic strains of the prowess of the forefathers, and mourns that he should have survived them and fallen on an evil time. 'When I think of the men who were so brave, I feel cheerless, without friendship for my heart. Here I am weak, living after the Fenii and Fionn MacCumhal. Small is my esteem for thyself and clergy—O holy Patrick of the crosier. I have greater regard for the white-handed king of the Fenii—but he is not near me now.' The saint has little

---

[1] This poem is found in various forms. One version is in the Book of Lismore. We quote from a very interesting translation by Simpson, in *Poems of Oisin, Bard of Erin.*

sympathy with his regard for the heroes of other days—he warns his listener that he has not long to live—his great forefather died a pagan and is in hell, and he will soon follow him unless he accepts the Christian faith.

'He is now shut up in torment; all his generosity and wealth do not avail him now for lack of piety towards God— for this he is in sorrow in the mansion of pain.' The old bard rises in incredulity and indignation, and there is something pathetic in the way he refuses to accept the cruel dogmatism of his teacher. 'Is Fionn in hell—the hero mild who bestowed gold! in forfeit for sins against the great God—is *he* in the house of torment under sorrow? I do not believe it possible for God, though great his power and his strength, nor for any devil who came ever, to put under lock Fionn of the Fenii— Fionn the hospitable to be under locks! heart without malice and without aversion; heart stern in defence of battle! It is plain your God does not delight in giving gold and food to others. Fionn never refused strong or weak, and shall he receive hell for his abode!' The saint contends against such unorthodox views with an earnestness which would do credit to some modern theologians. 'However much he may have divided gold and venison, hard are his bonds in the den of pains; no glimpse of light for him, no sight of brightness such as he first received from God!' The bard replied that he would rather be in hell with his forefathers than in the heaven of the saint.

'I would rather return to the Fenii once more, O Patrick, than go to the heaven of Jesus Christ to be for ever under tribute to him. I would rather be in Fionn's court hearkening to the voices of hounds in the morning, and meditating on hard-fought battles, than in the court of Jesus Christ.' The dialogue goes on at great length. What we have quoted is probably sufficient to indicate its character—the heathen clinging to his old beliefs; the saint entreating him to 'smite his breast and shed tears, and believe in Him who is above him.' It exhibits in poetic form the meeting of the old and new. It belongs to the transition time; the dawning hour; the twilight of Scottish Christianity.

Another memorial of the same time comes to us from Saxon sources, and refers to the Saxon kingdom now incorporated in Scotland. In a council of the wise men of the court of Edwin—who gives the name to our own city—of his aldermen and thanes and nobles, the Christian teacher stood ready to plead his cause. No scene in the history of missions is fuller of romance[1] than that which ensued. Coifi, the high-priest of Woden, arose and confessed that he was moved by the new doctrines. He had served his gods long and faithfully, yet there were those in the kingdom who were richer and greater than he—if the deities had power, he would have been richest and greatest of all. He asked that the new doctrine should be explained to them. The missionary declared his message to the assembly, and at the close of his address the high-priest exclaimed: 'Long since have I known full well that what we have been worshipping is naught, and the more diligently I sought after truth therein, the less I found it; but now in what this stranger preacheth I openly confess there shineth forth such truth as can confer on us life, salvation, and eternal happiness. I advise therefore, O king, that we straightway break and burn down those temples and altars which we have hallowed, and whence we have gained no good.'[2]

The advice was followed. The temple of Woden was thrown down by the high-priest himself, who hurled his spear at it, and bade his men break down the temple, and burn the hedge; but before this demolition of shrines was agreed to, one of the assembled thanes gave his opinion in words that are full of deep feeling, and cannot fail to touch us still, though so many centuries have passed away since they were spoken. They are words which speak, on the one hand, of the hopeless-

---

[1] M'Lear's *Conversion of the English*, p. 51. [2] Bede, *H. E.*, ii. 9.

ness of the old religion, and of the gleam of hope which the new threw on the life and destiny of man. 'The life[1] of man in this world, O king,' said the speaker, 'may be likened to what happeneth when thou art sitting at supper with thy thanes in the time of winter. A fire is blazing on the hearth, and the hall is warm; without, the rain and the snow are falling, and the wind is howling. There cometh a sparrow, and flieth through the house. She entereth by one door, and goeth out by another. While she is within the house, she feeleth not the howling blast; but when the short space of rest is past, she flieth out again into the storm, and passeth away from our eyes. Even so is it with the brief life of man; it appeareth for a little while, but what precedeth it or what cometh after it we know not at all. Wherefore, if this new lore can tell us aught, let us hearken to it and follow it.'

What that new lore told them regarding the present life and destiny of man we know, for we have heard it ourselves. The contrast between the paganism of that time and the civilisation of to-day is so overwhelmingly great as to be indescribable. The change in social life—political organisation—the rise of art—the discoveries of science—these things mark the distance we have travelled since the first Christian missionary set foot upon our shores. Year by year there has been a steady advance in all that pertains to the elevation of man; and the Scotland of to-day is as unlike the Scotland of that early time, as the well-tilled and cultivated fields are unlike the rough forests, swamps, and morasses, in which our wild ancestors were wont to dwell. How difficult it is for us, as we travel through some of the more fertile parts of our country, to think of them being formerly only inhabited by painted barbarians, living by the spoils of the chase; and that where now the busy city stands—its spires and noble buildings springing up against the sky—were groups of huts in which they lived in all the

[1] M'Lear's *Conversion of the English*, p. 51.

squalor of savage misery. It is impossible to deny that it is Christianity that has been the chief source of all that has made our country great; that it caused barbarism to be exchanged for purity of life, and the heroism of savages for the virtues of Christianity; that it gave an impulse to civilisation that has not yet spent itself. Above all, it brought comfort to those who knew no mitigation of human sorrow, and hope to those for whom the future was full of dread. It is well for us who now hear the sound of peaceful industry and the chime of the church bell, where once ascended the screams of devil-worshippers and the smoke of sacrifices, to remember how the change has come, how mighty it has been, and to have faith in the power of the same cause ever to produce the same result. Heathenism still confronts us in many quarters of the globe with which we have a close connection and a direct interest—heathenism, many of the forms of which recall that from which our own country was delivered. Let us not deny to those that 'sit in darkness' the same blessings that have in God's mercy come to ourselves. 'You have seen,' it has been eloquently said,[1] 'the fresh spring bursting up from the earth, and after it has filled its own little basin, overflowing into a rill that causes fertility and bloom all over the neighbouring valley. Like this is the living water of the love of Christ, that gleams and leaps with life, and then starts forth to convey its fullness and exuberance to barren places. The church that has no love to spare is the standing pool that "creams and mantles" with unwholesome things bred in its bosom by reason of its deadly stillness.' If this imperfect sketch which we have given you to-day of the paganism of old Scotland, make you more earnest in striving to enlighten that which still exists even in the Scotland of the present day—the heathenism in the heart of the Christian Church and under the shadow of our temples, and which sheds its baleful shadow over so large a portion of

---

[1] *Word, Work, and Will*, by W. Thomson, Archbishop of York.

the globe; if it fill you with a sense of gratitude to Almighty God for your own privileges, and deepen a sense of your responsibility to extend these privileges to others; if it bring you into greater sympathy with those who are seeking to extend the kingdom of Christ; if it lead you even 'to hold the rope' for those who bravely go down into the pit, I shall not have spoken in vain. If, looking to the past and to the present, we can say with the Psalmist: 'Blessed be the God of Israel, who only doeth wondrous things; and blessed be his glorious name for ever,' we will surely not refuse to add also with him the prayer: 'And let the whole earth be filled with His glory. Amen and amen.'[1]

[1] Psalm lxxii. 18, 19.

ST GILES' LECTURES.

FIRST SERIES—THE SCOTTISH CHURCH.

LECTURE II.

EARLY CHRISTIAN SCOTLAND, 400 TO 1093 A.D.

By the Rev. A. K. H. BOYD, D.D., First Minister of St Andrews.

MY time is short; and I have to tell you the story of six hundred and ninety years; from the beginning of the fifth century to near the end of the eleventh: a period which may be taken as including the Introduction of Christianity into Scotland, and its progress till earlier organisations were merged in the great Mediæval Church. Not one sentence, therefore, of introduction, save this: that it would be easier to compile a moderate volume than to prepare the thirty-two pages to which these lectures are restricted. For the materials, though often unreliable, are more than abundant. They are sometimes of deep interest. Above all, they afford opportunity of fighting over again still-continuing controversies under ancient names. But this is just what I am not going to do. My course is plain. For having, by aids quite familiar to most scholars[1] (there is no room here for original investigation), gained a fairly-clear idea for myself of that period, I wish to set it as clearly as may be before you; the truth uncoloured by any bias. I do not hold a brief.

I take for granted that you know what was said in this place as to Heathen Scotland to the Introduction of Christianity. It is generally supposed that during the Roman occupation of Britain, the Christian religion had made its way into the country. For Christianity, after Constantine, was part of the constitution of the Roman Empire; and the British Church, such as it was, was part of the Church of the Empire. The better faith was gradually undermining the ancient paganism. But of the *personnel* nothing whatever is known. The late Bishop Forbes of Brechin tells us that there was 'a regular hierarchy, with churches, altars, the Bible, discipline;' but there is no authority whatever for the statement, except in so far as the existence of Christianity may be taken to imply all these; and the names of the earliest preachers and priests have absolutely perished.

[1] The following are the authorities from which the facts stated in this Lecture have been derived:

1. *Celtic Scotland: A History of Ancient Alban.* By William F. Skene. Volume II. Church and Culture. Edinburgh: 1877.

2. *Lives of St Ninian and St Kentigern: compiled in the Twelfth Century.* Edited from the Best MSS. by Alexander Penrose Forbes, D.C.L., Bishop of Brechin. Edinburgh: 1874.

3. *Life of St Columba, Founder of Hy. Written by Adamnan, Ninth Abbot of that Monastery.* Edited by William Reeves, D.D., M.R.I.A., Edinburgh: 1874.

4. *Scoti-Monasticon. The Ancient Church of Scotland.* By Mackenzie E. Walcott, B.D., F.S.A., Precentor of Chichester. London: 1874.

5. *The History of Scotland.* By John Hill Burton. Volume I. Edinburgh: 1867.

6. *Scottish Abbeys and Cathedrals.* An Article in the *Quarterly Review* for June 1849. Known to be by the late Dr Joseph Robertson.

7. Some information has been derived from various writings of the late Robert Chambers, LL.D., notably from the article *Icolmkill* in his *Gazetteer of Scotland.* Glasgow: No date.

The first, whose name and career are in any way known to us, is St Ninian. In a troubled time, when the Empire was pressed by outlying barbarians and had yielded before them, shrinking within that northern frontier formed by the wall drawn across the country from the Forth to the Clyde in 369 A.D., Ninian founded a Christian community on the north shore of the Solway Frith. There, at a place which took the name of Whithern, and which still abides with slight change in name, the Saint built a church of stone, the first built of stone in that region, which was called *Candida Casa*, the *White House*. The title tells us how it looked in the eyes of the rude inhabitants of Galloway: how it looked to such as saw it rising on its promontory above Wigtown Bay.

It is a faint outline, the figure of St Ninian: it is hard to realise him as a living and working man. It is said that his father was a British king. It is more certain that through many years he was trained at Rome in the doctrine and discipline of the Western Church. It seems established that he laid the foundation of his church at Whithern in 397 A.D. Tradition gives the derivation of the name. Coming into Galloway, he asked a night's lodging of a churlish smith and his son: and being denied, the Saint fixed his staff three fingers'-length in the anvil, so that no human strength could move it. Terrified, the smith and his son besought pardon. The staff was removed. And Terna and Wyt (for such were their names) hastened to offer their land to the Saint, who called it *Wytterna* in memory of its givers. St Ninian's object was the conversion of the Picts who inhabited Galloway. He accomplished his end and more. The inhabitants of Scotland, as far as the Grampian range, renounced idolatry and became Christians. Many churches and altars received his name: some places bear it still.

The Roman occupation of Britain ended in 410 A.D. From this time, for many years, all historical information ceases. It does not seem that Ninian's years in Galloway were many. There is mention of the name of Palladius, a Bishop sent by Pope Celestine in 430. By this time Ninian was gone. But his work remained, for a while: and it reached beyond what is now called Scotland. Ireland comes near to Galloway: and the inhabitants of Ireland were the only race then called *Scots*. Into that country the Church of St Ninian extended: A Church closely connected with the Gallican, and doubtless recognising the Bishop of Rome as its head.

No detail remains of St Ninian's work or worship. There is no trustworthy account of what like man he was. We are told, indeed, that he wrought many miracles: and we may believe that the story is true that he, like many great religious workers, and like the Master of all such, gained strength for his work by seasons of lonely prayer. Like St Regulus at St Andrews, he chose a cave by the sea-side for his oratory: one such is still pointed out in the parish of Glasserton. We do not know his methods of evangelising. It would be profoundly interesting if we knew exactly how he set himself to his great work. No doubt he worked by many hands and many voices besides his own. He built his church: he gathered around him a company of men like-minded: these pervaded the thinly-peopled region round, and they penetrated far. How did they tell their story to the ignorant heathen: how did they explain the errand on which they came: what did they say? Did they reason with these reasonless creatures, offering them something better than they knew as yet: or, prophet-like, speaking with authority, did they command the poor pagan what to think and what to do? One thing seems plain, as concerning the conversion of tribes and peoples in those days: the missionary-preacher aimed at the conversion of chiefs and kings. These being gained, those under their authority followed their lead. There is something curious, and something touching, in the simple-minded fashion in which old chroniclers take it for granted that when the king was persuaded to be baptised, his subjects as of course followed. The surprise of both chief and missionary-saint would have been extreme, had any subject presumed to think for himself. Some survival of that old way, even into recent days, may be traced in the undoubting expectation of certain proprietors of the soil, that their tenants should vote, in matters political, as the proprietors might decide; and should even undergo very rapid conversion of views when the proprietors did so. But the conversion of large numbers to Christianity was a simple thing, and a rapid thing, in St Ninian's days. Only get one, and you got many. Draw the one: many would run after him. Conversion is a very different work, in an age wherein individual souls must be dealt with: each soul thinking for itself.

So rapid and wide must have been the work of conversion to the better faith, when in this same dimly-discerned age, Scotland sent Ireland her great missionary St Patrick; and all Ireland was converted in twenty-one years. About the year 372 Patrick was born, possibly at Kilpatrick near Dumbarton, of which place his father is said to have been Provost. At the age of forty-five Patrick was consecrated a Bishop: 'Patricius, a sinner and unlearned, but appointed a Bishop in Ireland,' is the good man's description of himself. His work lies beyond our range: and our range is too wide already. Indeed, little is certain concerning the Apostle of Ireland save that he was Scotch (as we now understand the word) by birth: that he did a great work in Ireland, with which country his name is indissolubly linked; and that he died about the year 458, having returned to die at the place where he was born.

You will think that the men and the events of that distant time look dim in the twilight of fable. But the light grows less. A hundred years pass between the death of St Ninian and the coming of the next great missionary-saint;—Columba. St Palladius, already named, possibly did his work in Scotland and in Ireland. He is called by some the first Bishop in Scotland: and one Servanus is named as his friend and associate. Tradition says Palladius died at Fordoun in Kincardineshire. But it is waste of time to dwell upon a period of which it is to be confessed that we know nothing for certain. This seems sure: that the work of St Ninian had been done too quickly to last; and that after Ninian and Patrick died, Scotland mainly relapsed into heathenism.

The work hitherto had been done by Churches, and a Secular Clergy. For that age, and that race, the system had been in great degree a failure. Another organisation came in God's Providence: and the Monastic rule succeeded where the Secular had failed.

Only the utmost prejudice, founding on the utmost ignorance, will deny the good work done by Monasteries and a Monastic Clergy in their day of purity, energy, and self-devotion: or will deny that they were admirably fitted to do the work they did. The Christian Church needed not only dissemination, but also strong centres. A Mission, set down amid a great surrounding Heathen population, demands these yet: It is impossible to imagine a case in which human nature more urgently needs the strengthening and comfort of the companionship of those like-minded. The Monastery, placed in a Heathen land, with its brethren reckoned in those days sometimes by hundreds, was in fact a Christian colony, into which converts were gathered under the name of Monks. And the Monks did good work in divers ways. They spread a zone of cultivated land around them, reclaimed from the morass and the forest. We remark time by time how beautiful is the landscape still abiding round the ruins of some ancient religious House, not always remembering what hands made it so. The Monasteries were quiet havens amid surrounding tempests. Amid the terrible insecurity of life, and the utter disregard of right and wrong, which we can discern to have been characteristics of Heathenism, here was comparative security, here were truth and righteousness. The Monasteries were places of Education: they were schools: the only schools for many a day. And while Printing was yet unknown, here a constant work went on of multiplying copies of

Holy Scripture: but for which the Bible might almost have perished. Nor need we forget, we who miss it so sadly, the ever-recurring hour of prayer and praise: the Psalms, notably, from beginning to end, kept familiar as they are to very few of us. The Monastery, in the age of which we are thinking, was no more than a gathering of rude huts, with a wattled chamber for a church, and a turf wall surrounding the settlement to keep off in some measure the invasion of savages. Yet it had its devout and earnest hearts: its masterful and statesman-like mind in its place of rule: It gave the mutual help and encouragement that come of brotherhood. It was a *Base of Operations:* the very best that could have been, then and there. Its analogues abide in the changed circumstances of the world: mankind will not readily part with them. The Heads and Fellows (supposing them to be what they ought to be) of a great University: the quiet learning, the elevated devotion, the available store of preaching and missionary and consultative power, of the ideal Cathedral Close: the workers (taking them for what they ought to be) of a modern Mission set down far in the depth of African heathenism and savagery, tilling the soil, curing the body, caring for the soul: the Brotherhood in faith and feeling and work after which many earnest men have longed, when constrained to work on in isolation, and which is aimed at by Unions and Societies and Guilds beyond numbering: the Quiet Days (let us not say *Retreats*) in some peaceful scene, where continual worship and kindly counsel strengthen the weary minister and advise the perplexed and lift up all hearts to God and send back to labour with fresh hope and energy: all these and more were in the Monastic System, while it was kept up to the purity of its idea.

You will say, the Monastic System soon fell far below its ideal. You will say, Monasteries were abused: and the day came when they did evil and not good. True: and then they went down and were swept away. But the abuse and degradation of a thing in itself good is not peculiar to any age or system. So he will judge who has seen the occasional working of what in this country are called *Church Courts:* who has heard a devoted clergyman, of undoubted Presbyterianism, declare in a loud voice that if his Presbytery then adjourned and never met again, the interests of religion within its bounds would not suffer at all: who has heard another clergyman, venerable by character and years, and devoted to the Church of Scotland, say how on his way to the Presbytery he visited a dying man and promised to see the dying man again on his way back; but that certain hours of that Court's deliberations wholly unfitted him to be of any use to any Christian soul. I might quote a much more vehement testimony, borne by an eminent preacher: but it is better not. And I might add a great deal more: but I will not. God forgive us all our many shortcomings in temper and speech. God forbid that what was intended for His glory and for the good of souls should ever be so perverted that it too must go.

At Clonard, in Ireland, there was a monastery of three thousand monks: a great training-school of missionaries, a great starting-point of missionary work: founded by St Finnian. St Finnian had twelve chief disciples, who filled the land with religious settlements, and who were known as the Twelve Apostles of Ireland. The names of eleven of these good men are of little concern to us: but the name of the twelfth must never be forgotten in Scotland. His name was Colum: the name was latinised into Columba: as a Colon of wider fame became Columbus. He was born on December 7, 521 A.D. at Gartan in Donegal: both father and mother were of royal descent. It is remarkable to what a degree Bishops and Abbots in those days were of royal race. Strict hereditary succession to worldly dignities and property was unknown among the Celts of that period. Two paths were open to energetic ambition. Should it be temporal king: or should it be spiritual leader? To such as Columba the latter path seemed the preferable. To rule a devoted community, which exercised a wonderful sway over men's hearts and souls, even though it lived an austere life in a settlement of rude huts of wattles and clay, had its attraction. And Columba, though mainly known to us as a religious leader, was deeply concerned likewise in the state affairs of his day.

As Scotland gave St Patrick to Ireland, so Ireland gave St Columba to Scotland. It remains a debated question, What brought St Columba here at all. Some would say, pure missionary and evangelistic zeal. But it appears at least as likely that he had made his own country too hot to hold him. There are terrible stories of the temper of the Apostle of Iona. He was a Saint: but there was in him a certain infusion of that which some folk call Devil: though like a certain great Duke, with whom it was likewise so, he became very mild and gentle when he grew old. I must tell you the story shortly. A great battle was fought in Connaught in 561 A.D. There was terrible slaughter. A Synod of the Saints of Ireland decided that Columba was responsible for all this evil: and that he must needs win from Paganism as many souls as had perished in battle ere he could be reinstated. Besides the work assigned to him, the penance was imposed of perpetual exile from Ireland. He sailed away, with twelve disciples. He landed first upon Colonsay. But, ascending a hill, he found Ireland was still in view; and he must go farther. Finally, in 563 A.D., being now in his forty-second year, he arrived with his followers at a small island, separated by a narrow channel of a mile in breadth from the greater land of Mull. The island has been variously known. It was *I*, it was *Ia*, it was *Hy*: these words each signifying *The Island:* but it came to bear the musical and never-forgotten name of *IONA, The Island of the Waves.* On Whitsun-Eve, in that year the Twelfth of May, St Columba landed at Iona: which was to be his home for six and thirty years. Christianity was there before him. He found two Bishops: Bishops of that singular kind of Collegiate Church which had arisen in Ireland in St Patrick's days: a Collegiate

Church of Seven Bishops, apparently co-ordinate. We do not know how they got on together. These two Bishops were willing to welcome Columba. But he refused to recognise the validity of their orders: and apparently reasoned the matter with them. The result was one very unusual in ecclesiastical controversy. The two Bishops saw they were wrong: and they departed, leaving the island to the Saint. Speedily Columba succeeded in gaining a grant of Hy: apparently from one King Connall: to whom it probably did not belong.

Pilgrims without number have in recent years visited Iona. Those who have thoroughly explored it say it is a pleasanter island than hasty visitors know it for. It has picturesque bays: quiet dells: green hills: plains not unfruitful. It is three miles and a half in length: a mile and a half in breadth. Divers isles are in sight: Mull looked like the mainland. Did Columba resolve to abide here; and to christianise the lands he saw? As with lesser men, probably he was guided by circumstances: probably his way opened before him as he went on. From that stand-point St Columba did in fact christianise all Scotland north of the Forth and Clyde. For a hundred and fifty years the Church of St Columba was in truth the National Church of Scotland.

I suppose it would not do, in speaking of the place, the man and the work, to omit a famous passage known to many who otherwise have little knowledge of either. In the autumn of 1773 A.D., Johnson, attended by Boswell, came to Icolmkill, *The Island of Columba of the Churches*. They found no convenience for landing, and were carried by Highlanders to the strand.

'We were now treading that illustrious island which was once the luminary of the Caledonian regions, whence savage clans and roving barbarians derived the benefits of knowledge and the blessings of religion. . . . That man is little to be envied, whose patriotism would not gain force upon the plains of Marathon, or whose piety would not grow warmer amid the ruins of Iona.'

Dr Johnson records that even Boswell was 'much affected' by the sight of the ruins. And he hazarded the conjecture that in the revolutions of the world, Iona 'may be sometime again the instructress of the Western regions.' It may be appointed so. I have heard the most renowned of modern Anglican preachers, looking upon the ruins of St Andrews Cathedral, say: 'This church will be rebuilt, stone for stone.' It does not appear likely, in these days of payment by results. One could but say Amen, Amen.

What-like Church was the Church of St Columba? Was it Episcopal? Was it Presbyterian? Was it neither one nor other?

It was an Episcopal Church of a peculiar type. The system was essentially Monastic. There were no territorial Bishops. There were no Bishops' Sees. There were indeed Bishops, who were recognised as of a higher grade spiritually; but who, anomalously, were placed under the authority of the Abbot. They could do what the Abbot could not. They could ordain: but they must ordain as they were ordered. And in St Columba's own day, there was no Bishop at Iona at all. Anything which needed a Bishop to do, Columba got done in Ireland. When the days came in which St Columba's rude buildings of wattles and wood gave place to the Cathedral of red granite from Mull and to the divers halls and apartments of a fully-equipped monastery, and in which Iona was recognised as the Mother-Church of many fair daughter-establishments; still all the Province, and even the Bishops, were subject to the Abbot of Hy. The case seems strange: but it has its analogous cases to this day. Higher spiritual rank may be freely admitted in theory, while yet the holder of it shall be kept in his proper place; and that a humble one. You may have known the resident Chaplain in a noble family which held very high views of the spiritual powers of the priesthood, believing that whosoever's sins they remit are remitted and whosesoever's sins they retain are retained, yet declare himself in public to be no more than a humble retainer of that great House. And the only excuse for the expression of a humility thus approaching to the abject, was, that the lowly priest's statement of his own position was severely true.

No traces remain of the buildings which Columba raised more than thirteen hundred years since. We know their general character. There was an earthen rampart which inclosed all the settlement. There was a mill-stream: a kiln: a barn: a refectory. The church, with its sacristy, was of oak. The cells of the brethren were surrounded by walls of clay, held together by wattles. Columba had his special cell, in which he wrote and read: two brethren stationed at the door waited his orders. He slept on the bare ground, with a stone for his pillow. The members of the community were bound by solemn vows. They bore the special tonsure which left the fore part of the head bare. It looked well in front, we are told; but unsatisfactory in profile. The brethren were arranged in three classes: the Seniors, the Working Brothers, the Pupils. Their dress was a white tunic, over which was worn a rough mantle and hood of wool, left its natural colour. They were shod with sandals; which they took off at meals. Their food was simple: consisting commonly of barley bread, milk, fish and eggs, with seals' flesh. On Sundays and Festivals the fare was somewhat better.

It does not appear that Daily Service was maintained in the church. The Psalter was repeated continually, but from this the Working Brothers were excused. The chief service was the Communion, celebrated each Sunday: also on Festal Days. Easter was the great Festival of their Christian year. They used the sign of the Cross many times. They fasted on Wednesdays and Fridays in Lent. A peculiar form of austerity practised by some was to remain in cold water till they had repeated the entire Psalter. They lived a life of rule, and of constant self-denial. The unreasonable yet natural belief was ingrained with them, as with others beyond number, Roman and Protestant, Christian and Heathen, that the less they pleased themselves the more they pleased God: and that God, in His moral government, would never be hard on tortured creatures, who had been so awfully hard upon themselves.

But for Columba's purpose it was not enough that he and his brethren should so live. No doubt, the fame of their sanctity and austerity would spread around them. But what did the holy men of Iona do, beyond being thus holy? They found access, first, to the neighbouring Picts; both teaching and exemplifying better things than the savage race had known before. After two years St Columba gained a hold upon the king of that region, Brude, who dwelt near the river Ness. On his first visit, the king kept his gates shut against the Saint: but Columba made the sign of the Cross, the bolts flew back, and he and his companions entered. The king, in anger, drew his sword: but the same sacred sign made over his hand withered it into helplessness, till he became a Christian. Then the hand, now to be used to better purposes, was restored to him. The king being won, his people at once followed. Who were they, that they should know better than their Master? And might not he do what he liked with his own? The magicians were banished from Court: and Columba took their place, ruling the monarch both for his own good and the kingdom's. It was a supernatural power to which king and subjects bowed. For they believed that Columba wrought many miracles: uttered many prophecies: and was visited oftentimes by angels. The Saint was a despotic ruler, but a beneficent one. Nor was he lacking in worldly wisdom: in all its manifestations: from the highest and largest sagacity of the statesman, down to the homely tact which is serviceable in daily life.

In twelve years from his coming, Columba had done much. The community of Iona was large: it was zealous: it was docile: it was incorruptible. The Saint now began to found monasteries in neighbouring islands. He chose his agents wisely. They loved him sincerely, yet he inspired too a salutary fear. In 584 A.D. King Brude died: but Columba's influence was so established that there was no falling off through the loss of his royal protector. He pushed on his outlying settlements to near the river Tay. And Cainnech (the Saint of Kilkenny) founded a monastery in the Eastern corner of Fife, at a spot by the sea called Rig Monadh, the *Royal Mount.* Afterwards there arose here the great church and monastery of St Andrews: hence for long named Kilrymont.

In 597 A.D. St Columba was seventy-seven years old. At the end of May, carried in a litter, he visits the Working Brethren, busy on the other side of the island. He speaks to them with the gentleness which had been growing: and which, pleasant as it was, they were almost afraid to see. He tells them he would willingly have died in April, in the first of Spring: but that he was glad this had been denied him, lest his removal should have made the Easter Festival a season of mourning to them. Then, turning to the East, he blest the island and all its inhabitants: and from that day no venomous serpent could harm man or beast therein.

On Sunday June 2 he was celebrating the Communion as usual: when the face of the venerable man, as his eyes were raised to heaven, suddenly appeared suffused with a ruddy glow. He had seen an angel hovering above the church and blessing it: an angel sent to bear away his soul. Columba knew that the next Saturday was to be his last. The day came: and along with his attendant, Diormit, he went to bless the Barn. He blest it, and two heaps of winnowed corn in it: saying thankfully that he rejoiced for his beloved monks, for that if he were obliged to depart from them, they would have provision enough for the year. His attendant said: 'This year, at this time, father, thou often vexest us, by so frequently making mention of thy leaving us.' For like humbler folk, drawing near to the great change, St Columba could not but allude to it, more or less directly. Then, having bound his attendant not to reveal to any before he should die what he now said, he went on to speak more freely of his departure. 'This day,' he said, 'in the Holy Scriptures is called the Sabbath, which means Rest. And this day is indeed a Sabbath to me, for it is the last day of my present laborious life, and on it I rest after the fatigues of my labours: and this night at midnight which commenceth the solemn Lord's Day, I shall go the way of our fathers. For already my Lord Jesus Christ deigneth to invite me: and to Him in the middle of this night I shall depart, at His invitation. For so it hath been revealed to me by the Lord Himself.'

Diormit wept bitterly: and they two returned towards the monastery. Half-way, the aged Saint sat down to rest, at a spot afterwards marked with a cross: and, while here, a white pack-horse, that used to carry the milk vessels from the cowshed to the monastery, came to the saint, and laying its head on his breast, began to shed human tears of distress. The good man, we are told, blest his humble fellow-creature, and bade it farewell. Then, ascending the hill hard by, he looked upon the monastery, and holding up both his hands, breathed his last benediction upon the place he had ruled so well; prophesying that Iona should be held in honour far and near. He went down to his little hut, and pushed on at his task of transcribing the Psalter. The last lines he wrote are very familiar in those of our churches where God's praise has its proper place: they contain the words of the beautiful anthem which begins 'O taste and see how gracious the Lord is.' He finished the page: he wrote the words with which the anthem ends: 'They that seek the Lord shall want no manner of thing that is good:' and laying down his pen for the last time, he said, 'Here, at the end of the page, I must stop: let Baithene write what comes after.'

Having written the words, he went into the church to the last service of Saturday evening. When this was over, he returned to his chamber, and lay down on his bed. It was a bare flag: and his pillow was a stone, which was afterwards set up beside his grave. Lying here, he gave his last counsels to his brethren: but only Diormit heard him. 'These, O my children, are the last words I say to you: that ye be at peace, and have unfeigned charity among yourselves: and if then you follow the example of the holy fathers, God, the Comforter of the good, will be your Helper: and I, abiding with Him, will intercede for you: and He will not only give you sufficient to supply the wants of this present life, but will also bestow on you the good and eternal rewards which are laid up for those that keep His commandments.' The hour of his departure drew near, and the Saint was silent: but when the bell rung at midnight, and the Lord's Day began, he rose hastily, and hurried into the church, faster than any could follow him. He entered alone, and knelt before the altar. His attendant, following, saw the whole church blaze with a heavenly light: others of the brethren saw it also; but as they entered the light vanished and the church was dark. When lights were brought, the Saint was lying before the altar: he was departing. The brethren burst into lamentations. Columba could not speak: but he looked eagerly to right and left, with a countenance of wonderful joy and gladness: seeing doubtless the shining ones that had come to bear him away. As well as he was able, he moved his right hand in blessing on his brethren; and thus blessing them, the wearied Saint passed to his rest: St Columba was gone from Iona. The church was filled with the lamentations of the bereaved brethren. But the face of the Saint remained glorified by the heavenly Vision he had last seen.

He died on the Ninth of June, 597 A.D. 'I did not feel sorrowful,' said a good man, telling how he had stood by the open grave of a great Evangelist of later days: 'for he was weary, weary in the work.' Even so, looking on that still face,

They carried the mortal part of St Columba back to the chamber from which a little before he had come alive: and his obsequies were celebrated with all reverence for three days and nights. But only the inhabitants of the island he had ruled laid him in his honoured grave. Long before, a simple brother had said to the Saint that so great a multitude would flock to his burial that the island would be entirely filled. But St Columba said: 'No, my child, it will not be so. None but the monks of my monastery will perform my funeral rites, and grace the last offices bestowed upon me.' Sure enough, a storm of wind without rain made the Sound impassable through the three days and nights: and the sea grew calm whenever the Saint was laid to his last sleep; 'to rise again,' as his kindly biographer St Adamnan says, truly if the words were ever said with truth of any, 'with lustrous and eternal brightness.' Some days after, messengers from Iona came to a place in Ireland where Columba was held dear; and the question was eagerly put to them, 'Is he well?' 'Yes,' was the answer, 'he is well: he has departed to Christ.'

Yet, touched though we be by the beautiful picture of his end which Adamnan has given us, Adamnan the Ninth Abbot of the monastery of which Columba was the first, we cannot but acknowledge that the Saint left a memory not equally dear to all. He was a masterful man. He would have his way, and he had it: and there were those who did not like him at all. Others there were who could not speak too warmly of him. 'Angelic in appearance, graceful in speech, holy in work, with highest talents and perfect prudence;' such is their strain. There is but one account of his wonderful voice: wonderful for power and sweetness. In church, it did not sound louder than other voices; but it could be heard perfectly a mile away. Diormit heard its last words: the beautiful voice could not more worthily have ended its occupation. With kindly thought of those he was leaving: with earnest care for them: with simple promise to help them if he could where he was going; it was fit that good St Columba should die.

His prediction held true for many years as to the greatness and honour of Iona. Columba's monastery long retained the primacy of all the churches and monasteries he had founded in Scotland. But after his death, the succession breaks down; as it does still when a great man goes. You fill up his office; but you cannot fill his place. In a certain sense, no man is necessary. In a very true sense, there are those, there have been those, who will be missed at many turns till all are dead who knew them. Still, the work at Iona went on, with the impetus of its first outset and of its singular success. In due time they carried over the red granite from Mull: they chose out from the rocks of the island itself such material as might serve, the hornblende, the clay-slate, the gneiss: the marble altar-piece came from a more genial clime: the severely beautiful buildings rose: chapel, nunnery, monastery, and chief of all, what was the Cathedral Church of the Bishops of Iona, a church which was dedicated to St Mary. Good men and wise men ruled; but there was never another Columba.

The Columban Church spread into Northumbria. The first missionary-preacher was a severe man, who returned with the complaint, common to workers lacking in temper and judgment, that the Northumbrians were so peculiar a race that nobody could make anything of them. A wiser and more politic successor lived to tell a quite different story. St Aidan preached with great success; and he founded a see at Lindisfarne, which twice a day becomes an island as the tide rises, and is known as Holy Island. But the fame of the first Bishop of Lindisfarne is lost in the light which surrounds the great name of St Cuthbert. Twenty-seven years after St Columba died, in 624 A.D., Adamnan was born, who ruled Iona as the ninth abbot, and repaired all the monastery, bringing for that purpose oak-trees from Lorn. But evil days came. Sea rovers, caring nothing for Columba or his work, time after time plundered the settlement. And the time came, early in the eighth century, when the little ways which the Columban monks had kept as their own could be permitted no longer. The Roman tonsure must be adopted: no doubt far liker the Crown of Thorns than that hitherto used. And the Roman fashion of reckoning the day on which Easter should fall gained general acceptance: general, but not unanimous. Not frequently, in Scotland, has any ecclesiastical change been made with unanimity. And the lifting up of a testimony has not been confined to post-reformation times. The Columban monks refused to give up the ways which had come down to them from their predecessors. The upshot was that the whole of them were expelled from the Pictish kingdom, including probably those of St Andrews; and the primacy of Iona ended.

We pass to another great name. In the kingdom of Strathclyde, among its Cumbrian population, towards the close of the sixth century, a Christian church was founded, the great agent being St Kentigern. After the battle of Arthuret, on the border of what is now Cumberland and Dumfriesshire, in 573 A.D., a certain chief, Rydderch Hael, bearing a designation in after ages to become familiar, for he is called *The Liberal*, became king of Strathclyde. The story of St Kentigern's life is not so well known as is the story of the life of St Columba: for five hundred years passed before he found a biographer, and marvellous fables had gathered round his personality. He was the son of Thaney, or Teneu, or Thenaw: for in all these ways his mother's name is given: a name which has passed through a singular modification. The people of Glasgow are familiar with a church which they call *St Enoch's*. It need not be said to the least instructed in such matters, that there is no such saint in the Calendar: nor that it would be contrary to all rule if one who lived so long before Christ as the patriarch who 'walked with God' were recognised as a Christian saint. The church was *St Thenaw's:* and good folk who never heard of St Thenaw, but who were accustomed to pronounce the name of Enoch in a fashion which I can remember as still surviving in my student days, fell into a not unnatural error. The error, not creditable to Scotch hagiology, is likely to abide. For not merely has a remarkably handsome railway station at Glasgow assumed the erroneous name, but the builders of a beautiful church in Dundee thought the name so pretty, that they called their church by it; to the wonder of some.

St Thenaw was the young daughter of a Pagan king, who ruled somewhere in the Lothians. Her son, afterwards to be so renowned, was born at Culross, on the north side of the Frith of Forth: then a wild solitude. Here the mother and child were found by herds, attending on their cattle; and were brought by them to Servanus, a Christian evangelist who was preaching near. Servanus was prepared for their coming. That morning, at the hour of Kentigern's birth, he had heard the *Gloria in excelsis* sung, far above him, by a choir of angels: and in joy that one was born who was to do a good work for Christ, Servanus had burst, with a thankful heart, into that great hymn, now so familiar in our churches (thank God), in which Christian folk through many centuries have lifted up their hearts in supremest thanksgiving. We know it by its first words: as verses dear to Scotland are known by their last. It is the *Te Deum*. Servanus welcomed mother and child: exclaiming, at first sight of the infant, 'He shall be *my dear one:*' which in the language of his country is *Munghu:* in Latin, the biographer tells us, *Karissimus Amicus: Dearest Friend.* He baptised the two by the names of Taneu and Kentigern. But the short pet name would not go. It supplanted the grander: as *Homer* has Melesigenes: for Homer means merely *Blind Man*. And as Joceline, in his *Life of St Kentigern*, says that 'by this name of Munghu even to the present time the common people are frequently used to call him, and to invoke him in their necessities,' so it is still. The great city with which his name is linked has many times been called *The City of St Mungo;* never (in my hearing) *of St*

Kentigern. The beautiful church, which has seen every other building in Glasgow rise, and which will probably be standing in glory when every other building in Glasgow is in the dust, bears the Saint's homely pet name: not a Christian name at all. Not very many among the hundreds of thousands who live round Glasgow Cathedral know what is indeed the church's name. If the stranger in Glasgow were to ask his way to St Kentigern's Church, he might find it as difficult to gain the information desired, as if in Westminster he asked his way to St Peter's.

Kentigern grew up: and it does not sound unnatural when we are told that one who was so special a favourite of Servanus was regarded with some jealousy by his fellow-students: for Servanus was teaching a school of young divines. In divers ways they testified their ill-will: and though Kentigern easily held his own against them, yet he gradually found that for their sake, and his own, and his master's, it was better he should go elsewhere. The day came when he parted from the kind protector of his infancy and childhood, with deep regret and with mutual blessing: and they met no more. In a new wain, drawn by two untamed bulls, Kentigern made his journey, knowing that he would be guided to the place where God needed him. Straight as an arrow, through the wild region without a path or road, his singular team bore him: till they stopped, in a fashion that signified that here they were to stop, at a spot called Cathures, beside a burying-place which had been consecrated long before by St Ninian. The name of Cathures yielded to another which is likely to abide while the Empire stands: the place became Glasgow. Here Kentigern dwelt for a while with two brothers, who had inhabited the spot before his arrival. One brother was Kentigern's friend, the other his enemy: the friend, and his descendants for generations, were richly blest of God: the enemy speedily came to a violent end. Gradually, Kentigern's character matured, in wisdom and holiness; and his fame spread wide: so that the king and clergy of that thinly-peopled Cambrian region discerned in him the man who could restore their failing Church, and with one consent elected him their Bishop. Kentigern resisted the elevation, alleging his youth and his desire to give himself to holy contemplation: but he yielded in the end to their importunity, after the manner of ministers called to a larger sphere of usefulness: and a solitary Bishop having been brought from Ireland, after the fashion of the Britons and Scots of that day, he was consecrated to the episcopal dignity. His consecration was in several respects irregular: yet the judgment of the Church admitted it as sufficient.

There had been an earlier Church at Glasgow, of St Ninian's foundation: and Kentigern restored it. Fixing here his Cathedral seat, he gathered to himself a family of earnest and self-denying men, who lived without private property, in holy discipline and service. Gradually, he extended his diocese to the limits of the Cambrian Kingdom. He lived for a while peaceably at Glasgow, practising severe austerity. His food was the sparest: mainly bread and milk: and even this only on each third day. He was clad in the roughest hair-cloth: but over this he always wore priestly robes, to remind him of his ministry. It is curious to read in Dr Liddon's Life of the last Bishop of Salisbury that he too in his earlier work at Sarum wore his cassock all the forenoon till he went forth for his daily walk, with the like intention. So across the ages do the fancies of good men meet. St Kentigern's pastoral staff was not gilded and gemmed, but of simple wood, and merely bent. And in his hand he always bore his Manual-Book, ready to exercise his ministry whenever needful. As for his bed, he lay in a hollow stone, having a stone in place of a pillow, like another Jacob. Even this rigour did not suffice. When he lay down, he cast in a few ashes: and taking off his sackcloth, he took his snatch of sleep upon these. 'Verily,' says his biographer Joceline, 'he was a stanch combatant against the flesh, the world, and the devil.' At the second cock-crowing he arose, and stripping himself of his raiment, he plunged into the cold and rapid stream: and then, with eyes and hands lifted up to heaven, he chanted on end the whole Psalter. Wonderful health, both of body and soul, followed this severe discipline. And sometimes, ministering at the altar, when he said the *Sursum Corda*, and sought to lift up his own heart to Christ, a glory gleamed upon his face and form, so that he seemed like a pillar of fire.

His story must be briefly told. His growing influence at Glasgow stirred the wrath of a pagan king, one Morken. Morken seems to have been a specially unmannerly soul: and not without some power of metaphysical argument. When St Kentigern applied to him for temporal means, towards the support of the staff of Glasgow Cathedral, the king said to him: 'Is it not a favourite rule with you, "Cast thy care upon God, and He will care for thee?" Now,' he continued, 'here am I, who do not regard God at all, and yet riches and honours are heaped upon me, which are denied to you. Your doctrine is false.' The Saint endeavoured to make the king discern that worldly trial might be sent as a blessing, and that worldly wealth was no sure mark of the Divine favour. But the truth, it need not be said, was high above Morken's comprehension. The king understood better when a miraculous flood swept all his grain away, and laid it beside the little river Molendinar ready for Kentigern's service. His temper, however, was none the better for this experience of St Kentigern's power: and, beaten in argument and in practice, in an evil hour for himself the monarch kicked the Saint. Speedily judgment followed. The king's feet fell off, and he died: and something resembling gout was sent upon his descendants for generations. It is not quite clear why Kentigern, leaving Glasgow for a while, took refuge in Wales: he ought to have been safe anywhere. But he went to Menevia, now known as St David's. He founded a monastery at St Asaph's, in a valley which bore some resemblance to the Vale of Clyde. And when, after the Battle of Arthuret, and the accession to the throne of Rydderch, *The*

Liberal, Kentigern was recalled to Glasgow, he brought with him no fewer than six hundred and sixty-five monks. It was at Hoddam, in Dumfriesshire, that Rydderch met him: and there he abode for a while: but Revelation indicated Glasgow as his proper seat. Hence he converted Galloway: Alban (which means the North-East portion of Scotland): and even the Orkneys. Traces of the Saint's sojourn in Wales remain in certain Welsh names in the district which lies between the Mearns and Deeside—a wild and picturesque tract, not known as it deserves to be: and where doubtless the gospel had been preached by monks who came from St Asaph's.

Of the miracles wrought by St Kentigern after his return to Glasgow it would be unprofitable to speak. One may be named, the memory of which is perpetuated in the arms of the great Scotch city. A certain Queen, of small desert, besought the Saint's aid in respect of a ring which she had given away, and which her husband had demanded back from her, it having been cast into the water by himself. And a certain great fish, called a salmon, taken in the Clyde, was found to contain the ring. The Queen was saved from imminent destruction, thenceforward to live a better life. For the heaviest rain and snow, which probably in those days as in the present fell in even excessive measure on Glasgow, St Kentigern needed no protection: his garments remained untouched. A recent Anglican Bishop, being offered a pastoral staff by some zealous folk, is recorded to have greatly discouraged them by saying he would rather they gave him an umbrella: Not so with St Mungo. And an instance in which certain rams, stolen from the Saint, had their heads converted into stone, seems to be commemorated in the curious name long borne by one of the City Churches of Glasgow. Many can remember when St David's was generally called *The Ramshorn Kirk*.

There are traces of friendly intercourse between Kentigern and his great contemporary St Columba. It is recorded that they met, and exchanged crosiers. The meeting was at

Glasgow: but the record of it is brief. For several days, we are told, they conversed in kindly fashion, on the things of God and on what concerned the salvation of men. Then saying farewell with mutual love they returned to their homes, never to meet again.

The years of Kentigern's episcopal rule passed on, and he attained a great age. Tradition would make him live to a hundred and eighty-five: and Bishop Forbes suggests that temperance and sweet temper do much to lengthen life. But Kentigern's maceration of his bodily nature went far beyond healthful temperance: and though his disposition was gracious, it seems as if the eighty-five years, lacking the century, were a long span to one who had so toiled and so afflicted himself. On the octave of the Epiphany, January 13, 612 A.D., St Kentigern died. One of his last doings was the setting up of a great Cross of stone in the burying-ground of the Church of the Holy Trinity, which was his cathedral. The present name, it need not be said, would have been unseemly while the Saint lived. He had perceived, by the failure of the earthly tabernacle, that the end was at hand: he prepared himself by Holy Communion for the great change: and he told his brethren he must soon leave them. Great sorrow fell upon them, as they knelt before him, receiving his last farewell. But some among them were lifted up to the thought of the supreme blessing, named in the unforgettable words *In death they were not divided;* and they asked Kentigern if they might not all go together, the shepherd leaving not one of his flock, the father accompanied by all his children. 'God's will be done,' said the saint. And as his brethren watched by him through the night, expecting his departure, an angel appeared and promised that it should be even so. 'Because thy whole life in this world,' said the heavenly messenger, 'hath been a continual martyrdom, it hath pleased God that thy manner of leaving it should be easier than that of other men.'

The day dawned, a day on which yearly he had been wont

to baptise many into Christ: and the brethren, following the instructions the angel had given, prepared a bath filled with warm water, and gently placed their master therein. Then they stood around, expecting. Lifting his hands and eyes to heaven, and bowing his head as if to calm sleep, St Kentigern was gone. They lifted out his body, and one after another eagerly hastened to lie down where he had lain: where each, as peacefully, died. All had passed before the water grew cool. But there remained, there, or hard by, brethren enough to wrap the Bishop's body for the tomb, and to lay it, with all honour, at the right side of the high altar in Glasgow Cathedral: not the present great church, but a humbler one; yet honoured by the presence in life and in death of the best and greatest in the long line of the Bishops and Archbishops of Glasgow. In the cemetery of his church, they said, in old days, six hundred and sixty-five rest, each entitled to the good name of Saint: 'And all the great men of that region,' says his biographer, 'for a long time have been in the custom of being buried there.' A church rose, in due time, on the hallowed ground, far nobler and more beautiful than St Kentigern had ever imagined: but his shrine is there; and his name will abide while church and city remain. It became needful that what had been a beautiful country stream when the spot was fixed on, should be hidden away from sight. The next generation will know only from hearsay how the Molendinar used to flow under the East end of the Cathedral Church of Glasgow. But still, as in past centuries, it is the way to bury hard by the place where so many of Christ's saints sleep for the Great Awaking. And in a solemn burying-place, that awes one by its wide extent, with terraced walks and green slopes and rocky graves, a very City of the Dead, the good and wise of the vast City of the Living, and many of its fair and young no less, are laid, as of old, beneath the shadow of the great church of St Kentigern.

No record remains of his successors. But the cause prospered; and twenty-five years after St Kentigern's death the nation of the Angles was brought over to Christianity by Paulinus, who on Easter-day at York baptised their king. Aidan, of Lindisfarne, whose diocese reached to the Frith of Forth, established in Scotland two monasteries, one at Coldingham, one at Melrose. It was from this latter that the famous Saint and Bishop originated, to whom the Church of Durham is in a great degree indebted for its special pre-eminence. I mean, of course, St Cuthbert. His parentage is unknown. We first hear of him as a shepherd-boy in Lauderdale. A vision led him to devote himself to the monastic life, at the age of twenty-five. First, at Dull, in Strathtay: next, in the newly-founded monastery of Ripon; Cuthbert found occupation. He returned to Melrose, of which House he became Prior: but in the year 664 A.D. he left Melrose and became Prior of Lindisfarne. In both places, his life was one of severe austerity: and he preached in all the country far and near. A visit which he paid to the Solway is perpetuated in the name of *Kirkcudbright*. After twelve years at Lindisfarne, he withdrew from the monastery and for nine years lived as a hermit in a rude cell of unhewn stones and turf which he built for himself in the island of Farne. In 685 A.D., by the choice of the king and people of Northumbria, Cuthbert became Bishop of Hexham; which in the same year he exchanged for the see of Lindisfarne. Only for two years did St Cuthbert hold that office. They were years of indefatigable labour, and of visiting the wildest parts of his diocese to preach to the people, still half-heathen. Finally, feeling the approach of death, he returned to his solitary cell at Farne, where in a few weeks he died. This was in 687 A.D. He was buried at Lindisfarne: but found his final resting-place at Durham, 'where his Cathedral, huge and vast, looks down upon the Wear.' It was more than three hundred years after his death before he was laid there. When the seat of the Bishops of Northumbria was removed from Lindisfarne, it was first to Chester-le-Street, a few miles North of Durham:

and it was not till 995 A.D. that the great Anglican see of the North came to bear its present name.

But though St Cuthbert's fame be great, and though he was a Scotchman, we must leave him. For his great work was not done in Scotland. And my time draws to an end.

It was in the beginning of the eighth century, a few years after St Cuthbert died, that a name begins to appear, formerly wholly unknown, and of much interest in Scottish Church-history: the name of *Culdee*.

Within the Monastic Church there grew up a tendency to forsake the Monastic life for the life of the Anchorite, or Hermit. Severe as were the austerities of the Monastic life, when lived according to its first idea, there was something beyond it: there was a possible life of greater austerity still. Absolute loneliness might be added to the unworldly self-denial of the devout monastic. And the desolate cell of St Cuthbert on his uninhabited island, or the ocean-cave of St Regulus on St Andrews Bay, implied a harder and sterner life than did the wattled huts or even the beautiful towers of the monastery in its garden-like tract of cultivated land, where men might at least fast and watch and afflict body and soul in company. Here was more to suffer, if God was to be pleased by suffering, self-inflicted. Here was a discipline which might further lift up the soul, and cleanse the thoughts of the heart. Early in the history of the Christian Church this feeling came in: founding, doubtless, on something in human nature: founding, too, on an overstrained interpretation of certain words of holy Scripture. Having been trained for a while in a monastery, those who sought after perfection would pass to a lonely life. The famous 'unspotted from the world:' the mention of 'a chosen generation, a peculiar people:' were taken to point this way. Such a life was held also to be a devotion, a *cultus*, specially pleasing to God the Father. And hence the Anchorites came to be called *Deicolæ, God-worshippers*, in contrast to *Christicolæ, Christ-worshippers*, which all Christian people were held to be. These solitaries were especially *the people of God*. They were gradually brought under the monastic rule: and solitaries as they were, they were associated in a sense in communities. The *Deicolæ*, the *God-fearing* (to use a word not quite forgotten in homely Scotch speech), were called in Ireland *Ceile De:* in Scotland, *Keledei*. Whence, plainly enough, *Culdee*. At Culross, at Lochleven, at Dysart, they found their place. And in a spot more sacred and more renowned they have left their record and memorial: in the famous though little City of St Andrews.

In 710 A.D. Nectan king of the Picts placed his kingdom under the care of St Peter. But the day was to come when the Patron Saint of Scotland should be, as ever since, St Andrew, first-called of the Apostles, and brother of the more illustrious one on whom, as a Rock, Christ would build His Church. Each brother was crucified, but neither quite as was his Master. The legend is that it was at Patras, in Achaia, that St Andrew gained the Martyr's crown. St Regulus, a monk of Constantinople, and perhaps Bishop of Patras, three hundred and eighty years after St Andrew's death, carried away his bones, or part of them. He sailed away, voyaging among the Greek Islands for a year and a half, and wherever he landed erecting an oratory in honour of St Andrew. Finally, after a stormy voyage towards the North, on the Eve of St Michael's Day, he was wrecked on the Pictish shore at a place then called *Muckross, The Promontory of the Wild Boar*. Here he erected a cross which he had brought from Patras. King Hungus, or Angus, or perhaps his Queen, gave the ground to God and St Andrew His Apostle, 'with waters, meadows, fields, pastures, moors and woods, as a gift for ever.' In the presence of the Pictish nobles, King Hungus offered a turf on the altar of St Andrew in token of the gift. And the spot, having borne in succession the names of Muckross, Kilrymont, Kilrule, finally received that by which it is well known in the history of Church and Nation. It became St Andrews. And here, besides the group which consisted of Bishop Regulus, his Priests and Deacons, his Hermits, and certain Virgins, there was a community of the *Keledei*, God-fearing men, who are represented as having had wives, and as performing sacred rites after a manner of their own, differing from that of the Church Catholic. How far differing, it is quite impossible to say.

But the comfortless caves of the first God-fearing hermits had grown into comfortable cottages, in which each Culdee dwelt separately with his wife and children. Church-offices had come to be hereditary. The *cure* was coming to be lost in the *living*. And these metamorphosed Culdees held, as Provost and Chapter, the Church of St Mary of the Rock, now the most desolate among the many ruins of a city of ruins. They were likewise Vicars of the Parish Church of the Holy Trinity of St Andrews: still the Parish Church of that city, but now generally known by the less decorous name of the Town Church. It is yet a building of much interest, though it suffered miserably at the hands of ignorant meddlers a hundred years ago. But it is capable of restoration: and restoration will come in time, though perhaps not in our time.

It is near the end of the Ninth Century that we find the first mention of the *Scottish Church*. Certain privileges were given to it by Giric, king of Pictland. Giric was driven into exile: and his successors took the title of Kings of *Alban:* which means the region from the Forth to the Spey. There was but one Bishop, who ruled all the Scottish Church. His seat had been removed from Abernethy to St Andrews: and he was called Bishop of Alban. In 1005 A.D. Malcolm II. began his reign over Alban, now first called *Scotia*. And gradually the Bishop of the Scots came to be called indifferently of Alban and of St Andrews.

The days of the Celtic Church were drawing to an end. We have sometimes been told that the impending change was for the worse: that a pure and independent National Church was subjected to the tyranny of Rome. But the glory of the Columban Church had mainly departed. Its temporalities had been seized by laymen. It is a mistake to think that only at the Reformation the Church of this country was plundered by hypocritical robbers. Whenever the Church had anything to be seized, there were greedy hands to seize it. And much spiritual error was now mingled with the Church's teaching. The times cried aloud for Reform. The change came mainly through the work of one of the sweetest and gentlest souls named in our annals, the sainted Margaret.

In 1069 A.D. King Malcolm married Margaret, an English Princess, the representative of Alfred and the niece of the Confessor. They were married at Dunfermline. There is but one story of her touching beauty, of her unselfish and holy life, of her wonderful influence over the rude people among whom it was appointed her to live. 'In her presence,' says her biographer, 'nothing unseemly was ever done or uttered.' She was masterful, though so gentle. By goodness and sweetness she got her own way. She was profoundly attached to the Church of her birth and bringing-up; and by no means liked the rude ways of Scotland. Her time was short: she was married at twenty-four, and died at forty-seven: died, like some of the best of the race, broken-hearted. But for these years she set herself steadfastly to conform the Church of her adoption to the manner of Catholic Christendom. Her tact, her energy, her quiet resolution, were as her loveliness in body and soul. She enlisted her husband to her part. She called divers Councils: at one of these she held a three-days' discussion with the clergy; and (strange to say) convinced them. The special points she pressed are recorded. She shewed how Lent ought to begin on Ash-Wednesday and not on the first Sunday in it: stating the usual reason, too familiar for repetition. She restored the observance of the Lord's Day, long neglected. It is to St Margaret that Scotland owes her solemnly-kept Sundays. Specially, she condemned the evil custom which had crept in of celebrating the Communion without any one receiving it. The fear of eating and drinking judgment through unworthy communicating had led to a fashion so indefensible and unchristian that we might doubt its possibility did it not exist, along with certain kindred and gloomy superstitions, in some parts of Scotland still. Religious changes, when uncomplicated with political events, are slow: and St Margaret had seen only the beginning of the better way when she was called to her rest. In 1093 A.D. her health had failed through the severe discipline in which she lived. Lying one day on her bed, she had offered earnest prayer: when suddenly her son Edgar entered, returned from the army, which was besieging Alnwick Castle in Northumberland. 'How fares it with the King and my Edward?' she asked: and receiving no answer, she entreated the truth might be told her. 'Your husband and your son are both slain,' was the reply. The Queen lifted her eyes to Heaven, and said: 'Praise and blessing be to Thee, Almighty God, that Thou hast been pleased to make me endure so bitter anguish in the hour of my departure, thereby, as I trust, to purify me in some measure from the corruption of my sins. And Thou, Lord Jesu Christ, who, through the will of the Father, hast given life to the world by Thy death, have mercy on me.' And, saying these words, gentle St Margaret died. Never was worthier life or death.

In the same year, 1093 A.D., died the last native Bishop of Alban. The place remained empty for fourteen years. It was a time of strife and of transition. Then a line began, bearing the title of Bishops of St Andrews. The title of Archbishop did not come till the latter half of the fifteenth century. St Margaret's three sons, reigning in succession, the last the saintly David, carried on her work. The old Celtic element went. Churches were made territorial, not tribal. Parishes and dioceses came in. Bishops ruled and did not merely ordain. Sees were multiplied. The Culdees were absorbed, and in some cases suppressed. How, it falls to my successor to tell you.

ST GILES' LECTURES.

FIRST SERIES—THE SCOTTISH CHURCH.

LECTURE III.

MEDIÆVAL SCOTLAND, 1093 TO 1513 A.D.

By the Rev. JAMES CAMPBELL, D.D., Minister of Balmerino.

THE long period of four hundred and twenty years of our ecclesiastical history of which I have to give an account is marked by the rise and growth of so many institutions, and the occurrence of so many important events, as to preclude an exhaustive treatment of it in the limited space at my disposal. All that I can here attempt is to sketch in outline the reconstruction of the Scottish Church in the twelfth century after the pattern then prevailing throughout Western Christendom, and the further development of this system onwards to the time when, through internal corruption, it had lost its energy and usefulness, and only awaited the shock by which it was to be overthrown.

Students of the history of this period enjoy one signal advantage, which is denied to explorers of the previous ages. Of the four centuries extending from the days of Cumin and Adamnan, who wrote Lives of St Columba, to the death of Malcolm Canmore, we possess scarcely any of those native contemporary chronicles in which England and Ireland are so rich; and the inquirer must have recourse to the meagre and too often misleading information supplied by foreign annalists, or by legends and traditions which were not committed to writing till many centuries after the death of those to whom they refer. But when we reach the twelfth century we enter upon a new era. Land is then coming to be held by feudal charter; important transactions are set forth in formal documents attested by many witnesses; the endowments and privileges of religious houses and bishoprics are carefully inscribed in their registers; chronicles composed by churchmen make their appearance. Vast stores of such records have been preserved: very many of them have in recent years been printed; and the materials thus available bring us out of darkness into the light of authentic history.

It is this light, coming in with the twelfth century, which reveals the Celtic Church in a state of decay. While the greater portion of the endowments of the monasteries was held as private property by lay magnates who assumed the name of Abbot, the duties of that office were left to a Prior presiding usually over twelve Culdees, who enjoyed only certain minor revenues. This was substantially the state of things at St Andrews, Abernethy, Brechin, Monifieth, Dunkeld, and other places. In some cases the monastic community came to be represented by a solitary priest. In course of time the Culdee clergy were superseded, as we shall see, or otherwise disappeared.

The Church lands which were secularised were in some instances very extensive. The hereditary possessor of the great monastery of Applecross was able, with his vassals, to give Alexander II. such powerful assistance in war that he was rewarded by being created Earl of Ross. The lay Abbot of Glendochart ranked with the Earls of Atholl and Menteith. Most of the possessions of the monastery of Abernethy were held by a layman named Orm, ancestor of the baronial house of Abernethy. Crinan, the lay Abbot of Dunkeld, married Bethoc, daughter of Malcolm II., and thus became the progenitor of our Scottish kings. The Church lands were frequently termed *Abthane*—a word which some have erroneously understood as denoting an office—and in the name Appin, still applied to two widely separated districts, we have a memorial of the ancient monasteries of Dull and Lismore.[1]

The assimilation of the Scottish Church to the English, and thus to the Roman model, begun by St Margaret, and continued by her three sons and their successors, involved the extinction of the remaining Culdee clergy. But neither the causes which led to this change, nor the means by which it was effected, can be rightly understood without reference to a great though peaceful revolution which had commenced in the reign of Malcolm Canmore, and was destined to have a lasting influence both on Church and State. This was a migration, on a very extensive scale, of settlers from England. The tyranny of William the Conqueror drove many of his subjects, both Saxons and Normans, to seek a refuge in the northern kingdom, which possessed for the former an additional attraction after the Scottish sovereign's marriage to the Princess Margaret, sister of Edgar Atheling, the heir of the Saxon line. This immigration was greatly encouraged both by Malcolm himself and his successors, whose education and tastes were for the most part English. During several reigns the tide continued to flow across the Border. The land was being filled with strangers; especially its southern and eastern districts. The immigrants, many of whom were persons of rank, received grants of land from the Crown. They married Scottish

---

[1] I may here once for all refer to the following works as the authorities I have chiefly consulted, besides the standard Histories and Chartularies of Religious Houses: Mr Skene's *Celtic Scotland*, vol. ii.; Innes's *Sketches of Early Scotch History*; the same author's *Scotland in the Middle Ages*; W. E. Robertson's *Scotland under her Early Kings*; Keith's *Historical Catalogue of Scottish Bishops*; and Spottiswoode's *Religious Houses*.

heiresses. They obtained the highest public offices. The power and wealth of the kingdom were passing away from the Celtic people, who were henceforth to hold a subordinate place in the land they had ruled. Throughout a large portion of the country the Celtic language died out: the Celtic population was absorbed; and Scottish customs and institutions were being conformed to those of England. It was the commencement of a process which has been going on, with some interruptions, ever since: which is going on now, and with increasing rapidity, as intercourse with the South is becoming ever more extended.

The remodelling of the Scottish Church was carried out mainly by the establishment of Parishes, and the introduction of Diocesan Episcopacy and the Monastic Orders of the Church of Rome. These several processes went on simultaneously, and were closely connected with each other. But a distinct idea of them can perhaps be best given by describing them separately. The formation of Parishes may be taken first.

The organisation of the Celtic Church was monastic, not parochial. In many cases a tribe or a province possessed its own monastery, endowed by some former chief, and supplying Christian rites to the people around. There were also foundations which did not possess this tribal character. Sometimes a monastery had under its charge a group of neighbouring churches. Mortlach, in Aberdeenshire, with its five churches, was an instance of such an arrangement. Those structures have perished. Yet memorials of not a few of their founders still remain. We can often recognise the name of the first evangelist of a district in the saint to whom its church was afterwards dedicated; in the well at which he baptised his converts; in the 'fair' or festival (for such is the original meaning of the term) held on his 'day,' and still known by his name; in the stone seat on which the good man was wont to rest; or in the cave to which he retired for shelter or meditation. Such memorials are numerous throughout the Scottish mainland and islands.

Those primitive churches must, in many cases, have practically served as 'parish' churches by furnishing religious ordinances to the inhabitants of a definite territory. But parochial churches in the proper sense, mainly supported by tithes drawn from the district which they supply, were almost unknown till about the commencement of the twelfth century. The formation of parishes was promoted by the sovereigns, whose efforts were zealously seconded by the Norman and Saxon settlers. The proprietor of a manor built a church, or adopted one already existing, for the use of himself and his people, endowed it with the tithes of his land, and nominated a priest, with the sanction of the bishop, to serve it. His manor came to be regarded as a parish; and this was the origin of parishes, tithes, and patronage. We have an interesting example of the erection and endowment of a church, and the formation of a parish, in the case of Ednam, in the Merse. Thor, one of the new settlers from England, states, in a charter granted by him, that 'King Edgar gave to me Ednaham, waste, which I, by his assistance and my own money, have inhabited; and I have built from the foundation a church, which the king caused to be dedicated in honour of St Cuthbert, and endowed it with one plough of land.'[1] It appears that the tithes of the manor were also given to the church of Ednam—in short it constituted a parish. It is the first parish of whose formation we possess a distinct record. Six centuries later it was the birthplace of the poet of the *Seasons*, his father being its Minister.

Reasons of convenience frequently caused parishes to be subdivided. If a manor was extensive, one or more chapels would be erected in distant parts of it for the accommodation of the people residing there; and these chapels would in course of time acquire parochial rights. Or if an estate was divided among several proprietors, each of them would build a church

---

[1] *National MSS. of Scotland*, vol. i. No. xiv.

for his own people. In some cases a parish intersected by a river, or by mountains, required a church for each of its divisions. If a burgh arose within a parish, a new church would be required for itself. Thus the parish of Edinburgh was taken out of St Cuthbert's.

The institution of Parishes was the most valuable part of the organisation of the Mediæval Church; and it has proved to be the most lasting. No better expedient could have been devised for the instruction of the whole population. It is an interesting circumstance that after all the revolutions through which the Scottish Church has passed since the twelfth century, the Parochial system is at the present time not only in vigorous operation, but continuously undergoing that extension which is rendered necessary by the increase of the population. Its efficiency in the Middle Ages was, however, grievously impaired, as we shall see, by the bestowal of the revenues of Parish churches on Monks and Bishops.

Another part of the process of assimilating the Scottish to the English Church was the introduction of Diocesan Episcopacy, which, it is now generally allowed, had no existence in Scotland till the twelfth century. The see of St Andrews—as yet the sole 'bishopric of the Scots'—first claims our attention. On the accession of King Alexander, he proceeded to fill up the vacancy which had existed since the death of the last Celtic bishop, by appointing, with the consent of the clergy and people, Turgot, Prior of Durham, who had been his mother's confessor and biographer. This was the first of a series of Englishmen who filled the see. His appointment led to a controversy involving the independence of the Scottish Church. The Primate of York claimed the right of consecrating Turgot, on the plea that the province of York embraced the whole of Scotland. The King and clergy resisted this plea. The matter was ultimately settled by a compromise. Turgot was consecrated by the Archbishop of York, the rights of both Churches being expressly reserved. On the death of Turgot, Alexander, in order to prevent a repetition of the claims of York, requested the Archbishop of Canterbury to recommend a fit person for the office. Eadmer, a monk of Canterbury, was accordingly sent to St Andrews. But he, after his election, proposed to go back to Canterbury for consecration. The King, being resolved to maintain the independence of the Church, indignantly refused his consent to such a step. After a lengthened dispute, Eadmer resigned his appointment, and returned to Canterbury. Ultimately, Robert, Prior of Scone, was appointed to the see of St Andrews, and, after Alexander's death, was consecrated by the Primate of York on conditions similar to those agreed on in Turgot's case. Arnold, the next bishop, was consecrated in the Cathedral Church of St Regulus—King David being present—by the Bishop of Moray as Papal legate, though the pretensions of York were not abandoned.

The Church of St Regulus, with its square tower—to which a fabulous antiquity was at one time ascribed—was erected by Bishop Robert between the years 1127 and 1144. It was not twenty years old when Bishop Arnold commenced the building of the greater Cathedral, which, however, was not completed till 1318, when it was consecrated in presence of King Robert Bruce, who then endowed it with a hundred merks, out of gratitude for his victory at Bannockburn.

Two new dioceses were created by Alexander I.—those of Moray and Dunkeld. The former embraced the country beyond the river Spey. The see was successively at Birney, Kinneddor, and Spynie. In 1224 it was removed to Elgin. At Dunkeld there had been a monastery from very early times. Here Kenneth Macalpin, about the year 849, founded a church, and transferred to it the primacy of Iona, with a portion of the relics of St Columba; and it had been the seat of the Bishopric of the Picts, which was afterwards removed to Abernethy, and thence to St Andrews. Cormac, who, it appears, was now Abbot of Dunkeld, was made the first bishop of the diocese; and the Culdees were superseded by a Chapter of secular

Canons. The diocese was of vast extent, and embraced Argyll, as well as many detached places where there were anciently Columban houses, including Iona itself.

King David zealously pursued the same policy by still further dividing the country into dioceses. While heir to the throne, as Prince of Scottish Cumbria, he had founded or restored, about the year 1116, the bishopric of Glasgow, and appointed to it John, who had been his tutor. John was consecrated by the Pope, though, as in the case of St Andrews, a claim of jurisdiction had been advanced by the Archbishop of York. The diocese of Glasgow extended from the Clyde to the Solway and the English Border, and from Lothian to the river Urr, and included also the districts of Lennox and Teviotdale. On the spot where St Kentigern had preached the Gospel by the Molendinar Burn, Bishop John erected a Cathedral Church, which was dedicated in 1136. But this was afterwards burned down, and the crypt and choir of a new Cathedral—the stately structure still existing—were completed by Bishop Jocelin in 1197. The nave was erected between 1233 and 1258.

On David's accession to the throne he proceeded to create additional dioceses; and before his death six other sees had been founded—those of Aberdeen, Ross, Caithness, Dunblane, Brechin, and Galloway.

The bishopric of Aberdeen embraced the district between the Dee and the Spey; and the old Columban monasteries of Mortlach and Cloveth formed part of its endowment.—The seat of the diocese of Ross was at first either at Rosemarky, where a monastery had been founded in the sixth century, or at Fortrose.—The remote province of Caithness, which embraced the territory forming the modern counties of Caithness and Sutherland, was held by the Norse Earls of Orkney in nominal subjection to the Scottish crown. In founding the bishopric of Caithness, David probably designed to strengthen his own authority in the district. The seat of the diocese was at Dornoch. John, the second bishop, had his tongue and eyes dug out at Skrabister by the Earl of Orkney. Adam, his successor, who had been too rigorous in exacting his tithes of butter, was set upon by the people on a Sunday, apparently with the connivance of the Earl, and burned to death in his own kitchen at Halkirk. For this outrage Alexander II. inflicted severe punishment.—The see of Dunblane was founded by the Earl Palatine of Stratherne. The diocese appears to have been formed chiefly out of that of Dunkeld.—At Brechin a church had been built towards the end of the tenth century; and it is supposed that the abbot of the monastery connected with it was made, as in the case of Dunkeld, the first bishop of the new diocese; while the Abbacy passed to his son, a layman, and became hereditary in his family. The Prior and Culdees formed for a time the Bishop's Chapter, till they were superseded by secular Canons.—At Candida Casa, or Whithorn, where St Ninian had built his white church, a see had been founded or restored in the eighth century; and as Galloway was then subject to the kings of Northumbria, the bishop was a suffragan of York. The see, long disused, was again restored by Fergus, Lord of Galloway, about the end of David's reign. The bishop was still subject to York, and remained so till the fourteenth century. The diocese of Galloway embraced the modern counties of Wigtown and Kirkcudbright, west of the river Urr.

The Diocesan system of the Church was now nearly completed. The only bishopric created after David's reign was that of Lismore or Argyll, in 1222. It was formed out of the diocese of Dunkeld, and embraced the mainland of Argyll. Its first bishop received the appointment because he could speak the Gaelic language of the people. The see of the diocese was first at Muckairn, on the southern shore of Loch Etive, and was thence removed to the island of Lismore, which was transferred from the diocese of the Isles to that of Argyll. The Western Isles originally formed part of the bishopric of Sodor and Man —'Sodor,' or the 'Sudreys,' signifying the southern, that is, those now called the Western Islands or Hebrides, as distinguished from the northern islands of Orkney and Shetland—and the bishop was a suffragan of the Archbishop of Drontheim, metropolitan of Norway. When Man was afterwards taken possession of by England, and the Western Isles were united to Scotland, the diocese seems to have been divided into two, and the northern diocese was united to the Scottish Church. The Benedictine Abbey Church of Iona was used as its Cathedral, though Iona itself continued to belong to the diocese of Dunkeld after the creation of that of Argyll. From about the year 1498, the Abbacy of Iona and the Bishopric of the Isles were held by the same person. In 1469, Orkney and Shetland were acquired by Scotland; and soon afterwards the diocese of Orkney, which had been subject to Drontheim, was annexed to the Scottish Church.

Most of the dioceses were divided into several Rural Deaneries: St Andrews and Glasgow into two Archdeaconries each; and these again were subdivided into Deaneries. The various sees were in course of time provided with Cathedral churches, and with Chapters usually embracing a Dean, archdeacon, chancellor, precentor, treasurer, and other officials. In the dioceses of Brechin, Ross, and Caithness, the chapter was at first composed of Culdees; but these were afterwards displaced, and ultimately a dean and secular canons formed the chapters of all the dioceses except St Andrews and Galloway, where their places were supplied by the prior and canons-regular of the monasteries there established. The cathedral constitutions were mostly borrowed from England. Glasgow and Dunkeld followed the model of Salisbury; Moray, Aberdeen, and Caithness, those of Lincoln. The Breviary and Missal of Salisbury formed the ritual of all the Scottish dioceses. It is believed that organs and choirs were introduced into Scotland in the thirteenth century.

Though the country had been divided into dioceses, it had as yet no Metropolitan or Primate. King David had endeavoured to procure from the Pope the erection of St Andrews into an archbishopric; but in consequence of the opposition of York, the attempt was unsuccessful. It was renewed by Malcolm IV., with no better result. In 1188, however, Pope Clement III. issued a bull by which the Scottish Church was declared independent of all foreign control, save that of the See of Rome. Having no metropolitan to preside over them, the Scottish clergy could not hold Provincial Councils without the presence of a Papal legate—an official whose visits and pecuniary demands were, both to the sovereigns and the clergy, objects of special aversion. In 1225, Pope Honorius III. authorised the holding of Provincial Councils without the presence of a legate, for the carrying out of the decrees of General Councils, and other purposes of discipline. Accordingly these councils now met annually for three days when necessary, and were opened with a sermon preached by each of the bishops in his turn. They were composed of all the bishops, abbots, and priors; to whom were added in later times representatives of the capitular, conventual, and collegiate clergy. One of the bishops was chosen for a year as Conservator of the canons or statutes of the council, with power to enforce them. The Conservator also summoned the council, and presided in it, or, in his absence, the oldest bishop. Two doctors of the civil law attended as representatives of the sovereign. In course of time these Councils framed a body of statutes which regulated the proceedings of the Church till near the Reformation.[1] In 1472, the Pope at length erected St Andrews into an archbishopric, with the other twelve bishops as its suffragans. As this was done on the suit of Bishop Patrick Graham, without the knowledge or consent of the king or bishops, a conflict ensued which proved fatal to him; and he—the first Archbishop—ended his days as a prisoner in Lochleven. In 1487, Schevez, his successor, was made Primate of all Scotland and legate *natus*. Five

---

[1] They have now been printed under the title *Concilia Scotiæ*, with Preface by Dr Joseph Robertson (Bannatyne Club Series).

years later the Bishop of Glasgow was raised to the rank of Archbishop, with the bishops of Dunkeld, Dunblane, Galloway, and Argyll as his suffragans. These proceedings led to bitter strife between the two archbishops, which continued till the Reformation.

There were also Synods of the clergy of each diocese, presided over by their own bishop. The Diocesan Synod of St Andrews (*Scottia*, Senzie or Seinyé) was held either at St Andrews in the Senzie Hall, or at Edinburgh in the Abbey Church of Holyrood.

The next part of the process of remodelling the Scottish Church which I have to describe is the introduction of the Monastic Orders of the Church of Rome, with their more thorough organisation and severer discipline, in place of the now effete Culdees. This movement was connected with a remarkable revival of deep religious feeling, which had recently occurred throughout Western Christendom, and now reached our country, impelling vast numbers of devotees to embrace the monastic life, which they regarded as the highest form of piety. The discipline of the cloister was observed with increasing strictness. One leader after another appeared in different countries of Europe, practising some new form of asceticism, whose 'rule' was quickly and enthusiastically adopted by thousands of followers. Those who did not themselves assume the monkish garb, reckoned it a duty and a privilege to found, or to contribute to the endowment of a religious house. Kings and nobles bestowed on these establishments their most fertile lands, and built for the dwellings, and for the religious rites of their inmates, the most stately and beautiful edifices. The people regarded the monks with veneration and affection, and believed that their prayers possessed extraordinary efficacy. The Monastic Orders enjoyed the special favour and protection of the Roman Pontiffs, of whose power and supremacy they were, in turn, the devoted supporters. In bestowing endowments on a religious house, the donors acted under the combined influence of piety and superstition. Sometimes they would stipulate for the privilege of being buried within its sacred precincts: or they hoped at some future day to find in the cloister a retreat from the strife and cares of the world. A powerful motive to liberality was the reward which they believed this would secure for them; and benefactions were usually bestowed for the salvation of the souls of the donor, his parents and ancestors, his children and descendants, as well as for the glory of God and the honour of the blessed Virgin, or of the Saint to whom the house was dedicated.

The members of the monastic fraternities were called Regulars, as being bound by the 'rule' (*regula*) of their Order; and were known as Canons, Monks, or Friars—all other clergy being styled Seculars. The two most celebrated Orders were the Augustinian canons, who followed the rule of St Augustine; and the Benedictine monks, who adopted that of St Benedict. Each of these embraced several species, whose names were derived from their founder, the place where they took their rise, their dress, or some other circumstance. The Augustinians comprehended the Regular Canons of St Augustine, the Præmonstratensians, the Red Friars, the Dominicans or Black Friars, and the Canons of St Anthony. The Benedictines included those of Marmoutier, styled Black Monks; of Cluny; and of Tiron; the Cistercians, or White Monks; and the Monks of Vallis-caulium. There were also the Carmelites, or White Friars; the Franciscans, or Grey Friars; the Carthusians, and others. Of these numerous Orders, most had ample endowments for their maintenance. Such were termed Rented Religious. The Dominicans, Carmelites, and Franciscans, who subsisted chiefly on alms, were called Mendicant or Begging Friars. The greater houses were styled Abbeys; the lesser, Priories: presided over by an Abbot and Prior respectively. An Abbot's deputy in his own monastery was also called a Prior. Many of the Priories were subject to the larger Abbeys.

While the several Orders differed from each other in various ways, they were all bound by the three rules of poverty, chastity, and obedience. Their members could hold no private property, but were permitted in their corporate capacity to receive lands, and other possessions and privileges. They were all subject to strict regulations in regard to their food and dress, and the disposal of their time. Daily they performed their devotional services in church seven times together, and also assembled in the Chapter-house for discipline. During meals the Holy Scriptures or other edifying books were read aloud to the assembled brethren by one of their number. The rest of the day was devoted to some useful occupation, such as the copying and illumination of manuscripts, works of art connected with the buildings or decorations of the monastery, or the practice of gardening and agriculture. Members of the brotherhood were set apart to certain conventual offices, such as chamberlain, refectioner, cellarer, almoner, infirmarer, hospitaller, librarian, treasurer, porter, master of the novices. For the management of their secular business, a certain number of lay brethren, called *converts*, were admitted into the community. Over all ruled the Abbot or Prior, chosen by the suffrages of the monks, and wielding extensive authority. The Superiors of the greater houses possessed the privilege of wearing the mitre, which carried with it the power of conferring minor Orders on the members; and in general the monasteries were independent of the bishop of the diocese, and were accountable only to the General Chapter of the Order, subject to review by the Pope.

Though St Margaret founded a church at Dunfermline, neither she nor her royal husband founded any Religious house. Her sons, in different degrees, distinguished themselves in this way. King Edgar, about the year 1097, restored the monastery of Coldingham, which, after experiencing a strange and romantic history, had for centuries been ruined and abandoned. He erected it into a priory, and placed in it Benedictine monks, whom he brought from Durham—the first of that order who were introduced into Scotland. After a brief reign, Edgar was succeeded by Alexander I., who pursued a similar policy. At Scone there had been a monastery of great antiquity, and there was now a church dedicated to the Holy Trinity—a place rendered famous by the coronation there of the Scottish kings on that 'fatal stone' which was believed to have served Jacob for his pillow, and still lends a peculiar interest to the Coronation Chair at Westminster. Here Alexander founded an abbey for canons-regular of St Augustine, who were now brought into Scotland for the first time, from St Oswald's, near Pontefract. Robert, an Englishman, was the first Superior of the house. The king bestowed on the new foundation a priory of the same order, which he established in an island in Loch Tay, where his consort, Queen Sibylla, daughter of Henry I. of England, was buried. Yet another religious house owed its existence to Alexander. Having on one occasion, while crossing the Forth during a storm, been cast on the island of Æmonia, where there lived a hermit who followed the discipline of St Columba; and having with his attendants subsisted for three days on the hermit's humble fare of milk, small fishes, and shell-fish, the king founded there a monastery, which he dedicated to St Columba, to whom he believed he owed his escape from shipwreck; and the island thereafter was known by the name of Inchcolm, or Columba's Isle. One of the abbots of this house was Walter Bower, the continuator of Fordun's *Scotichronicon*.

With the view of establishing at St Andrews a monastic fraternity of the Anglican type, Alexander restored to its church the lands called the Boar's Chase; and caused

> 'His comely steed of Araby,
> Saddled and bridled costlily,'

and covered with a mantle of rich velvet, to be led up to the altar, and, along with his Turkish armour, shield and spear of silver, and many precious jewels, presented as a symbol of possession. The monastery was, however, not actually founded till the following reign.

The most munificent patron of the monks was the saintly King David; and many of the houses founded by him also were restorations of decayed Columban institutions. While he was yet Prince of Cumbria, he founded two monasteries—those of Selkirk and Jedburgh. The former was soon removed to Kelso, and was supplied with Reformed Benedictine monks from Tiron in France. Its mitred Abbots at one time claimed precedence of the heads of all the religious houses of the kingdom. To Jedburgh David brought Augustinian canons-regular from Beauvais. After his accession to the throne, he converted his mother's church at Dunfermline into a monastery for Benedictine monks, whom he brought from Canterbury, and its first abbot was Geoffrey, Prior of Canterbury. The abbey of Dunfermline succeeded Iona as the burial-place of the Scottish kings. David also founded for Augustinian canons-regular the abbey of Holyrood, so called from the famous Black Rood which he presented to it. This crucifix, which was believed to inclose a portion of the true Cross, was brought into Scotland by St Margaret. For canons of the same Order brought from Aroise, near Arras, King David founded Cambuskenneth Abbey; and for Cistercian monks, Melrose, Newbottle, and Kinloss; besides several more monasteries for other Orders. Melrose got its monks from Rievaux in Yorkshire, and was the mother of most of the Cistercian houses in Scotland.

In 1144, King David co-operated with Robert, Bishop of St Andrews, in founding in that city a priory for Augustinian canons, who were brought thither from Scone. A great portion of the secularised revenues of the ancient monastery of St Andrews—of which King Constantine, two centuries before, having retired from the world, had become the Abbot—was eventually bestowed on this new community of regulars, who were placed there that they might supersede the Culdees. King David now ordained that the latter should be admitted into the Priory as canons, if they were willing to become canons: if unwilling, they were to be allowed to retain their possessions during their life; and as they died out, canons-regular were to be instituted in their place, and their endowments transferred to the Priory. Soon afterwards, the Pope deprived the Culdees of their right of electing the bishop. They, however, stoutly resisted these changes, and for more than a century maintained, with more or less success, their right to share with the canons in the bishop's election. It was not till 1273 they were finally deprived of this privilege. In 1258 they lost their position as vicars of the parish church of St Andrews, and became eventually known as the Provost and prebendaries of 'Our Lady College of the Heugh,' or the 'Church of the Blessed Mary of the Rock'—the Chapel-Royal of Scotland—the Provost continuing to be instituted, not by the Bishop, but by the finger-ring of the lay patron, the King of the Scots. The Priory of St Andrews rapidly rose to the first position, in wealth and honours, among the religious houses of the kingdom. Its Superior was mitred, and in the time of King James I. obtained precedence in Parliament above all Abbots and Priors.

Harsher treatment than that received by the Culdees of St Andrews was now the lot of their brethren of Lochleven, who had there for centuries kept alive the knowledge of religion, and had received endowments from several Celtic bishops and sovereigns, including Macbeth and his wife Gruoch. In the tenth century this interesting community, with Ronan their abbot, had made over their monastery to the Bishop of St Andrews, on condition that he would supply them with food and raiment. This transaction enabled Bishop Robert now to bestow on the priory of St Andrews the abbacy of Lochleven, with all its revenues, and its little library of sixteen manuscript volumes—the names of which are preserved—that a body of canons-regular might be there established. In a charter to the same effect, King David ordains that 'the Culdees who shall be found there, if they consent to live as

F

regulars, shall be permitted to remain in society with, and subject to the others; but should any of them be disposed to offer resistance, his will and pleasure is, that such shall be expelled from the island.' A priory of Augustinian canons was now therefore settled in Lochleven. One of its Superiors was Andrew Wyntoun, author of the *Orygynale Cronykil of Scotland*. The Culdees of Monimusk, who also were connected with the church of St Andrews, were in a somewhat similar manner superseded by a community of Augustinian canons-regular, as were likewise the Culdees of Abernethy.

To King David also is ascribed the introduction into Scotland of the Military Orders—the Templars and Knights of St John—instituted for the defence of the Temple of Jerusalem against the infidels, and for the entertainment of pilgrims. The principal house of the former order was at Temple in Midlothian, and that of the latter at Torphichen. The Templars were suppressed by the Pope in 1312, and their possessions, which were numerous in this country, were bestowed on the Knights of St John.

The most important of the royal foundations subsequent to David's reign was the great and richly endowed abbey of Arbroath, begun by William the Lion in 1178, seven years after the death of Thomas à Becket, to whom it was afterwards dedicated. Its founder was buried before its high altar in 1214. Fifteen years later, his widow, Queen Ermengarde, founded a Cistercian abbey at Balmerino. This house, which was beautifully situated on the south shore of the Firth of Tay, was dedicated to St Mary and St Edward the Confessor, and was associated with memories of subsequent Scottish queens. Before the high altar of the Abbey Church, Queen Ermengarde was interred in the year 1233, in presence of her son Alexander II. Towards the end of the twelfth century, the abbey of Lindores was founded for Tironensian monks by David, Earl of Huntingdon, brother of William the Lion, on his return from the Crusades.

The nobles of the land followed the example thus set by the royal family, by founding other religious houses, or by adding to the endowments of those already existing. Next to King David, the most munificent friend of the monks was Fergus, the semi-independent Lord of Galloway, who founded monasteries at Soulseat—to which he brought canons from Premontré—Whithorn, St Mary's Isle, Tungland, Holywood, and Dundrennan; and on being defeated in an insurrection which he raised against Malcolm IV., was compelled to end his days as a canon of Holyrood. The abbey of Paisley—at first a priory—was founded for Cluniac monks who came from Wenlock in Shropshire, by Walter, son of Alan, the Lord High Steward. Reginald, Lord of the Isles, founded at Iona a Benedictine abbey and nunnery. It is supposed that the Culdees in Iona adopted the Benedictine rule, and became monks of this abbey. The existing ruins on the island are the remains of these two houses. The last abbey founded in Scotland was a Cistercian house in Galloway; and its name was derived from a touching circumstance. The Prior of Lochleven tells us that Devorgilla, daughter of the Lord of Galloway, and wife of John Balliol, founded this monastery in the year 1275; and that when her husband died, she had his heart embalmed and placed in a coffer of ivory, which was daily set before her as a memento of him who was gone. And she gave orders that when she died, she should be buried in the abbey she had founded, with the coffer placed upon her breast. Her commands were obeyed, and the house received the name of Sweet Heart Abbey.

The number of monks in each house varied at different times. It is said there were in Melrose, in 1542, two hundred. Probably the larger monasteries contained usually fifty or sixty. The number was greatly diminished on the eve of the Reformation.

Of nunneries of various orders upwards of twenty were established in Scotland. We know little of the history of those communities of pious virgins who 'departed not from the temple, but served God with fastings and prayers night and day.' Let us hope that many of their members were successful in securing those higher spiritual attainments for which they erroneously forsook the innocent enjoyments, and declined the responsibilities of life.

In the foregoing brief survey I have mentioned by name only some of the chief monasteries. The various orders of Augustinian canons had forty-eight, and those of Benedictine monks thirty-one houses. There were at least a hundred and fifty religious houses of all kinds, including those yet to be specified. Many of them were richly endowed. A large portion of the best soil of the country was in the hands of the regular clergy. And the effects of this at first cannot be regarded as injurious to the nation. The monks not only gave much attention to agriculture, but were the first to grant long leases of their lands on easy terms to tenants, who were not, like those of lay proprietors, bound to give military service, except on very special occasions. The clergy had a direct interest in the maintenance of peace, and could not be deprived of their estates by forfeiture or other sudden changes, which were productive of great misery to the tenants of lay lords. The monks were the friends of the serfs, the poor, and the helpless; their charity and hospitality were bestowed with lavish profusion. Each monastery was a centre from which religious and civilising influences of various kinds radiated into the surrounding district. An important service rendered by the monks was their cultivation of learning at a time when no Scottish baron could sign his own name, or would have reckoned it other than a degradation to possess such a monkish accomplishment. In the monasteries the flickering lamp of knowledge was kept alive when 'there was darkness over the land, even darkness which might be felt.'

Having become possessed of enormous wealth, the monks began to relax the strictness of their discipline, and declined in popular esteem. It was for this reason the Mendicant Orders were instituted. The Dominican and Franciscan Friars took their rise in the thirteenth century. The latter were also termed *Fratres Minores*, Minor Friars, or Minorites. The Dominicans were specially styled Preaching Friars, because they devoted themselves particularly to preaching, which was scandalously neglected by the clergy. The Popes, perceiving how admirably the Mendicant Orders were fitted to strengthen the Church, permitted them to preach wheresoever they chose, without license from the bishop, or consent of the curates, and made them responsible to the Papal see alone. They also granted to them the right of administering the sacraments; of hearing confession and granting absolution; and of selling indulgences in order to eke out their means of subsistence. The attention of the people was arrested by the appearance of barefooted men, wearing a coarse robe and cowl, with a rope round their waist, expatiating on the love of God, and the duties of religion. Supplying a real want at the time, the Friars became rapidly popular; and their influence was soon felt throughout the whole of Christendom. They were the favourite spiritual guides of the people, especially the more ignorant, who everywhere flocked to their churches. This brought upon them the hatred of the bishops and parochial incumbents, whom they supplanted in popular esteem, and whose flocks they drew away from their ministrations. They soon exhibited the usual effects of such prosperity. They were filled with pride. They poured contempt on the other clergy. Their own fraternities were split into contending factions. At length, by the laxity of their morals, they became, in a greater degree even than the monks, a source of weakness and scandal to the Church, and were objects of animosity and ridicule to all who longed for its reformation.

In the reign of Alexander II. the favour which had hitherto been shewn towards canons and monks began to be transferred to the Friars, who had eventually forty-six houses of the various Orders, which were mostly situated in towns. The houses of the Trinity or Red Friars were termed Hospitals or Ministries.

I have already alluded to the practice of conferring on religious houses the revenues of parish churches. It commenced, indeed, previous to the reform of the twelfth century. Some time before the reign of Alexander I., the churches of Markinch, Scoonie, and Auchterderran had been bestowed on the Culdees of Lochleven by the Celtic bishops of St Andrews; and the monks of Iona had four churches in Galloway. But the system was adopted to an enormous extent in the twelfth century and subsequently. In the reign of William the Lion thirty-three parish churches were bestowed on the abbey of Arbroath. Dunfermline had as many; Paisley, thirty; Holyrood, twenty-seven; Melrose, Kelso, and Lindores, nearly similar numbers. The revenues of bishoprics were increased from the same source. In the early part of King William's reign, the Bishop of Glasgow possessed twenty-five churches, and several more were afterwards acquired by it. In Fife there were not more than eight rectories at the Reformation; all the other parishes were vicarages. Seven hundred Scottish parishes—probably two-thirds of the whole number—were vicarages—that is to say, the greater tithes of corn, &c. went to the monks and bishops; while the vicar, who performed the parochial duties, got only the lesser tithes or a very small money stipend. The evil effects of such a system may be easily imagined. The underpaid curate was despised for his poverty, which disabled him from worthily ministering to the varied wants of his parishioners; while those emoluments which would have provided a comfortable subsistence for a resident clergyman were carried off to the distant Monastery or to the Bishop's palace.

The assimilation of the Scottish to the English Church embraced also its architectural styles. As our country received its faith chiefly from Ireland, so its earliest monastic structures resembled those of that country. The only remaining monuments of the old Celtic Church, possessing any architectural pretensions, are the round towers of Abernethy and Brechin, which are evidently of the same class as the numerous round towers still existing in Ireland, and were doubtless used as bell-towers and places of security. The now roofless church of Egilshay in Orkney, with its round tower, is probably also of Irish origin.

The Norman Conquest was followed in England by a remarkable increase in the number, and an improvement in the architecture of churches. In Scotland, similar effects resulted from the Norman and Saxon immigration. In place of the little Celtic edifices, frequently built of wood, and thatched with straw or heather, there were now reared for the worship of God the most magnificent structures which any age has given to our country, and richly provided with all the materials of an imposing ritual. The church erected at Dunfermline by St Margaret, of which the nave still exists, is the earliest embodiment of the loftier aspirations now evoked, and the first example of the substitution of English for Irish or native influence in Scottish church architecture. This fabric is of the Romanesque or Norman style brought into England about the time of the Conquest—easily known by its round-headed doors and windows, heavy round pillars, and, in its later stages, by profuse 'zigzag' and other ornamentation. Additional examples of it may be seen in the oldest portions of the cathedrals of Kirkwall and St Andrews, and of the abbeys of Jedburgh and Arbroath; in Kelso Abbey; in the rural parish churches of Dalmeny and Leuchars, and St Margaret's chapel in Edinburgh Castle, which shew the semicircular apse.

Towards the end of the twelfth century the Norman style, both in England and Scotland, gave place to the Early English or First-Pointed, characterised by the pointed arch, long narrow lancet-headed windows, clustered pillars, and less massive walls supported by projecting buttresses—though in our country the semicircular arch, round pillar, and certain other Norman features, occasionally appear both in this and subsequent styles. Most of our cathedral and abbey churches—including the greater portion of the stately fabrics of St Andrews, Glasgow, Arbroath, and Elgin—are of the First-Pointed style, which continued with us, as in England, for about a century, and embraced the latter half of the reign of William the Lion, and the reigns of the second and third Alexander— a period which has been justly termed Scotland's Golden Age, when peace and plenty, law and justice prevailed, and a great advance was made in the consolidation of the Church and the civilisation of the people. A striking proof of the activity in church-building which prevailed in the thirteenth century is found in the fact, that Bishop David Bernham of St Andrews consecrated, in the space of ten years, no fewer than a hundred and forty churches in his own diocese—nearly one-half of the whole number it contained. Yet it is a singular circumstance —explain it how we may—that by far the greater number of ancient parish churches, of which fragments still exist, are of the Norman style of the twelfth century.

The First-Pointed style gradually merged into the Second-Pointed or Decorated, in which Gothic architecture in England reached the perfection of majestic beauty. This style, distinguished by mullioned windows filled either with geometrical or flowing tracery, enriched doorways, and elaborate mouldings, prevailed in the South during the whole of the fourteenth century. It had been introduced into Scotland, and was used to a limited extent, before the War of Independence. During that great struggle such of the clergy as were of English extraction were driven from the kingdom; dignified ecclesiastics sometimes took the field at the head of their armed vassals; religious houses were ruthlessly destroyed by the invaders; and the peaceful arts were of necessity neglected. At the termination of the contest, the resources of the country were so much exhausted that a long period elapsed ere it could undertake great works in church-building. In this respect the fourteenth century is almost a blank. In the latter half of it, however, the monks of Melrose commenced the rebuilding of their monastery, which had been destroyed by the English. The church of Melrose Abbey is the most splendid example which Scotland possesses of the Second-Pointed Style, to which also the cathedral of Aberdeen is to be referred—both of them the work of a lengthened period.

In England the next style was the Perpendicular or Third-Pointed—having the mullions carried up in straight lines to the head of the windows—which continued from the beginning of the fifteenth century till the Reformation. This style can scarcely be said to have taken root in Scotland, though the choir of Melrose Abbey is a fine example of it. It was no longer from England but from France—our steadfast ally—our countrymen now took their architectural models; and the Scottish style which was contemporary with the Perpendicular in England was a modification of the French Flamboyant—so called from the flame-like forms of its window tracery. A specimen of this style may be seen in portions of Dunkeld Cathedral.

The ground-plan of the larger churches, whether cathedral or conventual, usually took the form of a Latin cross, having a choir as the head of the cross to the east, a nave to the west, and north and south transepts. The choir was the portion first built, the remaining parts being in most cases added at long intervals of time. Thus it happens that the architecture of a great church exhibits the changing styles of successive ages. Monasteries had a Chapter-house, refectory, dormitory, and other domestic buildings surrounding a quadrangular court on the south side of the nave of the church; but sometimes, for local reasons, on the north side, as at Melrose and Balmerino. Cathedrals served by secular canons had only the Chapter-house: the canons lived in their own separate manses around the Cathedral Close or Chanonry. The uniformity both of general design and minute details which exists in churches of the same age, but far removed from each other, strengthens the belief that those splendid memorials of the Middle Ages were the work of travelling guilds of Freemasons, though the designers of them were doubtless Churchmen, who were devoted to the study of architecture and kindred arts.

Collegiate churches or Provostries had their origin in the reign of David II. They were so called as consisting of a College or Chapter of secular canons or prebendaries presided over by a Provost or Dean, and instituted for the more orderly performance of divine service, and for the singing of masses for the souls of their founders and others. The prebendaries were frequently the clergy of the neighbouring parishes, the revenues of which, as also those of chaplainries previously founded in their churches, were applied to the endowment of the new institutions. The parish churches thus deprived of their proper incumbents, were, like those bestowed on religious houses, served by vicars. This new application of parochial tithes to non-parochial purposes still further extended the evils arising from the want of adequately provided and resident clergy. The earliest example of a collegiate church appears to have been that of Dunbar, instituted in 1342 by the Earl of March for a dean, arch-priest, and eighteen canons. There were in all thirty-three churches of this class. Most of them were founded in the fifteenth century, and were built in the Middle-Pointed or Flamboyant style of architecture, with the French feature of a three-sided eastern termination resembling an apse. Their plan is cruciform, but only in a few cases has the nave been actually erected. In 1466, St Giles', the parish church of Edinburgh, was erected into a Collegiate church by King James III. for a Provost, sixteen prebendaries, and other officials, who were endowed with the revenues of its chaplainries and altars, said to have numbered about forty. Gavin Douglas, the translator of Virgil's *Æneid* into Scottish verse, and afterwards Bishop of Dunkeld, was for some time Provost of St Giles'.

The clergy of the Mediæval Church may be said to have been in those days the sole promoters of education. Connected with most of the monasteries and cathedrals there were schools, taught or superintended by the monks. There were also many burghal schools at an early period, presided over, doubtless, by churchmen. In the twelfth century, or soon after it, there were schools at Abernethy, Perth, Stirling, Dundee, Glasgow, Ayr, Berwick, Aberdeen, St Andrews, and doubtless in other towns. About 1268, Balliol College, Oxford, was erected by the Lady Devorgilla, founder of Sweet Heart Abbey; and in 1326, the Bishop of Moray gave certain endowments to the university of Paris, which formed the beginning of the Scots College there. But as yet Scotland had no university of its own; and Scotch students could only acquire the higher learning of the time by repairing to the English or Continental universities, as it appears they did in considerable numbers, especially to Oxford.

The fifteenth century witnessed a wonderful revival of learning throughout Europe, and the Church promoted its diffusion by means of universities. The universities of Europe, established under Papal sanction, formed a vast brotherhood, open alike to rich and poor; and the scholar who had acquired a certain grade in one, was thereby made free of all. To Henry Wardlaw, Bishop of St Andrews, who had himself studied at Oxford, belongs the honourable distinction of having founded the first university for Scotland; and his episcopal city was chosen for its seat, as being in several ways admirably adapted for that purpose. The foundation charter was granted by the bishop in 1411, and this was confirmed in 1413 by Pope Benedict XIII. The Papal bull was received in St Andrews with the most exuberant demonstrations of joy. The 'Studium Generale,' as a university was then called, was instituted on the model of the university of Paris, for the study of theology, canon and civil law, medicine, 'and other lawful faculties,' with the power of conferring degrees. It was to be governed by a Rector, subject to an appeal to the Bishop and his successors, who were to be its Chancellors. The students, as at Paris, were divided into 'nations,' who, through their Procurators, elected the Rector; and they were lodged, as at present, throughout the city. The Professors were parochial clergymen, exempted from residence in their parishes; and their benefices constituted their whole income, there being neither fees nor endowments. Their work was at first carried on in rooms in different parts of the city, there being no central buildings yet provided for the University. In 1430, a Pædagogium was erected for the Faculty of Arts. The university soon acquired celebrity, and the number of its students rapidly increased. It was greatly encouraged by King James I., who countenanced by his presence the disputations of the students, and invited to it distinguished Professors from the Continent. Separate Colleges were afterwards founded—St Salvator's, in 1450, by Bishop Kennedy; St Leonard's, in 1512, by Archbishop Alexander Stewart and Prior Hepburn; and St Mary's, in 1537, on the site of the Pædagogium, by Archbishop James Beaton. These Colleges being well endowed, the masters and students were maintained within their walls. The result, however, of this more exclusive system was a falling off in the number of students. The university of Glasgow was founded in 1450, by Bishop Turnbull, and that of Aberdeen in 1494, by Bishop Elphinstone; the constitution of both being in most respects similar to that of the Mother university. King's College, Aberdeen, was erected in 1506, and Hector Boethius, the Scottish historian, was its first Principal.

The erroneous doctrines of the Mediæval Church, and the superstitious observances founded upon them, form too large a subject for discussion here. I can only refer to some of those peculiarities which come under our notice most frequently in narratives of the period. Of this description are the honour and worship which were given to crosses and crucifixes, to pictures and images of the saints; the belief in Purgatory; and the masses and penances performed in order to obtain deliverance from its fires. The intercession of the Saviour was practically obscured by a belief in that of the Blessed Virgin and the saints. We meet with an affecting instance of this in the case of good Bishop Brown of Dunkeld, who, on his death-bed—in the year 1515—expressed himself as assured of the safety of his soul, not for his own merits, but through the sufferings of Christ, and the intercession of the Virgin, and of St Columba (patron-saint of Dunkeld.) The 'day' of the patron-saint of a church —the anniversary of his death—was celebrated with religious rites, and frequently with a procession, in which his image was borne aloft amid the reverence and genuflexions of the people. The local fair was also held on this day. As regards the Sabbath, when the religious services were ended, the remainder of the day was usually devoted to marketing and games, in which the curate sometimes joined with his parishioners. A peculiar feature of those times was the religious Play or Mystery, as it was termed, in which some portion of Scripture was dramatised, the characters being personated by priests. These plays, in which the modern drama had its origin, were first instituted by the clergy for the purpose of impressing the events of sacred history on the minds of a rude and ignorant people who were destitute of books; but they too often degenerated into mere buffoonery. Another practice very characteristic of the Middle Ages was that of making pilgrimages to the shrines of certain saints, whose intercession was believed to possess exceptional efficacy, and to whose bones were ascribed miraculous powers. The shrines which enjoyed the greatest celebrity were those of St Ninian at Whithorn, St Adrian on the Isle of May, St Palladius at Fordoun, St Duthac at Tain, St Mary at White-kirk, and Our Lady of Loretto at Musselburgh. From Chaucer's tales of pilgrims travelling to à Becket's shrine at Canterbury, and from the numerous sums of money given by

King James IV. to musicians and others while he was on pilgrimage to Tain and Whithorn to expiate his sins, we may see how on those journeys amusement was combined with devotion. Pilgrimages were also made by our countrymen, as by others, to the Holy Sepulchre at Jerusalem; and though the Crusades, which the Popes so zealously promoted for the rescue of Palestine from the sway of the Infidels, excited less interest in Scotland than elsewhere, yet contributions both of brave knights and of money were oftener than once made towards the Holy War.

There is now left to me only room for a few general remarks, with which I shall conclude. The remodelling of the Scottish Church in the twelfth century was undoubtedly for that period a beneficial reform. Some portion of the ancient endowments was recovered, and new benefactions were bestowed with a degree of liberality which has never been equalled in our country's history. The people were more systematically supplied with the ordinances of religion. The clergy, both regular and secular, were brought under stricter discipline. Divine service was celebrated with greater solemnity; while in the doctrines then inculcated there was probably but little more admixture of error than in those held by the later Celtic clergy. In its subsequent development the Scottish Church followed that of Western Christendom, with which it was now united. The establishment of Papal supremacy over the nations of Europe was gradual; and Scotland, partly from its remote situation, partly from the character of its people, maintained its independence longer than most countries. Our sovereigns frequently resisted the domination of Rome; and two of them —William the Lion in 1180, and Alexander II. in 1217—thus drew upon themselves and the nation the dreaded punishment of a Papal interdict, whereby the churches were closed, and the rites of religion were suspended throughout the land. If Scotland at length placed itself under Papal protection, it did so in order to escape subjection to English metropolitans.

The clergy, on almost all occasions, helped to preserve the stability of the State by giving their support to the throne, whether the contest was with Rome, with England, or with overbearing Scottish barons. During many generations the Mediæval Church exercised an unbounded ascendency over the minds and conduct of our ancestors; and its influence, in those rude and turbulent times, was, on the whole, greatly beneficial to the nation. With all its errors and shortcomings, the Church was for a lengthened period zealous in restraining the vicious, caring for the poor, civilising the people, and teaching them to fear God, and to prepare for a life beyond the present. Its bishops and abbots were frequently chosen to fill high offices of state, for which they alone were fitted by education and training. Amongst its clergy of all ranks there were not a few men of saintly lives, and eminent usefulness in their day. But in course of time, the Church declined in purity and zeal. Amongst the causes of this declension were the great wealth of the clergy, and the law of celibacy by which they were bound. The War of Independence also was injurious to religion. The clergy—especially the higher orders of them—while taking part in that patriotic contest, neglected their proper functions; and the relaxation of discipline which ensued gained strength from the disorganised state of society resulting from the same struggle. By-and-by, church benefices came to be bought and sold at the Roman Court; and all attempts to put a stop to this evil failed. From the reign of James III. the Monks were seldom, if ever, allowed to exercise their canonical right of electing their Abbots, or Cathedral Chapters their Bishops; and the sovereigns, adopting the Papal practice, disposed of these offices for pecuniary or other considerations to persons who, in too many cases, were unworthy of them, and unable to perform the duties they involved. This led the way to further abuses. Pluralities abounded: livings were held *in commendam;* and the spiritual interests of the people were disregarded. Bishoprics and

Abbacies were made use of as a provision for the natural sons of the sovereign and nobles. Preaching was almost entirely neglected, except by the Friars. Attempts were made to remedy this evil by some good men, such as Bishop Kennedy of St Andrews, who preached regularly throughout his diocese, and obliged the parochial clergy to remain at their churches, and attend to their duties. But such cases were rare. The Monastic Orders, too, were becoming more and more degenerate; and the nobles were beginning to hanker after their immense possessions. Thus the Church, which in the twelfth century had been assimilated to the Roman model, had, at the commencement of the sixteenth, sunk, even more than its Celtic predecessor, from a state of purity and energy into one of corruption and decay. My successor will tell you further of the evils which now prevailed: but the darkest night is followed by the dawn of a new day; and he will also tell you of the introduction of evangelical doctrines, for which some had already suffered martyrdom. Though the Church still presented an aspect of external unity, there were everywhere symptoms of approaching change. Not only in Scotland, but throughout Europe the established religion was fast losing its hold on the conscience and intellect of the people. All things seemed tending towards some great crisis. On the 9th of September 1513, King James IV. and his bastard son, the youthful Archbishop of St Andrews—appointed to that high office when only sixteen years of age—with the flower of the Scottish nobility, lay dead on the field of Flodden; and the fires of persecution were rekindled in the following reign. The year of Flodden witnessed another event of wider import—the elevation of Leo X. to the papal throne—which proved the commencement of a new Chapter of surpassing interest and importance in the history of Western Christendom.

ST GILES' LECTURES.

FIRST SERIES—THE SCOTTISH CHURCH.

LECTURE IV.

PRE-REFORMATION SCOTLAND, 1513 TO 1559 A.D.

By the Rev. ALEXANDER F. MITCHELL, D.D.,
Professor of Ecclesiastical History in the University of St Andrews.

I CANNOT, like my predecessors, complain of the length of the period of which I have to treat. But events of the greatest interest and importance are crowded into it. With the exception of the introduction of Christianity into the world, the Reformation of the sixteenth century is the most glorious revolution that has occurred in the history of our race; and that period of earnest contending and heroic suffering which prepared the way for it, and the story of the men who, by God's grace, were enabled to bear the brunt of the battle, and at last to lead their countrymen on to victory, will ever have a fascination for all in whose hearts patriotism is not extinct nor religion dead.[1]

By the time at which Reforming influences began manifestly to shew themselves, that grand mediæval organisation

---

[1] Authorities consulted: Theiner's *Monumenta*, Robertson's *Concilia*, rare treatises of Alesius; Knox, Calderwood, Spottiswood, Petrie, M'Crie, Cook, Lee, Lorimer, Cunningham, D'Aubigné, &c.

which had supplanted the simpler arrangements of the old Celtic Church, had exhausted its life powers, and shewn unmistakable signs of deep-seated corruption as well as hopeless decay. Whatever good it may have been honoured to do in previous times in preserving knowledge of God and things divine in the midst of 'a darkness which might be felt,' in promoting civilisation, alleviating the evils of feudalism, and providing institutions which, with a purified Church and revived Christian life, were to be a source of blessing to many generations—yet now it had grossly failed to keep alive true devotion, or to give access to the sources at which the flame might be rekindled; it had failed to provide educated men for its ordinary cures, to raise the masses from the rudeness and ignorance in which they were still sunk, and even to maintain that hearty sympathy with them and that kindly interest in their temporal welfare which its best men in its earlier days had shewn. It continued to have its services in a language which had for ages been unintelligible to the bulk of the laity, and was but partially intelligible to not a few of its ordinary priests. It had no catechisms or hymn-books bringing down to the capacities of the unlettered the truths of religion, and freely circulated among them.[1] It did not, when the invention of printing put it in its power, make any effort to circulate among them the Holy Book, that they might read therein, in their own tongue, the message of God's love. No doubt it had its pictures and images, its mystery plays and ceremonies, which it deemed fit books for children and the unlearned. But it forgot that these children were growing in capacity, even if allowed to grow untrained; that 'to credulous simplicity was succeeding a spirit of eager curiosity, an impatience of mere authority, and a determination to search into the foundation of things;' and that if it was to maintain its place, it must not only keep

---

[1] The one catechism which at the last it ventured to issue was 'not to be put into the hands of lay persons without permission of the ordinary.'

abreast but ahead of advancing intelligence and morality. So far from doing this, it began greatly to decline just as the laity began to rise, and let slip the golden opportunity it got of itself initiating needed reforms during the century which followed the councils of Constance and Basel. It never grappled as it ought with the problem of the education of the masses; and what was done for those in more fortunate circumstances was done more by the efforts of noble-minded individuals than by any corporate action. It never grappled as it ought with the problem of easing the burdens which had long been so galling to the peasantry and poorer burgesses.

Not only had the life powers of the Mediæval Church been exhausted and decay set in, but corruption—positive and gross corruption—had reached an alarming height. There was indolence and neglect of duty, especially the neglect of preaching by the higher ecclesiastics and ordinary parish priests; the conferring of benefices on unqualified men and minors; luxury, avarice, oppression, simony, pluralities, and 'crass ignorance;' and above all, that celibate system, which nothing would persuade them honestly to abandon, though it proved to be a yoke they could not bear, and was producing only too generally results humiliating and disastrous to themselves and to all who came under their influence.[1] The harsh methods to which men themselves so vulnerable resorted to maintain their position, the shameless cruelties they perpetrated on men of unblemished conduct and deeply religious character, could not fail in the end to turn the tide against them, and arouse feelings of indignation which on any favourable opportunity would induce the nation to sweep them away.

The corruptions in the doctrine of the Church were hardly less notable than those in the lives of its clergy. The sufficiency and supremacy of the written word of God were denied, and co-ordinate authority was claimed for tradition. The blessed

[1] Robertson's *Concilia*, pp. xc. cxl. 283, 289.

Virgin and the saints departed were asserted to share the office which Scripture reserves for the one Mediator between God and man. Penances and external acts of work-righteousness were thought to co-operate in the pardon of sin with the 'one obedience' by which 'many are made righteous.' The sacraments were asserted to produce their effect *ex opere operato*, not by the working of God's Spirit in them that by faith receive them. The literal transubstantiation of the bread and wine in the Lord's Supper was maintained. The doctrine of a purgatory after this life and the virtue of masses for the dead were persistently taught. The Roman Church was held to be the mother and mistress of the Churches, and its head the Vicar of Christ.

Yet, even in these degenerate days, there were those among the ministers of the Church who wept in secret over the abominations that were done, and longed for the dawn of a better day—who, in their parishes or cloisters or colleges, sought to prepare the way for it, and succeeded in doing so with many of their younger comrades, and only made up their minds to abandon the old Church when all their efforts for its revival proved vain. Nay, the men who initiated or carried to a successful issue the struggle for a more thorough reformation—the martyrs, confessors, and exiles—were almost all from the ranks of the priesthood of the old Church, from the regular as well as from the secular priesthood; from the Dominican and Franciscan Monasteries as well as from the Augustinian Abbeys; and from none more largely than the Priory of St Andrews and its daughter College of St Leonard's. At least twenty priests joined the reformed congregation of St Andrews in 1559-60, and among them more than one who had sat in judgment on the martyrs and assisted in their condemnation.

How was the great revolution which was to bring the Church back from these corruptions of life and doctrine prepared for? Scotland had had no Grosteste, no Anselm or Bradwardine among its mediæval prelates—no Wicliffe among its priests.

But the earnest contendings of the latter for the reformation of the Church of England, could not fail to be heard of here. His poor priests, when persecuted in the South, naturally sought shelter among the moors and mosses of the North. The district of Kyle and Cunningham was 'an ancient receptacle of the servants of God,' where their doctrines were cherished till the dawn of the Reformation. In 1406-7, one of these priests is found teaching as far North as Perth, and for his teaching accused and condemned to a martyr's death. A similar fate is said to have befallen another in Glasgow about 1422; and in 1433 Paul Craw or Crawar, a Bohemian, for disseminating similar opinions, was burned at the market cross of St Andrews. These were not in all probability the only grim triumphs of Laurence of Lindores, who during so many years 'gave no rest to heretics,' but they are all of which records have been preserved. The facts that every Master of Arts in the university of St Andrews had to take an oath to defend the Church against the Lollards, and that the Scottish Parliament in 1425-6 enjoined that every bishop should make inquiry anent heretics and Lollards, speak even more significantly of the alarm they had occasioned than these sporadic martyrdoms. And in the very close of the century, and in the old haunt, we find no fewer than thirty processed, but through the kindness of the king more gently dealt with. Three of the most resolute—namely, Campbell of Cessnock, his noble wife, and a priest who officiated as their chaplain and read the New Testament to them, were released when at the stake.

It has not been very clearly ascertained how or when the opinions and writings of Luther were first introduced into Scotland. Chief among its doctors at that time was John Major, who taught with distinguished success in Paris as well as at home. He was a true disciple of D'Ailly and Gerson, and trained many to testify against the immorality and ignorance of the clergy. In the year 1523, Patrick Hamilton, having studied in Paris and Louvain, and taken the degree of M.A. in Paris, was admitted as a member of the faculty of Arts in the University of St Andrews. At that time he was probably more Erasmian than Lutheran, though of that more earnest school who were ultimately to outgrow their teacher, and find their congenial home in a new Church. He associated chiefly with the younger canons of the Priory and the members of St Leonard's College. Skilled in the musical art, he set himself to improve the service of praise, and composed a chant in nine parts, which was performed in the cathedral, and is said to have greatly delighted the hearers. He talked much of recalling philosophy to its fountains in Plato and Aristotle, and abandoning the scholastic subtleties which Major so greatly affected. He sought the imposition of hands, that he might be authorised to preach the pure word of God to the people, as well as to defend its teaching in the schools.

The years 1525 and 1526 were very unquiet years in Scotland, various factions contending with varying success for the possession of the person of the young king. In 1525 the Parliament passed its first act against strangers introducing the new opinions; and two years after, in consequence of a letter from the Pope, urging the young king to keep his realm free from heresy, the act was extended to natives of the kingdom.

In 1526 the Primate, having taken keen part in the political contentions of the day with the faction which lost, had to escape for a time from St Andrews, and disguised as a shepherd, to tend a flock of sheep for three months on the hills of Fife. It was at this juncture that copies of Tyndale's translation of the New Testament were brought over from the Low Countries by the Scottish traders. Most of them are said to have been taken to St Andrews, and put in circulation there in the absence of the Archbishop. Hamilton, who had long treasured the precious saying of Erasmus: 'Let us eagerly read the Gospel; yea, let us not only read, but live the Gospel,' seized the golden opportunity to impress the saying on others, and invite longing souls to quench their thirst at those wells of living water which had so marvellously been opened to them. His conduct could not long escape the notice of the returned Archbishop. I do not suppose that the latter was naturally cruel, nor after his recent misfortunes likely, without consideration, to embroil himself with the Hamiltons, with whom in the tortuous politics of the times he had often acted. But he had those about him who were both less timid and more cruel. He was himself ambitious and crafty, and about this very time was exerting all his influence to obtain special favours from the Pope. He knew that there was no more certain way to counteract the opposition of the king and to secure what he sought than by zeal against heretics. Still, he was anxious to perform the ungrateful task in the way least offensive to the Hamiltons. He would rather, if he could, rid the kingdom of the Reformer without imbruing his hands in his blood. And that result he attained by the summons he issued.

Hamilton, yielding to the counsels of friends and opponents, made his escape to the continent. His original intention was to visit Luther and Melanchthon at Wittenberg, as well as Frith, Tyndale, and Lambert at Marburg. At the time he arrived on the continent, however, the plague was raging at Wittenberg. So he went to study at Marburg, and publicly disputed those theses that most fully and systematically set forth the main doctrines which he taught, and for which at last he suffered. He was warmly beloved there, and urged to remain. But his heart yearned to return to his native land, and once more proclaim in it the truths which had now become to him more precious and engrossing than before. His faith had been confirmed, and his spirit quickened by living for a time among earnest and decided Christians; and in the autumn of 1527 he set out once more for his own country, prepared for any fate that might await him, not counting even life dear unto him if he might finish his course with joy, and bear faithful witness to his Master's truth, where before he had shrunk back from an ordeal so terrible. He appears first to have resorted to his native district, and made known to relatives, friends, and neighbours that Gospel of the grace of God which gave strength and peace to his own spirit. In his discourses and conversations, he dwelt chiefly on the great and fundamental truths which had been brought into prominence by the Reformers, and avoided subjects of doubtful disputation. His own gentle bearing gained favour for his opinions, and it won for him the heart of a young lady of noble birth, to whom he united himself in marriage.

Archbishop Beaton, if not at the king's express desire, then certainly, from his own wariness, did not at first venture formally to renew his old summons. He invited the Reformer to St Andrews to a friendly conference with himself and other chiefs of the Church 'on such points as might seem to stand in need of reform.' Hamilton accepted the invitation. At first he was well received; 'all displayed a conciliatory spirit; all appeared to recognise the evils in the Church; some even seemed to share on some points his own sentiments.' He left the conference not without hope of some other than the sad issue he had anticipated. He was permitted for nearly a month to move about with freedom in the city, to dispute in the schools, and privately to confer with all who chose to resort to him at the lodging which had been provided for him. It was evidently the intention of those who were determinedly opposed to him, that he should have ample time allowed him to express his sentiments fully and unmistakably, and even should be tempted by dissemblers to unbosom himself in private on matters as to which he refrained from saying much in public —on the many alterations required in doctrine, and in the administration of the sacraments and other rites of the Church.

At length the mask was thrown aside, and he was once more summoned before the ecclesiastical authorities in continuation of the former process. It is said that the Archbishop still desired that he should again save himself by flight; but he and his friends took the credit of the terrible deed as promptly as if they had planned and intended it from the first. They also assembled their armed retainers, that they might be able to hold their prisoner when once seized, against all attempts to rescue him. On 28th February he was seized, and on the 29th was brought out for trial, in the Abbey church or cathedral.

Among the articles with which he was charged, and the truth of which he maintained, the most important were, 'that a man is not justified by works but by faith; that faith, hope, and charity are so linked together, that he who hath one of them hath all, and he that lacketh one lacketh all; and that good works make not a good man, but a good man doeth good works.' On being challenged by his accuser, he also affirmed it was not lawful to worship images nor to pray to the saints, and that it was 'lawful to all men, that have souls, to read the word of God, and that they are able to understand the same, and in particular the latter will and Testament of Jesus Christ.' These truths, which have been the source of life and strength to many, were then to him the cause of condemnation and death; and the same day the sentence was passed, it was remorselessly executed. 'Nobly,' I have said elsewhere, 'did the martyr confirm the minds of the many godly youths he had gathered round him, by his resolute bearing, his gentleness and patience, his steadfast adherence to the truths he had taught, and his heroic endurance of the fiery ordeal through which he had to pass to his rest and reward.' The harrowing details of his six long hours of torture have been preserved for us by Alesius, himself a sorrowing witness of the fearful tragedy. 'He was rather roasted than burned,' he tells us. It may be, his persecutors had not deliberately planned thus horribly to protract his sufferings; though such cruelty was not unknown in France either then or in much later time. They were as yet but novices at such revolting work, and all things seemed to conspire against them. The execution had been hurried on before a sufficiency of dry wood had been provided for the fire. The fury of the storm, which had prevented the martyr's brother from crossing the Forth to rescue him, was not yet spent. With a wind from the east sweeping up the street, it would be a difficult matter in such a spot to kindle the pile and keep it burning, or to prevent the flames, when fierce, from being so blown aside as to be almost as dangerous to the surrounding crowd as to the tortured victim. They did so endanger his accuser, 'set fire to his cowl, and put him in such a fray, that he never came to his right mind.' But through all his excruciating sufferings, the martyr held fast his confidence in God and in his Saviour, and the faith of many in the truths he taught was only the more confirmed by witnessing their mighty power on him.

The Archbishop thought that by this cruel deed he had extinguished Lutheranism. The university of Louvain applauded his deed, and so also did Major, the old Scottish Gallican, then residing at Paris, and preparing for the press his commentary on the four Gospels. But, according to the well-known saying, 'the reek of Patrick Hamilton infected all on whom it did blow;' his martyr death riveted for ever in the hearts of his friends the truths he had taught in his life. This was especially the case with the younger alumni in the colleges, and the less ignorant and dissolute inmates of the Priory and other monastic establishments in the city where he suffered. As at a future period they made sure of detecting a stern Covenanter, if he refused to admit that the killing of Archbishop Sharp was to be regarded as murder, so they thought it sufficient mark of an incipient Lutheran if they did not get him to acknowledge that Patrick Hamilton deserved his fate. One on this sole charge, and that he had a copy of the English New Testament, was subjected to long imprisonment and a violent death; another, for simply preaching, as Major would, of the corruptions of the clergy, had to escape for his life; and a third, whose history, after being long forgotten, has been again brought to light in our own day, was for the same offences subjected to many cruelties, and at last forced to flee from his native land, and plead with it by his writings.

The original name of this confessor was Alexander Alane; but he afterwards obtained from Melanchthon the name of Alesius or the Wanderer, and by that he has been commonly known ever since. Born in Edinburgh on the 23d April 1500, of honest parents, he received the first rudiments of education in his native city. He was sent early to the university, and entered St Leonard's College when opened in 1512. In due course he took his degree, and probably after acting for a few years as one of the regents of the college, he was drafted into the Priory as one of its canons. When Major came to St Andrews, he studied theology under him, and made great progress in acquaintance with the schoolmen and fathers of the Christian Church. He was, like most of the young scholastics of the time, fond of disputation, and probably imbibed from his able teacher that combative attitude towards the new opinions which at this period of his life he shewed. He thought it would be an easy task to convince Patrick Hamilton of his errors, and had various discussions with him. 'Hamilton, who had before him nothing but the Gospels, replied to all the reasonings of his opponent with the clear, living, far-reaching words of Scripture. Alesius was embarrassed, and at length silenced; not only was his understanding convinced, but his conscience was won, and the breath of a new life penetrated his soul.' He continued to visit the Reformer while he lived, and to cherish his memory when cut off. When his opinions and martyrdom were the subject of conversation among the canons, several of the younger of whom loved to speak of him, Alesius refused to condemn him.

His silence or reserve in regard to the martyr brought him under the suspicion of his more bigoted associates, and gave special offence to his superior, Prior Patrick Hepburn, a violent, coarse, immoral young noble, emulous of the debaucheries and vices as well as of the hauteur and polish of the young French ecclesiastics among whom his youth had been passed, and, like them and young Beaton, a cruel persecutor of the Reformers. Knox has drawn a graphic if severe account of the revelries of this young Prior and his gay associates, more in keeping with what we should have expected from the sons of Tarquin in heathen Rome, than from the *élite* of the young ecclesiastics in a Christian primatial city, and under the eye of an aged Archbishop. The representation of Alesius on the same subject is only the more credible because the more restrained, and combines with the other in shewing to what a low ebb morality had sunk among the aristocratic ecclesiastics of the old Church ere it was swept away.

The more Christian lives of the younger canons could not but be felt to be a standing rebuke by their superior, and doubtless were one main cause why he bore them such a deep grudge, and gave way to such fierce outbursts of passion in his intercourse with them. He denounced them, and especially Alesius, to the Archbishop; and soon after got him appointed to preach the sermon at the opening of a Synod of bishops and priests which was held in St Andrews, probably in the spring of the year 1529. Alesius says he inveighed earnestly against immoral priests; but he adds that, as he said nothing in a disloyal spirit, and attacked no one by name, the sermon gave no offence to good men. But his irate superior imagined that the sermon was specially intended to hold him up to ridicule before the assembled prelates and clergy; and having already defied the Archbishop, he was not likely patiently to brook such conduct on the part of one of his subordinates. An opportunity soon occurred to him of repaying with interest the insult which he imagined had been done to him. The canons had determined to lodge with the king a complaint of the cruelty of their Prior. When this came to Hepburn's ears, he rushed with a band of armed attendants into the place where they were met, ordered Alesius to be seized, and himself drew his sword, and would have run it through him had not two of the canons dragged him back and pushed aside his sword.

The affrighted canon was hurried off to prison, whither his companions speedily followed; but on a remonstrance by certain noble friends, the king gave orders that they should be released. These orders were soon carried out with respect to all save Alesius. So far from being set free, he was thrust into a more filthy dungeon, called in one of his little treatises *teterrimo specu subtus terram inter bufones et serpentes*, and in another a *latrina* or sink, to which nothing corresponding has yet been found in St Andrews, save the lately discovered roughly hewn cavern stretching to the northwards of Castle Street, going down by its southern entrance into the solid rock by thirty somewhat irregular steps, and terminating in a small chamber of rounded or oval form. This chamber had in its roof a circular opening eight or ten inches in diameter, which has now been enlarged, and to which a low rock-hewn passage from the castle leads down. No cry from that chamber deep in the rock could reach the upper air, and he might well abandon hope who entered it. In this or some similar place yet undiscovered, the poor canon was confined for eighteen or twenty days; and when released was enjoined to tell nothing about the treatment to which he had been subjected. Alesius, however, would not conceal the truth, and for that he was again seized and kept in confinement for nearly a year. This, probably, was within the priory itself, and when the Prior was absent, the canons occasionally had the prisoner brought out, and even allowed him to take a leading part in their service at the altar. On one occasion, the Prior came back when he was not expected, and seeing what went on in his absence, ordered his victim into ward again, threatening on the morrow to have him off to the place where his life had been so nearly sacrificed before.

The canons, now satisfied that horrible torments and certain death awaited him if he did not at once escape, gathered around him as soon as their superior had left for the night, and urged him to seek safety in flight. With reluctance he yielded to their wishes. Then followed a parting scene only less affecting than that of St Paul from the disciples on the sea-shore of Phenicia, and shewing that even then goodness and charity were still strong in the hearts of not a few left under the rule of Hepburn. Only, the Apostle, though in a heathen land, could in open day kneel down on the sea-shore and commend his friends in prayer to God, and they could openly take leave of him at his ship; while these, though living in a Christian land, had secretly to bring out their friend under cover of the night, and with a few words of comfort, send him forth alone. 'Secretly,' he says, 'they bring me forth and supply me with provisions for the journey. So when with tears we had bidden each other farewell, and they had somewhat alleviated my sorrow by sweet mention of the illustrious and holy men who, giving place to tyranny, had abandoned their native country, I set out on my way.'

In solitude and sadness he plodded on his way, under cover of thick darkness, to that broad Firth which on this same Sunday last year was the scene of such sad disaster to trustful travellers, if haply he might find on its shore some tiny boat, or on its bosom some friendly craft, to convey him without loss of time beyond the reach of his implacable persecutor. In both respects he was successful, and with earliest morn got safe on ship-board. *Quidam homo germanus*, which some translate 'a certain man, a German,' others render 'a certain man, a kinsman,' kindly received him and affectionately nursed him in his sickness during the tedious and stormy voyage, on which he started before the horsemen sent to recapture him arrived.

Thus Alane left his native land and the friends to whom he was so deeply attached. 'Could any one have whispered in the ear of the disconsolate fugitive that he was on the road to far more extensive usefulness' and happiness than had yet been his lot; that under his new name and in his new home he would gain many true friends, and be honoured to do much good work for Christ; that he would not only be the first by his writings to plead for the free circulation of the vernacular Scriptures in

Scotland, and one of the first to aid Cranmer in England in asserting the authority of the word of God, and Hermann von Wied in his noble effort to introduce the Reformation at Cologne; but that he would be also privileged to be the special friend of Luther and Melanchthon, to command at the same time the respect of Calvin and Beza, to attend many of the great conferences of the leaders of the Reformation on the continent; to labour as a professor of theology, first in the university of Frankfort-on-the-Oder, and then in that of Leipsic; to write commentaries on the Psalms, the Gospel of St John, the Epistle to the Romans, and the Pastoral Epistles, and live and die honoured and beloved in the land of his exile—'how incredible would it all have seemed to him.' Yet it was thus God meant it, and thus he brought it to pass. And if there was one among the Scottish confessors of that age who was less embittered than another towards his persecutors in the old Church, more willing to yield to them in things of minor importance, if only he could hope to secure their favourable regard for truths of highest moment and immediate concern to the welfare of his native land, it was this cruelly harassed fugitive. He was unquestionably the most learned, as well as the most conciliatory of the Scottish reformed theologians of the sixteenth century. It was to his persistent advocacy, perhaps, more than to any other human instrumentality, that his countrymen owe the concession of the precious privilege of reading the Scriptures in their mother-tongue. Had he done nothing more than successfully pleaded for that concession, he would have given them abundant reason to remember him still. But in addition, he pled with them, before the author of the *Complaynt of Scotland* did so, to lay aside their animosities, to have more confidence in each other, and less dependence either on England or France, if they would secure a happy issue from their troubles, civil or ecclesiastical. No monument has yet been reared to his memory, even in this city of statues—the city of his birth, which he has described so well—but I hope the day may yet come when Anderson's suggestion may be acted on, and a statue of the exile erected, bearing on its pedestal that scene from *The Cottar's Saturday Night*, still so dear to the hearts of his countrymen.

From the time that Alesius fled, down to the death of James V., there was almost continuous inquisition for those who were suspected of having heretical books, including the New Testament in the vernacular, or who otherwise shewed a leaning towards the new opinions. In 1532, as is generally supposed, Henry Forrest, who like Hamilton was a native of the county of Linlithgow, and had associated with the martyr in St Andrews, was the first to share his fiery baptism. He was burned at the North Kirk Stile there, that the heretics of Angus might see the fire and take warning from it. In the same year, 'there was a great abjuration of the favourers of Martin Luther in the Abbey of Holyrood.' In 1534 a second great assize against heretics was held in the same place. The king, as the great Justiciar, was present in his scarlet robe, and took part in the proceedings. About sixteen are said to have been convicted, and had their goods forfeited. James Hamilton, the brother of the martyr, had been ordered by the king to flee, as he could not otherwise be saved. His sister was persuaded to submit to the Church. Norman Gourlay, a priest who had been abroad and had imbibed the new opinions, and David Stratoun, the brother of the laird of Laureston, were burned at the Rood of Greenside. In the same year, Willock, M'Alpin, and M'Dowall had to escape into England. In 1536, when the king and the Cardinal were abroad, there was comparative peace. In 1537 several were convicted in Ayr and had their goods forfeited, among whom was Walter Steward, son of Lord Ochiltree. In 1538-9 many were accused and convicted in various burghs, and many sought safety in flight. Among these last were Gavin Logie, who in St Leonard's College had done good to many under him; John Fife, who became Professor of Divinity in the university of Frankfort-on-the-Oder; George

Buchanan, who at the king's command had written the *Franciscanus*; also George Wishart, who had taught the Greek New Testament; John and James Wedderburn of Dundee; and Thomas Cocklaw, John and Robert Richardson, and Robert Logie, canons of the Augustinian Abbey of Cambuskenneth. Cocklaw, Knox tells us, for marrying a wife, had been shut up within stone walls, but his brother came with crowbars and released him. 'Large numbers of the wealthy burgesses were stripped of their possessions, even after they had abjured, among whom the burgesses of Dundee were conspicuous. Nor was the good town of Stirling far behind Dundee in the race of Christian glory. She had less wealth to resign, but she brought to the altar a larger offering of saintly blood. On the 1st of March 1539, no fewer than four of her citizens were burned at one pile on the Castle-hill of Edinburgh. At the same stake with them perished one of the most sainted and interesting of Scotland's martyrs—Thomas Forret, Dean of the Augustinian Abbey of Inchcolm, and Vicar of Dollar.' He taught his parishioners the Ten Commandments, penned a little catechism for their instruction, preached every Sunday, and shewed them that pardon of sin could only be obtained through the blood of Christ. When he pulled from his sleeve his New Testament, his accuser exclaimed: 'This is the book that makes all the din and pley in our Kirk.' The same year two were condemned and burned at Glasgow.[1]

During all these anxious years, the measures against the Reformers had been really directed by the man who comes more into public view towards their close. This was David Beaton, the nephew of the Primate, and by this time Abbot of Arbroath and Bishop of Mirepoix in France, coadjutor to his uncle, and Cardinal of St Stephen on the Cœlian Mount. I can but abridge here what I have elsewhere said of him.

---

[1] Then also Mr John Brown, patron of the Chaplainry of St Francis' Altar, within the College Kirk of St Giles, was convicted of heresy, and his goods and patronage assigned to Mr James Foulis, of Colinton.

He was a man not only of large intelligence, consummate ability, unbounded ambition, and indomitable energy; but also of polished manners and considerable scholarly attainments. He did not, it is true, belong to the school of Pole and Contarini, who would have made concessions to the Reformers in respect of doctrine; nor to that of the disciples of D'Ailly and Gerson, who were pressing for a reformation in respect of morals. His associations and sympathies were rather with the Italian or French Humanist school, both in its virtues and vices. He was versed in the study of canon and civil law, as well as of the classics. He was a great stickler for the liberties of Holy Church, and for years refused to pay the tax imposed on him for the support of the College of Justice. It was no doubt by his advice that heretical processes from the first were carried on under the canon law, rather than under the acts of the Scotch Parliament. His time, from 1514 to 1524, was passed abroad—the later years in the diplomatic service of his country; and he had no sooner returned home than the same measures of restraint began to be adopted here, which had already been put in practice in France. Even some of the hardest sayings of the king were but the echo of those of the king of France. Like many of the high dignitaries of the Scottish Church of that time, he was of incontinent habits, but he was never, so far as I know, guilty of such shameless excesses as were the boast of his comrade Hepburn; nor did he ever allow himself to sink into the same indolent and unredeemed self-indulgence. He was above all a 'hierarchical fanatic,' devoted to the cause of absolutism, who would shrink from no measures, however cruel, to preserve intact the privileges of his order, and to stamp out more earnest and generous thought, whether having in view the reformation of the old Church, or the building up of another and better on her ruins. If we may not say that he had sold himself to France, which had pensioned him with a rich bishopric, and helped him to his honours, we must say he had lived so long in it, and had got so enamoured of it, that he was three parts French and 'all Popish.' He had mingled not only with its scholars, but with its nobles; and he loved their society —loved and resolved to imitate their ways, even down to their way of treating heretics. He made no earnest effort to reform the old Church; and it was not till towards the close of his life that he began to apply for the building of St Mary's College, the money which his uncle had set apart for it.

For the suppression of evangelical Christianity, the Cardinal needed the support of his sovereign, and he spared no efforts to gain him over to his side, and to detach him from his nobility and his uncle. There was much in the king's character to encourage such efforts. With good natural abilities, and a frank and amiable disposition, he had been encouraged by his guardians in sensual pleasures, and never to the last freed himself from his evil habits. 'Dissolute as a man, prodigal as a king, and superstitious as a Catholic, he could not but easily fall under the sway of superior minds, who promised to free him from the worries of business, to regard his failings with indulgence, and to provide him with money.' These things Beaton and his party endeavoured to do; and lest he should be tempted to follow the example of his uncle, and appropriate the property of the monasteries and other religious institutions, or set the Church lands to feu, as he once threatened, they repeatedly presented to him lists of those who were suspected of heresy, urging that they should be prosecuted without delay, and their goods, on conviction, be escheated to the crown. They made large contributions from their own revenues to aid him in the wars with England, which obedience to their counsels had brought on him. They procured dispensations from the papal court to enable his sons, though illegitimate and infants, to hold any benefices inferior to bishoprics, and on reaching a certain age, to hold even the highest offices in the Church.

But though James shewed little indulgence to the Reformers, and little favour for their doctrine, he seems to the last to have had no great liking for the priests of the old faith. No bribery, no flattery, no solicitations, could reconcile him permanently to those who for their selfish ends dragged him into courses from which his own better impulses at times made him revolt. 'He incited Buchanan to lash the mendicant friars in the vigorous verse of the *Franciscanus*. He encouraged by his presence the public performance of a play which, by its exposure of the vices of the clergy, contributed' greatly to weaken their influence. 'He enforced the object of that remarkable drama by exhorting the bishops to amend their lives under a threat that, if they neglected his warning, he would deal with them after the fashion of his uncle in England. He repeated the exhortation in his last Parliament, declaring that the negligence, the ignorance, the scandalous and disorderly lives of the clergy, were the cause why the Church and Churchmen were scorned and despised.'

So, notwithstanding all measures of repression, the desire for reformation grew and spread throughout the nation, especially among the smaller landed proprietors in Angus and Mearns, in Perth and Fife, in Kyle and Cunningham, as also among the more intelligent burgesses in the cities and burghs, and above all, among the *élite* of the younger inmates of the monasteries and of the alumni of the universities. When the poor monarch, almost as much sinned against as sinning, at last died of a broken heart, and the Earl of Arran looked about for trusty supporters to defend his claims to the regency, he deemed it politic to shew not a little countenance to the friends of the Reformation and of the English alliance. We should hardly be warranted to assert that even then he meant to rank himself among Protestants. But he chose as his chaplains preachers who inclined to their opinions, he encouraged their chief men to frequent his court, and he ventured to lay hands on the haughty and unscrupulous Cardinal. He consented to pass through Parliament an act expressly permitting the people to have and to read the Scriptures of the Old and New Testaments in the vulgar tongue, and despatched messengers to all the chief towns to make public proclamation of the act. The little treatises of Alesius had done their work, and he himself thought of returning and completing what he had so well begun. The friends of the Reformation imagined that the hour of their triumph was at hand. They did not know on what a treacherous prop they were leaning, nor that the Regent, within six weeks after the last of the messengers was despatched with the above-named proclamation, secretly sent off others to inform the Holy Father of his accession to the regency, to put himself and the kingdom under his protection, and to ask permission to have under his control the income of the benefices of the king's sons till they should come of age. The love of money was with him the root of this evil, as the fear of man was of others; and so he went from bad to worse, till in the dim light of the Franciscan chapel at Stirling, 'that weak man, to whom people had been looking for the triumph of the Reformation in Scotland, fondly fancying that he was performing a secret action, knelt down before the altar, humbly confessed his errors, trampled under foot the oaths which he had taken to his own country and to England, renounced the evangelical confession of Jesus Christ, submitted to the Pope, and received absolution from the Cardinal.'

Even in June he had entered in the books of the Privy Council an ordinance against Sacramentaries holding opinions of the effect and essence thereof tending to the enervation of the faith catholic, in which they were threatened with loss of life, lands, and goods. He had not dared to proclaim this openly, though perhaps his friend Henry VIII. would not have blamed him greatly for doing so. But no sooner was he under the power of the Cardinal, than he shewed in open Parliament 'how there is great murmur that heretics more and more rise and spread within this realm, sowing damnable opinions contrary to the faith and laws of Holy Kirk, and to the acts and constitutions of the realm;' and exhorted 'all prelates and ordinaries . . . to make inquisition after all such manner of persons, and proceed against them according to the laws of Holy Kirk;' promising to be ready himself at all times to do what belonged to his office. This promise he was soon called to fulfil. On the 20th January 1544, he set out in company of the Cardinal, the Lord Justice and his deputy, with a band of armed men and artillery, to Perth, where a great assize was held. Several were convicted of heresy, and their goods forfeited. Several were condemned to die. The governor was inclined to spare their lives, but the Cardinal and the nobles threatened to leave him if he did this. So, on 25th January 1544, Robert Lamb, James Hunter, William Anderson, and James Ronaldson were hanged. The wife of the last-named was refused the consolation of being suspended from the same beam with her husband, and put to death by drowning, after she had consigned to the care of a neighbour the infant she carried in her arms. Dundee was next visited, but the suspected citizens had taken the alarm and fled, leaving only their books to be burned.

It was about this time that a new evangelist arrived in the country, singularly fitted to impress on the hearts of men the lessons of the holy book to which they had now free access in their native tongue. This was George Wishart, a younger brother of the laird of Pittarrow in the Mearns. He appears to have been born about 1512, and to have received his university training in Aberdeen, or abroad. He acquired a knowledge of Greek—at that time a very rare accomplishment in Scotland—from a Frenchman brought by Erskine of Dun to Montrose. While acting as schoolmaster there, Wishart had read the Greek New Testament with some of his pupils, and in consequence had been cited by the Bishop of Brechin to answer to a charge of suspected heresy. Like many others at that time, he thought it best not to appear, and escaped to England. He was thereupon excommunicated and outlawed. He is found at Bristol in 1539, involved in fresh troubles. After that he visited several of the Continental Reformed Churches, especially those of German Switzerland, and brought home and translated into English the First Helvetic Confession. He is supposed to have returned to England before the close of 1541, and shortly after his return, to have entered into residence in Benet College, Cambridge. To one of his pupils there we are indebted for our fullest account of his appearance and habits; and in one of its stained-glass windows, place has been found for a worthy memorial of him. He 'was a man of tall stature . . . black haired, long bearded, comely of personage, well spoken after his country of Scotland, courteous, lowly, lovely, glad to teach, desirous to learn, and was well travelled. . . . His charity was unbounded; he studied all means of doing good to all, hurt to none.' He was not only of rare graces, but 'learned in all honest human science.'

Such was the evangelist who—in 1543 according to some, in 1544 according to others—returned to his native land, and for two years testified of the Gospel of the grace of God throughout Angus and Mearns, Ayrshire and the Lothians, but whose favourite fields of labour were to be the towns of Montrose and Dundee. A portrait of him has been preserved and engraved, and the expression of the face harmonises well with what his pupil has said of him. It is supposed that for a short time after his return he lived quietly at Pittarrow, and being an accomplished artist, occupied himself in adorning the ancestral mansion with several significant paintings, which, after being long covered over by the wainscot, were again brought to light in the present century, but unfortunately were destroyed before their value was perceived. The most remarkable of them was a painting of the city of Rome, and a grand procession going to St Peter's. Below the picture were written the following enigmatical lines on the Pope:

> Laus tua non tua fraus, virtus non gloria rerum
> Scandere te fecit hoc decus eximium ;
> Pauperibus dat sua gratis nec munera curat
> Curia Papalis, quod more percipimus.
> Hæc carmina potius legenda, cancros imitando.

It was about the same time that he formed that kirk or congregation which at a later period we shall find he came to salute, and began his labours as a preacher by expounding the Ten Commandments, the Lord's Prayer, and the Apostles' Creed. This was in the town of Montrose, the scene of his early scholastic labours. At that time it was frequented by some of the nobles and many of the landed gentry around who were favourable to the Reformation and the English alliance; and their hearts could not fail to be cheered and their courage raised by the exhortations of the evangelist. Dundee, however, was the chief and favourite scene of his ministrations, and it was from the great success which attended these that it gained the name of the Scottish Geneva. It was even more decidedly attached to the new opinions and to the English alliance than Montrose; and a Reformation, as it was called, including the sacking of the monasteries in the town and neighbourhood, took place shortly before or soon after his arrival. He preached for a time in Dundee with great acceptance, expounding systematically the Epistle to the Romans, the full significance of which the recently published commentary of Calvin had deeply impressed on the minds of his co-religionists in various lands. At length he was charged by one of the magistrates in the queen's name and the governor's to desist from preaching, depart from the town, and trouble it no more. This was intimated to him when he was in the pulpit surrounded by a great congregation. Thereupon he called God to witness that he intended not their trouble but their comfort, and felt sure that to reject the word of God and drive away his messenger was not the way to save themselves from trouble.' He then left the town, and 'with all possible expedition passed to the west land.' There he pursued his labours in the same kindly spirit, refusing to allow his followers to dispute possession of the churches by force, and choosing rather to preach in the open air wherever he found a convenient place and audience fit, than go where he was not welcome.

Soon after he left Dundee, the plague extended its ravages to that place. Wishart, on hearing this, returned to the afflicted town, and its inhabitants received him with joy. He announced without delay that he would preach to them; but it was impossible he could do so in a church. Numbers were sick of the plague; others in attendance on them were regarded as infected, and must not be brought into contact with those who were free from infection. The sick were lodged in booths and the 'lazar-houses' near St Roque's Chapel, outside the East or Cowgate Port of the town. Wishart chose as his pulpit the top of this port, which, in memory of the martyr-preacher, has been carefully preserved, though, like Temple Bar—so long tolerated in London—it is now in the heart of the town, and an obstruction to its traffic. The sick and suspected were assembled outside the port, and the healthy inside. The preacher took for the text of his first sermon the words of Psalm cvii. 20: 'He sent His word and healed them;' and starting on the key-note that it was neither herb nor plaster, but God's word which healeth all, as Knox tells us, he so raised up the hearts of all who heard him, that they regarded not death, but judged those more happy that should depart than those that should remain behind; considering that they knew not that they should have such a comforter with them at all times.' John Wedderburn, as well as others who had fled from the town in the persecution of 1539, had before this time returned, and no doubt they were co-operating with Wishart in his work. Then in all probability came out in rudimentary form the 'Psalms of Dundee,' and that beautiful funeral hymn which passed from the Bohemians to the Germans, and from the Germans to the Scotch, and which in the Scottish version contains certain additional stanzas, having unmistakable reference to the circumstances in which it originated in a plague-stricken town, which had just before been occupied by the soldiers of the Cardinal and the Regent, and might well dread a similar visitation:

> Though *pest or sword* wald us prevene,
> Before our hour to slay us clene,
> They cannot pluck one little hair
> Furth from our head, or do us dare.

Wishart concerned himself not only about the souls, but also about the bodies of his hearers in that sad time, fearlessly exposing himself to the risk of infection, that he might minister to the diseased and the dying, and taking care that the public funds for the relief of the destitute should be properly administered. He forgot himself only too much, and the terrible risks to which, as an excommunicated and outlawed man, he was exposed in so near proximity to the Cardinal.

One day as the people were departing from the sermon, Knox tells us that a priest, bribed by the Cardinal, stood waiting at the foot of the steps by which the preacher was descending from the top of the port, with his gown loose, and his dagger drawn in his hand under his gown. Wishart, most sharp of eye and swift of judgment, at once noticed him, and as he came near, seized the hand in which he held the dagger and took it from him. Immediately the rumour spread that a priest had attempted to assassinate their favourite preacher, the sick outside burst open the gate, crying: 'Deliver the traitor to us, or else we will take him by force.' But the preacher put his arms around his would-be assassin, exclaiming: 'Whosoever troubles him shall trouble me, for he has hurt me in nothing, but has let us understand what we may fear in time to come;' 'and so he saved the life of him that sought his.'

Like Dr Lorimer, I cannot persuade myself that the man who spoke and acted thus is the same as 'a Scottish man called Wishart,' who is mentioned in a letter of the Earl of Hertford, in the spring of the year 1544, as privy to a conspiracy to assassinate Cardinal Beaton, and as employed to carry letters between the conspirators and the English court. There were other Wisharts in Scotland, and even in Dundee, at that time, also friends of the English alliance. It is unjust, therefore, to charge the Reformer with any participation in such a dastardly plot, without a particle of positive evidence to support the charge. As an outlawed man, he came down to Scotland under protection, and seems never to have travelled in it save under protection; and so he was one of the last men likely to be chosen for a secret mission. If anything more than the able essay of the late Professor Weir, in the *North British Review* for 1868, were needed to prove that 'the pure lustre of the martyr's fame is still unsullied,' it seems to me to be furnished by himself in his affecting address at the stake: 'I beseech the Father of heaven to forgive them that have of any ignorance, or else of any evil mind, *forged any lies* upon me. I forgive them with all my heart.'

From this time forth, the Reformer had a clearer view of the perils which beset him, and a mournful conviction of the issue which awaited him if he would not flee or flinch. By his success in Dundee, the rage of his adversaries was lashed into fury, which appalled his friends and partisans in various districts; but none of these things moved him, that he might finish his course with joy, and make full proof of his ministry. As soon as the plague abated, heedless of the warnings of his northern friends as to the risk he ran in leaving, he administered the communion in both kinds at Dun, and took his last farewell of the churches of Montrose and Dundee. At all hazards, he was determined to fulfil his engagement to meet with his western friends in Edinburgh, prosecute his work there under their protection, and engage in public disputation with certain of the popish clergy, who about that time were to meet in synod in the capital. Disappointed of their presence and protection, he laboured for a brief season in Leith, Inveresk, and East Lothian with varying success. At last, forsaken by many of those who should have stood by him, he was seized at Ormiston under cover of night, and promise of safe keeping by the Earl of Bothwell, Sheriff-Principal of the county. The earl pledged his honour not to give him up to his enemies, but was persuaded to deliver him to the governor, as the governor was to hand him over to the Cardinal, though finally protesting against his being tried or condemned in his own absence. A full account of these transactions has been given by Knox, who rendered his first service to the cause of the Reformation by attending on him, bearing a two-handed sword, and was dismissed on the night of his betrayal with the significant words: 'One is sufficient for a sacrifice.'

I cannot enlarge on these things, nor on the sad scenes which took place at St Andrews on the 28th February and 1st March 1546, when the Cardinal, regardless of the remonstrances of the Regent, and the murmurs of the people, tried and condemned him; nor on his last touching interviews with the Sub-Prior of the Monastery and the Captain of the Castle. Throughout all these trying scenes he comported himself as nobly as Hamilton had done, and not less plentifully did his blood prove the seed of the Church, so that, as he said, not many should suffer after him. Within three months his persecutor was surprised in his stronghold, and 'cut off by a fate as tragical and ignominious as any that has ever been recorded in the long catalogue of human crimes.' No doubt this cruel martyrdom hastened the removal of the tyrant, who set himself above all restraint of law, and breathed forth threatenings against the saints of God; though that removal had not been plotted by Wishart, nor would have been approved by him. The words attributed to him at the stake by Buchanan are not generally regarded as authentic.

The remembrance of Wishart was fondly cherished, especially in that district where he chiefly laboured, and where he wrought a work not less memorable than that M'Cheyne and Burns were honoured to do in our own day. His influence was but deepened by his cruel fate, and 'he lived again,' as Dr Lorimer has said, 'in John Knox.' 'This zealous disciple, who had counted it an honour to be allowed to carry a sword before his master, stood forth immediately to wield the spiritual sword which had fallen from his master's grasp, and to wield it with a vigour and trenchant execution superior even to his.' God sent them comfort after him, as he said.

It belongs to my successor to tell of the triumph and portray the character of him whom Mr Froude has pronounced to be 'the grandest figure in the entire history of the British Reformation.' All that I must attempt, in closing, is to give the briefest account of his preliminary labours.

Knox was born at Giffordgate in Haddington in 1505, and matriculated at the University of Glasgow in 1522. From that date up to 1545, when he appears as sword-bearer to Wishart, his life is to us almost a blank. Like Elijah the Tishbite, he comes into view only to enter on his public work. Whatever his early training may have been, he had by this time thoroughly mastered the subjects in controversy between the two Churches, and possibly, as Bayle supposes, the writings of the two greatest doctors of the Western Church. 'He received his first taste of the truth' from his fellow-townsman, Thomas Guillaume, one of the Regent's chaplains, as he received his political principles from his early instructor, John Major, also a native of East Lothian. Ever since he had cast in his lot with Wishart, he had been so harassed, that but for a refuge unexpectedly opened up, he would have found it necessary to leave Scotland. This refuge was the Castle of St Andrews, which the conspirators had determined to hold, and in which numbers of those friendly to the Reformation and the English alliance had already taken shelter. Knox arrived about Pasche, 1547, in charge of the sons of certain lairds in East Lothian. At that time there was a truce between the citizens and the 'castilians,' as they were called. The reforming citizens had access to the services in the castle, and the chaplain of the garrison at times made his way into the parish church and preached to the people. Knox resumed there the system he had followed with good effect in East Lothian, expounding in a colloquial manner the gospel of St John, and making his pupils give account of their catechism in public, that even people who could not read, by hearing it often repeated, might gain familiarity with it.

His great abilities as a teacher, and his wonderful gift of persuasive speech, soon attracted notice. Private efforts failing to move him, a formal call to the ministry was addressed to him from the pulpit by the chaplain in name of the rest. Yielding to this, he soon made full proof of his ministry not only before the rude garrison of the castle, but before the doctors of the University and the citizens in the parish church. By his sermons, catechisings, and disputations, the new doctrines gained a hold on the minds of learned and unlearned which they never really lost. But times of trial were to come ere the cause should finally triumph. They who had taken into their hands 'the sword of God' were made to suffer by the sword, and had to surrender the castle to the representative of the French king. Those who had come to it for shelter, as well as those who had conspired against the Cardinal, were dealt with as criminals of the worst class. For nearly twenty months our Reformer had to work in chains on board the galleys. Even then he maintained unshaken faith in God; but he would have been more than human if the iron had not entered into his soul, and traces of the sternness thence arising had not long been visible in his character. Early in 1549 he was released by English influence. He was sent to Berwick, where he was as near to his countrymen as it was safe for him to go, and where many of them were able to resort to him. He preached not only to the garrison and citizens of Berwick, but also throughout the northern counties, proving himself a true successor of those early Scottish missionaries who had originally won over to the Christian faith the Saxons of Northumbria.

His fame as a preacher and defender of the new doctrines spread southwards, and he was appointed one of the royal chaplains. In the autumn of 1552 he preached with great power and faithfulness before the court of Edward VI., and with his fellow-chaplains aided in the revision of the English Articles and Prayer-Book. He refused a bishopric and a London rectory, and continued to labour devotedly as a preacher unattached. He had a presentiment that the time he would have to do so would be brief, and he improved it diligently. When 'the bloody Mary' succeeded to the throne, Knox, as a foreigner, was especially warranted to leave the country and reserve himself for happier times; and he did so when it was only not too late. The few years he spent abroad were to be richly blessed to himself and his fellow-exiles. He at least had not gone there to have his views of doctrine or church order changed, but to have his spirit refreshed by counsel and communion with brethren, and nerved for further achievements in the service of their common Lord. He would have settled down to quiet study in Geneva, but Calvin persuaded him to go to Frankfort as pastor of the English congregation there; and on disputes arising in it, he secured an asylum for him and his Puritan brethren beside himself. Knox returned to his native land to pay a short visit to his friends, and to bring his wife and her mother to Geneva. But he was obliged again and again to prolong his visit. The cause of the Reformation had made quiet progress in the immediately preceding years, without the voice of the living preacher or any agency but the private study of the Scriptures and the circulation of hymns and poems. 'If he had not seen it with his own eyes, he could not have believed it.' Night and day they sobbed and groaned for the bread of life, and now his preaching came to them in demonstration of the Spirit and with power, and was greatly blessed to many in Angus and Mearns, in Ayrshire and the Lothians, and other parts. He administered the Lord's supper to 'them, persuaded them to give up attending the Popish worship, and bind themselves to uphold the truth, and defend their brethren who did so.[1] He urged the Queen Regent to undertake the reformation of the Church, but with-

---

[1] Knox's *History*, vol. i., page 251.

out success. He urged the nobles to do their duty, and promising to return when they deemed the time had come for this, he at length departed to his charge at Geneva. Before he left, he had been summoned to appear before the bishops, but this summons was 'cast.' Soon after his departure, he was summoned again, and in his absence was condemned and burned in effigy.

Archbishop Hamilton, who had succeeded Beaton as primate, continued to hold council after council, to make feeble and fitful efforts for the revival of the Church—to provide a catechism and other helps for the priests in their work, and to execute with rigour the laws against heretics. But all availed not to save the Church or stem the tide which had set in. Time was when reasonable concession and speedy reform might have done so. Patrick Hamilton and Alexander Alesius had come pleading for the free circulation of the Word of God, and the free preaching of the great truths it contained; and the one had been burned, the other forced into exile. George Wishart had come to reiterate the plea, and to contend for the right doctrine and administration of the sacraments; and he also was put to death. Willock and the reforming nobles had come even in 1558 to plead for a *minimum* of reform, which if granted, might have saved the old organisation, and brought the new life into it, as in England. But this too was refused. The gnarled old tree was rotten to the core, and could not take in the fresh sap. And now came Knox, not to 'sned the branches,' but to lay his axe at the root of the tree and cut it down as a cumberer of the ground. 'It was not a smooth business,' as Carlyle says, 'but it was welcome surely, and cheap at that price; had it been far rougher on the whole, cheap at any price as life is. The people began to *live;*' and as another has it, from being one of the rudest, poorest, most turbulent races in Europe, became one of the most educated, prosperous, orderly, and upright.

ST GILES' LECTURES.

FIRST SERIES—THE SCOTTISH CHURCH.

LECTURE V.

THE REFORMATION, 1559 TO 1572 A.D.[1]

By the Rev. DONALD MACLEOD, D.D., Minister of the Park Church, Glasgow; and one of Her Majesty's Chaplains.

IT may be well to give at the outset a brief *résumé* of the chief events between 1559 and 1572. Mary of Guise, who acted as Regent for her daughter, had put the preachers of the Reformed doctrine 'to the horn'—a process equivalent to proclaiming them rebels. This led to a civil war between the Lords of the Congregation, who had espoused the new opinions, and the Regent, assisted by a strong body of French veterans. In June 1560, the Regent died, and during the following month the Protestants, with the aid of an English army, obtained the mastery. The *Confession of Faith* was immediately afterwards accepted by the Scottish Parliament. Next year Queen Mary

---

[1] The following authorities, among others, have been consulted: Laing's edition of Knox's Works; *Booke of the Universall Kirk*; Sir David Lindsay's Works; Peterkin; *Register of the Scotch Privy Council*; the Histories of Wodrow, Calderwood, Keith, Tytler, Robertson, M'Crie, Froude, Cunningham, and Burton; Sprott's preface to *Book of Common Order*; Schierns' *Bothwell*; *Life of Kirkaldy*, &c.

arrived from France, and began gradually to increase her influence in the hope of ultimately restoring Romanism. Her marriage to Darnley was connected with this design, and might have led to serious results, had not the assassination of Rizzio in 1566, and the murder of Darnley in 1567, plunged the country into new confusion. The surrender of the queen at Carberry-hill, and her defeat at Langside the following year, completed for a time the ruin of Mary's power in Scotland. The Regent Moray, during his brief career, gave for the first time the sanction of the Crown to the Reformation; but his death in 1570 involved the country again in civil war. Until 1573, the Queen's party, under the leadership of Maitland of Lethington and Kirkaldy of Grange, held Edinburgh Castle. In the five years from the abdication of Mary at Lochleven, till Edinburgh Castle fell in 1573, no fewer than four regents were appointed; and of these two were assassinated. The war was bitter and bloody, but ended in the final overthrow of the hopes of the queen, and, with her, of the Romish Church in Scotland.

The time had now arrived when the final issue betwixt Romanism and Protestantism was to be tried in Scotland.

It was June 1559, and Perth was full of determined men, who, laying aside for the time steel jacket and morion, so as not to appear openly in arms against the government, had gathered to display their sympathy with the Reformers. The Queen-Regent, Mary of Guise, had mustered her forces at Stirling, and had vowed that though 'the preachers preached as truly as St Paul,' she would silence them. On the 25th of the month John Knox arrived at Perth, and the cause of the Reformation passed into the strong hands of the man who, within a year, was to carry it to victory.

When Knox began the great struggle of his life, he was upwards of fifty-four years of age. He had passed through many experiences. For ten years he had been a priest of the

Romish Church: he had stood sword in hand beside George Wishart, when he, so soon to become a martyr, preached in the Lothians: he had shared the rough fortunes of the garrison of St Andrews: he had been for nearly two years a galley-slave, now sweltering under the burning sun of the Loire, and now chained to the oar on the German Ocean: for four years he had ministered in England, and, alien as he was, had risen through sheer force of character to be one of the king's chaplains and his personal friend, to find himself consulted on delicate affairs affecting the Church, and to have a bishopric within his gift: he had lived for several years on the Continent in close intercourse with some of the keenest intellects of that or any other age; and when he now left his foreign home, it was amid the 'weeping of grave men' who had learned to love as well as to venerate him. Although he had hitherto been only for a comparatively short period actively engaged as a preacher in his native land, yet he was already recognised as the leading man of his party. His correspondence abroad had been extensive, and his influence powerful. Thus ripe in experience and worn with hard service, he threw himself into the front rank of the Reformation; and, as if possessed of some inherent right, he was accepted from the first as its chief. 'I assure you,' said Randolph, years afterwards, in a letter to Secretary Cecil, 'the voice of that one man is able, in an hour, to put more life in us than six hundred trumpets continually blustering in our ears.

To know John Knox is to know the Scotch Reformation, for he embodies at once the virtues and the faults which characterised the movement. It is no exaggeration to say that during the stirring period under review his voice was more powerful than that of the sovereign or of any statesman. He was pre-eminently patriot as well as preacher, statesman as well as ecclesiastic. Many of the state-papers now preserved in the English Records Office are in his handwriting, and are known to have been his composition. His influence, while founded on the response which the conscience of the nation gave to the truth he preached with a voice of thunder, did not lack the support that such carnal weapons as sword and spear supplied. He had only to issue his summons, and thousands of steel bonnets were ready to march across moor and over mountain to enforce his policy. For years the General Assembly was more representative of the popular will than was the secular government. It is true that the preachers did not always gain the day against the barons; but when they failed, it was on points which were not calculated to rouse enthusiasm. It was not to be expected that the people would rush to arms when the question in dispute was the amount of stipend to be paid to ministers and schoolmasters, or when the sackcloth sheet was to be enforced on the unwilling lords. On these two points, the Church certainly failed in its contention with the Privy Council and the Parliament; but on all others the voice of the General Assembly was practically the voice of the nation. And Knox was the very soul of the Assembly. There were others there—Willock, Craig, Winram, Erskine of Dun, men of learning and force of character—whose names are not unworthy to be compared with his. The Reformation certainly owed much to the great ability and statesmanship of the Regent Moray; but Knox was its embodiment. We shall therefore deal with the Reformation and Knox as identical terms, and speak of the *Confession of Faith* as Knox's Confession; of the *Book of Common Prayer* as Knox's Liturgy; of the Genevan Catechism and Psalm-books as Knox's Catechism and Psalm-books; and of the *Book of Discipline* as an expression of his genius. We shall in this way be able, without any sacrifice of historical truth, to create a more living picture of the forces then at work, by investing them with a certain personal interest.

I propose to direct your attention to two chief topics: I. The Church system and general polity of the Reformation; and II. The character and work of Knox.

I. The fundamental principle of the Reformation was the paramount authority of Holy Scripture. Not the Church alone, but the nation and every member of the nation were bound to obey the Word of God. The Church and the nation were with Knox identical terms; and not with him only, for indeed neither Romish Church nor Protestant, no statesman or theologian of that time, ever dreamed of civil government being purely secular. Voluntaryism in the modern sense was not even discussed. The battle, therefore, which had primarily to be waged, was between the authority of Scripture and the authority of the Pope. The Reformation under Knox did not turn on questions of ecclesiastical order, like the later contest between Prelacy and Presbytery. The peculiar claims of Presbytery were as yet scarcely asserted, though they were acted upon. Nor did it turn then, as it did nearly a century afterwards, on the lawfulness of Liturgies. It was a contest, as Knox would unhesitatingly have phrased it, betwixt the authority of God as given in His Word, and the authority of all the Bishops, Cardinals, and Councils who dared to oppose or add to that Word. The one was true, the other was false; the one was of God, the other of man. With such convictions regarding the absolute rule of Scripture, he could make no compromises. The duty of the Church was to make known what the Scriptures taught; and, unless contrary Scripture could be shewn, it was the duty of king and people to submit.

This principle was entirely different from that which primarily determined the Reformation in England. With Henry VIII. the chief question was the supremacy of the crown, and as long as authority was transferred from the Pope to the English monarch, he cared little for any change in doctrine or in ritual. For many years the mass was virtually retained, and the desire of the king to preserve historical continuity prevented all sudden changes in public service. But in Scotland the Reformation was the work of the people, and effected in spite of the Executive. The barons, with a few exceptions, cared little for the doctrines of the preachers. Nearly all of them were governed by purely selfish motives, and many of them were ready to return to Rome, as some did return, when the Reformation no longer served their interests. The movement was essentially a popular movement, consequent on newly awakened religious convictions, and partaking of the excitement which usually accompanies such outbursts. A great modern authority has told us that the law of reaction is the true key to history, and the saying finds a vivid illustration here. The rupture with the past was complete. At one bound the Church leaped over ten centuries, and went back to the Scriptures and the early Fathers. Much that was beautiful and reverent may thereby have been sacrificed, but the principle was the only logical one by which the popular movement towards reform could then have been conducted.

The greatness of Knox can be measured better by what he tried to build up than even by his intrepidity and firmness in attacking the errors and corruptions which had demoralised both the Church and Society. We stand amazed at the rapidity with which the Church of the Reformation was furnished not merely with a Confession of Faith, but with a richness and variety of instrumentality, in startling contrast to the denuded and unsystematic condition of the Church now.

We shall describe the system which it was then proposed to establish, under the following heads : (1) The doctrine of the Church ; (2) The worship of the Church ; (3) The discipline of the Church.

(1) In four days after Commission had been given by the Scotch Parliament of 1560 to Knox and his four associates to draw up a statement of doctrine, they were able to lay before it a Confession of Faith which may in many respects be favourably compared with the later symbol of the Westminster Divines. It was not the first experience which Knox had in drawing up a doctrinal system. He had assisted at the revision of the English

Articles of Edward VI. in 1552, and had himself compiled a Confession for the English congregation of Geneva. The Scotch Confession, however, while betraying acquaintance with other models, is original, independent, and masterly. It is divided into twenty-five sections, treating of the principal subjects with which it is the province of theology to deal. The general scope of the treatment is Calvinistic, as might have been expected from the relationship of Knox and the Reformers generally to the great Genevan doctor; nevertheless, the spirit of the whole is broader, more human, and, if we might use the expression, more modern than that of the Westminster Standards. So satisfactory did it appear to such a man as Edward Irving, that he used to read it twice a year to his London congregation. 'This document,' he says, 'is written in the most honest, straightforward, manly style, without compliment or flattery, without affectation of logical precision or learned accuracy, as if it came fresh from the heart of laborious workmen, all day long busy with the preaching of the truth, and sitting down at night and embodying the heads of what they continually taught. Its doctrine is sound; its expression is clear; its spirit is large and liberal; its dignity is personal and not dogmatic, and it is redolent with the unction of holiness and truth.' So also does another authority, widely removed from Irving, speak of it. 'As far back as the Reformation,' says Dean Stanley, 'there were indications of deeper insight—exceptional and quaint, but so expressive as to vindicate for Christianity, even then, the widest range which future discoveries may open before it. In the first Confession of John Knox, the Reformers had perceived what had been so long concealed from the eyes of the Schoolmen and the Fathers—that the most positive expressions, even of their own convictions, were not guaranteed from imperfection or mutability; and the entreaty with which that Confession is prefaced, contains at once a fine example of true Christian humility, and the stimulus to the noblest Christian ambition:

"We conjure you if any man will note in this our Confession any article or sentence repugnant to God's Holy Word, that it would please him of his gentleness, and for Christian charity's sake, to admonish us of the same in writing, and we upon our honour and fidelity do promise him satisfaction from the Holy Scriptures, or due reformation of that which he shall prove to be amiss."' For nearly a hundred years this Confession was the only recognised standard of the Church of Scotland. The greatest battles the Church ever waged were fought under it. It was the authoritative creed of the Melvilles, the Hendersons, the Rutherfords, and must ever be regarded as an extraordinary evidence of the intellectual grasp and theological attainment of those who, in four days, drew up such a document to be adopted by the legislature of their country.

(2) But Knox had mature views regarding the necessity of furnishing the Church with a suitable guide for its worship, as well as its faith. Hitherto, the Protestants had been in the habit of using the English Liturgy of Edward VI.; but John Knox had had a twofold experience regarding Liturgies. He was intimately acquainted with the Anglican Prayer-book of that time; and he had been forced more than once to discuss its merits. He was also familiar with the Liturgy of Geneva, and as soon as he could assert his influence, he did not hesitate to recommend the substitution of the Swiss Prayer-book for that of England. He disapproved of what he termed the 'mingle-mangle' of the Anglican Liturgy. He noticed how much room was still given in it for customs that might lead back to superstition, and for statements that might naturally reintroduce in substance the very doctrines of priestly power against which he had contended. And, in spite of all that England owes to her Prayer-book—the grandest devotional service ever furnished to a Christian Church—we cannot, in the light of modern controversies, deny that Knox had some ground for the suspicions which he entertained as to the dangers that might accrue from the ambiguous character of many

passages. He accordingly persuaded the Assembly to take the Genevan Prayer-book as a basis; and in four years afterwards, what is popularly termed Knox's Liturgy became the Service-book of the Church of Scotland. With the exception of one or two passages that are coloured with the passionate feeling of the time, it is a dignified and impressive Liturgy, not altogether unworthy to be compared with that of the sister Church. The services are copious and varied. There are forms of prayer for public worship, for the administration of the sacraments, for marriage, for visitation of the sick; besides services for special occasions, such as the ordination of ministers, the observance of fasts, and the administration of ecclesiastical discipline. A comparatively large provision was also made for praise, hymns as well as psalms being printed with fixed tunes, and care taken that the people should be taught to sing them well. After the issue of the *Psalter* in 1564, there commenced those interesting institutions called 'Sang Schules,' which not only stimulated the study of music in Scotland, but secured great efficiency in congregational singing. We find, for example, an instance of as many as two thousand people singing the second version of the 124th Psalm, to the very music to which it is still sung, and able to do so with a harmony in four parts.

The Liturgy of Knox was not imposed with exclusive strictness, for it might be used merely as a guide, and room was expressly afforded after sermon for extempore prayer. Yet there can be little doubt that the practice of the Church for many years was towards a comparatively strict use of the Prayer-book. It was enjoined that in all large towns prayers should be read daily in church, except when the week-day sermon was preached; and in other places, not supplied with a fixed ministry, the 'reader' was to gather the people at least once a week, for the reading of the Holy Scriptures, and of the prescribed prayers. For a hundred years this Liturgy of Knox was the law of the Church of Scotland, and for about seventy years it was universally observed. Its abandonment was in consequence not of Scotch or Presbyterian influence, but from the teaching of English sectaries; and by a strange reversal of modern associations, it was rebuked by the General Assemblies of that time as an 'innovation.' As in the case of the *Confession of Faith*, still more in regard to the devotional equipment of the Church, we may look back to the earlier years of her history with feelings of regret, that what appears the healthier, richer, and more efficient system of our first Reformers should ever have been superseded. Besides the Liturgy, a Catechism was supplied for the instruction of children, to which were attached forms of prayer for daily use in the household, for grace before meat, and for special occasions. The Church thus took a powerful grasp of the religious necessities of the country, and met its requirements with an almost imperial plan of Christian training. Nothing essential was left to the amateur efforts of individuals or voluntary societies, but a well-considered scheme was at once established, practical and far-reaching, and fortunately not hindered in its application by sectarian division within the dominant Protestantism.

(3) The *Book of Discipline* is perhaps even a greater testimony to the patriotism and statesmanship of Knox. It was a book of discipline in the sense of the Latin *Disciplina*—a book of training—the statute-book of the Church, in which his plan for educating the people as a Christian commonwealth was exhibited. It therefore embraced not merely the correction of morals, as the term 'church discipline' usually signifies, but the whole polity of the Church, as distinct from its creed or the order of its worship. It includes the organisation of the Church in respect of its office-bearers; the regulation of schools and colleges with their endowments, and the nature of the education to be imparted; the maintenance of the poor; and the principles on which ecclesiastical censures are to be administered. We shall take a brief survey of each of these important subjects.

(a) *The Organisation of the Church.*—It would be difficult to rank under any of the usual ecclesiastical systems the type of Church organisation which prevailed during the first twenty years of the Reformation. Knox did not entertain any very strong beliefs as to the necessity of ordination, although his views respecting the sacraments were 'higher' than what are now practically held. He did not believe that any special grace or Apostolic descent of authority was received from the mere laying on of hands. Personally, he regarded the call of the people of God (for from the first the Church recognised the popular voice in the election of ministers), the trial of gifts by the Church, and due appointment, as all that was necessary for valid orders. But whatever value may lie in the doctrine of Apostolic succession, the Church of Scotland, in the days of Knox, and certainly the Church since 1638, did possess it through its presbyters. Nearly all the first ministers of the Church had previously been priests, and although irregularity in the form of ordination crept in during the first twenty years of its history, yet this quickly vanished with the *Second Book of Discipline*, and the High Church Presbyterianism of the Melvilles. The validity of orders through the line of Presbyters was then recognised and acted on by the Church of England, and by all the churches of the Reformation. The framers of the Thirty-nine Articles, and such divines as Tillotson, Grindall, and even the High Church Bancroft, acknowledged the position of those ordained by presbyters alone. Presbyterian ministers were freely admitted, and even made bishops, without reordination.[1] But the point of orders was subordinate in the days of Knox to the more difficult problem, as to how the spiritual wants of the country were to be overtaken at all. The first General Assembly consisted of forty-two members; and of these only six were ministers. On counting up the names of all

---

[1] See a series of papers on Apostolic Succession in the *Christian Instructor* for 1838; also a Sermon preached in 1873 before the Synod of Aberdeen, by Rev. Geo. W. Sprott.

those, lay or clerical, throughout the country, who, in addition to the members of Assembly, were considered suitable for acting as ministers or readers, only forty-three could be named. There were therefore not ninety persons in the whole country on whom the first General Assembly could rely for assistance in the great work committed to its charge. Common-sense dictated the one course which was fitted for utilising these small resources. The basis of the Church system was Presbyterian, for it consisted of the three offices of presbyter, elder, and deacon—whose functions were similar to those now associated with the names—but following the example of some of the foreign Churches, Scotland was divided into ten dioceses or districts, over each of which it was proposed that a Superintendent should be appointed. These superintendents were not in any sense bishops. They might be laymen, were under the authority of the Assembly, and had no exclusive right to ordain. There was also another extremely useful office recognised—namely, that of Readers. Teachers or Doctors were also recognised as Church functionaries. This system was the best possible for the time. It is stamped with the common-sense of Knox, who, anything but an ecclesiastical doctrinaire, took the readiest instruments for accomplishing the work in hand. The effect justified the practical wisdom of the Reformer, for so great was the advance that, in 1567, there were about two hundred and eighty-nine ministers and seven hundred and fifteen readers, with five superintendents, labouring in the Church.

(*b*) The provision made for ecclesiastical discipline was ample, through all the various stages of humiliation, from privy censure to excommunication. The severity with which it was exercised is a painful feature in the history of the Reformation. It was one of the few customs of the Romish Church which the Protestants preserved. But while we may feel justified in condemning them, we must not forget that such efforts were urgently needed in order to create a higher public tone on questions of morality. Everything we know tends to prove that all ranks of society were steeped in shameless coarseness. The Reformers, as Christian men, could not admit the excuse that other countries were equally bad, or that such was 'the habit of the times.' They had their Bibles in their hands, and knew what God required of His Church; and so they determined to purify it by reproving wrongdoers, as well as by preaching the gospel. It is to their credit that they were impartial as well as brave in their rebukes. No class was spared. The Lord High Treasurer was dealt with as faithfully as the humblest peasant; and on none did the hand of the Church fall with greater severity than upon any minister overtaken in a fault. The result, for a time at least, and so far as appearances went, justified the stern *régime*. Knox could challenge the verdict of his contemporaries as to the beneficial effect upon society.

(*c*) The rest of the *Book of Discipline* referred chiefly to the uses to which the revenues of the ancient Church were to be applied. The property of the Romish Church was enormous, amounting to about one-half of that of the whole kingdom, and the Church, the poor, and the education of the people, were the three objects to which it was proposed to dedicate a proportion of these resources. A modest but sufficient provision was to be laid aside for the decent sustenance of the ministry; the deserving poor were to be supported in their own parishes at the sight of the elders and deacons; and the very highest possible education—far higher than ever has been attained since—was to be supplied to the people. The commonwealth had a right, Knox said, to assert a paramount claim on every child, and to compel it to be educated. If poor, their expenses were to be paid; but no father, of whatsoever estate or condition, was 'to use his children at his own phantasy,' but must 'be compelled to bring them up in learning and virtue.' Schoolmasters were accordingly to be attached to every church; while in 'upland' districts, the reader was to attend to the necessities of the young. Grammar or secondary schools were to be erected in every considerable town; and the whole system linked on to the universities. In the parish school, instruction was to be given, not only in elementary subjects, but in the rudiments of Latin; while in the grammar-schools, the tongues—embracing Latin, French, and perhaps Greek—rhetoric, and philosophy, were to be taught. Once every quarter the pupils at all the schools were to be examined, and any scholar, however poor, shewing aptitude for learning, was to be directed in his studies, through the grammar-school to the university. The curriculum for such students was long and thorough, extending, in the case of the learned professions, to at least the twenty-fourth year of a man's age. Liberal endowments were proposed for the teachers and professors, and a splendidly equipped staff was to be appointed to each of the universities. For the maintenance of this magnificent national system, embracing the support of the poor, the efficiency of the Church, and the education of the whole body of the people, it was proposed to take as much as was requisite from the enormous endowments of the ancient Church. A grander scheme for the elevation of a people never emanated from the brain of patriot or statesman—and it was a scheme whose accomplishment was then quite within the power of the nation. If Scotland was, in one aspect of the polity, to be made a kind of modern theocracy, in which all departments of government were to be guided by Scriptural texts and examples, it was, according to another part, to be raised to the front rank among educated nations. The former design would undoubtedly have broken down when the relative functions of the civil and ecclesiastical jurisdictions came to be determined. For Knox drew no very distinct line betwixt the two. The State was as much bound to govern the Church and enforce Scriptural rule on its observance, as the Church was bound to press Scriptural rule on the State. But the educational project sketched by Knox is magnificent.

Such were the system, the creed, the worship, the polity of the Church of the Reformation; and when we contemplate the massive structure thus planned in the space of four years, chiefly by the genius of one man, we know not which is the more prominent feeling—astonishment at the grandeur of the system, or indignation at the unprincipled cupidity of the nobility and barons which prevented its execution. For the barons, who were ready to adopt the *Confession of Faith*, refused the *Book of Discipline*. It was 'but a devout imagination,' said worldly-wise Lethington; and he was right. Assent to abstract doctrines was very different from submission to any interference with dissolute living, and still more from thwarted avarice. 'The belly hath no ears,' replied Knox, who felt that reasoning and principle were alike thrown away upon the hungry landowners who had enlisted in the army of reform for the sake of the plunder consequent on its victories. There were doubtless conscientious and patriotic men like Argyll, Moray, and Glencairn among them, who were in full sympathy with the preachers; but they were the exception. For years they had as a class been bribed either by England or France; and they now displayed a rapacity, the disgrace of which can only be equalled by the injury inflicted upon the country. In vain the preachers protested. They alone remained pure of the taint of avarice. For years the ministers, cheated by false promises and resolutions of the Privy Council, and denied possession even of manse or glebe, lived in honourable beggary.

II. *Character and Work of Knox.*—Two figures stand out from the crowd in the stirring scenery of the Reformation in Scotland. John Knox and Queen Mary are the historical representatives of the two great currents of opinion and policy which then contended for the mastery. They were each endowed with an intellect of unusual vigour, with keen political insight, and with a most resolute will. Mary was in her own way almost as remarkable as Knox. To quickness of perception, subtlety of project, and heroic bravery, she added a beauty and fascination which supplied exquisite instruments for her skilful and ceaseless diplomacy. She had all the artistic grace and charm of the Stuarts; and if some of their faults also, these were combined with greater mental power and force of character than were found perhaps in any other of her race. Every one must regard with generous pity the young girl whose misfortune it was to be cast into a position for which by temperament and education she was so utterly unfitted. We must admire her devoted loyalty to her creed—a virtue by which some others of her race also lost their crowns. But while doing so, we join issue with the romantic school which, affecting a sentimental loyalty to the Stuarts, would canonise Mary as a saint and martyr. We have a very different conviction regarding her. From the first, she only lacked opportunity to have extinguished the Reformation in a sea of blood; and in all her coquetting with the Protestants, the smooth glove she wore covered a gauntlet of steel. She had been taught as a girl to gaze upon the martyrdoms of which the Huguenots were the victims. For some time after her arrival in Scotland, she acted her part skilfully and without guilt; but the barbarous assassination of Rizzio, perpetrated under circumstances of the coarsest brutality, seems to have demoralised her finer nature. That terrible scene, when the poor wretch, clutching at his mistress for protection, was dragged forth to his doom by the hard-featured barons, and the still more terrible discovery of the complicity of her husband Darnley—had awakened a fierce desire for revenge. The malign influence of Bothwell completed the moral injury she had sustained, and all ended—God knows alone through what gradual steps she was led on !—in the terrible crime of Kirk-o'-Field.

John Knox has been the object of almost as keen detraction as Queen Mary, but the closer our examination, the more we are forced to recognise in him one of the noblest men—sincere, truthful and brave—our country ever produced. He has been described as a rigid Puritan who frowned down laughter and innocent amusements; a ruthless iconoclast, to whom we are indebted for roofless cathedrals and ruined abbeys; as intolerant as any cardinal or inquisitor, exchanging the infallibility of the Pope for that of himself and the General Assembly. Men suppose they can trace the influence of Knox in the miserable barns which have taken the place of the old Gothic churches, and throw upon him the blame of the ugliness which has so long characterised our ecclesiastical system.

Now, we would not conceal the faults with which Knox is fairly chargeable. The language he employed—sometimes in public prayer—regarding the religion and character of Mary, seemed even to his contemporaries needlessly coarse and strong. His interviews with the Queen were marked not by the dexterity of the courtier, but by the unflinching faithfulness of a man to whom a great cause was intrusted. 'I know that many have complained,' he said on his death-bed, 'much and loudly, and do still complain of my too great severity; but God knows that my mind was always free from hatred to the persons of those against whom I denounced the heavy judgments of God. . . . For a certain reverential fear of my God who called me, and was pleased of his grace to make me a Steward of divine mysteries . . . had such powerful effect as to make me utter so intrepidly whatever the Lord had put into my mouth, without any respect of persons. Therefore I profess before God and his own holy angels that I never made gain of the sacred word of God, that I never studied to please men, never indulged my own private passions or those of others, but faithfully distributed the talent intrusted to my care for the edification of the Church over which I did watch. Whatever obloquy wicked men may throw upon me respecting this matter, I rejoice in the testimony of a good conscience.' 'It was unfortunately not possible,' writes Carlyle, 'to be polite with the Queen of Scotland, unless one proved untrue to the Nation and Cause of Scotland. A man who did not wish to see the land of his birth made a hunting-field for intriguing ambitious Guises, and the Cause of God trampled underfoot of Falsehoods, Formulas, and the Devil's Cause, had no method of making himself agreeable.' It must, however, be remembered that this method of speaking to a sovereign was not uncommon in that period. It may be paralleled by the language Latimer privately addressed to King Henry VIII., and by the sermons preached by Reginald Pole regarding the marriage of Anne Boleyn. There are indeed things which Knox has written that we wish he had never penned. The models he put before him were unfortunately borrowed more from the Old than from the New Testament; and Samuel slaying Agag, Elijah executing the priests of Baal, the Israelites exterminating the Canaanites, and such-like events, were recognised not only as teaching general principles, but as affording to himself title to apply the principles, and to act towards Mary and her co-religionists with the rigour of ancient Judaism. The man, indeed, felt he had no choice. The true key to his severity is to be found in nothing personal, but in his deep awe of God's word and in the belief that he was God's prophet, sent to apply that word to every political as well as religious matter that might occur. 'I find no more privilege granted unto kings by God, more than unto the people to offend God's majesty,' were his grave words to Lethington; but he adds: 'When kings do expressly oppose themselves to God's commandment, the people are bound to execute God's law upon them.' Such principles, when cautiously interpreted, are undoubtedly true, but they become dangerous if their application is to be left in the hands of every self-constituted judge of the occasion which renders their vindication necessary.

But without concealing those defects and exaggerations, we believe that Knox was the very opposite of what a certain type of detractors would fain represent him. So far from being a sour Puritan, his history shews a man full of humour and *bonhommie*, with an intense sense of the ludicrous. Our space does not admit of our giving illustrations of the humour with which his history abounds. We would simply refer to the descriptions of the carrying 'the young Sanct Geile,' and of the fray between the partisans of the two bishops in Glasgow Cathedral.

There was surely something of the geniality of Luther in one who on his death-bed caused a visitor 'pierce ane hoggit of wine which was in the cellar, and willed the said Archibald to send for more as long as it lasted, for he would never tarry until it were drunken.' He indeed denounced dancing at the court, and put down Maid Marian and the May-pole; but we have too much evidence as to the character of the dancing and of the popular sports of those times, not to attribute his condemnations to other causes than harsh Puritanism. He was certainly intolerant, but toleration in the modern sense is an anachronism in the sixteenth century. He insisted on the suppression of the mass, whether in the Queen's chapel or in the remote Baronial keep. On the authority of a verse in the Old Testament, he even urged the execution of the 'mass-mongering papists' as idolaters. But putting aside doctrinal beliefs, we must not forget that the mass was then the symbol of a system which was pledged to exterminate Knox and every Protestant. The Council of Trent was then issuing its decrees for the extinction of heretics, and the Catholic powers, including Queen Mary herself, were leagued for their execution. The dark-minded Philip was filling Spain with *autos-da-fe;* Alva was ravaging the Netherlands; the Duchess of Parma was crushing liberty in Holland; France was preparing for St Bartholomew; even Elizabeth of England was but a half-hearted Protestant. It would have required superhuman toleration in a man of the keen political insight of Knox to remain indifferent to the possible destruction of faith and liberty, of which every mass that was celebrated was practically the pledge. Even now we could not view with calmness a Queen in visible opposition to the Protestant faith, and bringing her priest with bell and candle to every castle she visited. Knox saw how Mary from the day of her arrival in Holyrood was by her bewitching grace acting as a solvent on the stern convictions of his associates. Moray for a time was fascinated; Lethington was won over. The men who tried to 'swim betwixt two waters' were increasing; Popery began to shew itself! It was necessary for Knox and the preachers to stand firm. The mass was idolatry; and if the country would escape the judgments with which God had visited the sins of the Kings of Judah and Israel, the Queen must not be privileged to disobey Jehovah. But his intolerance was in word only, for whatever he may have said or urged, it must be remembered that there was no martyrdom during the time Knox had influence. He was certainly intolerant in the modern sense; but it was precisely such intolerance as could alone have produced the Reformation. The colourless 'Liberal Thought' of the present day, with its hesitation as to all religious beliefs, would never have emancipated Scotland. It required the firm, almost relentless, grasp of determined men, who had no doubts, but who could boldly say, 'Thus saith the Lord,' as they hurled falsehood and superstition from their seats, and built up religion and political freedom.

It has long been the habit to refer every ruined shrine in Scotland to the vandalism of Knox and the Reformers; and there is perhaps no class of Scotchmen who condemn Knox on this account more than the landed gentry, who stand aloof from the Church of Knox. There is no class, however, who are less entitled to be heard in accusation. Knox did his best to check 'the rascal multitude' which ruined the churches of Perth and destroyed Scone. Cathedrals, abbeys, and churches were undoubtedly cleansed of their images, altars, and other superstitious symbols; and monastic establishments and one or two cathedrals received even a rougher handling. But the destruction effected by the Reformers in a time of great popular excitement is not to be compared with that caused by the invading armies of England, and was infinitely less than what was produced by the sacrilegious penuriousness and carelessness of the Scotch heritors. Were we to trace the causes to which we must attribute, on the one hand, the utter ruin of so many ancient and noble piles, and on the other, the meanness of so many of the edifices which now serve as parish churches, it would be found that the connection is very slight with the Reformation or with any principle inherent in Presbyterianism. One of the keenest controversies Knox had with the Privy Council was to secure the repair of churches, 'in such a manner as appertaineth as well to the majesty of the Word of God as unto the ease and commoditie of the people.' The spirit of Puritanism imported into Scotland a century afterwards, undoubtedly did much to destroy the feeling of art among the people; but the expense of upholding the ancient buildings, the value of the lead and slates which protected them, and their convenience as quarries from which ready-made materials might be had for erecting farm-houses or mansions, have demolished our churches and abbeys infinitely more than ever Knox did.

But without dwelling further on the misrepresentations of which Knox has been the subject, let us glance at the work he accomplished besides that already sketched. One work of Knox was the creation of a new class in Scotland—the seed of the nation that was to be—religious, educated, strong in conviction even to bigotry, self-reliant, industrious and bold. Hitherto the feudal system had placed all the power of the country in the hands of the great lords and barons. The burghs had perhaps more than a semblance of freedom from feudal dependence, but it was little more than a semblance. Neither the lesser barons, living in their 'Peels,' round which clustered the cots of hinds and shepherds, nor the villagers dwelling near the parish church or by the great abbey, ever dreamed of asserting their individual opinions or their rights. There was no middle class, there were no Commons to form a Third Estate along with the Crown and the temporal and spiritual peers. But the Reformation, as it was founded on an appeal to 'every man's conscience in the sight of God,' accompanied by enlightened instruction in Divine truth, produced the natural result of kindling a sense of personal responsibility in all who received it, and of emancipating the manhood of the country from the bondage of blind obedience to priest or baron. After the religious revolution of 1560, when the country was covered with evangelists, when the policy of the General Assembly found living voice in every pulpit, and when the mind of the leaders of the Church was expounded by every superintendent, minister, and reader, in all corners of the land, there came a mighty stirring of the slumbering masses. Men commenced to think for themselves, and to recognise their responsibility to God as members of the commonwealth. Conviction grew into devotion, and the Scotch small proprietors, burghers, artisans, and peasantry, beginning to breathe somewhat of the indomitable spirit which afterwards secured the freedom of their country and their faith, now grew into a powerful middle class —firm through conviction. 'It was not for nothing,' says Mr Froude, 'that John Knox had for ten years preached in Edinburgh, and his words been echoed from a thousand pulpits. Elsewhere the plebeian element of nations had risen to power through the arts and industries which make men rich—the commons of Scotland were sons of their religion. While the nobles were splitting into factions, chasing their small ambitions, taking security for their fortunes, or entangling themselves in political intrigues, tradesmen, mechanics, and poor tillers of the soil had sprung suddenly up into consciousness, with spiritual convictions for which they were prepared to live or die. The fear of God in them left no room for the fear of any other thing, and in the very fierce intolerance which John Knox had poured into their convictions, they had become a force in the State. The poor clay, which a generation earlier the haughty barons would have trodden into slime, had been heated in the red-hot furnace of the new faith . . . . Scotch Protestantism was shaped by Knox into a creed for the people; a creed in which the Ten Commandments were of more importance than science, and the Bible than all the literature in the world; narrow, fierce, defiant, but hard and strong as steel.' The middle class which John Knox was inspiring with his own convictions, was the beginning of that Scotch people to whom we belong. The Scotch people have grown with the Scotch Church. The Church has been the palladium of popular liberty, the mother of education, the trainer of the people in truthfulness and in an independence regulated by a supreme loyalty to the Word of God.

The work of Knox in Scotland was felt far beyond the country in which he laboured. The entire population of Scotland at that period was about the same as that of Glasgow in the present day. But the victory of Protestantism in Scotland was more complete than in any other country in Europe, except perhaps the Republic of Geneva. The German Protestant States were as yet part of the Catholic Empire; the Protestants of Holland and the Netherlands were struggling to relax the grasp with which Spain was attempting to strangle their new beliefs; the policy of England was hesitating; but Scotland at one stride had passed out of the most corrupt ecclesiastical system in Europe into the purity of the primitive faith. This had its influence on contemporary history. It had a very marked influence then and afterwards upon England, and many a despairing heart abroad got new courage from the spectacle. But the political as well as religious principles which were then expounded scattered a seed which took root in other times and places. Cromwell, the Puritans—maligned as they are by those who enjoy the fruit of their struggles—the English Revolution of 1688, the constitutional monarchy of the present day, and America as it now is, may trace the stream of their history to its fountain-head in the victory of Knox over absolutism and in the assertion of the supreme rule of Scripture.

The position of Knox and of the Reformation was long critical, and the difficulties which had to be contended with were enormous. Knox was well acquainted with the ceaseless diplomacy and 'practices' going on among the Catholic powers for the extirpation of heresy, but he could not have realised the danger in which his country more than once stood. The perils to which the Church was exposed from parties in Scotland were small compared with that which was threatened by larger movements, which, if successful, would have crushed liberty and religion from John o' Groat's to the Land's End.

There were two occasions on which foreign intrigue so supported the designs of Mary and the Catholic party in England and Scotland as to bring affairs to the very edge of a precipice over which Protestantism and liberty would have been hurled, and on both of these occasions the danger was averted by the occurrence of great crimes. Immediately before the assassination of Darnley the train had been skilfully laid for something being done 'for the restoration of the auld religion,' as the Queen herself confessed in her letter to Archbishop Beaton, her ambassador at Paris. We cannot here describe the particular steps which had prepared the possibility of her success. Point after point had been gradually reached, until the goal of her ambition was all but attained. Such of the Scotch Lords as had been the very soul of the Reformation were in banishment, and their estates were about to be confiscated; the power of the sword was for the first time in her hand; she had been able to restore the Bishops to their seats in Parliament; several powerful nobles had returned to the old faith; the mass was being celebrated with startling freedom, and friars were preaching in Holyrood; it was even said that new altars were ready to be placed in St Giles'. But at the very moment when the plot had reached its crisis, Rizzio was assassinated, and the kingdom thrown into confusion. Had the Queen possessed the skill to have used that crime to her advantage, it might have been the means of strengthening her throne and of advancing her designs. But Mary could not forgive the outrage she had sustained at the hands of her husband, and her mad attachment to Bothwell, followed by the atrocity of Kirk-o'-Field, her subsequent reckless bearing, and her surrender at Carberry, led first to her compulsory resignation, and finally to her imprisonment in England. She was branded by the populace as an adulteress and murderess, and as far as the commons of Scotland were concerned, her influence sank with her reputation. The Reformation passed safely through its first great peril, and the Regency of Moray for a time gave security and the formal sanction of the crown to the Church as restored to purity.

Even the partisans of Mary, shocked by her follies, if not her complicity in the actual murder of Darnley, for a time abandoned their plots in her favour. But it was only for a brief time. Fotheringay, with its fair prisoner, soon became the centre of new 'practices.' Conspirators were busy among the English Catholics, and Spain once more took up the thread and began to spin new combinations for the overthrow of Elizabeth and the establishment of Romanism under Mary. She was to marry Norfolk, and Norfolk was to lead the Catholics of England to her side. Scotland became broken up into contending factions. The Queen found the ablest of all her counsellors in Maitland of Lethington, and he 'practised' with such effect among the nobles—who for different reasons, chiefly selfish, were jealous of the Regency—that a strong force was organised for the maintenance of her cause. Kirkaldy of Grange held Edinburgh Castle in her name. Dumbarton Castle, until taken by the extraordinary daring of Crawford of Jordanhill, protected her interests in the West. The Hamiltons, Buccleuch, Fernihirst, the reivers of the Border, Huntly, and the men of Aberdeenshire and the North-east, espoused her cause. The country was for a time steeped in bloodshed. Money was freely poured into Scotland—now from France, and now from Spain—and used according to the policy of the moment. As the plot thickened, darker measures were projected. The Spanish Armada was to be anticipated. Plans were laid for the reception of a Spanish force, which the Duke of Alva was to land in Aberdeenshire. Had it not been for Knox and the men from Angus to the Lothians, from St Andrews to Glasgow and Galloway, who would have died for their religion, Maitland might possibly have secured the country. Alva was, as usual, dilatory. He perhaps recognised the difficulties which the firmness of the Reformers presented to the success of his project, but delay he did until the second great crime occurred in the Massacre of St Bartholomew, which blasted for ever the hopes of Mary and of Romanism in the kingdom.

Knox was indeed 'inflexible,' as Lethington wrote to the Queen. Although shattered in body through a stroke of apoplexy—having 'tacken gude nicht of this world,' and 'creiping upon his club' as he went to the kirk-session in St Giles'—yet the unquenchable fire flamed into its old strength as it was stirred by the treachery and danger he beheld on every side. For years the minister of this same church of St Giles—then the only church in Edinburgh—he had preached in it twice every Sunday, and thrice during week-days. It was here that in the ears of lords and courtiers the impassioned preacher rang out the brave words that shaped the policy of the time. It was of his pulpit in this church he said: 'I am in the place where I must speak the truth, and the truth I will speak, impugn it who so list.' We cannot look round on these walls without seeing them repeopled with the men whose names still live—the young Lord James, the subtle Lethington, the wretched Darnley, the rough Bothwell, or the fierce Huntly drawing back with a scowl and 'tugging his bonnet over his eyes' as he winced under the fervid denunciations. It was here that the dark crowd of three thousand men gathered to listen to the funeral sermon over the dead Regent of happy memory. And now Knox, struggling with weakness, strove as of old to warn friends and foes. Edinburgh was then as a beleaguered city, and he was in the midst of danger. The roar of cannon disturbed the midnight as well as the day. The retainers of the Hamiltons, who bore him no good-will, might at any time stab him as they jostled along the causeway. A gun-shot came crashing into his room as he sat in his house down there in the Canongate. Kirkaldy of Grange did his best to protect him. His friends offered to form a bodyguard for his defence; and chiefly to save them the risk of injury, he yielded to their petitions and went for a time to St Andrews—the city to him of so many memories. After he left Edinburgh (May 1571), it was for a time given up to the conflict between the castle and the supporters of the king. The Church was closed. Cannon were mounted on St Giles' steeple, and nothing was heard but the 'ringing of artillery.'

We cannot forbear giving here the well-known and graphic picture which James Melville, then a young student, draws of Knox's appearance when in St Andrews: 'I heard him teache there the prophecies of Daniel, that simmer, and the wintar following. I haid my pen, and my litle buike, and tuk away sic things as I could comprehend. In the opening up of his text, he was moderat the space of half an houre; but when he enterit to application, he made me so to *grew*, and tremble, that I could not hald a pen to wryt. . . . I saw him, euerie day of his doctrine, go hulie and fear, with a furring of marticks about his neck, a staff in the an hand, and gud godlie Richart Ballanden, his servand, halding up the uther oxter, from the Abbey to the parish kirk, and be the said Richart, and another servant, lifted up to the pulpit, whar he behovit to lean, at his first entrie; bot, er he haid done with his sermone, he was sae active and vigorous, that he was lyk to ding the pulpit in blads and flie out of it. . . . Mr Knox wald sum tyme com in and repose him in our college yeard, and call ws schollars unto him, and bless ws, and exhort ws to knaw God and his wark in our contrey, and stand be the guid cause, to use our tyme weill, and lern the guid instructiones, and follow the guid exemple of our maisters.'

While in St Andrews, events were hurrying on which gave Knox the greatest anxiety. The dangers from without were only a little worse than those from within the Church. The Regent Morton, who was the embodiment of the grasping spirit of the Scottish nobility, had managed, partly by threats and partly by reasoning, to persuade the Church to restore the bishops. Some of the reasons for such a step were at the time obvious. The loss of the spiritual estate in parliament would have destroyed the balance of power and implied a serious revolution in the Constitution. Although it should be only in name, the seats vacated by the bishops and abbots must be filled up. There were other causes less honourable. The restoration of the old ecclesiastics, or rather the institution of 'Tulchan' bishops and abbots, was a device whereby the barons might more securely drain the Church of its property. This event, however, properly falls to be discussed by my successor. Knox made no formal protest to the Assembly against their appointment, although in his public preaching and in private conversation he 'discharged his conscience that the Kirk of Scotland should not be subject to that order.' He tried, however, to secure the arrangement from some of the evils he suspected would arise, for he counselled the Assembly to take order that the bishops should account to the Church and not to the nobles for the revenue of their dioceses, and earnestly warned them against the sin of themselves entering into simoniacal compacts. Had his counsels been acted upon, many a future scandal and trouble would have been saved.

Knox felt that his time on earth was short. A truce between the contending factions, accompanied by an earnest request by the people of Edinburgh for his return, brought him back once more to his old charge. He was too feeble to make his voice heard in the Cathedral Church, and a smaller place was appointed for his services. His sermon at the induction of his colleague Lawson was the last he ever preached.

Scarcely had he returned to Edinburgh before the country was startled with horror by the intelligence of the Massacre of St Bartholomew. 'At first, it was the news of the assassination of Coligny which arrived; but post followed post, bringing fresh accounts of the most shocking and barbarous cruelties. It is believed that seventy thousand persons were murdered in one week. For several days the streets of Paris literally ran with blood.' When the tidings of this horrible butchery (for which a solemn procession to be made to the church of St Louis, the patron saint of France, a *Te Deum* to be sung, and a year of jubilee to be observed, were ordered by the Pope) reached Scotland, the effect was profound and universal. John Knox and the Reformers, many of whose personal friends were among the victims, were appalled. All parties in the state were horrified. Those who had hitherto supported the Queen, felt now that her cause was doomed. The wavering Elizabeth of England was startled from her trickeries. Kirkaldy and Lethington still held out in the castle, but they knew that their days were numbered. Lethington indeed was dying. For months he had been a living miracle, for never did keen intellect consort so strangely with an exhausted frame. The two men, dying within so short a distance of each other, who had once been friends, were now separated by greater differences than political feuds. 'Never,' wrote the English Randolph, after visiting Maitland in the castle, 'have I found in so weak a body, a mind less mindful to God, or more unnatural to his country.' Unable to bear the noise of the guns, he, with his little lapdog, was carried down to one of the cellars; and eleven days after the castle was taken, he died, it was supposed by poison administered by his own hand.

The Massacre of St Bartholomew, which was intended to

crush Protestantism in France, saved Protestantism to Scotland and England. As the murder of Darnley five years before occasioned a reaction of horror which frustrated the plans of Mary and her foreign advisers, and by placing Moray in power, led to the recognition of the Reformation as the religion of the State, so now the crime of the Medici destroyed for ever the influence of Mary and Romanism in Scotland. In less than a year Edinburgh Castle fell, and the brave Kirkaldy, reconciled to his old friends, died on the scaffold under circumstances of weird interest.

But long before the taking of the castle John Knox entered into his rest. For months before the end came, almost every letter he wrote bore touching proof of his weariness of life and his desire to depart. 'John Knox with my dead hand and glad heart preising God.' 'Wearie of this world and thirsting to depart.' 'Call for me, deir brethern, that God in his mercy will pleis put an end to my long and painful battell. For now being unable to fight as God sometimes gave me strenth I thrist an end, befoir I be moir troublesum to the faithful; and yet Lord let my desyre be moderat be the Holy Spirit.' These and such-like are the expressions which occur frequently in his writings at this time.

There are few more touching records than the account of his last hours, preserved by his faithful servant Richard Bannatyne. The simple pathos of the narrative reveals the personal and tender affection which Knox inspired in those who knew him— an affection of which we have many incidental notices, disproving the popular belief that he was distinguished by a harsh and repulsive nature. On the Tuesday after he preached his last sermon at the induction of Lawson, 'he was stricken,' writes Bannatyne, 'with a grit hoist,' which so enfeebled him, that he had to leave off his ordinary reading of the Bible; 'for ilk day he red a certane chepteris, both of the Auld Testament and of the New, with certane psalmes, quhilk psalmes he passed through eucrie moneth once.' . . . 'The Friday, which was the 14 day, he rose above his accustomed dyet; and yit when he did ryse, he could scairse sit in a stuile: and then being demandit what he wald doe up? said, he wald goe to the Kirke and preich, for he thocht it had been Sonday; and said that he had been all nicht meditating upoun the resurrectione of Christ, which he sould haue preichit after the death of Christ, whilk he had finishit in his last sermonde the Sonday befoir; for oft and monie tymes he wishit—and desyred of God that he mycht end his dayis in the teiching and meditatioune of that doctrine, quhilk he did.' . . . 'On Sonday, the 16 day, he kept his bed and would not eat,' having mistaken it 'for the first Sonday of the Fast,' on account of the Massacre of St Bartholomew.

'Upoun Fryday, the xxi day, he commandit Richard to gar make his kist (coffin) whairin he was borne to his burial. Sonday, the 23 day (which was the first Sonday of the Fast), at efternoune, all being at the kirke except thame that waited upoun him. . . . He said the Lordis Prayer, and the Beleife, with some paraphraise, upon euerie petitione and article of thaim; and in saying "Our Father which art in heaven," he says, "Who can pronounce so holie wordis?" . . . He wald oftin burst furth, "Live in Christ!" and "Lord grant us the rycht and perfyte hatred of syn, alsweill be the document of thy mercies as of thy judgmentis." "Lord grant trew pastoris to thy Kirke, that puritie of doctrine may be reteaned." . . . A litill efter none, he caused his wyfe reid the 15 Chapter of the First Epistle to the Corinthianis off the resurrectione. A litill efter he sayes, "Now, for the last, I commend my saule, spreit, and bodie (pointing upoun his thrie fingeris) unto thy handis, O Lord!" Thaireftir, about fyve houris, he sayis to his wyfe, "Goe reid whair I cast my first ancre!" And so shee read the 17 of Johnes Evangle; quhilk being endit, was red some of Calvinis Sermondis upon the Ephesianis. We, thinking that he was a sleip, demandit gif he heard? Answerit, "I heir, and understandis far better, I praise God." . . . Half ane houre eftir ten, or thairby, we went to our ordinar prayeris (whilk was the longer or we went to thame, becaus we thocht he had bene sleipand); quhilk being endit, . . . Robert Campbell sittis downe befoir him on a stule; and suddanlie thairefter he sayis, " Now it is cum!" for he had gevin ane long siche and sobe. Then Richard sitting doun before him, said, " Now, sir, the tyme that ye have long callit to God for, to wit, ane end of your battell, is cum! And seeing all naturall power now failes, remember upon these comfortable promises, which often tymes ye have schawin to us of our Salviore Jesus Christ! and that ye may understand and know that ye heir us, make us some signe." And so he lifted up his one hand, and incontinent thairefter randerit the spreit, and sleipit away without ony paine, the day afoir said, about ellevin houris at evin.'

In this manner died John Knox on the 25th November 1572. Within a few yards of this place where we are now met, he lies buried in that grave over which it is reported that the Regent Morton pronounced the well-known and well-deserved eulogium: 'There lies one who never feared the face of mortal man.'

'It seems to me hard measure,' says Thomas Carlyle, 'that this Scottish man, now after three hundred years, should have to plead like a culprit before the world: intrinsically for having been, in such way as it was then possible to be, the bravest of all Scotchmen! . . . He is the one Scotchman to whom of all others his country and the world owe a debt. He has to plead that Scotland would forgive him for having been worth to it any million "unblamable" Scotchmen who need no forgiveness.'

'What I have been to my countrie,' wrote Knox himself, 'albeit this unthankful aige will not knowe, yet the aiges to come will beir witness to the treuth.' It will be our shame, and the shame of Scotland, if that confidence is not justified.

ST GILES' LECTURES.

FIRST SERIES—THE SCOTTISH CHURCH.

LECTURE VI.

EPISCOPACY, PRESBYTERY, AND PURITANISM IN SCOTLAND, 1572 TO 1660 A.D.

By the Rev. JOHN CUNNINGHAM, D.D., Minister of Crieff.

THE sixteenth and seventeenth centuries were times of fierce religious conflict. In the period immediately preceding 1572, the struggle was between old Romanism and nascent Protestantism. In the period following 1572, and stretching on to the very close of the next century, the struggle was between Presbyterianism and Prelacy. The first of these conflicts was short, sharp, and decisive. The second was protracted and indecisive, and, like a slow fever, simply kept the country in a state of continual unrest.

In 1572, when my lecture begins, Scotland was in as chaotic a state, socially, politically, and ecclesiastically, as it well could be. The king was a boy of six years old. The deposed Queen-Mother was a captive in England. The government was in the hands of a Regency; but the first Regent, the Earl of Moray, had been shot on the streets of Linlithgow in 1570; the second, the Earl of Lennox, was killed, in what we would now call a *coup d'état*, at Stirling in 1571; the third, the Earl of Mar, died in 1572; and before the close of the same year, the fourth and last, the Earl of Morton, occupied the dangerous pre-eminence, and ruled for a time with a rod of iron; but in the end he was more unfortunate than all his predecessors, for he died a traitor's death. In 1572 there had been four regents in little more than two years, recalling the time when Galba, Otho, Vitellius, and Vespasian successively wore the Roman purple in a similarly short period.

The Reformation may be said to have been now legally completed, for the Regent Moray had given as much legal validity as he could to the new Church: the Confession of Knox was the Confession of the Nation; and to say a mass was death. But a relapse was possible—even probable. Men are not able all at once to tear out of their hearts religious ideas deeply rooted there—above all, women are not able to do so; and we may be quite sure the women of the Reformation Period had still a strong hankering after their priests, their masses, their confessionals, their indulgences, and their religious processions. The great wave which had surged over the country had swept them out of the ancient Church; but there were thousands who had been carried out in the crowd almost against their will; and another wave, if the tide began to recede, might wash them back again. Everybody recognised the possibility of this. The Guisian relatives of Queen Mary plotted for it; and the diplomatists of Queen Elizabeth plotted against it.

Though the practice of the old religion had been declared to be illegal, the framework of the old Church remained almost entire. Most of the abbeys had been wrecked, most of the cathedrals sadly defaced, and all the parish churches purged of their images; but otherwise the face of things remained much as before. The bishops were still drawing two-thirds of their revenues; the parsons were still living in their manses, and in large districts of the country, more especially in the northern and south-western counties, keeping possession of the churches and barring them against the Protestant preachers. The Church of which the foundations had been laid by Queen Margaret, and which had been defended to the last extremity by Cardinal Beaton, was now like a useless shell lying on the beach, almost entire, and outwardly as beautiful as ever, but with all its inner life gone.

But what was to be done with the Church's rentals and teinds as the bishops, abbots, and parsons died out? The Reformed clergy had claimed these as their inheritance, but the lords and lairds had destined at least a considerable portion of them for themselves. It must be told that there were many among the Lords of the Congregation who hungered and thirsted more after the corn-fields of the monks than after righteousness. But however this may be, as the law stood, it was only bishops who could draw the episcopal revenues—only abbots who could lift the rents of the abbey lands. To the lay mind, it seemed that to destroy these orders, was to disturb the balance of the Constitution, by removing the Third Estate, and to annihilate the tenure by which a great deal of the property of the kingdom was held. This feeling lay at the bottom of the arrangement so well known in Scotch ecclesiastical history as the Concordat of Leith. According to this Concordat, concluded between the Church and the State on the 1st of February 1572, Archbishops and Bishops, Abbots and Priors, were to be continued as parts of the Spiritual Estate, but with restricted powers, and subject to the jurisdiction of the General Assembly. This compromise being made, the vacant bishoprics were soon filled; but it was everywhere whispered that the patrons had bargained with the presentees that a portion of the episcopal revenues was to be handed over to them. This led to their being stigmatised as Tulchan Bishops—they were no better than stuffed calves set up to make the cow give her milk.

Such was the state of the country and the Church when Andrew Melville returned home after a residence of many years at the universities of Paris, Poitiers, and Geneva. He had already a great reputation as a learned man; he had been the intimate friend of Theodore Beza, the successor of Calvin, not only at Geneva, but in the Reformed Churches everywhere; and Glasgow was fortunate in securing him as the Principal of her University. Here he taught not only Divinity and Oriental languages, but Greek, Logic, Rhetoric, Arithmetic, Geometry, Aristotle's Ethics, Politics and Physics, and Plato's Dialogues—a whole Senatus Academicus in himself. Students came in such numbers that his class-room was crowded.

Melville came to Scotland with strong Genevese proclivities, and it was not long till he threw down the gage to the Episcopal party in the Church. The battle began in the Assembly of 1575, and here he obtained his first victory from his accurate knowledge of his Greek Testament. The Assembly declared that the name 'bishop' properly belonged to all who had charge of a flock; and all scholars are now agreed that, according to Apostolic usage, the Assembly was right. But Melville was not content with this. In 1578 he pushed his advantage further, and in 1580 he obtained his crowning victory. The Assembly then unanimously declared the office of a diocesan bishop to be 'unlawful, and without warrant in the Word of God,' and called upon those who held the office forthwith to demit it. It was a wonderful triumph to be obtained so quickly by one man against the influence of the Regent, the simoniacal nobility, and the bishops whom they had set up.

Looking back upon it now, after three centuries, is it a triumph of which we should be glad, or which we must regret? It is tolerably certain that if the dignities and offices of the old Church had remained, the greater part of the wealth of the old Church must have remained with them. By their abolition it was lost. It is also certain that the country would have been saved the convulsions and throes through which it had to pass in the next hundred years. Moreover, thus early, before Presbyterianism was distinctly stamped upon the Scottish

Church, that religious uniformity between England and Scotland would have been secured which many thoughtful men in all the centuries have earnestly wished to see, and which many thoughtful men even still would sacrifice much to realise. To those who regard all forms of Church polity as indifferent—and these in Scotland are now a large class—it may seem that Scotland has paid too high a price for the discovery that diocesan bishops were unknown in the Apostolic Church. We have lost our episcopal revenues and our abbey lands; the clergy have lost their places in Parliament and on the bench; the country has come through agonies of which the traces still remain; and England and Scotland, long united politically, are still divided ecclesiastically. All this has come of Melville's victory.

Such is one aspect of the question. But there is another aspect which we must also look at. The Presbyterian Church was the home of freedom and independent thought all through the seventeenth century—on two different occasions it was their last asylum when they had been driven out everywhere else. From it there issued the forces which established the Commonwealth and afterwards led to the Revolution; and it is questionable if there had been Commonwealth or Revolution without it. Without it the Stuarts might have been still upon the throne, doing as the Stuarts always liked to do. One Church might have been established over all the island, undisturbed by the muttering of dissent, but dead, stagnant, with no breath of God blowing over it; and Great Britain been as king-ridden and priest-ridden as Spain. Unless, perchance, the revolutionary fiends, held back for more than a century, and breaking out with all the more fury because of it, swept away both Monarchy and Church—as happened in France—reading to all Churches and nations a salutary lesson for all time. I am inclined, then, to think that after all we did not pay too high a price for our Presbytery, though it cost the clergy their dignities and lands, and the country some bloody agonies.

Having swept away the Episcopal polity so far as an Act of Assembly could do it, Melville and his party set themselves to build up the Presbyterian. The *Second Book of Discipline* was compiled and approved of by the Church. It is curious that in this famous constitutional document only four ecclesiastical assemblies are mentioned—the Œcumenical, the National, the Provincial, and the Congregational. The Œcumenical was never realised till the Pan-Presbyterian Council met in Edinburgh three years ago. The National is the General Assembly which from that time till this, save in times of suppression, has held its sittings annually. The Provincial is the Synod. The Congregational Court or Eldership appears to agree in its main features with the Kirk-session. But what of the Presbytery—the most rudimental court of the Presbyterian Church? It is not once mentioned. The truth is, it was not yet clearly conceived of as a court separate from the kirk-session. More than one-half of the parishes were yet without regular ministers. One minister, in many cases, dispensed the sacraments in four or five different parishes, where there were only readers to read the *Book of Common Order* on the Sundays. There was one Eldership for such a group of congregations. But as the parishes were gradually supplied with ministers, an ecclesiastical development took place which resulted in every congregation having its own kirk-session and every district its own Presbytery. The original Eldership parted into two separate organisations.

Up to this time there had been no such thing as a Presbytery in Scotland; but even while the *Second Book of Discipline* was being debated in the Assembly, Presbyteries were being constituted in different parts of the country. They at once attracted the attention of the Court. Some of their moderators were summoned before the Privy Council, jealous of this new ecclesiastical judicature, and ordered to produce their minutes. But the work of constituting Presbyteries went on, and they soon existed everywhere. As they increased, the occupation of the Superintendent was gone.

The king was now a lad of fifteen, and a very precocious lad. He had nominally at least assumed the reins of government. Morton had laid down the regency, and soon afterwards was compelled to lay down his neck under the knife of the Maiden; and his head now grinned from the highest gable of the Tolbooth. Two gay young men had become the constant companions of the king—Esmé Stuart, generally known as Mons. D'Aubigny; and Captain James Stuart, a son of Lord Ochiltree's. The first was a Frenchified cousin of the king; the second, a worse than Frenchified brother-in-law of John Knox—a curious conjunction. The one soon became Duke of Lennox and the other Earl of Arran, for James was prodigal of titles to his favourites. These two ruled everything. The English Court was alarmed, and so were the Scotch Presbyterian ministers. And there was good cause. The bishops who had not demitted their office, were maintained in their cathedrals and dioceses in defiance of the mandates of the Church. It was rumoured that Popery as well as Prelacy was about to be re-introduced; and the public recantation by D'Aubigny of his popish errors, did not allay the panic. It was regarded as a sham. The horrors of St Bartholomew's Day, still fresh in the memory, intensified the feeling. It was at this crisis the Raid of Ruthven took place. The royal lad was wheedled to Huntingtower, near Perth, and kept a virtual prisoner by the Earl of Gowrie and other Presbyterian lords; Lennox and Arran were obliged to flee for their lives, and almost every pulpit in the kingdom proclaimed the deliverance of the Kirk and the king from the hands of their enemies. But it was a short-lived jubilee. Within a year James managed to escape from his keepers, and was soon surrounded by his old friends. The Raid was declared to be treason. Most of the barons hastened to make their submission, and were forgiven; but not so the ministers. Many of them still justified the deed in their sermons, and foremost among these was Melville, who, with his fierce elocution, told the king to be warned by the fearful examples of Belshazzar and Nebuchadnezzar. He was summoned before the Privy Council, but declined its jurisdiction, and ventured to be contemptuous. Ordered to enter himself as a prisoner at Blackness Castle, he thought it safer to cross the Border and seek a refuge in Berwick.

It is certain that James had already contracted a dislike of Presbytery; and the Raid of Ruthven and the plain speaking of the preachers had deepened the feeling. In 1584 the Acts were passed by the Estates which are known in history as the Black Acts. They ratified the jurisdiction of the Three Estates; they declared the king to be supreme in all causes and over all persons; they placed the chief ecclesiastical authority in the hands of the bishops. These enactments struck at the root of the most cherished principles of Presbytery. Some of the ministers left the country; the most of them sullenly submitted, for what else could they do? For eight years from this time there was ecclesiastical chaos in Scotland—Episcopacy and Presbytery jumbled confusedly together.

But strange to say, at the very time when the fortunes of Presbytery were at the lowest ebb, an Act of Parliament was passed, which made a well-endowed Episcopate for ever after impossible in Scotland. In 1587 the Act of Annexation was passed, which attached the temporalities of all benefices to the crown. The teinds still remained sacred, but the lands were secularised. It was the first direct act of disendowment connected with the Reformation. If the rich estates which had maintained the splendour of the Pre-Reformation bishops and abbots, had remained with the crown, for national uses, we might not so much have lamented it; but many of them were soon squandered by the prodigal James among his favourites, and now they only increase the acreage of some of our great proprietors. When the next act of disendowment comes, how much of the teinds will go in the same way?

During all this time Presbyterianism and Episcopacy were struggling for supremacy, and now Presbyterianism managed to throw its antagonist. But how, it is difficult to say. James had got married to a Danish princess, and had been engaged in drinking-bouts with the Danish nobles, forgetful of Episcopacy and Presbytery alike. When the young husband returned, he was immensely pleased with everything and with everybody, for the Presbyterian ministers and people had given him a right royal welcome. In the Assembly of 1590, he delivered his celebrated speech. As Calderwood has it, 'he fell forth praising God that he was born in such a time as the time of the light of the Gospel, to such a place as to be king in such a Kirk, the sincerest Kirk in the world. The Kirk of Geneva,' he continued, 'keepeth Pasche and Yule; what have they for them? they have no institution. As for our neighbour Kirk in England, it is an ill-said mass in English, wanting nothing but the liftings. I charge you, my good people, ministers, doctors, elders, nobles, gentlemen, and barons, to stand to your purity; and I forsooth, so long as I brook my life and crown, shall maintain the same against all deadly.' This speech is very like our Scotch King Solomon, and yet it is altogether unlike everything else he ever said or did. It gives the lie to all his past and all his future. But for the time being he was sincere. Two years afterwards, in June 1592, the Act was passed which is known as the Magna Charta of the Presbyterian Church in Scotland. It annulled the Black Acts so far as they infringed upon ecclesiastical jurisdiction in spiritual affairs; it gave legal sanction to the Presbyterian Courts, and provided that presentations to benefices should henceforth be laid before the Presbyteries, who were instructed to take the presentees on trial, and give them collation should they be found qualified. This last clause made the presbyters of those days to rejoice with exceeding great joy, for it stripped the bishops of the most essential attribute of their office, and gave it to the Presbyteries; and yet, strange to say, it was this very clause which, in 1843, split the Church asunder, from the Church's refusal to take on trial the presentee to Auchterarder. It does not seem to have occurred to Andrew Melville, stickler for spiritual jurisdiction though he was, that it was wrong for the Parliament to impose this upon the Church; it was rather a thing for which the Church should be devoutly thankful; but the successors of Andrew Melville, two hundred and fifty years afterwards, thought differently, and read the clause as putting a yoke on their necks, which they could not and would not bear. The bishops who were dispossessed in 1592, were avenged in 1843.

In 1592 Presbytery was supreme, but it did not long maintain its supremacy. It abused its power. The king wished to be lenient to some of his great nobles in the North who were still attached to Popery. The ministers would have no mercy upon them. They would confiscate their estates and drive them into exile. The pulpit then performed the work which the press has usurped now, and fierce philippics were pronounced against the king and his courtiers. David Black, one of the ministers of St Andrews, preached a sermon denouncing king, queen, court, council, in language which would hardly be used now by the most violent republican demagogue. He was summoned before the Privy Council, but he declined its jurisdiction. As the altar consecrated the gift, so, in those high days, it was thought the pulpit sanctified every word that was spoken in it, however libellous or treasonable it might be. Notwithstanding his declinature, he was found guilty, and banished north of the Tay; for our Highland glens were regarded then as Siberia is now among the Russians, or as Botany Bay was lately among ourselves. But the matter did not end here. The whole Church had been excited by the trial, and the excitement culminated in a riot in Edinburgh, in which James thought his royal life was endangered. He came to the conclusion that Presbytery could not be bridled, and that it must be destroyed.

He carried out his plans with considerable kingcraft. He shifted the meeting-place of the Assembly from Edinburgh to the North, where a love for Prelacy and even Popery still lingered. Moreover, it was hoped the turbulent spirits of the South and West would not travel so far—for a long journey it then was. The first Assembly was held at Perth, but the king's design was there veiled under general propositions. Soon afterwards, another Assembly met at Dundee, and there a standing Commission was appointed of some of the most eminent and ambitious ministers of the Church—one of them bearing the name and, I suppose, the blood of our present Premier. In the month of December of that same year, 1597, these Commissioners, who seem to have understood well the part they were to play, appeared before the Estates, and craved that some of their number should be admitted to Parliament as the Third Estate. The crave was granted; but it was provided that if they entered Parliament it must be as bishops, abbots, or priors, as in the olden time. This was exactly what was wanted, and indeed just what had been arranged. Again an Assembly was summoned to meet at Dundee. The king was present, and protested that he did not wish to see 'papistical or Anglican bishops,' but only some of the wisest of the ministers to sit in Parliament and Council, and 'not to be standing as poor supplicants at the door.' The proposal sounded well, and was carried, notwithstanding the resolute opposition of some of the more sturdy Presbyterians. It was remarked that it was the Northern ministers who had decided the vote. Caithness and Orkney led the ring. The Southern ministers bitterly complained of this, just as some people are complaining at this present moment of the preponderating vote of the North in a somewhat different matter. Thus had James very dexterously managed to insert the thin edge of Episcopacy into the Church. Of course, it was something for a parish minister to sit in Parliament, and become a member of the Privy Council, and a lord of Session. It was scarcely in flesh and blood to resist these honours when they were thrust upon them. How many of us would resist them now? And why then should we severely blame these ancient presbyters when their ambition had been stimulated and the consciousness of a Parliamentary power, to be still further developed in their descendants, was already stirring their blood?

Five years after this, James succeeded to the throne of Elizabeth; and from being a petty king, brow-beat by his clergy and intimidated by his nobles, he suddenly found himself the almost absolute monarch of a great kingdom. In Church affairs he had all along been influenced by Anglican examples; but now when he was surrounded by bishops and deans, and felt the strength which his new position gave him, he set himself with more earnestness than ever to the work of religious uniformity. It was a natural and excusable ambition, had he gone about the matter in a kindly and constitutional way. But that was not James's way—especially now. He dissolved Assemblies which he thought would be unruly; and cast the ministers, who met in spite of him, into jail. He called other Assemblies, when and where he pleased, by his own kingly prerogative, and packed them with his own creatures. In this way the work was easily and effectually done. In an Assembly which met at Glasgow in 1610, the Presbyterian polity was pulled down, stone by stone, by the hands of Presbyterian ministers, and the Episcopal polity set up in its room. The Parliament had been still more prompt than the Assembly. In 1606 it had repealed the Act of Annexation so far as the episcopal lands were concerned, and in 1612 it gave full legal status to the episcopal order.

But could Parliament or General Assembly make bishops? Up to this time they had both made and unmade them. But different ideas upon this point were now prevalent in England, and James had inhaled these. Archbishop Bancroft had bitterly attacked the Scotch Church, as an institution of Genevese origin. It had no divine right, no apostolical succession. The Scotch ministers designated to the Episcopate must therefore go to England and receive the Episcopal grace, and through the English line of succession link themselves with the Apostles. Spottiswood, Lamb, and Hamilton went; and having been consecrated by the Bishops of London, Ely, and Bath, they returned, bringing with them a true Church. Shall we blame them for their subserviency? Not much, for 'he that desireth the office of a bishop, desireth a good thing;' and we must remember that Anglican ideas were at that time telling powerfully on the Scotch clergy through kingly and courtly influences. Anglican influences are acting upon us now, and they always will.

But what of that unflinching presbyter, Andrew Melville? He was not a man to be bribed by mitres. He was not a scholar to be daunted by Bancroft, albeit he was an Archbishop. He had already pulled down a whole hierarchy; and when James, timid and testy, would not listen to him, he had taken him by the sleeve and told him he was 'God's silly vassal.' James knew he must either be won over or got rid of. He was invited to the English court, and put through a course of Episcopal divinity—a very farcical proceeding; but it appears to have done him harm rather than good. He amused himself with writing a Latin lampoon upon what he had seen in the Chapel-Royal. It unfortunately found its way into the king's hands, and the too witty presbyter was found guilty of a misdemeanour by the Privy Council, and sent to the Tower. There he lay for three years, when he was allowed to retire to France and accept a professorship at Sedan, now famous for the destruction of the French army and empire. He never saw his native country more. That was the way in which James used his invited guest—the ablest and honestest ecclesiastic in his kingdom.

Melville is undoubtedly one of the most massive figures in Scotch ecclesiastical history. In scholarship and manly grasp of mind, he excelled Knox. In courage and disinterestedness, he was equal to him. He was the great Northern apostle of high Church principles—the Hildebrand of Presbytery. These principles were not in much favour in England in those days, for

Henry would have taken off the head and Elizabeth would have torn off the frock of any priest who disputed the royal authority; and James, though not so violent in his way, had quite as high conceptions of prerogative, in all causes, ecclesiastical as well as civil. But had Melville lived in our own more tolerant day, he might have been hailed as the greatest champion of the spiritual power on both sides of the Border.

The Church of Scotland was now Episcopal—more Episcopal than it had ever been since the Reformation. But its worship was somewhat balder and barer than in the sister Church. There were no sacerdotal vestments, no choral singing, no organs. James was determined there should be uniformity in all things. In 1617 he revisited his native country after an absence of thirteen years, and he took care that the service in the chapel at Holyrood should be conducted with all the splendour of the Anglican ritual. He explained to the bishops and nobles his views as to the future worship of the Church, told them he might make the changes by virtue of his own royal prerogative; but that out of deference to popular prejudices, he would leave it to the General Assembly. Next year, 1618, the Assembly met at Perth, and a famous Assembly it was. The Dean of Winchester brought before it Five Articles which the ecclesiastical monarch had drawn up, and which he wished the Assembly to pass into law. They were: (1) That the sacrament of the body and blood of Christ should be received kneeling; (2) That it might be administered in private to the sick; (3) That infants might be baptised at home when they could not conveniently be brought to church; (4) That all children of eight years of age, after having learned the Lord's Prayer, the Creed, and the Ten Commandments, should be brought to the bishop to be blessed; (5) That the days commemorative of Christ's birth, passion, resurrection, and ascension, and of the descent of the Holy Ghost, should be observed as holidays.

These Five Articles would not stagger us very much now

unless, perchance, the first. Two or three of them are less or more a part of our modern Presbyterian usage. But they did stagger and distress our ancestors two hundred and sixty years ago. They regarded the Articles as a reversion to Popery; and, moreover, they did not like to have them thus forced upon them by the king. Nevertheless, they were passed by the Assembly, for both bribery and intimidation were employed, and the cringing courtiers outvoted the independent ministers. But it was soon found that it was more easy to make such regulations than to get people to keep them. Some kept Christmas and Easter, others did not. Some ministers gave the sacrament to kneeling communicants; others adhered to the old communion table, in scenic representation of the last supper at Jerusalem. In many churches there were confusion and distress from the conflict between the old forms and the new.

So far as we can trace, the revolution which had set up the hierarchy had never greatly stirred popular passion. The jealousies and grudges, the ideas and arguments which it evoked, had not penetrated much below the clergy and the lairds. But these new questions about worship touched every man, woman, and child. Those who did not care a straw whether the ministers in the cathedral towns were called presbyters or bishops—it was no matter of theirs—did care that the worship to which they had been accustomed from their infancy should not be disturbed by king or courtier. We know what is happening in England at this day in many churches where an elaborate Ritualism is being introduced—the heart-burnings, the rioting, the appeals to the law-courts—and it may help to illustrate the state of feeling in Scotland for years after the Assembly of 1618. It was plain that a revolution of the national worship was not to be effected so easily as had the revolution of the Church's polity.

And yet, now in the nineteenth century, we feel it might be possible to conform the worship of the Church of Scotland to that of England; but its polity—never. Not that we think Presbytery divinely right and Episcopacy essentially wrong; but because we think no form of Church government has a prescriptive right, and that that form, be it Episcopal, Presbyterian, or Congregational, is the divinest and the best which works the best. We can never now belie our history by surrendering our Presbyterianism, or renounce our reason by believing that religion depends upon a trinity of Orders.

In 1625 James died—not much lamented in his native country. He was succeeded by his son Charles I., a man of graver manners, and greater earnestness, but bigoted and obstinate in the last degree. From this time on till 1633 the history of the Scotch Church is a dead flat, with no incidents of much interest rising above the ordinary level. In 1633 Charles came to Scotland to be crowned with the crown of his ancestors. He was accompanied by William Laud, then Bishop of London, and on the fair way to be Archbishop of Canterbury. On Sunday the 23d of June he came to this church (St Giles') to worship, but the ordinary officials were hustled out of their places; two English chaplains, in surplices, read the lessons and the prayers; and the Bishop of Moray, also in a surplice, preached the sermon. How different from this the conduct of our gracious Queen, when she goes to the humble church of Crathie, and joins in its worship according to the usual simple ritual of the country!

Charles was not idle while in Edinburgh, for he had resolved on a great deal of legislation, some of it of rather an explosive kind. An act which continued to him the paternal tailoring prerogative of prescribing vestments for the clergy, excited violent opposition. Curious that clerical costumes should have excited such agitations in all ages and all churches. But if Carlyle and other philosophers who have written about clothes, be right, perhaps chasubles, albs, stoles, birettas, hoods, capes are worth all the commotion they have caused.

There was another matter which caused still greater alarm in a different quarter: the king had set his heart on recovering the Church lands and tithes, more especially those granted during his father's minority, but found he had undertaken an impossible task. The possessors held on to them with a death-grip; but they were greatly alarmed, as they well might. He had, however, devised the scheme by which the stipends of the clergy are still paid out of the teinds of their parishes, and the Parliament of 1633 gave it its sanction. It was at the time a great improvement upon the older methods, and so far the Church is Charles' debtor; but as it made the valuation of land at that time the valuation for all time, although the real value might have increased twenty-fold, it owes him no thanks. Every one is now crying out for a change in the teind laws.

Another good thing he did—he laid in that parliament one of the chief foundation-stones of our parochial school system.

There was another thing he did; and I suppose that in this building, I must say it was a good thing too. He erected Edinburgh into a bishopric, for, strange to say, while such paltry towns as Dunkeld and Dunblane were bishops' seats, the metropolis, up to that day, was not. As the bishop must have a cathedral, the Collegiate Church of St Giles was by royal charter erected into the Cathedral Church of the diocese, with all the rights, liberties, and immunities belonging to a cathedral. There was still another thing which I suppose I must also say was good, though the Presbyterian writers of the time are against me. 'He did cause demolish the partition wall betwixt the Great and Little Kirk. Neither ministers nor magistrates in Edinburgh,' said honest Row the historian, 'did shew tokens of grief or sorrow for this; but many good Christians, both in Edinburgh and the country, did heavily complain of it to God, knowing it to be an evident beginning of a huge desolation to come, for Edinburgh had too few kirks before, and now this was unfitter for hearing nor it was before.' But more than this. In order that the new cathedral might be made in every way worthy of its position, the Town

Council despatched the Dean to Durham, to sketch the choir of the cathedral there; but before these plans were carried out the country was in confusion; and it has been reserved for Dr Chambers to restore this noble church to its pre-Reformation beauty.

But another matter was arranged during the royal visit which led to much more important results than all the others. The Scotch bishops were instructed to prepare a Liturgy, after the model of the Anglican one, and transmit it to London for revisal. It was this which had brought William Laud to Scotland.

No student of Scotch history now makes the mistake of supposing that up to this time there was no Liturgy in the Scotch Church. Knox's *Book of Common Order* had been in ordinary use from the Reformation down to the time we speak of. It was read every Sunday morning by the Reader in this church, and in almost every other church in the kingdom; only the rubric gave the officiating clergyman liberty to diverge from it. There was, therefore, no national prejudice against a liturgical service; but there was a nervous dread of Popery, and a nervous dread that the national usages were to be abolished, and Anglican ones substituted in their stead, without the sanction of Parliament or Assembly, and simply by a stretch of the royal prerogative. The old stubborn spirit of independence—bred in the bone and hardened by the wars of Wallace and Bruce—could not stand that.

It was July 1637 before the Prayer-book was prepared and revised, and all the arrangements made for its introduction. But on the 23d of that month it was to be used for the first time in this church. At ten o'clock, the dean, in his surplice, entered the reading-desk, but he had scarcely begun to read when the congregation was in a state of wild uproar. The storm which had been slowly gathering since 1618 now burst out. 'They are bringing in Popery,' shouted some. 'Woe, woe!' cried others. The shrill voices of women were uppermost. The half-mythical, half-historical Jenny Geddes hurled the stool upon which she had been sitting at the dean's head, screaming: 'Fause loon, dost thou say mass at my lug?' Other missiles of a similar character went hurtling through the air. Spottiswood, the Archbishop of St Andrews, who was present, and Forbes, the new Bishop of Edinburgh, tried to appease the people, but they only made matters worse. At length the magistrates managed to eject the principal rioters; and Forbes preached a short sermon, with closed doors, and amid comparative quietness. But when the church dignitaries came out to the street, they were mobbed by the people, hooted, hustled, stoned, and glad to escape with their lives. Sitting where you are, you must have a dull imagination if you cannot realise the whole scene as if it were happening before your eyes.

This riot was the spark which set the whole country in a blaze, and indeed kindled the civil war in England as well as Scotland. Knowing what they had to fear, the people began to organise themselves for defence. THE TABLES were formed; these being, in fact, four Committees representative of the Nobles, the Gentry, the Clergy, and the Burghers. But as the sky grew darker—and everything looked more threatening —it was felt this was not enough. The whole nation must be bound together in a religious covenant—such covenants having been well known and often used before this time, both for good purposes and for bad. The National Covenant was accordingly framed, in which the Covenanters swore by the great name of the Lord their God that they would continue faithful to the doctrine and discipline of the Church against all errors and corruption, that they would be loyal to his Majesty in defence of the laws, and true to one another.

On the 1st of March a solemn fast was called, and a vast assemblage gathered in the Church of the Greyfriars. After the religious services usual on such occasions, the Covenant was produced and eagerly subscribed by all who were present, amid immense enthusiasm. It was then hawked through the city, then despatched to every Presbytery in the provinces, and everywhere it was received and signed amid prayers and tears. There was a volcanic outburst of religious feeling, and in the white heat generated thereby the whole population was welded together and became as one man. The excitement was not confined to any one class—almost all the nobles, the barons, the burgesses, as well as the clergy, had signed the Covenant. Aberdeen only and some of the Glasgow professors held back, and they were regarded as the opprobrium of the nation.

News of all this was swiftly carried to London, where some advised that fire and sword should be used as a remedy; but it was felt that this might be a dangerous experiment, more especially as the king 'had fish to fry at home,' as the people said, and so it was thought safer to send down the Marquis of Hamilton as a royal commissioner, to do what he could to punish or appease the rebels. The people demanded that there should be a General Assembly and a Parliament to settle their affairs; and after long hesitation and with much reluctance, the commissioner made the concession.

On the 21st November 1638, the General Assembly met in the Cathedral Church of Glasgow. No Assembly had met for twenty years, or, as many said, for more than thirty years; for they would not recognise as Assemblies the meetings from 1606 to 1618, which, at the dictation of the king, had overturned Presbytery and set up Episcopacy. But now there was a General Assembly once more. It was a wonderful gathering of all the notables of the kingdom. It consisted of one hundred and forty ministers, seventeen nobles, nine knights, twenty-five landed proprietors, and forty-seven burgesses. No Parliament which could have been convened at that time would have so fully represented the national feeling. The Marquis of Hamilton acted as the Lord High Commissioner; Alexander Henderson, minister of Leuchars, was raised to the Moderator's Chair; and he had deserved the honour by his heroic defence of Covenanting principles, as well as by his moderation and learning. He is still honoured as one of the chief worthies of the Covenanting time.

The temper of the Assembly was evident from the first. It resolved to put the bishops on their trial; and when the Lord High Commissioner found he could not prevent this, he dissolved the Assembly in the king's name, and withdrew. But there was not a moment's hesitation—the business went on just as before. The Five Articles of Perth, the Book of Canons, and the Service-book were abjured and condemned. The bishops were all deposed from their bishoprics, and eight of them were excommunicated—'given over to the devil for the destruction of their flesh, that their souls might be saved in the day of the Lord.' The whole fabric of Episcopacy was thrown down, and Presbyterianism in its power and purity restored.

It was indeed a remarkable Assembly—remarkable for its courage, its thoroughness, its contempt of all authority but its own. It can only be compared to the French Convention at the outbreak of the Revolution. What did it matter to it that the hierarchy had been established by Acts of Parliament? It crumpled up Acts of Parliament like waste-paper. It treated king and council and the whole Three Estates as if they had no voice in the government of the realm. But it had good reason for its high-handedness. The country was with it.

Another thing is very remarkable about this Assembly—the rancorous hatred exhibited against Episcopacy. Episcopacy had now existed in Scotland for upwards of thirty years—the lifetime of a generation. Three-fourths of the clergy must have entered the Church during its existence, and received ordination from the bishops. The remaining fourth must at least have acknowledged the jurisdiction of their diocesans in many ways, and lived at peace with them, though it is possible some old men may have looked back with longing to 'the former days.' But now they were one and all seized with a revolutionary fury, and not only overturned the religious system under which they had lived all their days, but charged their former patrons and friends with all imaginable and unimaginable crimes. The only possible explanation is, that the chief motive power in the Assembly was lay rather than clerical. The one hundred and forty ministers, though forming a majority of the Assembly, were scarcely a full representation of the Church; and scarcely a match for all the baronial and burghal power of the kingdom. We know that before the Assembly met, the Clerical Table had more than once come nearly to a rupture with the other Tables, more especially regarding the method of choosing representatives. That the laity, and especially the great landed proprietors, had for the nonce conceived a violent dislike of the bishops, is certain. Episcopal writers assert that the revocation of the Act of Annexation, and the fear of losing their Church-lands, lay at the bottom of the whole matter. There is certainly a curious contrast between the subserviency of the nobles in helping on the Episcopal schemes of James, when he was silent regarding the episcopal revenues, and their opposition to the schemes of Charles, when he told them that if there were to be bishops, they must be supported by the bishops' lands. However this may have been, it is certain the great body of the people still retained their affection for Presbytery and its simple ritual, or there would never have been such a general revolt. Episcopacy in their minds was associated with despotism and the loss of national independence.

When the Assembly had done its work and dissolved, a humble petition to the king, which had been agreed upon, was despatched to London, and the Marquis of Hamilton, after some hesitation, presented it on his bended knees. On hearing it, Charles said: 'When they have broken my head, they will put on my cowl;' and would not vouchsafe any other reply. Civil war was inevitable, and the Scotch army was soon encamped on Dunse Law Hill overlooking the Tweed. His Excellency Field-Marshal Leslie—'a little crookit soldier,' who had been trained to war under Gustavus Adolphus, and borne a distinguished part in the terrible battles with Wallenstein and Tilly—held the chief command. Almost all the colonels were noblemen, who led their own vassals. At each tent-door there floated a flag, with the motto, 'FOR CHRIST'S CROWN AND COVENANT.' There was psalm-singing everywhere; preaching continually; but still strict discipline and daily drill were maintained; and the king, who was on the other side of the river with an English army, not very enthusiastic in his cause, began to think it would not be wise to test the fighting powers of the Covenanters. Accordingly, after some negotiation, articles of peace were agreed upon, the king undertaking to call a General Assembly and Parliament to settle the affairs of the country. It is characteristic of the time that the obligation to disband the forces and deliver up the strongholds of the country to the king, was signed by three noblemen, two ministers, and the Clerk of the Assembly. Things being thus arranged, the wags in the English camp said the Scotch bishops had been sent about their business, neither by canon law nor civil law, but by Dunse law.

Next year (1639) the General Assembly met, and Lord Traquair appeared as the Lord High Commissioner, to give to its proceedings the stamp of regal authority. As the king persistently declined to acknowledge the Assembly of 1638, this Assembly, to pleasure his Majesty, did all its work over again. It declared the Assemblies of 1606, 1608, 1610, 1616, and 1618 to be no Assemblies; it condemned the Book of Canons and the Service-book; it declared Episcopal government unlawful 'in this Kirk;' it revived the Presbyterian polity. The Parliament afterwards virtually ratified all that had been done by the General Assembly. They went further; they declared that the country was threatened both by land and by sea, and appointed a committee to look to its defence.

In 1640 it was known that the king was doing his best to muster forces for the invasion of the kingdom; and the Covenanters resolved to anticipate him. In the month of August they were again marching southward, and now crossed the Tweed—the Marquis of Montrose being the first to dash into the river; and in a few days more they were in possession of Newcastle. This bold step compelled the king to call the Parliament, now so well known as the Long Parliament. In the troubles which ensued, and which were daily becoming more menacing, Charles now saw that it was clearly his interest to conciliate his Scotch subjects. In 1641 he came to Scotland—a different man from what he was in 1633. He humbly took part in the Presbyterian worship; he agreed that none should sit in Parliament till they had signed the Covenant; he gave his sanction to the Acts of the Parliament of 1640; and finally showered honours and Church-lands on those who had thwarted him in everything. It must have been a bitter draught for him.

Next year the great Rebellion broke out in England. It is not for me to trace the ebb and flow of the bloody tide; but I may mention that even before the royal standard was erected at Nottingham in August 1642, the English Parliament had sent commissioners to the Scotch Assembly, craving its sympathy and friendship. Again, in 1643, commissioners from the English Parliament appeared in the General Assembly, asking its prayers and its help in the struggle they had begun. They narrated their achievements—how they had ejected the bishops from the House of Lords, overthrown Episcopacy, summoned an assembly of learned divines to meet at Westminster and settle the doctrine and worship of the Church. All this was music to the ears of the Scotch Covenanters. It is true the king had granted them all they had desired. But these Parliamentary commissioners promised them still more. There was to be Presbytery not only in Scotland, but in England and Ireland too. And had they not shewn they were in earnest by what they had already done! And what a proud thing it would be for Scotland—for the General Assembly to give religion and law to the three kingdoms! The Scotch divines became drunken with the thought. The English deputies hinted at a civil alliance; but no—it must be a religious covenant which would bind the nations into one. The Solemn League and Covenant was accordingly framed, and the Assembly with one voice gave it their assent. The Estates were sitting at the same time, and they also, on the same afternoon, gave it their sanction; for the Parliament in those palmy days existed only to register the decisions of the Church. Next month it was sworn to by the English Parliament and the Westminster divines, and thus a solemn league, a holy alliance, was formed to extirpate every form of religious faith but one, and to drive Papistical Irishmen, Prelatic Englishmen, and Presbyterian Scotchmen into the one Church—by fire and sword if needful. The full meaning of the International Covenant was seen when in January 1644—two or three months after it was sworn to—the Scotch army crossed the Tweed and marched into England.

It would not become me, in this place, to follow the fortunes of the war—to describe the battle-fields in England and Scotland, where Cavaliers and Roundheads, King's-men and Covenanters struggled together. I would rather sit as an auditor in the Jerusalem Chamber at Westminster, and report the debates of the assembled divines when they were formulating the faith, worship, and discipline which our Church has inherited, though the Church of England has repudiated them. But neither my time nor my text allows me to go beyond Scottish ground. I can only look at these stirring incidents from this side of the Border. In 1645, the *Directory for the Public Worship of God* was laid before the General Assembly, and accepted by it, with a trifling exception regarding the administration of the Lord's Supper. It is curious that the Assembly never once refers to its own *Book of Common Order*—the Liturgy of the Church up to that time. But that book seems never to have taken a hold on the Scottish heart; it had fallen in estimation since the disputes about prayer-books had begun and extempore prayer had come into vogue, and so its very existence was ignored.

The same Assembly gave its sanction in a general way not

exactly to the Westminster form of Church government, but to 'the propositions concerning the officers, Assemblies, and government of the Church, and concerning the ordination of ministers brought unto us as the results of the long and learned debates of the Assembly of Divines sitting at Westminster.' It protested, however, that certain points were to be open questions—admitting further discussion; for the Scotch Church did not wish to bind itself hand and foot for ever. The fact is, there had been bitter disappointment that the Presbyterian polity had not been settled more definitely and declared to be *jure divino*. We may be glad it was as it was, thanks to the Independents and Erastians.

It was not till 1647 the *Confession of Faith* was laid before the Assembly. The Assembly approved of it, but in a very guarded away. They found it 'agreeable to the Word of God,' 'in nothing contrary to the received doctrine' necessary 'for the intended uniformity in religion.' They further judge it to be 'most orthodox,' and agree that it be a 'Common Confession of Faith for the three kingdoms.' They, however, take exception to its teaching on two different points, more especially regarding the authority of the civil power in ecclesiastical affairs. Knox's Confession is never referred to. Everything was to be sacrificed to the mad desire for Uniformity.

It is clear from all this the Scotch Church did not view these Westminster documents as absolutely true or as universally binding. They were to form the common basis, the rallying-point, the articles of union, the colours of the great united Church of the three kingdoms—nothing more. No attempt was made to compel every minister and elder to subscribe them. The Westminster divines had themselves disclaimed infallibility. Looked at in this light, they are worthy of high praise. The Confession is a logical compendium of the Calvinistic theology of the period; while the Directory and Form of Government are plainly a compromise between the ideas prevalent among the English Puritans and Scotch Presbyterians regarding worship and discipline. They will ever form a great landmark in the progress of religious thought; but how long a way have we travelled since they were set up! Looking to the new questions which have been opened since that time, they look like the cast-off slough of controversies long since dead.

While divines at Westminster and Edinburgh were thus fixing the religious faith and worship of a Church which was never to exist, the terrible arbitrament of war was going against the king. In May 1646, he came as a fugitive within the Scotch lines; on the 30th of January 1647, he was given over to the tender mercies of his English subjects; and on the same day of the same month in 1649, he was beheaded in front of Whitehall. Oliver Cromwell reigned in his stead as Lord Protector of the Commonwealth of England, Scotland, and Ireland. But the Scots were almost as loyal as they were religious. They refused to acknowledge the new government. They proclaimed Charles II. king, and invited him to come over from Holland and be crowned. He came, professed himself a Presbyterian, signed the Covenant, listened to no end of sermons in some of which the blood-guiltiness of his father and mother was proclaimed, and promised everything he was asked. The less shrewd of the Covenanters were rather proud of their convert; but they paid for it with their best blood at Dunbar and Worcester.

Cromwell was now supreme; and as he knew the General Assembly had for the last ten years overridden the Parliament and managed everything, he resolved to put it down. As he himself had shortly before entered the Long Parliament and stamped on the floor, and put an end to its palaver, so now by his orders one of his colonels in 1653 entered the Assembly, asked by what authority they met, and then told them to begone. And it was for this the Church of Scotland had given up its own Confession, its own Prayer-book, its own traditions! The glorious vision of a great united Church, on the Presbyterian model, in Scotland, England, and Ireland, had vanished for ever; and sectaries of every kind, who scorned the Covenants and preached universal toleration, carried everything before them.

Under the stern rule of the Protector, the Church of Scotland found the same liberty of faith and worship which was accorded to all who did not violate the law or shew themselves dangerous to the state. But it was torn by internal dissensions. The troublous times through which it had passed had left a legacy of bitterness behind. The religion of Scotland at this unhappy period, sometimes so much vaunted, consisted mainly in the rival parties hating, cursing, and excommunicating one another. There were Engagers, Remonstrants, Resolutioners, and Protesters, all symbolising special feuds, and doing their best to propagate them. The man who happened to differ from the prevailing party in any political or ecclesiastical affair was stigmatised as a Malignant, and compelled to do penance in sackcloth at the church-door before he was admitted to the meanest office in Church or State. And all this uncharitableness blossomed and bore its fruit in an atmosphere heated with religion, or at least what was thought religion at the time. Some of our worst bigotries—still living, though now fast dying—were generated amid these malarious exhalations.

Ever since the days of Melville, Presbyterian Scotland had been gradually becoming more and more Puritanic. In the days of Knox, our Church was emphatically a broad Church, anxious to be on good terms with every reformed Church of Europe, and more especially with the Church of England. Untroubled itself with any controversy about Vestments, the General Assembly in 1566 addressed a letter to the English bishops begging them not to press the use of 'surcloath, cornet, cape and tippet' upon those whose consciences rebelled against them. It speaks of these things as 'vain trifles'—will not determine 'whether such apparel is to be counted among things simple and indifferent or not;' but 'in the bowels of Jesus Christ they crave that Christian charity may prevail,' seeing 'how tender a thing the conscience of man is.' This is truly admirable. But the course of events naturally drew the English Puritans and Scotch Presbyterians closer and closer together. Most of the Puritans were in fact Presbyterians; and the anti-Episcopal policy of Melville naturally widened the gap between the two national Churches. Bancroft's pamphlet—*Dangerous Positions, or Scottish Genevating and English Scottizing for Discipline*—betrays the jealousy of the Anglican prelate. The Scotch Church was regarded as exercising a bad influence upon England, and as fostering Puritanism. It is evermore to be regretted that this rupture between the two Churches began, for otherwise they might have acted and reacted beneficially on one another. From this time a somewhat gloomy view of Christianity—a somewhat stern conception of Sabbath-keeping and church-going—began to grow up. What we now call the æsthetical was banished more and more from the Church services, and great virtue was attached to long sermons and prayers almost as long.

In so far as the clergy of those days did their best to enforce the Ten Commandments, we must heartily applaud them; and there was need for their severity; but some of their efforts in this direction seem strange to us now. They had great faith in the power of shame; and the pillory, the jougs, and the cutty-stool were the instruments they employed for reforming the manners of the age. Their excommunication was as terrible as the anathemas or interdicts of Rome. We see them busy at work in the minutes of the Assembly and of the inferior courts. The elders and deacons who attended Robin Hood Plays on the Sunday were put under discipline. All markets and fairs on the Sunday—all work, even in harvest-time—were forbidden. And the Church was no respecter of persons. Earls and Countesses frequently appeared before the kirk-session, and had to stand at the church-doors clothed in sack-cloth for their sins. The ministers, as often as occasion presented, took it upon them to rebuke King James for his swearing propensity; and he seems generally to have taken it well, and to have laughed at them good-naturedly. In 1591, a deputation of ministers visited Holyrood to see if the royal household was religiously conducted, and they urged upon James to have the Scriptures read at table both at dinner and supper. In 1596, he again had his sins set before his face, for he does not seem to have benefited by the advice he had received five years before. It would appear he frequently omitted to say grace before and after meat, that he rarely came to the week-day sermon, that he was 'bloated with banning and swearing,' and encouraged his courtiers by his evil example to do the like. It would further appear that the queen was little better than himself; for she did not repair to the Word and Sacraments as regularly as she might, and was fond of balls and such-like amusements.

In the Assembly of 1638, among the crimes charged upon the bishops was Sabbath-breaking, playing at cards and dice, dancing, and the omission of worship in their families. It would appear the doing or not doing these things distinguished the Episcopalians and Presbyterians of those days. When Episcopacy was brushed away, and the high-flying Remonstrants and Protesters ruled the country, still stricter notions of Sabbath-keeping and church-going began. It was not unusual for the elders to make a round of the public-houses during divine service to see if there were any delinquents who preferred tippling beer to hearing the word; and private houses were sometimes visited in this way too, and lazy housewives without an excuse were summoned before the session. The well-meaning but somewhat officious elders never hesitated to penetrate into the sanctities of domestic life; and these intrusions were generally meekly submitted to.

But perhaps the most characteristic feature of the time was the stress laid upon days of fasting, preaching, and prayer. The diaries of the time are full of notices of such days with their protracted services. Spalding says 'the people were "vexed to death" with their continual fastings and thanksgivings.' Bishop Burnet tells us of his uncle Johnstone of Warriston, that 'he would often pray in his family two hours at a time,' and that 'he had very high notions of lengthened devotions, in which he continued many hours a day.' And speaking elsewhere of the Presbyterians, he remarks: 'Long sermons and much longer prayers came to be the distinction of the party. This they carried even to the saying grace before and after meat sometimes to the length of a whole hour.' It is probable there is a little exaggeration in this, but it is certain there is much truth in it, and the practices of those days have in some quarters floated down to our own. We should not wonder at these excesses in fasting, preaching, and praying, when we remember how heated the atmosphere was both politically and ecclesiastically. They were the natural outcome of the existing conditions. It was an earnest age, and required to be so. These men who thus fasted and preached and prayed all the day long, were not vulgar ranters or hollow hypocrites; they were terribly in earnest, and they were wrestling with God for the salvation of their country and their Church. And we must remember that preaching then—when the country was all astir with emotion—must have been much more exciting than it is now. There were then no penny papers—no political leaders—no letters from special correspondents. The pulpit was the only source of 'light and leading.' The burghers in the towns, and the farmers in the rural parishes, sat for hours while the ministers declaimed against the vices of kings and courts and parliaments, or described the marching and the fighting of the Covenanted armies, or bewailed the victories of Montrose, or gave thanks to God for his defeat at Philiphaugh. The preachers of those days preached to the times, and therein lay their power. They educated the whole people to think as they did. It is impossible to deny that the influence of the pulpit was in the main good. It was all on the side of morality and liberty. It has never been charged with venality or time-serving.

The counsels of the Church during these stormy days were guided by a band of men, undoubtedly distinguished for learning and eloquence, though none of them rose to the rare altitude of greatness. The times were scarcely such as to make greatness possible. Knox and Melville were both great, partly from the times in which they lived. Knox pulled down Romanism, Melville set up Presbyterianism; and these were feats which could not be performed every day. Henderson, Douglas, Gillespie, Rutherford, Baillie, all did their part well; but after all, it was only in the see-saw struggle of Presbyterianism and Episcopacy. They were all ardent lovers of liberty, and Rutherford is well known to have been in principle a republican. It was in their time the great party-name of Whig was first used.

The fierce controversies and civil strifes I have described were only the ground-swell which necessarily followed the storm of the Reformation. It was impossible that after such a terrible upheaval, things should settle down all at once into calm, and contentment, and order. The Reformation in Germany was followed by the Thirty Years' War, the traces of which are said to be visible still, in tracts of land previously cultivated but now lying waste, and villages then burned and still unbuilt. Let us be thankful that though Montrose swept over our country like a fiery meteor, and though Cromwell made many a gallant though fanatic Scotchman bite the dust at Dunbar, all the physical vestiges of the struggle have long since disappeared; and though we may be still to some extent influenced by the traditions of the times, it is not altogether to be regretted, for they have given intensity to our religious faith and feelings. We are none the worse of having a little of the Covenanter in us to modify the indifferentism of the nineteenth century.

ST GILES' LECTURES.

FIRST SERIES—THE SCOTTISH CHURCH.

LECTURE VII.

THE COVENANT, 1660 TO 1690 A.D.

By the Rev. ROBERT FLINT, D.D., LL.D., Professor of Divinity in the University of Edinburgh.

THE later, like the earlier, stages of the Covenanting period of Scottish Church History still awaken very different feelings in those who contemplate them from different party points of view. But, of course, the true point of view from which to contemplate them—the only properly historical point of view—is one higher and more general than any which can be appropriated by a party. To this point we must seek to rise. The views obtained from lower elevations will be comparatively narrow and perverted; and we may be assured that in so far as they do not include truth they cannot be useful, and that in so far as they contain error they must be hurtful. Few things are likely to injure a people more than the misinterpretation of any important chapter of its own history. How much humiliation and unhappiness has France suffered during the last fifty years because large classes of her citizens would persist in looking back at her first Revolution and the career of her first Napoleon from the low levels of party prejudice, and through the distorting media of passion, exaggeration, and fiction. No social organisation is more dependent for its welfare on the recognition of historical truth than the Church, which, in so far as it truly lives at all, lives by the truth. Nothing but the truth in regard to its history will do any honest Church real good; and the whole truth, pure and simple, will be always more welcome and more profitable to such a Church than a part of the truth or a mixture of truth and error.

The partisan spirit in dealing with the period of history under consideration shews itself by deviation from the line of historical justice towards one or other of these extremes—a judgment wholly favourable to the Royalist and Episcopal side, or to the popular and Presbyterian side. It is, in consequence, apt to flatter itself that it is promoting the interests either of monarchy and Episcopacy or of popular freedom and Presbytery. In thus judging, however, it is mistaken. No great cause or party can at the present day be benefited by its advocacy. Monarchy and Episcopacy have certainly nothing to gain by defending the conduct of the last two Stuart kings and of Sharp and his coadjutors. The men who sought to force Episcopacy on Covenanting Scotland by physical constraint and pressure were the worst enemies Episcopacy has ever had in Scotland. No Episcopalian need feel specially concerned to defend their memories; and no fair-minded Presbyterian will hold Episcopacy responsible for their measures. On the other hand, it only tends to discredit Presbyterianism in the eyes of persons who care for truth and accuracy, to indulge in those indiscriminate and unqualified panegyrics on the Covenanters which conceal the fact that some of their principles and many of their proceedings were unjustifiable. Every Presbyterian denomination in this country now rejects doctrines which the Covenanters deemed of vital importance.

Few Presbyterian Christians, it is to be hoped, would now, under any circumstances, commit some of the actions which the Covenanters thought they were bound by the law of God to perform.

In order to follow intelligently the course of events in Scotland from 1660 to 1690, the state of the country at the Restoration must be clearly realised. At that date, then, Presbyterian Scotland had been held for nine years as a conquered province by Puritan England. The strong man armed, who humbled the military pride of the nation at Dunbar and Worcester, remained its absolute master to the day of his death, and left it in the power of his soldiers. The rule of the alien was as just and lenient, perhaps, as the circumstances allowed, but, of course, it was hated, although outwardly obeyed. The nation, notwithstanding its sharp controversies with its kings, was, on the whole, sincerely Royalist. Few of the people of Scotland did not wish to have their own hereditary monarch, although many of them wished to have him only if he would subscribe the Covenant and obey the Kirk. The soldiery maintained order in the land, so that life and property were perhaps safer than they had ever been before; the civil and judicial administrations were vigorous and impartial; but the statement of various historians that the condition of the country was one of physical prosperity, must be rejected. That trade and agriculture were in a most depressed state; that taxation was felt to be intolerably severe, although the revenue raised by it was only about half of what was required to meet the civil and military expenditure; that great poverty prevailed; that a gloomy despondency overspread the community—might be shewn by a mass of evidence. The nobility had suffered most. Its chief representatives had been slain or had fled the country, or were lying imprisoned in England, or were hiding in the Highlands. The rest were living in obscurity, afraid to make a movement which would remind their enemies of their existence. Most of them had been spoiled of their estates; hardly any of them were not overwhelmed with debt. Argyll alone, perhaps, had been able to keep hold of what belonged to him; and even he was 'drowned in debt and obloquy.'

The religious condition of the country was less lamentable than the political, but it was utterly unlike the picture which Kirkton and other historians have drawn of it. Gross wickedness and great crimes were not rare. Cloaks of piety were worn by many whose ungodly passions they only partially concealed. Religious profession was general, and religious sincerity was, as the subsequent history fully proved, the rule and not the exception; but there was a terrible lack of that highest Christian grace, the charity so worthily eulogised by St Paul. Presbyterianism was dominant, but, as explained in the previous lecture, was broken up into parties which hated and reviled one another. The enthusiasm for Presbyterianism had greatly declined in consequence of its internal dissensions and the national misfortunes to which they had led. The clergy were, however, in general, notably faithful and earnest ministers of the Word; and their flocks were sincerely attached to them. The favourers of Episcopacy were numerous in the North, and increased among the upper classes as it became more and more obvious that their only hope of deliverance from worldly ruin lay in the success of a Royalist reaction. The 'sectaries,' as they were called, came in with, and were almost confined to, Cromwell's troopers; their doctrines made few converts. Religious toleration was enforced; but this was felt to be a sore grievance and a deadly sin.

The restoration in 1660 of Charles II. to the throne of his ancestors was hailed in Scotland as in England with enthusiastic joy. England welcomed it as a deliverance from the military despotism, the severe morality, and the religious peculiarities of Puritanism, all of which had gradually become hateful to the large majority of Englishmen. Scotland welcomed it as the recovery of national independence and the commencement of an era of peace and prosperity. In the month of June 1660,

Scotland was in great excitement. In the churches there were thanksgivings; in public halls there were banquets; at the market crosses there were crowds drinking claret to the health of the king and the Duke of York; bonfires blazed on the hill-tops, and the streets were gay with flags by day and brightly illuminated by night; over all the land there were piping and dancing and immoderate mirth; and on the roads to London there were numbers of Scotchmen of all ranks and degrees eager to congratulate his Majesty, and anxious to secure preferment and emolument. At the fireworks on the Castle-hill, an effigy of Cromwell chased by an effigy of the devil till the former was blown up, gave particular satisfaction. At a bonfire near the Tron Church, the Janet Geddes who in 1637 threw a stool at the head of a dean, now presided at the burning of her 'chair of state' and 'all her creels, baskets, creepies, and furms.' Times had changed, and men and women had changed with them. In the minds of the thoughtful, however, joy was not unmixed with disquietude. This question could not be evaded: What will be done as to religion? And the consideration of it could not fail to produce anxiety. Probably no person or party either in Scotland or in England anticipated what really and speedily happened, but every sincere and intelligent Presbyterian must have felt in some measure that the situation was a critical one.

The Resolutioners, who formed the largest and most moderate Presbyterian party, had, as soon as they perceived it to be likely that the monarchy would be restored, intrusted the representation of their interests with the king and his advisers, to one of their number who had acquired by his conduct in former difficult transactions a reputation among them as a trusty and skilful negotiator. This dexterous ecclesiastical diplomatist was the Rev. James Sharp of Crail; and his instructions were, in the main, these: 'To use his endeavours that the Church of Scotland should enjoy the freedom and privileges of its judicatories, as ratified by law; to represent by all prudent and lawful means the sinfulness and offensiveness of the toleration then established; and to attempt to secure the right application and increase of the ministers' stipends.' From the middle of February to the end of August he was out of Scotland, and chiefly about the Court at Breda and London, professedly carrying out these instructions. According to the view given in the numerous letters which he wrote to the Rev. Robert Douglas and other leaders of the Resolutioners, he soon saw that the idea of getting Presbyterianism established in England was altogether chimerical, and that even its claims to establishment in Scotland must be urged with caution and moderation; found, as time went on, the gale always blowing stronger for Prelacy and Erastianism; was much thwarted by influential persons, lay and clerical, who wished to bring in Episcopacy into Scotland; much saddened and wearied out by what he heard and saw; but at length obtained from the king, who was personally averse to meddling with the Church government, a promise that Scottish Presbyterianism would not be disturbed.

With this promise in the form of a letter from the king, directed to Mr Douglas, to be communicated to the Presbytery of Edinburgh, Mr Sharp returned to Scotland, reaching Edinburgh on the last day of August. On the 3d of September the letter was read. In it the king said: 'We do resolve to protect and preserve the government of the Church of Scotland, *as it is settled by law*, without violation.' He also stated that he intended to call a General Assembly as soon as affairs permitted, and to consult with Mr Robert Douglas and some other ministers as to what might further concern the affairs of the Church. This letter, in accordance with a command which it contained, was transmitted by the Presbytery of Edinburgh to all the other Presbyteries in the kingdom, and was, of course, received by them with great satisfaction. It was a distinct pledge that the existing Church government would not be unsettled.

Just a week before Sharp reached Edinburgh, a few zealous Protesters—ten clergymen and two laymen—met in a private house in the city. Among them was Mr James Guthrie, the leader of the Protesters. They drew up a very characteristic document in the form of a supplication and address to the king. In it they implored his Majesty to 'extirpate Popery, Prelacy, superstition, heresy, schism, profaneness, and everything contrary to sound doctrine and the power of godliness;' to 'fill all places of trust, not only in Scotland but in England and Ireland, with those who had taken the Covenant and were of known affection to the cause of God;' and to 'remove the beginnings of stumbling that had already been given, by taking away the ceremonies and Service-book from his own chapel and family, and other places of his dominions.' This was still the Protesters' ideal of good government. But the general body of Presbyterians had not been so blind to the teaching of experience. If the king and his councillors had left the Presbyterian government of the Church undisturbed, and the petitions of the Protesters unnoticed, Protesters would have rapidly diminished. Unfortunately this was not the course they took.

It so happened that the Committee of Estates began to sit on the day on which the Supplication mentioned was being drawn up, and one of its first acts was to cause the assembled Protesters to be arrested and imprisoned. On the following day a proclamation was issued against meetings and conventions which had not been specially authorised by his Majesty, and against seditious petitions and remonstrances. Later, the Committee imprisoned various other Protesters, prohibited the owning or promoting the Remonstrance, ordered the *Lex Rex* of Rutherford and the *Causes of God's Wrath* of Guthrie to be called in and burned, and shewed in various ways that the spirit of the governing classes was now very different from what it had been on the day when the National Covenant was signed in the Greyfriars Churchyard.

The Scottish Parliament, with the Earl of Middleton, a rough, imperious, dissolute soldier, as Royal Commissioner, met on the 1st of January 1661. It shewed itself slavishly and madly Royalist. It proclaimed the supremacy of the king over all persons and causes. It forbade the renewing of the Covenant. It passed a marvellous Rescissory Act which expunged from the statute-book all legislation later than 1633. Thus at one stroke every law which the Presbyterians and Covenanters had passed was swept away. This Act was carried on the 28th of March, almost unanimously. As early as the 10th of January there had been eager Royalists to suggest this measure, but Middleton checked their zeal.

On the 16th of April, the Marquis of Argyll was brought before the bar of the House on the charge of high treason. The trial ended on the 25th of May with his condemnation to death. The sentence was executed two days thereafter. Argyll had played such a part in the history of his country that his trial and condemnation seemed to be the trial and condemnation of Covenanting Scotland. There may easily be different opinions as to various parts of his conduct. There can be but one as to the moral grandeur of his death. That death freed the king from the only man in Scotland whose intellect and power he had much reason to dread; and yet, perhaps, it injured him more than anything Argyll could have done against him. For years before the Restoration, Argyll was generally distrusted and disliked; his death gratified many personal enemies, but it caused multitudes to remember only his services and great qualities.

Four days after it, Mr James Guthrie was executed. He had done more, I think, than any man of his time to divide and weaken the Presbyterianism which he loved so well; he was a persecutor in principle, and ready to be so in fact; he had clamoured for the blood of conscientious men whom he called malignants; but he was a sincere and heroic man, and, according to the light he had, a most pious man. He was willing to sacrifice everything, even to the laying down of his life, for every principle which he held. He had certainly been very troublesome to the Royalist cause in Scotland; but he had also been warmly attached to it, and had done much to keep affection for it alive when the hearts of less courageous men were failing them for fear of Cromwell. Nothing on earth could frighten James Guthrie. In London, four years before the Restoration, he had stood up in public debate against Hugh Peters, Cromwell's chaplain, and had, in the presence of Cromwell's officers, maintained the right of the king. That might have been remembered now. He died despising death; speaking for an hour on the ladder as calmly as if he had been preaching in the pulpit; reasserting the principles to which he had so often testified and from which he had never wavered; and declaring that 'the covenants could be loosed or dispensed with by no person or power on earth, but were still binding upon the three kingdoms, and would be so for ever hereafter.' His last words were: 'The Covenants, the Covenants, shall yet be Scotland's reviving.'

The Synods of the Church met in April and May. The southern Synods protested, some more and some less decidedly, against the Rescissory Act, but even at this critical time there was bitter strife in them between Resolutioners and Protesters. Some of these Synods were forcibly dissolved by Royalist noblemen. The northern Synods were in favour of the restoration of Episcopacy, or, at least, not opposed to it. Presbyterianism had been forced upon the North, and had no claim to expect support from that quarter.

In the month of August Charles intimated to the Privy Council his intention to interpose his royal authority to establish government by bishops, as it was previous to the late troubles; and in doing so he actually referred to his letter of the previous August to the Presbytery of Edinburgh, as if he were now implementing the promise it contained, seeing that Parliament by its Rescissory Act had rendered the Presbyterian form of

Church government no longer that which was settled by law. The moral obtuseness and shamelessness thus displayed tended to confirm the opinion that his letter to the Presbytery had been a deliberate falsehood, never meant to be fulfilled in its plain literal sense, but craftily contrived to throw Presbyterians off their guard. This is the view generally held; but it cannot, I think, be said to have been proved, and, of course, we are not entitled to believe even the most despicable man more guilty than the evidence shews him to have been. Admitting, however, that his letter was probably not the treacherous lie commonly supposed, his conduct in regard to the promise which it contained was disgraceful.

The new system was rapidly set up and brought into operation. Long before the year 1662 was out, it was complete and vigorously at work. Bishops were selected, and consecrated, and seated in Parliament, and all the rights and powers of the judicatories of the Church were put into their hands, as being the agents and officers of the king; the royal supremacy in all matters spiritual was affirmed; and when that was done, the task of Charles and his councillors was accomplished. A simpler system than the new one there could not be. It needed no change in creed or liturgy, and little or no change in organisation. It needed only a king and bishops. The absolute obedience of the clergy and laity to the bishops, and of the bishops to the king—that was its sum and substance. Recognition of the royal supremacy in all religious and ecclesiastical questions—that was its life and soul. Erastianism, naked and not ashamed, was what the Church of Scotland now found itself confronted with.

Could the disastrous revolution which had been thus rapidly effected have been prevented? Not in the actual circumstances. To have prevented it, the Presbyterians of Scotland would have required to have been more united and better led, and at once more reasonable and more decided, than they were. The strife of Protesters and Resolutioners, the demand of the Protesters to have the Covenants everywhere enforced in their entirety, and the mistake of the Resolutioners in trusting to negotiations with the king, instead of arousing by every means in their power the people to a sense of the seriousness of the situation, and to a recognition of their duties to the Church and nation, were ruinous errors. Had there been a Knox or a Henderson in the country, affairs would doubtless have been differently managed, but no man of their stamp was vouchsafed at this crisis. The fanaticism of the loyalist and irreligious reaction, instead of being restrained and counteracted, was allowed almost free course.

James Sharp was placed at the head of the new ecclesiastical establishment as Archbishop of St Andrews and Primate of Scotland. Soon after his return from London, on the occasion already mentioned, the rumour began to circulate that he had, while professing to act zealously on behalf of the Church of Scotland, been, in reality, selfishly undermining it and joining in a plot against its existence. This rumour continued to spread in spite of the many contradictions which he gave to it; and when he accepted the Archbishopric, few Presbyterians, at least, doubted its truth, and Protesters and Resolutioners alike looked on him with horror as a perjured traitor of the deepest dye. It is still the prevalent view taken of his conduct. My time does not allow me to discuss the question of its truth or falsity; but I have considered the evidence which bears on it with some care, and have only been able to come to the conclusion that the common opinion is not warranted; that Sharp's decision to abandon Presbyterianism was only made after Presbytery had been disestablished by the Scottish Parliament, and the strength of the royalist and anti-covenanting reaction had plainly declared itself; and that, consequently, perjury cannot, in this connection, be justly imputed to him. Scotland was, at this time, untrue to herself, and therefore disposed to believe that she had been betrayed by individuals. Sharp's desertion of the Presbyterian cause, however, cannot be excused. Self-interest was obviously his chief inducement to the step. He must have foreseen that he would carry to the archiepiscopal throne a reputation for treachery, which would blacken and discredit it, and that, as the Primate of the new system, he would be required to labour for the destruction of the independence and liberty to which the Church was entitled. His own letters shew us that he believed the sphere of the Church to be an independent kingdom on which the State ought not to encroach, and he had no right to accept a position in which his practice could not fail to be in continual contradiction to this belief.

The other bishops were much inferior to Sharp in practical ability. Some of them were in every way unworthy of their positions. Only one of them was eminently endowed with ministerial gifts and graces. He was so pre-eminently. As far as I can judge, a purer, humbler, holier spirit than that of Robert Leighton never tabernacled in Scottish clay. He was 'like a star which dwelt apart,' while the storm raged below; or, like a fair flower of Paradise dropped amidst the thorns and thistles on some bleak mountain-side. His character was of an almost ideal excellence, and so divinely beautiful, that men, while attracted by it, were also awed by it, as beyond what imitation could hope to reach in the earthly state of being. His works, owing to the marvellous fullness and perfection of the spiritual life which pervades them, are worth many times over all the writings of all his Scottish contemporaries. There is nothing nearly equal to them in our devotional literature from its rise until now. Once minister of Newbattle, afterwards Principal of Edinburgh University, he was at this time persuaded, or rather constrained, to accept the bishopric of Dunblane. There is no room for doubt as to the purity or disinterestedness of his motives. He looked on his office not as an object of ambition, but as a heavy cross which Providence called him for a season to bear. He cared little for forms of ecclesiastical polity, but rather preferred the episcopal, and he believed that the bishops could, by humility, gentleness, moderation, and the maintenance of the rights of the Christian people, unite all ranks and classes of men in Scotland in the acceptance of a mild and modified Episcopacy, whereas adherence to simple or strict Presbyterianism would keep them divided. He failed to understand the circumstances of the time and the characters of the men around him, but was not chargeable with any graver error.

What, now, was to be done with the clergy of the disestablished Church? Three methods presented their competing claims. The first was Leighton's. Displace no one; coerce and oppress no one; enact and enforce no subscription which can offend any man's conscience; let the bishops renounce all pomp and pride of office, and confine themselves strictly to spiritual duties; let them be guided by the clergy in their deliberations, and by the people in their presentations; and let their great aim be to secure, by example and persuasion, that public worship be more beautiful, preaching simpler and less controversial, individual piety more diffused, and religious divisions gradually healed. This was the method which he sought to commend to his colleagues, as he and they journeyed from London to Scotland to take possession of their bishoprics; but he soon found that he would receive no help from them in carrying it out; and hearing that they intended to make a grand entry into Edinburgh, he quitted them at Morpeth, 'very weary of them, as he supposed them to be of him,' and went quietly to the sphere of work which had been assigned to him. There he practised his method, not without success; and to his dying day he believed that it might have succeeded over all Scotland, if it had been patiently and consistently tried. Possibly it might, if the other bishops had been Robert Leightons, or his equals; but being only what they were, this plan had no chance. The second method was Sharp's. Self-sacrifice was not one of its principles. He meant to take full advantage of his position, and to rise in the world as high as he could. So far from despising even pomp and parade, when he rode from Leslie to St Andrews to take possession of his see, it was with an earl on each hand, and between seven and eight hundred mounted gentlemen in his train. But Sharp was a clear-headed, worldly-wise man, and he wished a cautious, temporising, step-by-step procedure, which would result in getting rid gradually of those most opposed to the new system, and supplying their places with those more compliant. The method actually adopted, however, was neither that of the saintly pastor nor that of the politic ecclesiastic, but a high-handed and reckless method which commended itself to the domineering and inebriated minds of Middleton and his boon-companions. They were under the delusion that by strongly asserting the Royal Supremacy in ecclesiastical causes, by enforcing the abjuration of the Covenants and adhesion to the new system, by making it apparent to the Presbyterian clergy that they were under the power of the civil rulers, and by passing stringent laws accompanied with formidable threats, they would prevent the rise of any serious opposition to the government, however arbitrarily it might choose to act. The whole legislation of the Parliament of 1662, and the whole course of procedure of the Privy Council in connection therewith, were expressions of this delusion.

That Parliament passed various laws which were insulting and unjust to the Presbyterian part of the nation. The most foolish of them was this Act: 'All ministers entering in or since the year 1649, at which time patronages were abolished, are declared to have no right to benefice, stipend, manse or glebe, for this year 1662, or hereafter; but their kirks to be vacant, unless they receive presentation from the patron, and collation from the bishop.' The clergy against whom this enactment was directed, at first took no notice of it; but the Privy Council decided to enforce compliance. The immediate result was one of those great incidents which nations remember with a legitimate pride. Upwards of three hundred of the ministers sacrificed their worldly all, rather than be untrue to their principles. During the closing months of the year 1662, over large districts throughout all the Lowlands of Scotland, the parish churches were shut, and the sounds of public worship on the Lord's Day unheard. Edinburgh was left with a single minister, Mr Robert Lawrie of the Tron Church, who, on account of his conformity to Episcopacy, was nicknamed the 'Nest Egg.' The men thus driven out of their charges composed the great body of the younger and most energetic portion of the clergy, and had gained the respect and affection of their flocks. Their places had to be supplied; and this could only be done with men in all respects inferior to their predecessors.

These new incumbents, or curates, as they were termed, were, in fact, probably the worst set of clergymen which the Protestant Church in Scotland has ever had. They were, for the most part, needy, ignorant young lads, hurriedly drawn from the northern parts of the kingdom, and thrust into positions for which they had no intellectual, moral, or religious qualifications. More difficult positions to fill, however, than those assigned them can scarcely be conceived. Placed between hostile parishioners, despising and hating them, frequently insulting and occasionally assaulting them, and civil and ecclesiastical superiors, commanding and constraining them to act as informers against the disaffected and to aid in carrying out oppressive measures, they would have required the most angelic gentleness to gain the affections of the former, the most heroic courage to resist the tyranny of the latter, and to mediate between the parties a wisdom altogether superhuman. Being only what they were, they, of course, sided with their own supporters. Many of them, having probably no better society, consorted with 'the baser sort of the gentry,' and fell into the vicious habits so prevalent at this time.

The expulsion of the ministers and the intrusion of the curates led to the parish churches being almost deserted, and to multitudes attending religious services, conducted by the ejected clergy in their own houses or in the open air. How was this fact to be dealt with? Middleton was not required to consider it, for he was supplanted by Lauderdale and replaced by one of Lauderdale's faction, the Earl of Rothes. Lauderdale had been a leading man among the Covenanters. Had he died before the Restoration, or even before 1663, his life would probably have been in *The Scots Worthies,* where it might have been a suitable companion picture to that of the Earl of Loudon. He lived too long, however, to have his name handed down to us as that of a saint. He is known to us instead as what he really was, a most unscrupulous and depraved man, hypocritical, avaricious, licentious, a mass of vices associated with the abilities most fitted to make them dangerous and disastrous—a man whose soul was far more repulsive than his body was uncouth. During the last twenty years of his life, he above all men was a shame and curse to Scotland. Rothes was the son of the celebrated Covenanting Earl. Both father and son were bad men. The former made great religious professions and kept on good terms with the clergy, but was a secret libertine. The latter was openly dissolute. He was a favourite with the king, and resembled him both in person and character. He had alike the genial qualities of Charles and his shameful vices. The fall of Middleton and the rise of Lauderdale and Rothes promised little good, and brought none.

The history which we have to consider is from this point onwards to the Revolution very easy to understand. It is, on the one side, a continuous series of attempts made by the government to force an ecclesiastical system of a kind inconsistent either with civil or religious liberty on a people to whom it was obnoxious; and, on the other side, the series of acts by which that people resisted the pressure so long, so uninterruptedly, and so heavily brought to bear on them. The government during the whole of this time treated the Presbyterian community as if it were a piece of iron which had to be beaten into a particular shape, and it transformed itself, as it were, into a hammer and anvil for the purpose; and the question of questions for Scotland was just this: Will hammer and anvil shape the iron, or will the iron break the hammer and anvil? On a people so circumstanced the chief demand is that it be firm, tenacious, patient, or what the oppressor will call stubborn, *dour*. That the Covenanters were so, is their glory.

As the history of the period is so simple, the rapid glance along its course, which is all that my time permits me to give, may be sufficient to shew its general drift. It was resolved to compel attendance on the services of the Episcopal clergy. Accordingly, the parliament of 1663 decreed as follows: 'Hereby it is ordained, that such as ordinarily absent themselves from their parish kirks on the Lord's Day incur these penalties: each nobleman, gentleman, and heritor, the loss of a fourth of each year's rent; and each yeoman or tenant, the loss of such a part of their movables as the Lords of Council shall modify, not exceeding a fourth; and every burgess his liberty, and the fourth of his movables; and the Council is to execute this Act against all who, after admonition of the minister before two sufficient witnesses, and by him so attested, shall be given up to them, with power to them to inflict further corporal pains, as they shall judge necessary, and to do every other thing for procuring obedience to this Act, and for the executing thereof.' The Council was quite willing to try its utmost to execute the Act; indeed, thought it not comprehensive enough. It said nothing about women, who then as now formed the largest portion of most religious assemblies, and nothing about the ejected clergy, whose devotions and instructions were preferred to those of the 'curates.' The Council, therefore, supplemented it by resolving that husbands were to be held responsible for the church attendance of their wives, and by enacting that no recusant minister should reside within twenty miles of his old parish, six miles of Edinburgh or any cathedral town, or three miles of any royal burgh, on pain of being treated as a seditious person. With these appendices of the Privy Council, the Act of Parliament was not badly entitled to its familiar designation of 'the Bishops' drag-net.'

The penal legislation needed by the new ecclesiastical establishment seemed now tolerably complete. The next problem was how to apply it so as to secure the end its authors desired. This was soon seen to be a most difficult problem. The Privy Council, Court of Justiciary, and lower tribunals were overburdened with the additional work the new legislation imposed upon them. The Court of High Commission was revived to deal with ecclesiastical offenders, but the powers given to it were so large and so indefinite, its proceedings were so harsh, and it was altogether so unpopular, that it had speedily to be suppressed. Recourse had to be taken to military law and military force. Troops of soldiers, under the command of a fierce and drunken officer, Sir James Turner, were sent to punish the disaffected Remonstrants of the south-west, and, as was admitted some years afterwards by the Privy Council itself, they conducted themselves in the most lawless and barbarous manner, fining and plundering promiscuously in whole parishes where there were no persons accused. Their severities occasioned the insurrection called the Western Rising, which broke out on the 12th of November 1666, at Dalry in Galloway, and was completely crushed down on the 28th of that month at Rullion Green. Sir Thomas Dalziel, with his three thousand 'well-appointed horse and foot,' took four or five hours of that 'fair frosty day' before he could break and scatter the nine hundred almost undisciplined and ill-armed men commanded by Colonel Wallace. The eagerness shewn by the peasants of the neighbourhood to capture or kill the fugitives was some evidence that the revolt was premature, and also that Mid-Lothian was far from as warmly Presbyterian in 1666 as it had been not very long before. The prisoners were mercilessly treated by the government. None shewed themselves more cruel and revengeful than the Archbishops of St Andrews and

Glasgow. None—it is right to add—shewed himself more humane than Dr Wishart, the Bishop of Edinburgh. He had been barbarously persecuted by the Covenanters in their day of power, and yet he not only urged that the prisoners should be forgiven, but daily supplied them with provisions.

The severities which had caused the insurrection were for a time continued, and even increased and extended. Sir Thomas Dalziel, a man of the sternest stamp, whose reputation as a soldier had been gained by fighting for the Czar against Turks and Tartars, and whose fanaticism for the royal cause almost amounted to frenzy, was sent into the west with his forces, in order to compel the people of Ayrshire and Dumfriesshire to attend their parish churches. He did his work of violence and extortion with zeal and thoroughness, and cut his mark so very deep on these counties that it is hardly yet effaced. It is admitted that he filled the churches.

The fall of Clarendon in England was followed by a change for the better in Scotland. Rothes was dismissed from office; Sharp had to confine himself to his diocese; the expostulations of Leighton and others had some effect on the king; worthy men like the Earl of Tweeddale and Sir Robert Murray acquired an influence in the conduct of affairs. About forty of the outed ministers who had lived peaceably were indulged, as it was termed, or allowed to go back to their charges, on condition of not discussing public questions. Many of them were among the most esteemed; two of them, Robert Douglas and George Hutcheson, were among the most eminent of the Presbyterian ministers; but by a large number of people their acceptance of the Indulgence was regarded as a base compliance with a sinful course of action. On the other hand, Archbishop Burnet of Glasgow and many of the Episcopal clergy were enraged because the Indulgence allowed benefices to be held without a direct acknowledgment of the authority of the bishops. Burnet pushed his opposition to the measure so far that he got ejected himself. Leighton was put in his place, with permission to attempt to bring about an accommodation between the two conflicting parties.

Accordingly, in the year 1670, there was much negotiating between Leighton and the most considerate and reasonable of the Episcopalian clergy on the one side, and the Presbyterian ministers on the other, with a view to agreement on a scheme of comprehension. There was no difficulty as to the mode of worship, the bishops having in that respect introduced no innovations of consequence. The difficulty was as to bishops themselves. Leighton was willing that they should be little more than perpetual Moderators of the Church courts; that Presbyterians by conviction should not be required to renounce their opinion about Church government; that intrants should be ordained at the parish churches and not at the cathedrals; and at their admissions should not be engaged to any canonical oath. Leighton failed to bring about the result which he desired. The Presbyterian brethren were not prepared to concede even the requirements in his plan. Doubtless, they had little confidence that what was promised in it would be performed, even if they did accept. Leighton could be implicitly trusted so far as his power went, but to depend on the king's sanction being given merely because it had been pledged, was to trust to a reed very likely to break and wound the hand which leaned on it. Sharp and most of the bishops were keenly opposed to a scheme which implied their loss of so much power and dignity. Leighton was sorely disappointed. It was not long before he renewed a former request to the king to be allowed to resign. With much difficulty he obtained the royal permission; and with great thankfulness he retired to spend the rest of his years in study and devotion at Broadhurst in Sussex.

The lull in the storm was brief and partial. Lauderdale was the real master of the situation, and he had other ends in view than the peace of the Church or the good of the nation. Under his leading, the Parliament of 1670 passed several atrocious Acts against conventicles. Death and confiscation of goods for whoever preached at them; ruinous fines for whoever attended them; imprisonment or banishment for all who refused to reveal what they knew regarding them; five hundred merks reward to any one who captured a conventicle preacher; and severe penalties for having a child baptised by an outed minister, or for being absent for three successive Sabbaths from the parish church, were the terrors now fulminated by law over the land. There was no slackness in the application of the law. Magistrates were held responsible for conventicles within their burghs. Heritors were punished for meetings on their grounds. Heads of households had to answer for the church attendance of their dependants. Arbitrary and enormous fines were laid upon offending individuals and districts accounted disaffected. They were a most lucrative source of revenue to Lauderdale and his associates, who fattened and rioted on the miseries of their country. Persons who failed to appear when cited by the Council were *intercommuned* or outlawed. In 1675, letters of intercommuning were issued against one hundred individuals. To give food, drink, or shelter to those thus excommunicated, or to hold intercourse with them by word or writing, was a criminal offence. Then, as if worthily to crown all this, Lauderdale, in 1678, actually let loose on the West some ten thousand soldiers, of whom six or seven thousand were Highland clansmen. For three months the Highlanders pillaged at pleasure. They might have done so longer had they not, fortunately perhaps, been unable not only to distinguish between *meum* and *tuum*, but between the friends and enemies of the government. The wonder is, considering the animosity which then existed between Highlanders and Lowlanders, that they did not murder as well as plunder.

And yet, notwithstanding all these devices and efforts of the government, conventicles were not put down. On the contrary, the very means employed to suppress them converted them into truly formidable assemblages. Small private meetings, little local gatherings, had to be abandoned; but in their place sprang up large armed conventicles to which people came from great distances, at which many wore weapons and were ready to repel force with force, and which were addressed only by the most resolute of the Covenanting preachers—men who saw in King Charles and his ministers only the enemies of King Jesus—who would hear of no compromises, who regarded the indulged as traitors, and attendance on their ministry as a sin, and in whose discourses pathetic and fervent offers of the Gospel were mingled with stern denunciations of their rulers and the prelates. Conventicles of this sort were found to have strong attractions. A passion for their excitements grew up and spread. No government, of course, can be reasonably blamed for attempting to suppress armed conventicles. The condemnation of the government of Charles II. is that it so acted as to create them.

The tempers of the persecuted had by this time become embittered and dangerous. The Covenanters were from the first, on the whole, a stern and harsh race of religionists. They never acknowledged, either in theory or practice, the principle of toleration of others, although they perceived so clearly their own right to liberty. In the days of their ascendency they had slaughtered, imprisoned, and despoiled their opponents, on the ground that it was a plain dictate both of Scripture and of conscience that those who resisted the cause of Christ should be punished by the law. The Protesters, in particular, had always vehemently contended against leniency towards non-Covenanters. It was, accordingly, only too natural that many of the harassed field-conventiclers should come to the conclusion that their persecutors might righteously be cut off without law, and that no mercy ought to be shewn to the active enemies of the truth. It was by a band of men possessed with this conviction that Archbishop Sharp was murdered on Magus Moor, near St Andrews, on 3d May 1679.

No person was so abhorred by the Covenanters as the

Primate. They believed him to have basely betrayed the Presbyterian Church; to have been the chief instigator of the cruel measures taken against the faithful; to be a sorcerer and a man of flagitious life. In this belief there was much exaggeration. He meanly deserted the Presbyterian cause, but proof is wanting that he betrayed it. He took a prominent part in the enactment and execution of the laws passed against the Covenanters, but his influence in this connection was not nearly so great as that of several of the lay lords. The history of the period would probably have been little different if he had never been born. His private life was irreproachable; the statements to the contrary are plainly calumnious fabrications. He was not a moral monster; nor was he a man to be morally admired. He was self-seeking, scheming, unforgiving; he was too pliant where principle was concerned, and too persistent where mere interest was concerned; he fawned on the strong, and was unsympathetic towards the weak. His assassination had been attempted as early as 1668 by a fanatic named Mitchell; and one of the individuals who took part in his murder on Magus Moor confessed to have twice previously sought an opportunity to slay him. The circumstances connected with that murder are known in their minute details, but willingly we turn away from so foul a deed so foully done. The assassins—of whom Hackston of Rathillet and his brother-in-law, Balfour of Kinloch, better known as Burley, were the leaders—escaped to the West and joined themselves to those who approved of their action.

On the 29th of May—the anniversary of the Restoration—some eighty horsemen, headed by Robert Hamilton, brother of Sir William Hamilton of Preston, entered Rutherglen, extinguished the bonfires blazing in honour of the king, denounced and burned the Acts of Parliament in favour of Episcopacy, and affixed to the market-cross a document entitled 'The Declaration and Testimony of the true Presbyterian Party in Scotland.' Three days afterwards—June 1—these and other armed men to the number of several hundreds, among whom some, such as Hackston, Balfour, Hall of Haughhead, and young William Cleland, possessed decided capacity for fighting, were at a large conventicle at Drumclog, when John Graham of Claverhouse with his dragoons came upon them. But, as he himself writes, his meeting with them was 'very little to his advantage.' Although a trained soldier, he was new to this kind of work—probably underrated the martial qualities of his opponents—certainly fought rashly and in ignorance of the nature of the ground—and was outgeneraled, and so badly beaten, that he had to flee on a wounded horse, hotly pursued, leaving thirty-six troopers dead, while the Covenanters lost only three of their number. Mr Robert Hamilton, who commanded the Covenanters, was of quite the same way of thinking as the murderers of Sharp. It appeared to him to be plainly the Divine will that 'Babel's brats' should be destroyed. He put to death with his own hand one of the prisoners, and was greatly grieved that, contrary to his express orders, five others were let go. The Covenanters, hopeful that the hour of deliverance was near, flocked from all sides to his standard. Ere a week elapsed, he had, according to his own account, 'betwixt five and six thousand horse and foot drawn up on the moor besouth Glasgow, all as one man and of one mind, to own the Rugland testimony against all opposers.' They were not long 'as one man, and of one mind.' Bitter dissensions broke out among them regarding the Indulgence, although none of the indulged ministers joined them. Their camp was a scene of ecclesiastical wrangling. They appear to have been on the point of breaking up into two parties and separating, when they learned that the Duke of Monmouth, with an army twice as strong as their own in numbers, and vastly superior in all military respects, was close at hand. No one among them, probably, was capable of handling with soldierly efficiency so large a body of men as seven or eight thousand. Mr Hamilton, their nominal commander-in-chief, was certainly quite incompetent for such a task. Yet he must have had a strong expectation of victory, seeing that he allowed a banner to be carried which bore on it in scarlet letters the words, 'No quarter for the active enemies of the Covenant,' and had a large gibbet erected in the midst of his camp, with a cartful of new ropes at the foot of it. No opportunity, however, presented itself either for the refusal of quarter or the use of the gibbet and rope. The Covenanters acted at Bothwell with such a want of sense and vigour, that, had it not been for the brave fighting of the three hundred under Hackston at the bridge, the affair of June 22, 1679, might have been called a rout, but could not have been called a battle. Had the merciless Dalziel, and not the humane Monmouth, commanded the royal forces, it would in all probability have been a massacre. About four hundred persons were slain in flight; above a thousand were taken prisoners, of whom seven were executed, while the others were confined for months in the Greyfriars Churchyard; and then those who consented to acknowledge the rising in which they had been engaged as rebellion, and to promise to keep the peace in future, were released, while those who refused were shipped off to the plantations.

The schism which was on the point of breaking out at Bothwell, split altogether the Covenanting ranks soon afterwards, and was widened and aggravated by the grant of a new indulgence on terms which none of the extreme party could regard without abhorrence. This party now stood strictly and sternly apart from those of more moderate views, and uncompromisingly proclaimed and carried out its own principles. Donald Cargill was its oldest leader; Richard Cameron, his son in the faith, supported it with a fervent zeal and heroic courage which led to its being called *Cameronian;* young James Renwick caught up its banner when it dropped from Cameron's dying hand, and guided its Secret Societies with a rare genius for organisation and government.

Never did men cling more consistently and tenaciously to their creed, or suffer more for the sake of conscience than the members of this party—the Hillmen, the Wanderers, the Faithful Remnant, the Wild Whigs, the Cameronians, &c., as they were variously designated. Whatever may have been their faults, their fidelity to conviction has been seldom equalled in the history of the world. Nor can there be any reasonable doubt as to the chief source of their steadfastness and strength. It is impossible to read the reports of their sermons, or any of the writings which they penned, without being impressed by the obvious sincerity, thoroughness, and assuredness of their faith in God and Christ—by the directness, self-consciousness, and closeness of their sense of communion and personal relationship to Jehovah. There may be differences of opinion as to how far their piety was at various points enlightened, but a denial that their piety was singularly real and operative must be traceable either to ignorance or to religious unsusceptibility.

They were not content merely to resist certain measures and defy certain commands of the government. They entirely renounced allegiance to it. They held themselves to be bound by none of its laws. They declared war against it. They proclaimed that the king, by his covenant-breaking, vicious life, and tyrannical rule, had forfeited the throne. They taught that he and other persecutors might justly be put to death. Hackston of Rathillet, until his capture at Ayrsmoss, was a leading man among them, the honoured companion of Cameron and Cargill. Their preachers hesitated not to represent God as calling upon persons of all ranks and classes to imitate Jael and Ehud, by executing judgment on the wicked rulers of the time. Mr Forman expressed the same doctrine clearly and concisely by an inscription on his knife: 'This is to cut the throats of tyrants.' Most of the party were willing to die rather than acknowledge the killing of Sharp to have been murder, or that it would be a crime to kill the king and his brother.

These resolute men took the steps which they considered requisite to make known their position towards the government. When Hall of Haughhead was killed in a scuffle at Queensferry, 3d June 1680, there was found on his person an unsigned paper, the rough draft of a public declaration, in which the king and his associates in the government were solemnly rejected, monarchy repudiated, and an administration of God-fearing judges proposed. On the 21st of the same month, twenty men, amongst whom were Donald Cargill, Richard Cameron and his brother, and Hackston, entered the old burgh of Sanquhar on horseback, rode with drawn swords to the cross, and there proclaimed: 'We, for ourselves and all that will adhere to us, the representatives of the true Presbyterian Church and covenanted nation of Scotland, do, by these presents, disown Charles Stuart, who has been reigning, or rather tyrannising, on the throne of Britain these years bygone, as having any right, title to, or interest in the crown of Scotland, or government, as forfeited several years since, by his perjury and breach of Covenant with God and His Kirk, and by his tyranny and breach of the fundamental rules of government in matters civil. . . . Also we declare a war with such a tyrant and usurper, and all the men of these practices, as enemies to our Lord Jesus Christ and His cause and covenant. . . . And we hope, after this, none will blame us, or offend at our rewarding those that are against us as they have done to us, as the Lord gives opportunity.' Just a month afterwards—July 22—Cameron was slain and Hackston taken prisoner by the dragoons of Bruce of Earlshall at Ayrsmoss. Two months later, at Torwood in Stirlingshire, Cargill 'excommunicated, cast out of the true Church, and delivered up unto Satan,' King Charles, the Duke of York, the Duke of Monmouth, the Duke of Lauderdale, the Duke of Rothes, Sir George Mackenzie (King's Advocate), and Thomas Dalziel of Binns. In January 1682, a band of fifty armed Society men entered Lanark, burned the Test and Succession

Acts, and published a declaration of their principles. In November 1684, a celebrated Apologetic Declaration was affixed to several market-crosses and parish churches in Galloway, Dumfriesshire, Ayrshire, and Lanarkshire, in which warning was given that all who took part in the work of persecution would be regarded as enemies to God and His covenanted work, and punished as such. 'Let not any think that (our God assisting us) we will be so slack-handed in time coming to put matters in execution, as heretofore we have been.' 'Call to your remembrance, all that is in peril is not lost, and all that is delayed is not forgiven.'

The strict Covenanters looked upon those Presbyterians who were not prepared to go the same length as themselves as time-serving and hypocritical. They denounced the indulged ministers more frequently and more severely than the curates. They represented attendance at their meetings as a sin no less ruinous to the soul than theft or adultery. This was just what was to be expected from men with their convictions and in their circumstances. We ought, however, to beware of being misled, as many have been, by their denunciations of the more moderate brethren. The indulged ministers may have felt quite as conscientiously that the preachers who held armed conventicles and declared war against the government were going too far, as these preachers felt that the ministers did not go far enough. There was need for both parties. Just as the Italy of our own generation required, in order to obtain her unity and liberty, not only uncompromising and heroic enthusiasts like Mazzini and Garibaldi, not only martyrs like Ugo Bassi and the brothers Bandieri, but watchful, calculating, and prudent politicians like Cavour and his friends, so the Scotland of the Restoration period needed, in order that she might be prepared for and profited by the Revolution epoch, alike her idealists and her moderates. The wandering Hillmen rendered services which well deserve national gratitude; but if all the Presbyterians of Scotland had been as they, Scottish Presbyterianism would have rashly taken up the sword, and might have perished by the sword. It is right to remember what we owe to them for having resisted unto death the encroachments of the Civil Power on the rights of the Church and the tyranny of the king over the community; but it is not right to forget that they also strove for much which was unjust and unattainable. Cargill, Cameron, Renwick, and their followers, entertained not a doubt that it was God's will that all in these lands, from the king to the peasant, should be made subject to the Covenants; they had no firmer conviction. Who can believe so now? If the course of Divine Providence, as traceable in the history of the last two hundred years, affords any indication of the Divine will, *that* was *not* the Divine will. To have imposed these Covenants on the nation at the Revolution, or at any period since the Revolution, could manifestly have only led to wrongs and cruelties as great as were those against which the Covenanters protested and struggled.

Charles II. died February 6, 1685. Few men have had such opportunities of conferring happiness on others, and leaving behind him a loved and honoured name, and few men have been more richly endowed with the qualities fitted to secure popularity and affection; but through yielding to self-indulgence, and allowing the lusts of the flesh to overrule the higher principles of the spirit, he so wasted his advantages, so misused his gifts, so degenerated in nature, so sank into the slough of vice, that it is hard to find in history a life more painful to contemplate, more ignoble, depraved, and mischievous than his. The last year of his reign was, perhaps, that during which the persecuted Presbyterians of Scotland suffered most. Things came to such a pass that the most awful of judicial functions, along with complete executive power, was intrusted to common soldiers. On mere suspicion, men could be arrested in the fields or on the highways by the humblest agents of the government, and, on refusal or failure to answer in a particular way certain questions, immediately shot. The transference of the sceptre to the hands of his brother, James VII., brought little improvement. The three years of this monarch's reign were also 'killing times.' The Acts of indemnity and of toleration which he published did not prevent, and were not meant to prevent, the slaughter of Cameronians. Claverhouse, Grierson of Lagg, Bruce of Earlshall, and others, engaged in that work with an activity and rigour which caused them to be regarded as almost demons incarnate. That much which passes for history in regard both to the persecutors and the persecuted has no claim to the character must, I believe, be admitted. The loads of martyrological tradition collected by Wodrow and other writers require to be far more thoroughly and critically examined and weighed than they have yet been before historians can safely use them. The common estimate of their historical worth appears to me to be far too high. Leaving them altogether aside, however, there remains ample evidence in the official records of the government itself, and in the still extant letters of its agents and officers, that the violence inflicted and the suffering endured in this period of persecution were enormous.

The hour of deliverance came at length. With the Revolution, night fled and day appeared. The main cause of the Revolution was neither the sufferings nor the strivings of the Presbyterians in Scotland or the Nonconformists in England. It was fear of the spread and triumph of Romanism. The nation bore with strange equanimity the evils inflicted by the last two Stuart kings so long and in so far as they were wrought in support of the arbitrary personal power of the monarch and in favour of Episcopacy; but as soon as there appeared to be serious danger of the Royal Supremacy being applied to the establishment of Romanism, all classes of the people arose in determined antagonism, combining their powers and efforts with wonderful rapidity, and with a force so irresistible that William of Orange, instead of having to cut his way to the throne of Britain, had merely to march to it in a triumphal procession. As soon as the Church of England, alarmed at the measures taken by James in favour of Romanism, turned suddenly and in its collective strength against him, his fate was sealed. The action then taken by the Church of England was what more than anything else insured the fall of Episcopacy and the rise of Presbytery a second time in Scotland. Even in Scotland, hatred of Romanism was a much stronger passion than love of Presbytery; immeasurably stronger than admiration of the Covenants. The most servile courtiers and cruel persecutors among the Scottish nobles and judges shewed an independence and sensitiveness in regard to Acts and measures constructively favouring Romanism which were little to have been anticipated. The example of Edinburgh itself is instructive. Throughout the whole period of the persecution it sided with the Anti-Covenanters, although the execution of a sufferer like young M'Kail might cause an evanescent and exceptional outburst of human sympathy. It turned out howling mobs to insult the prisoners brought into it after the battles of Rullion Green and Bothwell Bridge. At the same time, it was intensely Protestant, or, at least, intensely Anti-Romanist. Neither the presence of the Duke of York nor fear of the fury of General Dalziel could keep its students, aided by its apprentices, from burning an effigy of the Pope; its baker-boys would pelt with mud a pervert Countess of Perth, and a mild attempt of the authorities at punishment of the offence was followed by manifestations of resentment which might have been more usefully displayed in rescuing a martyr at the Grassmarket. Long noted as one of the most turbulent towns of Europe, it was exceptionally quiet from 1660 to 1690; but its one great riot during the time was on occasion of the sacking and demolition of the Chapel-Royal at Holyrood, into which James had introduced Roman Catholic worship. The nation was resolved not even to tolerate Romanism. James was resolved not only to tolerate but to favour it. Being the weaker party, he fell.

On the fall of James, the outraged Covenanters and oppressed peasantry of the west of Scotland rose in mobs and drove the Episcopal clergy from their parishes. This 'rabbling of the curates' began on Christmas Day, 1688, and lasted for some months. About two hundred persons were thus expelled. No lives were lost; but this must rather be ascribed to the curates having almost no support, and consequently making scarcely any resistance, than to the self-restraint of the rioters. In order not to judge too harshly the 'rabbling of the curates' in 1688, we must remember the ejection of the ministers in 1661; but in order not to judge of it too leniently, we must also remember that the ejection of the ministers had been itself preceded by the expulsion of the Episcopal clergy in 1639, and that one reason why there were so few Non-Covenanters in certain districts of the West was that the war-committees of the Covenanters in 1640 had driven so many of them away and left them nothing to which to return.

During the whole period which has been under our consideration, the economical resources of the country, as well as literature, science, and art, were almost entirely neglected. Yet we shall err, I believe, if we deem it to have been either an unnecessary or unfruitful period. Nations, like individuals, cannot live by bread alone, or by the truths of science and the comforts and charms of art alone. Nations, like individuals, if they will only look thoughtfully over their histories, will not fail to acknowledge that the times which they could least have spared have been their times of affliction.

ST GILES' LECTURES.

FIRST SERIES—THE SCOTTISH CHURCH.

LECTURE VIII.

THE REVOLUTION SETTLEMENT, 1690 TO 1707 A.D.[1]

By the Rev. ROBERT HERBERT STORY, D.D., Minister of Rosneath.

IF Episcopal benediction and subserviency could have saved King James VII., he would have been saved from the consequences of his own fanaticism and tyranny. Two days before the Dutch deliverer landed at Torbay, the Scotch bishops were engaged at Edinburgh in concocting a letter to the king, whom they poetically addressed as 'the darling of heaven,'

---

[1] The authorities for the period of the Revolution and the Union, to which the general reader may be referred, are Wodrow's *History of the Sufferings, Analecta,* and *Correspondence*; Dalrymple's *Memoirs*; Burnet's *History of His Own Time*; Defoe's *Memoirs of the Church of Scotland*; with the recent histories of Mr Hill Burton and Dr Cunningham. So much of the same ground is traversed in the present writer's *William Carstares: a Character and Career of the Revolutionary Epoch*, that at two or three points short passages therefrom have been adapted to the uses of this lecture. Readers, who wish to make a more minute acquaintance with the period, may consult the *Coltness Collections*; the *Caldwell Papers*; the *Leven and Melville Papers*; the *Lockhart Papers*; the *Marchmont Papers*; and the *Carstares State Papers.*

assuring him of their unquenchable loyalty, praying God to give him 'the hearts of his subjects and the necks of his enemies,' and promising to do their best to promote in all his subjects 'an intemerable and steadfast allegiance' to his Majesty 'as an essential part of their religion.' The prayers of the right reverend fathers in God did not obtain for his Majesty the two impossible gifts they besought; nor could all the devotion of their order avail to thwart the will of a nation, whose strongest passion, burning most strongly in its noblest hearts, was a zeal for liberty—for liberty of conscience and of life. At the root of the long struggle against the manifold misgovernment of the Stuarts, as of all the least practical fanaticisms of the Hillmen, with their visionary Covenant, lay a deep conviction of the human right of personal freedom and personal responsibility, compared with which all assertions of divine right, whether of kings or prelates, were weak as water—strong for a time, no doubt, in the possession and unscrupulous use of brute force, but weak in all elements of moral strength, the only strength that endures, because having in it some measure of that will of God which 'abideth for ever.' King James fell in spite of his bishops' prayers; and his system of absolutism in Church and State fell with him. The convulsion which overthrew him was not a political revolution merely. It was an upheaval and change of the whole national life. The motive power in it was a religious, more than a political, force. It is not too much to say that of all the factors in the Revolution of 1688, Scottish Presbytery was the most radical, the most indomitable, the most triumphant; Scottish Presbytery, not simply, or mainly as the opponent of Prelacy, but as the representative and champion of the rights and liberties of the people.

Since those days in the summer of 1639, when the Scots army under Leslie encamped upon Dunse Law, until the hour that saw King James a refugee in France, the Ark of the Covenant of civil and religious liberty had been guarded by the strong hands of that inextinguishable Presbyterian remnant, whom no diplomacy could cajole, and no persecution extirpate. Liberty, dear to them, as to all people of their blood and race, was specially dear because the possession of it was bound up in the same bundle with the most sacred treasures of their religion. What the Pilgrim Fathers had crossed the Atlantic to find beyond the seas, they were resolved to attain at home—freedom of life and thought; above all, 'freedom to worship God.' Their detestation of a certain order in the Church was no jealousy of hierarchical rank. It grew up in them and possessed them, too wholly perhaps, because they saw in that order the most offensive stumbling-block in the way of the triumph of their noble cause.

It is altogether an error to believe that preference for a non-liturgical service was implied in the popular enmity to the Prelacy, which got its death-blow in 1688. The error owes some of its vitality to the magic pen of Sir Walter Scott; but it is mainly traceable to that general ignorance of Church History, which allows people to suppose that because the present service of the Church of Scotland is non-liturgical, it has always been so; and that one of the chief differences between Episcopacy and Presbytery is that the one does, and the other does not, use forms of prayer. Like the Reformed Churches of the Continent, our National Church possessed, as you have already heard, its national Liturgy for nearly one hundred years after its reformation. It surrendered that invaluable possession to the sinister influence of English Puritanism; and the Prelacy of the Restoration made no effort to recall the unhappy forfeiture. The Revolution found Scotland without a Liturgy either among the established Episcopalians, or the disestablished Presbyterians. 'We,' says Sir George Mackenzie, speaking of the former—'we had no ceremonies, surplice, altars, cross in baptism, nor the meanest of those things which would be allowed in England by the Dissenters, in way of accommodation.' Such scraps of liturgical order as the use of the

Lord's Prayer and the Gloria Patri, the disuse of which had vexed the soul of Henderson more than forty years before, might be found among some of the Episcopalians; but in general, as far as ritual was concerned, there was as little to distinguish the Presbyterian service from the Episcopal, as there is, at the present day, to distinguish the service of the average Free Church congregation from that of the average parish church, perhaps not so much. In the parish churches, at the date of the Revolution, the Sunday's service commonly was begun by the precentor's reading, after the manner of the earlier 'Reader,' two or three chapters of the Bible; after which the curate entered the pulpit, and a psalm was sung. Then followed an extempore prayer, and a sermon, generally unread. After the sermon there was a second prayer, concluding with our Lord's Prayer. Then came another psalm, and the benediction; and this was all. In the meeting-houses of the Indulged, the service was the same, except that the Lord's Prayer had no place. The Holy Communion was administered by the curate, as well as by the 'outed' or the 'indulged' minister, to recipients who sat about a table, and never thought of kneeling. At prayer, the attitude seems to have been sitting too. During the sermon, the Presbyterians were in the disrespectful habit of putting on their hats or bonnets. I do not know if the Episcopalians exhibited the same irreverence, or not. The prolonged services preliminary to the Communion, on the Fast-day and Saturday—the lengthy 'preachings' in the church and from the 'tent' on the Sunday, and the thanksgivings of the Monday—were unknown among the Episcopalians, as they were among the earlier Presbyterians. They originated with the Protesters, and established themselves pretty generally throughout the Church, soon after the Revolution.

The ritual of the conventicle was naturally subject to no law. The order which I have described as that of the usual Sunday's service, you will recognise as virtually in agreement with that prescribed in the *Book of Common Order* and in the

Westminster Directory, which is the basis of our more comely and elaborate usage in the present day. It lacked the liturgical element common to the Reformed Churches, and it excluded the people from that large share in the service, which adds unction and power to the inflexible devotional forms of the Anglican Church. Its weak point was the almost absolute power it confided to the minister, who, knowing no guide and no restraint except that of a general but not authoritative custom, could deal with the service in all its constituent parts pretty much as he chose. The traditions of days when, filled by Knox or Henderson, the pulpit had been a great political force—of the times of persecution, when the most stirring call to the defiance and resistance of a degrading tyranny had been the voice of the outlawed preacher on the bare hillside—were cherished in an age when preaching had lost its former political importance, and when its fiery testimony for freedom was no longer needed. The preacher still thought it fair and right to discuss in the pulpit all questions of public and local interest; but when such discussion no more affected national policy or involved personal danger, the independence which had before been courageous and noble could not retain that character. The pulpit was too often degraded to the uses of personal ill-will, sectarian spite, or professional intolerance; and, for a time at least, forfeited much of its power to edify and elevate the public mind.

The establishment of Episcopacy had wrought as little change upon the subordinate government of the Church as upon its ritual. That court of the Church which has generally been regarded as the most prominent feature of Presbytery—the Kirk-session—lasted throughout the whole of the Caroline Prelacy. Not only so; but King Charles, moved possibly by a pious admiration of the discipline of that court, had, on finding that the eldership was not a popular office under the 'curates,' issued a proclamation empowering them to make their own selection of elders in their respective parishes, and ordering those so chosen to accept office, within fifteen days, 'under pain of rebellion.' The second court of the Church, the Presbytery, continued to hold its constitutional position and to discharge its ordinary duties, with the exception—no doubt, a radical exception—of ordaining candidates for orders. The Presbytery examined the candidates, but referred their ordination to the bishop, who also had the right of nominating the moderator. The Synods met as usual, but under the presidency of the bishop. There was no General Assembly. The ordinary parochial and Presbyterial government of the Church went on, as though the bishops had not existed. The restoration of Presbyterianism required to make no alteration beyond abolishing the bishops, and reopening the General Assembly.

Neither was it called to effect any change in doctrine. The Westminster Confession, which had been accepted by the General Assembly of 1647, had since that date retained, without dispute, such ecclesiastical authority as that acceptance implied, and had never been repudiated or renounced in any of the voluminous oaths which the government of Charles demanded from the clergy. The Revolution found it where the Restoration had found it. On the ritual, the subordinate government, and the doctrine of the Church, twenty-six years of Prelacy had left no mark. If anything could add emphasis to the national repudiation of that Prelacy, it is this simple fact.

'What have I done to be so loved?' said Louis XV.—Louis 'the well-beloved'—when he rose from his sick-bed at Metz. The poor perplexed bishops of the Stuarts might have asked: 'What have we done to be so hated?' as they gathered their tattered skirts around them and fled into those coverts from popular ill-will, which justified Dundee's sarcasm that they had become 'the Kirk invisible.' I find the answer in the words of the most dispassionate and sagacious of English historians— Henry Hallam—who, reviewing the Scotch Episcopacy of the seventeenth century, in calm and philosophical survey, says:

'There was as clear a case of "forfeiture" in the Scots Episcopal Church as in the royal family of Stuart. . . . It was very possible that Episcopacy might be of Apostolical institution; but for this institution houses had been burned and fields laid waste, and the Gospel had been preached in wildernesses, and its ministers had been shot in their prayers, and husbands had been murdered before their wives, and virgins had been defiled, and many had died by the executioner, and by massacre, and in imprisonment, and in exile and slavery, and women had been tied to stakes on the sea-shore till the tide rose to overflow them, and some had been tortured and mutilated; it was a religion of the boots and the thumbscrew, which a good man must be very cool-blooded indeed, if he did not hate and reject from the hands that offered it. For, after all, it is much more certain that the Supreme Being abhors cruelty and persecution than that he has set up bishops to have a superiority over presbyters.'

The representatives of a vicious system may sometimes be able, by their own personal character, or genius, or merits, to redeem their office from popular odium and contempt; but the prelates of 1688 had no such power. Of the twelve deprived bishops, none could raise a voice to which the nation would listen, or exert the slightest sway over the turbid currents of revolution. There was not one of them round whom the people of his own diocese, even, would rally. 'And shall Trelawney die?' chanted the Mendip miners, when they heard that James had sent their bishop to the Tower:

'Then twenty thousand under ground will know the reason why.'

The incarceration of all the bishops in Scotland would have evoked no such loyal sentiment, in any region between Whithorn and Kirkwall. Not a hundred of their countrymen could have been found to strike a blow for them. They fell, and no one held out a hand to lift them up. They were hustled out of Church and Senate, and no man bade them stay, or said

God bless them, as they and their hated order and tarnished honours passed away.

The mind and conscience of the country felt relieved when they were gone. Men breathed more freely. It became easier to believe in that old article of the Reformers' creed—a divine government and a righteous Kingdom of Christ—when the mean curate, with his weekly list of defaulters from his Sunday's services, no longer sought the alliance of the sergeant of dragoons to coerce his recreant flock; when the victims of the boot and the thumbscrew were no longer watched, during their torture in the Laigh Parliament House, by the cruel eyes of the right reverend fathers in God of the Privy Council.

The Scotch people had, at the time of the Reformation, and for several years after it, no fanatical hatred of Prelacy—not even any bitter jealousy of it. Knox himself exercised his ministry, for a time, in the English Church; and when asked by the Privy Council to explain his refusal to accept the preferment offered him by King Edward, he never alleged that Anglican Prelacy was at the bottom of it. The early Scottish Reformers communicated, without scruple, in the Church of England, and in their own worship used her Liturgy. The altered feelings of a later age owed their birth to the fact, emphasised by the Duke of Argyll in his *Presbytery Examined*, that while the Scottish Prelacy of the Regencies was without any principle, Scottish Presbytery was not. 'It was founded on passionate conviction; and every opposition it encountered, springing from motives less earnest than its own, tended to strengthen that conviction, and give to all its principles additional value in its sight. If, in the main, those principles were great and true positively, every scrap of them appeared great and true by contrast.' This, true of the earlier, was doubly true of the later, Prelacy. Its existence had been an outrage on the liberties of a people whose passion for liberty had sometimes raged with even too fierce a flame. Its overthrow lifted the weight of a nightmare-like oppression from the national breast.

At the same time, we must not overlook the fact that, by the end of the twenty-six years of the Caroline Prelacy, the policy of the Stuarts and the bishops had not altogether laboured in vain, or spent its strength for nought. Hanging, shooting, torturing, banishing, imprisonment in foul dungeons, confiscation of goods, ruinous fines, all the agencies of a reign of terror, had done their part. Persecution had rooted out of the population thousands—how many thousands, it is hard to tell now—of its best and bravest—had cowed many into a sullen submission. Many others, moved probably by dread of new changes, or under the influence of the Court, or finding Episcopacy most in accordance with their political principles, had become the partisans of that form of government. The Revolution Settlement met with little or no favour among the nobles and gentry, that had been the minions or adherents of the Court; among the party that hated popular rights, and believed in the *jus divinum* of kings; and among the half-civilised Highland clans, many of whom had no religion but their loyalty to their chief, and among whose glens and islands the Reformation had left not a few savage retreats, as wholly Papal as the passes of the Apennines or the Pyrenees.

The only Lowland region (besides some districts of Aberdeenshire, Banffshire, and Moray) where Episcopacy had gained a decided hold on the general community, was that which stretches from the Tay to the Dee, between the Grampians and the ocean; a region even then still liable to the incursions of the Gael, and, except in the towns of the sea-board, exhibiting but a moderate standard of civilisation. The country from the Tay to the Border—and especially the well-peopled and strong-minded west and south-west—was enthusiastically Presbyterian, and rejoiced to see the State renounce the ecclesiastical associate of regal despotism, and prepare to restore its former establishment and endowment to a free Church in sympathy with a free people.

The populace in several districts, exasperated by the memories of twenty-six years of outrage and injury, did not wait till the orderly process of the law should expel the alien 'curate.' Giving the rein to their own indignant sense of ill-usage, and in the first turbulence of a recovered freedom, they took on themselves the work of driving the intruder from kirk and manse; in some cases with slight violence and insult, in none with even an approach to the brutality with which the soldiery of Dalziel and Claverhouse had harried the homes of the Covenanters. This was that 'rabbling of the curates,' over which their representatives and apologists may, to this day, be heard to bleat and whimper. Never were enormous wrongs so leniently retaliated. Never, in the day when power had passed from the oppressors to the oppressed, was the oppression so lightly revenged.

As soon as a Convention representing the true mind of the mass of the nation was summoned, Prelacy was doomed. The voice of righteousness and freedom was heard asserting the people's 'Claim of Right.' The Claim of Right formed the basis of the Revolution Settlement; and one of its clauses was, 'That Prelacy and the superiority of any office in the Church above presbyters is, and hath been, a great and insupportable grievance and trouble to this nation, and contrary to the inclinations of the generality of the people, ever since the Reformation, they having been reformed from Popery by presbyters; and therefore ought to be abolished.' This frank acknowledgment of the will and welfare of the Christian people as a higher law of Church polity than any *jus divinum*, royal or ecclesiastical, must have struck terror into the hearts of the bishops, who owed their existence to the king's will, and entrenched their office behind the Church's tradition. The terror must have deepened into despair when they found that the Parliament, into which the Convention was transformed, passed, among its earliest measures, an Act abolishing Scottish Prelacy— which was succeeded by another abolishing Charles II.'s 'Act of Supremacy.' The first steps of the free representatives of the people, acting in their constitutional capacity, were to abolish the office and order which had embodied ecclesiastical tyranny, and to rescind the servile concession by which a former Parliament had degraded itself to own the galling yoke of regal despotism.

We must, however, trace the stages of this history in more exact and chronological detail.

William was essentially an Erastian. Born and bred a Presbyterian, under the wing of that National Dutch Church, which is Presbyterian to this day, he had no covenanting enthusiasm for that, or for any form of Church government. He wished to gain the crown of Scotland, and to rule the Scottish people according to their own law, in Church and State. Had their ecclesiastical constitution been reconcilable with that of England, he would have been well pleased, knowing that this reconciliation would have been a strong element in that international union, which he foresaw must ultimately be effected, if Great Britain was to hold its proper place in Europe. As this reconciliation appeared to be impossible, he preferred that the nation should settle for itself what form of Church government should be established. Its choice would relieve him of an irksome responsibility, and would transfer to other shoulders than his own the load of that Anglican odium, which must follow the subversion of Episcopacy and triumph of Presbytery. Those exiles who had been around him in Holland were all Presbyterians; and had, no doubt, represented their party in Scotland as the only one to be consulted or recognised. In London, William met many representatives of Episcopacy, whose version of affairs in Scotland opened his eyes to the diversity of feeling and opinion beyond the Tweed. The Episcopal party there, after all, was stronger than he had supposed. He was beset by the pertinacious emissaries of both parties. Carstares introduced to him an influential deputation of the Presbyterian ministers. Sir

George Mackenzie and Bishop Rose, of Edinburgh, attended him on behalf of the Episcopalians. At this juncture, it is evident William was inclined to waver between supporting Episcopacy and supporting Presbytery. As I have said elsewhere, the ecclesiastical settlement of Scotland perplexed him. He saw that Presbytery had lost ground; and he saw also that Episcopacy was Jacobite and intolerant. He did not wish to put it down; but if it would not abjure Jacobitism and intolerance, it must be put down. He had the promise of hearty Presbyterian support. Rose might have given him a promise equally gratifying, on behalf of the Episcopalians. Those whom he represented were not the men to quarrel with his policy, if its result should be to keep them in safe possession of their sees. William, through Compton, Bishop of London, intimated to Rose that if the Scotch bishops and clergy would give him their support, he would give them his, and 'throw off the Presbyterians.' Rose would not take the hint. At length he was admitted to an interview. 'Are you going for Scotland?' asked William. 'Yes, sir,' answered Rose, 'if you have any commands for me.' 'I hope,' replied the Prince, 'you will be kind to me, and follow the example of England.' The bishop's answer was: 'Sir, I will serve you as far as law, reason, or conscience shall allow me.' William turned on his heel without a word; and the fate of the Scotch Episcopal establishment was virtually sealed.

The Convention of the Estates of the realm, summoned by William, met in March 1689. It consisted of one hundred and fifty members, of whom nine were bishops. When the resolutions declaring the throne vacant, and inviting William and Mary to ascend it, were proposed, only nine members voted against them. Of the nine, seven were bishops. When these resolutions had been carried, and the Claim of Right adjusted, three delegates of the Convention —the Earl of Argyll, Sir John Dalrymple, and Sir James Montgomery, were sent to London, empowered to offer the crown to William and Mary, and to tender to them the coronation oath. Argyll read the words of the oath, which they, with uplifted right hand, repeated after him, clause by clause. At the last clause, William paused, for it bound him to root out all heretics and enemies of the true worship of God. 'I will not,' said he, 'lay myself under any obligation to be a persecutor.' On the commissioners' replying that no such obligation was involved, 'In that sense, then, I swear,' said William; and the ceremony was concluded.

The incident was significant. It announced that the era of the Covenant was past; that the sword of the civil power was not again to be drawn at the bidding of the Church, or employed in ecclesiastical feud. This was gall and wormwood to the Cameronian remnant, who looked with indignation on the progress of a revolution which was to achieve results so far below the height of their Utopian principles, and which they felt they could neither control nor arrest. 'They held excited meetings and used violent language; but the dragoons no longer dispersed their conventicles, and their stern military spirit was judiciously allowed to expend itself in legitimate warfare. The "Cameronian" regiment, eight hundred strong, was drafted from their ranks, and under the gallant Cleland played a noble part in retrieving the disaster of Killiecrankie. The main body of the grim religionists, thus reduced in aggressive strength, and no longer stimulated by persecution, watched in sullen acquiescence the progress of events. They had done their work. Their injuries, their martyrdoms, their passionate protests, their inextinguishable vitality, their armed resistance to a "tyrant's and a bigot's bloody laws," had been powerful agents in producing the Revolution. But in the political settlement which followed it, the remnant of the Covenanters and the Protesters had no part; nor indeed were they fit to have any.' The General Assembly, at its first meeting, received their three remaining ministers into the Church. The fighting strength of the Societies themselves was dispersed, or absorbed into the army. The ideal of a Covenanted Reformation faded away. The Dutch king was hopelessly unlike the hero of a new crusade against Popery, Prelacy, and profaneness. I question if a sharper iron of angered and embittered disappointment entered into the heart of any Prelatist or Royalist, in these days of revolution, than that which pierced the proud, though fanatical, spirit of the Cameronians. To them, as they saw the Covenant quietly ignored by Laodicean politicians, while lukewarm Churchmen calmly looked on, it was small comfort to know that their old foe, Prelacy, fell in the same convulsion which ingulfed the ark of their testimony.

The Convention denounced Prelacy: the Parliament abolished it; but it did nothing more. Episcopacy was put down; but Presbytery was not set up. Nothing was done to evict the Episcopal incumbents, unless they shewed disloyalty by refusing to pray for the new king and queen, for which refusal one hundred and seventy-nine of them were expelled by the Privy Council. No steps were taken to call a General Assembly. A General Assembly indeed, such as the clergy in the North clamoured for, would have been too wholly Episcopal to be safely summoned. It was not till June 1690, that the Act was passed ratifying the Confession of Faith; settling Presbyterian Church government; and vesting that government in those ministers who had been ousted since 1st January 1661, and such other ministers and elders as they might receive into co-operation with themselves. 'This famous Act was not passed without some difficulty and opposition. When the House was about to consider the article which ratified the Confession of Faith, the Duke of Hamilton moved that the Confession itself "be read all over with a distinct and audible voice." The Laird of Craignish preposterously proposed that this should be done on the Lord's Day, if done at all. The Duke's motion was adopted, and the long Confession was read. When the reading was finished, it was proposed that the Catechism and the Directory for

Public Worship should come next. But this was too much for the wearied senators; the reading of the Confession was voted to be enough, and the Catechism and Directory were passed over, and so escaped embodiment in the Act. At various points the Duke of Hamilton offered an opposition to the Bill, in the interests of a more indulgent treatment of the Episcopal ministers, which did not fail to rouse the suspicion of being dictated by resentment at Melville's preferment to the commissionership, quite as much as by real charity and liberality. At last, before the House divided on the article which, with undeniable injustice, proposed to confirm the ejections by the "rabble," the Duke's temper gave way. "The vote should stand," he cried, "approve or not approve the deed of the rabble;" and when the article had passed, "he was sorry," he said, "that he should ever have sat in a Scottish Parliament where such naked iniquity was established into a law;" and, much in wrath, he marched out of the House, followed by several other members. As soon as he was gone, it was proposed to pass the whole Act *in cumulo*. A voice was heard: "Fie! make haste! despatch, lest he return again, and create more trouble." It came from a Presbyterian minister, who had made his way into the house, and in the excitement of the moment called out to the members near him. The hint was taken. The whole Act was approven, and laid on the table to await the royal assent. It erred, as the legislation of the Parliament of the Restoration had erred, in an assertion and in exercise of powers which, even though tempered by William's impartial tolerance, were too harsh and absolute. The extreme measures of the Restoration were sure to beget a reaction of like extremes when the oppressed gained their opportunity of becoming oppressors; and the knowledge of the near danger of Jacobite plots, which might overthrow the still insecure fabric of the Revolution, disposed William's Scottish supporters to be more jealous and rigid than their master.'

The legislature, having settled the government and creed of the Church, next adjusted its Patronage. The patronages were taken from the old patrons, and conferred upon the heritors and elders—in burghs, on the Town Council and elders—reserving to the congregation the right of laying objections to a presentee before the Presbytery, with whom should rest the decision of their validity. Now that Patronage, in its old sense, has finally been abolished in the Church, it is unnecessary to occupy time in criticising this stage in its chequered history. We cannot fail to see, however, that this settlement of it involved all the elements of that conflict between the Presbytery, the people, and the civil law, which came to its crisis in 1843.

The ground was now cleared for the meeting of a General Assembly. The clearance had been effected, in the most Erastian way, by the authority of the State alone. As in earlier crises of her history, secular policy had ruled the destiny of the Church, without her own assistance or consent. It is one of the ugliest features of the epoch, and worst signs of the generally low standard of the national religion, that it was obviously thought unsafe to trust the settlement of Church affairs to Churchmen. Such was the suspicion of their principles —of their patriotism—of their integrity; such the dread of their rancorous jealousies—of their lust of power—that the clergy of neither persuasion found the politicians ready to hand over to them the settlement of their own affairs, until there was comparatively little left to settle. The politicians themselves—we may remark in passing—were, as a rule, singularly corrupt and untrustworthy. The very bench of justice was defiled with bribery, favouritism, and servility. The religious contentions of the Church, or some other equally noxious cause, had been fatal to a high tone of public or private morality.

The General Assembly met on 16th October 1690—for the first time since Cromwell's dragoons had interrupted its debates thirty-seven years before—and was once more the Supreme

Court of an Established Church. It met in no very good humour. It had been made to wait the pleasure of the king. Though the Presbytery, which it represented, had been established as agreeable to the Word of God, the Prelacy, which it supplanted, had been deposed on no higher principle than because it was contrary to the inclinations of the people. The older members, who had been outed or exiled or ruined under Prelacy, and who still retained some of the 'protesting' zeal of earlier times, felt it chilled by the king's message recommending, above all things, 'Moderation.' 'Moderation,' said the royal letter, delivered by the Commissioners to the Assembly, 'is what religion enjoins, neighbouring churches expect from you, and we recommend to you.' This word, much needed as it was, and not yet of evil omen, was no doubt chosen by the king's confidential adviser and friend, the cautious, wise, and liberal Carstares.

The temper of this great Churchman's nature had been tested by a long course of political vicissitude and personal trial, of adversity, imprisonment, and exile. He had stood the cruel torture of the thumbscrews with patient courage, and had baffled the inquiries of his torturers with rare discretion. His sterling honesty, his diplomatic skill, his varied experience, and large sagacity, had long secured to him the thorough esteem and confidence of William. His influence was predominant in the settlement of the Scotch ecclesiastical affairs. He had been by William's side in Holland during all the delicate negotiations which preceded the invasion of England. He had crossed with him in the same ship from Helvoetsluys to Torbay. He had conducted, at the head of the army, the religious service which consecrated its first day's occupation of English soil. His counsel had guided the king through the critical time when the balance of policy wavered between Episcopacy and Presbytery; and he had revised, along with William, the drafts of the Act for the re-establishment of the Church. And now he came to Edinburgh, armed with the king's instructions, which were but the embodiment of his own ideas, to keep a watchful eye upon the doings of the resuscitated ecclesiastical court.

Upon the whole, the Assembly acted calmly and fairly on the advice of the king. It was inevitable that among men, the older of whom had borne the brunt of the persecution, the younger of whom had been either trained in Holland in enforced exile, or had exercised a fugitive ministry in defiance of the law, there should be some bitterness of feeling and warmth of prejudice. But these were held in check, partly by the influence of Carstares, partly by a common-sense, which convinced its possessors of the practical folly of indulging personal fanaticisms, or straining after unattainable ideals. The Covenant was dropped by the Assembly, as it had been dropped by Parliament. There was no anathematising of Prelacy as Satanic, or glorifying of Presbytery as divine. The ministers of the Covenanting remnant were, as I have already said, received into communion, on the one hand; and, on the other, full liberty to stay in their parishes was extended to all such Episcopal curates as should subscribe the Confession, and promise allegiance to the Presbyterian government. High-flying Churchmen would have liked much more rigid exclusions—much more dogmatic assertions of divine right—much sharper discipline. But 'men must take what they can have in a cleanly way, when they cannot have all they would,' wrote Lord Melville, the Secretary of State, to Lord Crawford, president of the Parliament, a stanch Presbyterian, with a keen eye and a tight grip for the rents of abolished bishoprics.

A moderate Presbyterianism, tolerant of rival theories and systems, a Church established on liberal and comprehensive principles, and not on extreme dogmas and rigorous exclusiveness, was all that was practicable; and what was practicable was what was most desirable. The devout theocratic imaginations of John Knox, the haughty Hildebrandism of Andrew Melville, the Judaic intensity of the leaders of the Covenant, had all passed away. It was a tamer and less heroic time than theirs—a time, not for the vehement assertion of absolute claims, or the desperate maintenance of imperilled causes, but for the quiet and patient reconstruction of a system of religion and framework of society, disordered and ruptured by long years of insolent oppression and exasperated resistance, of conflicting jealousies and misunderstandings, during which hearts had grown bitter and consciences perverse.

To prosecute this work of reconstruction, the Assembly, ere it rose, appointed two Commissions, the one for the regions lying to the south, and the other for those lying to the north, of the Tay. These Commissions, in virtue of the powers conferred on them by the Assembly, and by the Act of Parliament which had authorised the Assembly to correct the disorders of the Church by a system of visitations, were to go through the country, purging out all obnoxious ministers. Although an Act of the Revolution Parliament had taken what most people felt to be its sharpest sting from ecclesiastical discipline, by forbidding, for the future, any civil penalty to follow a spiritual sentence; yet the powers of this executive of the Assembly were very real, and extended to deposition from function and benefice. To the south of the Tay the visitation proceeded without disturbance or scandal. It was not so in the north. The moderation of the Assembly was not reflected in the Commission; and the Presbyterian fervour, which had bridled itself in Edinburgh, ran riot through the northern provinces, driving out ministers, shutting up churches, stirring evil and sectarian passions, under the cloak of enforcing ministerial purity and efficiency. Where the incumbent was Episcopal, it is to be feared charges of negligence, or immorality, or heterodoxy, were only too readily framed and sustained.

What with the number expelled by the Privy Council for refusing to acknowledge William and Mary, and those extruded on various pleas by the Commissions, the Church in the north was stripped of a host of her clergy, whose places no new race of candidates had yet arisen to supply. In some of the northern parishes, when substitutes for the deprived incumbents were found, the people, resenting the loss of the ordinances of religion through the expulsion of their old pastors, resisted, and sometimes successfully, for months, and even years, the induction of the new. At Inverness, for example, which, though the capital of the Highlands, was then but a wretched village of some five hundred thatched houses, the people defied for no less than ten years the attempts of the Presbytery to settle a minister among them. At Insch, upon the parish falling vacant, the parishioners called an Episcopalian curate, who did not even take the oaths to government, but who remained in possession of the living for many years. And these were not solitary cases.

Those Episcopal curates who had accepted the terms of the government and remained in their parishes, were not allowed to act as members of the Church courts. The Presbyteries, accordingly, in the north, where Episcopacy was strong, were mere skeletons. The whole Synod of Aberdeen, comprising eight Presbyteries, had to concentrate itself into one; and even after the lapse of seven years, could only muster sixteen clerical members. The desire to increase the strength of the Presbyteries, no doubt, was one of the motives which spurred the zeal of the Commission to substitute Presbyterian for Episcopal parsons. But the bad blood engendered by the process began to inflame the whole body of the Church and State.

William was inclined to suspect the Commissioners of harshness and injustice, and to blame the general temper and policy of the Presbyterians. The relations between the Crown and the Church became strained. The annual meeting of the Assembly was postponed by the royal command. The Church grumbled at this interference with its right of convening at its own pleasure. When at last the king summoned a meeting for 15th January 1692, the members assembled in a somewhat irritated and irreconcilable mood, which was not soothed by the receipt of a royal letter urging them to admit the Conformist Episcopal ministers into the Church courts, on subscribing a simple formula, of which the king sent them the draft. The Assembly consigned the formula to the consideration of a committee—a method of indirect strangulation still dear to the heart of that venerable court—and having by the 13th of February done nothing else, was abruptly dissolved by the Commissioner, who declined even to name a day for its next meeting. This was a direct repudiation, by the Crown, of the Church's claim of a right to hold its annual Assembly; and also rendered impossible that harmonious coincidence by which the Commissioner and the Moderator, each naming the same day, evaded any conflict of jurisdiction or confusion of dates. The Moderator, in spite of the Commissioner's refusal, appointed the next Assembly to be held in August 1693. This was a mere assertion of the Church's rights. When the day came, no attempt was made to hold an Assembly. Before the critical date, Parliament had intervened with an Act 'for settling the quiet and peace of the Church,' in which provision was made for the summoning of an Assembly by the sovereign. While, by this clause, the Act averted the impending danger of a direct collision between the royal and ecclesiastical authority; by another, it provided for the admission to a share in the government of the Church of those Episcopal incumbents who should subscribe the engagements set forth in the Act. One of these was the 'Oath of Assurance'—a new declaration which had been devised to circumvent those who made a distinction between a king *de facto* and a king *de jure*, and who were ready to own William in the one sense, but not in the other. The oath of assurance expressed allegiance to him as king both *de facto* and *de jure*. No one was to sit in the Assembly unless he had taken this oath.

This enactment, so far from helping to settle the quiet and peace of the Church, produced nothing but ill-will and clamour. It exasperated Presbyterian and Episcopalian alike. What right had 'Cæsar' to make a civil oath the condition of entrance to an ecclesiastical court? Was it to be borne that a king, by popular election, should wring from the exigencies of an ill-used priesthood a renunciation of the sacred doctrine of hereditary right? The remonstrances of the clergy, however, had no effect. The Assembly was summoned for the 29th March 1694; and the Commissioner was instructed to exact the oath, and if it was refused, to dissolve the Assembly. The crisis was perilous. The Crown was inexorable; the Church's patience was exhausted; the perfervid Scotch blood was stirred. But for some averting providence, Church and State must come into fatal collision, and the Revolution Settlement perish in the crash. The averting providence took the shape of the Church's best and wisest friend, William Carstares. Among the events of a somewhat monotonous and unpicturesque period, the episode of his interposition is sufficiently striking to excuse its being once more related, in the words of his first biographer, M'Cormick. The Commissioner, Lord Carmichael, he tells us, had been assured by the clergy that they could not and would not give in. He 'saw that all his attempts to bring them to better temper would be vain and fruitless. At the same time, he was sensible that the dissolution of the Assembly would not only prove fatal to the Church of Scotland, but also to his Majesty's interest in that kingdom. From a sincere regard to both, therefore, he undertook to lay the matter, as it stood, fairly before the king; and, for that purpose, sent off a flying packet, which he expected to return from London, with the king's final determination, the night before the Assembly was appointed to meet. At the same time, the clergy sent up a memorial to Carstares, urging him to use his good offices, in this critical conjuncture, for the preservation of that Church which he had so active a hand in establishing.

'The flying packet arrived at Kensington in the forenoon of that day upon which Carstares returned [he having been absent from Court]. But before his arrival, his Majesty, by the advice of Lord Stair and Lord Tarbat, who represented this obstinacy of the clergy as an act of rebellion against his government, had renewed his instructions to the Commissioner, and sent them off by the same packet.

'When Carstares came to Kensington and received his letters, he immediately inquired what was the nature of the despatches his Majesty had sent off for Scotland; and, upon learning their contents, he went directly, and, in his Majesty's name, required the messenger, who was just setting off, to deliver them up to him. It was now late at night; and, as he knew no time was to be lost, he ran to his Majesty's apartment; and, being informed by the lord-in-waiting that he was gone to bed, he told him it was a matter of the last importance which had brought him at that unseasonable hour, and that he must see the king.

'Upon entering the chamber, he found his Majesty fast asleep, upon which, turning aside the curtain, and falling down upon his knees, he gently awaked him. The king, astonished to see him at so late an hour, and in this posture by his bedside, asked him what was the matter? He answered he had come to ask his life. "And is it possible," said the king, " that you have been guilty of a crime that deserves death?" He acknowledged he had, and then produced the despatches he had brought back from the messenger. "And have you," says the king, with a severe frown—" have you indeed presumed to countermand my orders?" Carstares begged leave only to be heard a few words, and he was ready to submit to any punishment his Majesty should think proper to inflict.' He then entered into an exposition of the situation of the Church in Scotland, and of the arguments against the oath, which M'Cormick gives at length; and at the close of which, 'the king, having heard him with great attention, gave him the despatches to read, and desired him to throw them in the fire; after which, he bade him draw up the instructions to the Commissioner in what terms he pleased, and he would sign them. Carstares immediately wrote to the Commissioner, signifying that it was his Majesty's pleasure to dispense with putting the oaths to the ministers; and, when the king had signed it, he immediately despatched the messenger, who, by being detained so many hours longer than he intended, did not arrive in Edinburgh till the morning of the day fixed for the sitting of the Assembly.

'By this time, both the Commissioner and the clergy were in the utmost perplexity. He was obliged to dissolve the Assembly; they were determined to assert their own authority independent of the civil magistrate. Both of them were apprehensive of the consequences, and looked upon the event of this day's contest as decisive with respect to the Church of Scotland; when, to their inexpressible joy, they were relieved by the return of the packet, countermanding the dissolution of the Assembly. Next to the establishment of Presbytery in Scotland, no act of King William's administration endeared him so much to the Presbyterians as this.'

This incident, as I have remarked elsewhere, marked a crisis in the history of the Church. Henceforth the Presbyterians believed in William's honesty and good-will, as they had not believed before. They were now convinced of his firm intention to maintain Presbytery, and of their own secure position. Conscious of a confirmed power, they were able to use it with greater generosity. The Assembly proceeded to receive, and empowered its Commission also to receive, the Episcopal clergy who should apply for reception upon the reasonable terms recently approved by Parliament. Those who thus conformed were amicably admitted. Many of those who would not conform were allowed, and even entitled, under the protection of an Act of the Parliament of 1695, to remain, and to officiate in their parishes, though debarred from a place in the Presbyteries, Synods, and Assemblies, in which the Presbyterian government was vested. The waste and empty places were gradually reached, and filled up. In the north, force was no longer employed to expel Episcopal, or to intrude Presbyterian, incumbents. The complete organisation of one homogeneous establishment was left to the healing and restoring influences of time. That no harsh pressure was used to hasten the action of these, and that the policy and practice of the Church were vastly more lenient after the Revolution than after the Restoration, is sufficiently attested by the fact that even as late as 1710 there were one hundred and thirteen Episcopal ministers, of whom nine had not even taken the prescribed oaths to government, still ministers of parishes; and that the Sacrament of the Lord's Supper was not celebrated in Aberdeen, according to the Presbyterian use, until the year 1704. The Episcopal Church, as a Church, was now, however, practically broken up. Those of its clergy who conformed were henceforth politically powerless, and were merged, more or less completely, in the Establishment. Those who kept aloof, and who maintained a furtive relation to the surviving bishops of the deprived Episcopate, became, in the natural development of their original tendency, a body of political dissidents, whose bond of union was primarily Jacobitism, and only in a far inferior degree, Episcopacy. The lonely exile at St Germain's was the true source of the Scotch Episcopacy of the eighteenth century. The Scotch Episcopacy of the nineteenth has no longer any sympathy with, in few cases has it any knowledge of, its own historical ancestry. It retains no relic or recollection of its old Scotch simplicity of ritual, and of its Calvinistic creed. It acknowledges no admiration of the royal absolutism, to which it owed its temporary establishment. It has adopted the English Articles, and has clothed itself with all the forms of Anglicanism of which it could lay hold. It owes its vitality now to causes which did not exist, and were not even thought of in 1694; but it is still, as it has always been, essentially an alien on Scottish soil; and in any of the great movements of thought, whether theological or political, exercises but little influence. That midnight interview of Carstares and William decided that, for evil or for good, Scotland in future was to be emphatically Presbyterian.

Since that critical year of 1694, there has been no break in the regular annual meetings of the General Assembly, under the sanction of the sovereign, as represented by the Lord High Commissioner. There has been no attempt to subvert the arrangement by which—the Moderator and the Commissioner each naming the same day for its next meeting—the independence of the Church and the prerogative of the Crown are mutually recognised and adjusted.

The period between this year and that of the Union is not marked by any special interest. The Assembly of 1694 began a process (which was continued, with intervals, up to 1711) of exacting, with a growing stringency, from both ministers and elders subscription to the Confession of Faith. An overture approved by this Assembly contains the earliest draft of the formula, which was subsequently required from ministers and elders; and which, originally devised with a view to scare undesirable Episcopal applicants, or, at least, to entrap them into professions of orthodoxy, has bequeathed an embarrassment to the Church in days when no such safeguards are required. Orthodox zeal took a more untoward form, when it prompted the sacrifice on its cruel altar of a foolish lad of eighteen, who had rendered himself amenable to a savage law of Charles II., by spouting some juvenile irreverences about certain doctrines of the Church. A great deal has been made of his execution, as an index of the relentless and persecuting temper of the Presbyterian clergy. Lord Macaulay, in particular, has described their part in Aikenhead's unhappy fate, with much rhetorical exaggeration, and says, 'Wodrow has told us no blacker story of Dundee.' The lad, it must be remembered, was condemned, not by the Church, but by the High Court of Justiciary; and recent investigation has proved that the voice of the clergy was by no means raised so unmercifully and unanimously against him, as the eloquent historian has represented.

That the spirit of the dominant religion, as embodied in the clergy of the Revolutionary Epoch, was somewhat harsh, intolerant, and narrow, it would be vain to deny. Persecution does not favour the growth of 'sweetness and light.' Breadth of Christian culture and charity is not developed under penal laws. 'The ministers of the Revolution,' as Mr Hill Burton justly says, ' were no more a fair specimen of the literary fruit of the Presbyterian system, than the fugitives of a routed force are a fair specimen of the discipline and morality of an army.' Nor were they a fair specimen of that noble type of character, of which the Church had since the Reformation produced many shining examples, in which unselfish patriotism and varied learning illustrate personal piety and charity. It says much for the statesmanlike ability and governing power of Carstares, that out of the somewhat rough materials, that lay to his hand, he was able to build up the fabric of the restored Church so skilfully as he did, and to keep so steadily to the rule of ' Moderation.' It says much for the substantial reasonableness and good principle of the clergy—despite their defects in culture, in tolerance, in the ' philosophic mind '—that amongst a people which still believed in witchcraft there were no serious outbreaks of religious bigotry; that in a country seething with Jacobite intrigues, and national discontents, and preyed upon by a gigantic pauperism, there was no explosion of political or social disorder. The earlier fathers and leaders of the Church, of whom you have heard, reckoned among their number many men of marked genius, learning, and literary power. There is no greater name than Buchanan's among the names of the European scholars of the sixteenth and seventeenth centuries. Melville, Baillie, Rutherford, Calderwood, Gillespie, were all learned divines and accomplished men of letters; and there were many of the same class and character among the Churchmen of the first half of the seventeenth century. But we find no such names in the roll of the Revolution clergy. The greatest man among them, Carstares, was a good scholar, and had enjoyed the advantage of the best training that Holland—that generous nurse and shelter of Presbyterianism—could afford him; but his destiny and the bent of his mind led him to the region of diplomacy and politics—ecclesiastical and secular—and not of literature. The most prolific writer of the period, Wodrow, cannot take high rank among scholars and authors. The theological and literary dearth is not relieved by the superabundance of controversial pamphleteering—of all forms of literary activity the most barren and unedifying.

Yet it is to the Church at this era of intellectual sterility—as far as its literature is concerned—that we owe the measures which have done more than any other to develop the intellectual life of our country. Public education had been neglected during the internecine strifes of Prelacy and Presbytery. Now, however, the Assembly and the Parliament found time and opportunity to carry out, at last, one long-postponed portion of Knox's great scheme of Education. Since the Restoration, no effort had been made to establish the system of parochial schools: but the Church of the Revolution was not content until Parliament had passed an Act compelling the heritors of every parish to erect and endow a parish school; which was followed by an Act of Assembly enjoining Presbyteries to see this law obeyed. It was duly carried out, and the result was soon apparent. 'It made,' says Mr Lecky, in his *England in the Eighteenth Century*, 'the average level of Scotch intelligence superior to that of any other part of the Empire.' Now that the system, which brought such good for our forefathers, has been superseded by another, it is well to remember that they owed it to the Church of the Revolution.

The industrial and commercial life of Scotland, which had long been paralysed by the distractions of the country, began to revive after the re-establishment of the National Church, but had scarcely grown into any strength or stature, when it was stupefied by the crushing disaster of Darien. The only hope of its renewal lay in a union with England. Social and political ambition, commercial enterprise, and the desire to secure the Protestant succession to the throne, all pointed in the same direction.

The Church had no liking for closer connection with Prelatic England; but wise Churchmen knew that Established Presbytery had nothing to lose by being made a part of the constitution of the United Kingdom, and put under the protecting wing of the stable legislature of Great Britain. The Church's interests, in prospect of the Union, had often engaged the Scottish Parliament; and Belhaven and his friends had been zealous to maintain that the treaty offered no security to the Church adequate to the danger which she would incur. The Jacobites eagerly tried to fan the flame of discontent and apprehension; but the great majority of the clergy were wise, and were wisely counselled by Carstares, who after William's death had come to Scotland to be the Principal of the University of Edinburgh, and minister of this ancient church. They refused to be led away by the zeal of injudicious allies or the false sympathy of covert foes. The Commission of the General Assembly, which, in virtue of its ordinary powers, continued to act when the Assembly was not in Session, represented the Church during the progress of the treaty with calmness and dignity; and in its addresses to Parliament temperately stated those points in the measure which were considered defective. The Commission complained of the English Sacramental Test as the condition of holding civil and military office, and urged that no oath or test of any kind, inconsistent with Presbyterian principles, should be required from Scottish Churchmen. They recommended that an obligation to uphold the Church of Scotland should be embodied in the Coronation Oath. They represented the necessity of a 'Commission for the Plantation of Kirks and Valuation of Teinds;' and they concluded their fullest and most formal representation with an intimation that knowing, as they did, that twenty-six bishops sat in the House of Lords, which, on the conclusion of the treaty would have jurisdiction in Scottish affairs, they desired to state, with all respect, but all firmness, that it was contrary to the Church's 'principles and covenants' that 'any Churchman should bear civil offices and have power in the Commonwealth.'

These representations had due effect. The bench of bishops of course could not be removed. The operation of the Test Act in England could not be meddled with, though its scandal and injustice were undeniable; but as a kind of equivalent for this grievance, and to guard the Scotch universities and schools against the dreaded infection of Prelacy, it was enacted that every professor and teacher should, ere his admission, subscribe the Confession of Faith as the confession of his faith, and bind himself, in the Presbytery's presence, to conform to the discipline and worship of the Established Church. It was provided that the unalterable establishment and maintenance of the Presbyterian Church should be stipulated by an Act prior to any other Act that should ratify the treaty, and should then be embodied in the Act of ratification; and that the first oath the British sovereign should take, on his accession, and before his coronation, should be an oath to maintain 'the government, worship, discipline, rights, and privileges of the Church of Scotland.' The minor points, as to kirks and teinds, were satisfactorily disposed of, and the Church saw her firmness and moderation crowned with an adequate success.

A General Assembly had been held in the spring of 1707, ere yet the Act of Union had come into operation. There is no reference to the Union in its printed records; and we may conclude that its leaders, finding that their brethren would not bless the treaty, thought it best to pass it by in silence. Their patriotic calmness and self-control were highly appreciated by the government; which was well aware that had the clergy thrown their influence into the same scale with the popular passion and hatred of the Union, it never could have been accomplished.

By the time the Assembly of 1708 met, the ancient Parliament, which the ecclesiastical Convention had so often controlled, so often withstood, had passed away for ever. With the demise of the Scottish Legislature much of the strength and glory of the Supreme Court of the Church departed. The Assembly could never again expect to influence the British, as it had influenced the Scottish, Parliament. The leaders of Scotch political life, attracted to St Stephen's, and exposed there to all the influences of English society and of a powerful and predominant Episcopacy, were no longer likely to take their seats as elders in the Scotch Church court, and to lend their weight to its deliberations.

It was of importance that the first Assembly that met in these altered circumstances should choose as its president one whose Presbyterianism and Churchmanship had stood keen tests, and who yet enjoyed the confidence of the government, and had been a promoter of the Union, and who, by the worth of his character and dignity of his position, would do honour to the Moderator's Chair. The choice naturally fell upon Carstares.

The queen's letter to the Assembly made no special reference to the Union, although referring, in commendation, to the 'zeal and affection' which the Church had shewn, during the recent attempt at a French invasion in the Jacobite interest. Neither in the Acts of Assembly, nor in its address to the queen, is the great change in the constitution of the nation named. Carstares' opening speech is occupied with the threatened invasion, rather than with the abolished Legislature and the new condition of things. 'The Presbyterians of Scotland,' he said, 'have too great a concern for the Protestant Churches, and too great a detestation of Popery and tyranny, and see and hear of too many dismal instances of French government, not to have an abhorrence both of the designs of Versailles and the pretences of St Germain's.'

This avoidance of a subject which could not but be uppermost in all men's minds indicates no indifference to it, nor any unanimity regarding it; it rather reveals a state of feeling and opinion in which it was tacitly admitted that the subject could not be approached without danger. National pride had been too recently wounded, ecclesiastical jealousy too freshly irritated, the practical effects of the Union, in Church and State, in society and in trade, too little tested, to allow of any body of Scottish Presbyterians giving it an unprejudiced discussion. Carstares' wisdom and moderation were rewarded by, as they were reflected in, the dignified reticence of the first post-Union Assembly. The predominating control of that great Moderate party, which he had largely helped to consolidate, and which he now led—a control that was to last for more than a century—was already established.

I have reached my limit. If, throughout this lecture, and now at its close, I should be thought to have trenched too much on the domain of civil history, it must be remembered that the rights of the people were inseparably connected with their Church's cause; and that it was, in point of fact, the sturdy Presbyterianism of Scotland, of which their Church was the embodiment, that won the liberties of the Revolution, and secured the blessings of the Union.

ST GILES' LECTURES.

FIRST SERIES—THE SCOTTISH CHURCH.

LECTURE IX.

THE CHURCH OF THE EIGHTEENTH CENTURY,
1707 TO 1800 A.D.[1]

By the Very Rev. JOHN TULLOCH, D.D., LL.D., Principal of St Mary's College, St Andrews, and one of Her Majesty's Chaplains.

THE subject assigned me is a large one, requiring an extended canvas. In the short space allotted to me, I can only draw some of its salient features. It is, moreover, a difficult and critical subject, stirring questions of which we have not yet seen the end, and bringing before us for the first time fully developed parties, whose rival influence has modified the whole modern history of the Church of Scotland, and whose conflicts and jealousies survive to the present time. I must therefore not only work upon a reduced canvas, but with a very delicate pencil. Whatever use these St Giles' Lectures may be, one of their main intentions must be to soften, rather than to harden ecclesiastical prejudices, and to make the controversies and

---

[1] I wish particularly to express my obligations in the preparation of this lecture to Dr Cunningham's *Church History of Scotland*, vol. ii., and Morren's *Annals of the General Assembly from* 1739 *to* 1766—the more so that I have not given detailed references to either. I need not particularise my obligations otherwise. They appear partly in the course of the lecture, which has been completed with difficulty during illness, and makes no claim to research.

asperities of the past a warning for our better guidance, rather than a stimulus to our unspent feuds. The Lecturer must of course say what he thinks; but he must say it with discrimination, and in charity towards all.

With the cessation of the Scottish Parliament in 1707, Scotland ceased to have a separate political history. It remained in many respects still a distinct kingdom, especially in those social and religious characteristics which are deeper than any Acts of Parliament, which formal legislation may express and ratify, but cannot directly alter. The people themselves were distinct from their kindred across the Border; hardened into an independent nationality by long struggle with influences which they refused to accept, and having their independence rooted in the passionate, if narrow love, which is always lavished on that which has cost us dear. The judicial and administrative system of the country which centred in the Court of Session and its cognate functionaries, was distinct. And of course the Church was distinct, secured by definite statute in 1690, and again and very solemnly in the Act of Union. The Commissioners for the Union had been precluded from treating 'of or concerning any alteration of the worship, discipline, and government of the Church as by law established in Scotland.' Whatever was to be altered, the Presbyterian Church was not to be altered. And so, while the ancient Parliament of the realm disappeared, the Scottish Church not only remained untouched, but was continued, in the emphatic words of the Act of Union, 'without any alteration to the people of this land in all succeeding generations;' and the oath guaranteeing this settlement, as is well known, is the first that is taken by a new monarch on his or her accession to the throne.

Distinct as Scotland remained in national life at the beginning of the eighteenth century, the Church, thus secured by statute and the 'inclinations of the generality of the people, ever since the Reformation,' naturally became the chief organ for the expression of national feeling and activity. Such national diversities as existed were reflected in it, and came to a head in the management of its affairs in the General Assembly. The difficulties described in the previous lecture as to the Episcopal clergy who remained within the Church, were prolonged into this period; and others were added arising out of the Union and the natural influx of English officials which followed it. In the east and the north—in Forfarshire, Kincardineshire, Aberdeenshire, and even the far Ross-shire, where Presbyterianism of an extreme type is now so conspicuously found, Episcopacy possessed many entire parishes. In point of fact, there were parts of the Highlands and Islands where Popery, if not Paganism, still lingered; and to the acknowledgment of this fact the Society for the Propagation of Christian Knowledge owes its origin. It originated in the very year of the Union, was fostered by the Church, and received royal institution and sanction two years later. There are Highland districts even now, as every one knows, where Romanism has its contented and peaceful adherents. But in the beginning of last century, and in the view of a National Presbyterianism clothed with new statutory authority, such facts were naturally fitted to arouse anxiety. The terms of the Church's original establishment called upon it to purge out all such erroneous elements, as savouring of civil no less than of religious disaffection; and the royal letters addressed to the General Assembly emphasised the same duty of planting everywhere vacant churches with sound Protestant ministers. This part of its work, therefore, was expressly laid upon the Church; and it was no mere restlessness of zeal that impelled it to undertake the task of Presbyterian propagandism, in the course of which the visitors or agents of the General Assembly sometimes met with what Wodrow calls 'very inhuman treatment from those disaffected to the Establishment.'[1]

The Church was only doing its duty in planting, so far as it

[1] *Corresp.*, vol. i., p. 216.

was able, Presbyterian ministers in the face of local opposition; but it was undoubtedly wrong in resisting the rights of free worship and toleration to Episcopal clergymen like Greenshields, who desired merely to meet and hold divine service according to the forms of the Church of England. The persecution of Greenshields, from first to last, was a miserable business, reflecting credit neither on the General Assembly nor on the Magistrates of Edinburgh; and the Tory Parliament of Queen Anne, if not to be justified in much that it did, was fully justified in securing by statute that the Episcopal Communion in Scotland should not be disturbed in the exercise of their religious worship. The Toleration Act of 1712 was a statute of freedom, obnoxious as it was to the great body of Presbyterians. It confined the ecclesiastical power to its own sphere; and, while it left the Church its anathemas against schism and 'innovations in the worship of God,' protected all who chose to put themselves voluntarily beyond its pale from all forcible interference. It is melancholy to think that even the Church of Carstares did what it could to oppose such a law, and that it can be said with truth by the modern historian that the Scottish Parliament would never have ventured to pass it.

But the legislature of Queen Anne, unhappily, did not stop with the Act of Toleration. In the very same year it introduced the Act for the Restoration of Patronage, which has proved such a fertile and unhappy cause of division in Scotland. I need hardly say that I am not going to treat this subject in any controversial spirit; but the facts regarding it require to be clearly stated, if for no other purpose than because it forms the centre round which all the later external history of the Church of Scotland revolves. There are features of the Church in the eighteenth century which would no doubt have been the same although lay Patronage had not been restored; but the history of Scottish Presbyterianism would have been entirely different, if the Tory politicians of Queen Anne had only left undisturbed the settlement of the Patronage question made in 1690 by the same Parliament of William and Mary as re-established the Church. It is true that this settlement did not go so far as some had desired. It did not recognise the right 'of every several congregation to elect their minister,' as formulated in the *First Book of Discipline*, to which—although never sanctioned by law—a certain class of Presbyterians have always looked back as their special charter. Nor did it fall back upon the Parliamentary enactment of 1649, by which Patronage was first legally abolished, and the right of collation was left in the hands of the Church, acting 'on the call and with the consent of the congregation, on whom none was to be intruded against their will.' The Act of 1690 gave the initiative or right of nomination to the heritors and elders or kirk-session of each parish, who were taken bound to pay to the respective patrons a small sum of money, for which they were supposed to renounce their rights for ever. It is needless to ask whether this was a good settlement of the question in itself. It does not seem to have worked smoothly; but then no system could have worked smoothly at such a time when many parishes were still alienated from the dominant Presbyterianism, and disputes as to the succession of ministers were necessarily engendered. The one thing that demands our attention is, that the lay patron had disappeared under solemn statutory enactment. That form of Patronage which the Church, or at least those supposed most entitled to represent it, had always felt as a 'heavy grievance,' had been constitutionally removed. It had been unknown to Scottish Presbyterianism for upwards of sixty years; and it is hardly possible therefore to conceive anything more unwise or unjust than its restitution. Carstares did all he could to prevent it, but in vain. The well-known Act of Queen Anne finally passed both Houses of Parliament by large majorities, and received the royal assent on the 22d April 1712.

It was not immediately that the sad effects of this policy began to appear. The call survived untouched by the new legislation; and while the initiative was transferred to the lay patrons, the custom of consulting the wishes of the congregation was still maintained in force. It is not till some considerable time afterwards that we hear of special difficulties in the settlement of ministers. In fact, the first form which these difficulties took does not seem to have sprung from the people themselves, but from the rivalry of two parties within the Church, neither of whom in the beginning doubted that something more was required than the mere act of Patronage—something implying the assent of the parish or congregation—to constitute the right of entry to a ministerial charge. Neither party, in short, doubted the necessity of a call. The only question between them was as to the persons in whom the right of call was vested. Was it the congregation itself, or merely the kirk-session and heritors, according to the Act of 1690? It was not till 1732 that this question arose definitely in the Church. The inference to be drawn from this is, that while the restoration of Patronage in 1712 was probably intended as a movement in favour of the reactionary Jacobite policy of the latter part of Queen Anne's reign, such an intention was entirely frustrated by the accession of George I. and the Rebellion following in 1715. The Jacobite influences were effectually crushed for the time by the severities which the Rebellion called forth, and the renewed right of Patronage evidently remained for some time a dead letter, or nearly so.

But gradually with the consolidation of the Hanoverian dynasty, and the increasing attachment of many of the gentry to the Presbyterian Church as representing the established order of things, the Church itself, or at least a section of it, became more reconciled to Patronage and to its exercise within definite bounds. A new race of clergy began to appear—men to whom the troublous times before the Revolution were a dim retrospect, and who were animated, not so much by an enthusiasm for Presbytery, as by what they deemed a sober and enlightened regard to the peace and good of the country both in Church and State. This change may be said to date definitely from about 1720. The words *popular* and *moderate* party were not heard of as yet. It is at least twenty years later till they come into vogue, and much later before they assume the characteristics by which they are generally distinguished. But the germs of the divisions were perceptible at this earlier time.

Much has been said, and as it appears to me, not very intelligently, as to the growth of what is called Moderatism in the Church of Scotland. The word has unhappily become a by-word—a synonym of evil reproach—in the mouths of those who dislike the cause and the principles which it is understood to represent. I am not its apologist; but I desire this as well as all historical phenomena should be looked at rationally, as a product of natural forces working in the national mind of Scotland in the eighteenth century, and not as a mere combination of evil men for evil purposes, which is not only not a rational, but not an intelligible view of any historical movement. Whatever elements may have entered into the composition of the Moderatism of the eighteenth century, it was so far plainly a direct expression of the spirit of the age and the circumstances of the Church, extending as far back as the close of the first quarter of the century, and destined, as we shall see, to assume very distinct phases with the course of the century. It was impossible that the enthusiasms which had preceded and accompanied the Revolution should last, or that the more settled order of the time should not produce the natural fruits in a more settled temper and a disposition to adapt the machinery of the Church to its changed fortunes. But it is equally certain that a change of this kind would be unacceptable to many in the Church, in whom the old spirit survived—men like Wodrow, Boston, the Erskines, and others, who loved the old enthusiasms for their own sake, and could only see spiritual declension in a less fervent state of the spiritual atmosphere. Wodrow himself, in his lengthened and garrulous *Correspondence* and *Analecta*, is an unceasing witness to the alteration of feeling and sentiment that was going on around him. The new and the old are mingled in his pages in the most curious manner. He is himself the child of the age that is passing away. The dawn of the new age is unpleasant to him; yet he cannot wholly give his faith to the legends of the one, nor shut his mind against the larger light of the other. The trial of Simson, Professor of Divinity in Glasgow, and the 'Marrow Controversy,' from 1718 to 1722—are on the intellectual and theological side notable illustrations of the same conflict between the new and the old; the spirit of criticism and negation which was beginning to assail the old watchwords of the Faith, and the spirit of extreme Evangelicalism, which was its natural reaction. The 'Marrow Divinity,' although a direct continuation from the seventeenth century, was yet also something of a novelty in Scotland, as Wodrow himself felt. The voice was the voice of the Evangel, but its language was too perilously near to Antinomianism for the good minister of Eastwood—who loved not merely the old ways, but to stand in them in the old manner.

It is evident from all that we have said that the Church was in movement in the years that followed 1720, and that we are to trace back to this time the formation of distinct parties within her. Up to this time she had been so busy in settling her borders, planting vacant churches, and watching against the common enemies of Romanism and Episcopacy, that she had had no time to develop internal divisions.[1] Such divisions as

---

[1] This is the view of Sir Henry Moncrieff Wellwood, as shewn in the following passage (Appendix, No. I., p. 421) in his *Life of Dr Erskine*: 'An unbiassed reader who dispassionately examines the proceedings of the General Assemblies from 1690 to 1712, cannot but perceive the sincerity with which the great body of the clergy then united to promote the religious interests of the people and the general tranquillity of the country. There were occasional differences of opinion among them. But there do not appear any settled combinations, or indeed any offensive symptoms, either of party spirit or of political intrigue.'

existed had been inherited; they had come to her with the Revolution settlement which made her; and no doubt the force of these earlier divisions was perpetuated in the new. The survival of Episcopal curates in the Church may have in this way helped the nascent growth of Moderatism. But facts do not point to any such influence working within the pure leaven of Presbytery. By the year 1720, the Episcopal incumbents within the Church must have been rapidly dying out; nor is there any reason to believe either that they were likely to adapt themselves specially to the altered law of Patronage, or to become the exponents of a new theology. I cannot think, therefore, that Moderatism can have drawn almost anything of its strength or life from such a source. The truth seems to be simply, that with a new generation, Presbyterianism began to take a new colour. This is true of the popular, no less than of the moderate side of the Church. Even the fervid Evangelicalism which lived on was no longer quite the same. The tone was different, if not the principles. The spirit of the eighteenth century was insensibly moulding all parties within the Church, even those most opposed to it.

The difficulties which sprung up in the Church with the advance of the eighteenth century were partly doctrinal and partly administrative. We have already alluded to the case of Professor Simson. So far as mere prominence is concerned, he is quite a heresiarch in the history of the Scottish Church. He was twice the subject of trial. As early as 1714, his opinions were brought under the notice of the Church courts; and three years later, after the Presbytery of Glasgow had dealt with him at length, his teaching was formally censured by the General Assembly to the effect that 'he had vented unnecessary opinions and used expressions in a bad and unsound sense, and attributed too much to the powers of natural reason and corrupt human nature.' Ten years later, Simson was again arraigned for heretical tendencies of a quite different character. Formerly, his teaching was found inclined to Pelagianism;

now, it was Arianism or Semi-Arianism on the borders of which he seemed to hover.

It is difficult to express any definite opinion of Simson's case. On the one hand, he himself fails to interest us—even if we judge him in some degree a victim of persecution. He is throughout a veiled and vacillating figure, seldom appearing except in the background as an argumentative valetudinarian who makes endless explanations without reaching any result satisfactory to his accusers. Wodrow represents him as a man of restless argumentative tendency, who delighted to stir the theological atmosphere around him, without much real depth or reflective thoughtfulness. But his letters, and especially the first letter of date March 2, 1726, give a higher idea of his intelligence and learning, if they are also marked by a strangely querulous spirit. On the other hand, Simson's accusers seem captious and unfair in refusing to acknowledge the apparent honesty of many of his explanations, and especially in submitting the Glasgow students to a process of examination as to any unguarded utterances he may have used in the course of his teaching. The process did not end till 1729, when the General Assembly, heartily tired of it, as their minute implies, brought it to an issue by suspending the Professor permanently from his functions of teaching and preaching. As a whole, the case is highly significant of a certain restlessness of thought in the Church, and at the same time of the very narrow limits within which it was possible for this thought to express itself without incurring censure. Younger minds were beginning to move out of the old dogmatic restraints; but the great majority of the clergy had no idea of relaxing even the old modes of expression, far less the old doctrines.

When Simson's sentence of suspension was finally confirmed in May 1729, there was one minister of the old school who expressed his dissatisfaction and intimated his dissent from the judgment as too lenient. This was Thomas Boston, minister of Ettrick, the apostle of the 'Marrow Divinity,' and the well-known author of the *Fourfold State*. As the case of Simson marks the advance of a negative line of thought in the Church, the case of the 'Marrow men,' as they were called, represents the survival of the spirit of doctrinal enthusiasm. It was characteristic above all of this spirit, that the power of Divine grace should not only appear in the front of the Gospel system, but should so overlay the whole sphere of Christian life, as to seem to supersede all distinct activity of the human will. The Auchterarder formula, which was connected with the rise of the 'Marrow' movement, brings this out clearly: 'I believe that it is not sound and orthodox to teach that we must forsake sin in order to our coming to Christ.' The zealous Calvinists of the Auchterarder Presbytery required all candidates for the ministry to sign this formula, a proceeding which was properly reprobated by the General Assembly of 1717. There were a few zealous clergy, however, of the old school who approved of the formula, or at least of the faith it was supposed to indicate, and who of course dissented strongly from the sentence of the Assembly.

In the course of his parochial visits while minister of the parish of Simprin, Boston had come across a volume which greatly interested him as a highly interesting embodiment of his special views. The author of this volume was an Oxford gentleman-commoner of Brazennose College—Edward Fisher—who in the first triumphs of Puritan zeal had caught its dogmatic spirit in a very ardent form, and transferred it to his pages in a dialogue 'touching the Covenant of Works and the Covenant of Grace; and secondly, touching the most plain, pithy, and spiritual exposition of the Ten Commandments.' The dialogue is carried on by such speakers as Evangelista, a minister of the Gospel; Nomista, a Legalist, Antinomista, an Antinomian, and Neophitus, a young Christian; and the object is to explain the relations of the Law and the Gospel. The book, which bears the general title, *The Marrow of Modern Divinity*, is learned and, in a sense, lively, if no longer very readable. It contains much that is both true and sound in doctrine; but the form of it, as may be easily imagined, suggests paradox and overstatement. Many of its propositions were capable of a dangerous interpretation—such as that 'the believer was not under the law, and that he does not commit sin.' Nothing could seem more wildly Antinomian, and yet the intended meaning was probably no more than that Christ is all in all to the believer, and that God looks not upon the sinner himself but on Christ, in whom he is delivered from all sin. Here, as everywhere in theological controversy, if the terms could only be settled beforehand, the controversy might almost cease. The 'Marrow men' certainly did not mean to teach, any more, we suppose, than the Auchterarder Presbytery, that a believer is freed from the obligations of the Christian life, however incautiously they may have expressed themselves. It is not to be wondered at, however, that the General Assembly in 1720 condemned the book, and forbade it to be circulated or recommended. Of course the 'Marrow men' protested against this decision. They held a meeting at Edinburgh, at which both Ebenezer Erskine and his brother Ralph attended. They made a representation of their views to the General Assembly, and two years later that court so far modified their sentence, but at the same time condemned the representation and petition signed by the Erskines and others as containing 'injurious and undutiful aspersions cast upon the supreme judicatory of the Church. The General Assembly,' it is added, 'had no design to recede from the received doctrine of the Church;' but those who impugned its judgment had laid themselves open to suspicion that they favoured the Antinomian errors censured in the Act regarding the *Marrow of Modern Divinity*. The 'Marrow men,' who had now increased to a band of twelve, including the Erskines, were accordingly rebuked and admonished at the bar of the Assembly.

Much followed this Act of Assembly which we have no time,

however hurriedly, to notice. Of course the 'Marrow men' protested; and the Assembly refusing to receive their protest, there began a system of protest on the one hand, and of rejection and admonition on the other hand, the end of which could hardly have been otherwise than it was. The doctrinal complication was greatly aggravated by the Act of Assembly in 1732 regarding the mode of electing ministers where the patrons had failed to exercise their right of presentation. As we have already mentioned, this Act fell back upon the statute of 1690, and placed the call in such circumstances in the hands of the heritors and elders. This was strongly opposed by Ebenezer Erskine in the General Assembly, and so far on the valid ground that the overture on the subject which had been transmitted to Presbyteries by the preceding Assembly, had really not received the sanction of a majority of the Presbyteries of the Church. But the measure was also obnoxious to him and his friends on general grounds. 'What difference,' he vehemently asked in the course of the debate, 'does a piece of land make between man and man in the affairs of Christ's kingdom? We are told that God hath chosen the poor of this world "rich in faith."'

It is sufficiently plain that the banner of popular election was here raised[1] in the face of the Church; and this too just at the time that the yoke of Patronage, although still felt to be grievous, and declared to be so in successive Acts of the Assembly, was yet beginning to settle upon the Church, and to enter into its constitutional and practical working as it had never hitherto done. The Church in its corporate capacity continued to protest against Patronage, and to profess an

[1] According to Sir Henry Moncrieff Wellwood, this was the first time that the idea of the popular election of ministers *as a divine right* was heard of in the Church after the Revolution. 'There does not appear,' he says (Appendix I. to *Life of Erskine*, p. 434), 'during the whole interval from 1690 to 1712, the least vestige of a doctrine, so much contended for at a later period, which asserted *a divine right* in the people individually or collectively to elect the parish ministers.'

eagerness for legislative redress. It continued to do this even during all the time of Dr Robertson's administration in the heyday of Moderatism, even up to 1784. But long before, and even at the time which we have now reached, the Church had begun to adapt itself to this system. And it was the consciousness of this growing change of feeling, along with what also appeared to them as a decline of zeal for orthodoxy, which lay at the root of the impending schism which the Erskines were about to head.

Hitherto—if we except a small number of Covenanters who had stood aloof in impracticable isolation—the Church had remained unbroken. But now we approach a distinct crisis in its history—the formation of the first secession. The causes of this unfortunate event were obviously not one, but many, and these deeply laid in the Church's life and history. The majority of the clergy were plainly inclined, onwards from the close of the first quarter of the century, to accommodate themselves to the spirit of the age; if not to accept Patronage, yet to make the best of it; to welcome new modes of preaching in conformity with what seemed improved literary canons, more or less at variance with the popular taste; to relax or abandon the old rigorous precision of doctrine; and to indulge in generalities which may have helped to cover the half-doubts of some of them. All this change was in a high degree obnoxious to men like the Erskines, and they were already alienated in feeling from the Church before they came into actual collision with its courts. They saw in it, as they themselves said, 'a defection from Reformed and Covenanting principles.' It was in the interest of such principles, and as representing 'the true Presbyterian Covenanted Church of Scotland,' that they entered upon their struggle; and it was against such laxities, as well as particularly the support given to Patronage, as they said, by the Act of 1732, that they lifted their Testimony when they took their first step of secession and met under the name of the Associate Presbytery at Gairney Bridge, near Kinross, in December 1733.

It would carry us beyond our bounds to detail the various steps of this first unhappy secession. They have been amply described from different points of view. Ebenezer Erskine followed up his speech and protest in the General Assembly of 1732, by a sermon in the following autumn before the Synod of Perth and Stirling, which gave great offence to the majority of his brethren, who carried a vote of censure against the preacher, which was confirmed by the ensuing General Assembly. Along with three others—William Wilson of Perth, Alexander Moncrieff of Abernethy, and James Fisher of Kinclaven—he protested of course against this sentence. The Assembly retorted by summoning the brethren to appear before the August Commission, express their repentance, and submit to the authority of the Church. Still recusant in August, the Commission of Assembly, according to its instructions, suspended the four ministers from the exercise of their ministerial functions. In the following November, being still disobedient to the voice of authority, they were declared no longer ministers of the Church —a sentence which they met by a still more elaborate protest as to their principles; and in December of the same year the meeting of the Associate Brethren took place at Gairney Bridge, and the secession on their side was virtually complete. The following General Assembly sought to woo them back. The Acts of Assembly which had been specially obnoxious to them were repealed. Their synod was authorised to restore them to their ministerial position—the Presbytery of Stirling even went the length of electing Erskine as their Moderator, and appointing a deputation to urge the office upon him; but all to no effect. The seceding brethren met with a large popular sympathy. They were proud and confident of the position which they had taken up on behalf of what they believed to be the true principles of the Church of Scotland. They issued still another Testimony, known as their 'Judicial Testimony,' in the end of 1736—still further widening the breach between them and the Church. Finally, in 1738, the Church took the matter once more in hand, and summoned the seceding ministers, now eight in number, to her bar. They appeared—but as a corporate body or Associate Presbytery, with their Moderator at their head—declined the jurisdiction of an 'unfaithful Church,' and departed. In the Assembly of 1740—but not before—they were deposed; and from the side of the Church, the act of separation was completed, which had already long since taken effect on the side of the seceders themselves.

It is of no use, at this time of day, trying to judge the merits of this memorable quarrel on either side. If the Church was precipitate and high-handed, to begin with, in dealing with the scruples of the brethren, it certainly shewed a real wish to welcome their return. But ruptures which are easily made are not easily healed, and especially as in this case, where there are not merely ostensible causes of opposition, but alien principles in movement. The leaders of the first secession from the Church of Scotland were really the representatives of principles, partly popular and partly traditionary, which the Church of the Revolution embodied. But then the Church embodied other principles and tendencies as well of a more moderate and flexible character; and a struggle between the two lines of thought and policy was inevitable. Nothing could have prevented the collision. Whether a higher statesmanship, and a more Christian forbearance on both sides, might not have averted the catastrophe, it is needless now to speculate. But one thing may be said, that the action of the Church in reference to the first seceders, was of a far more generous and conciliatory character than in the case of the subsequent Relief secession twelve years later.

From this time onwards the two parties known as *popular* or *evangelical* and *moderate* rapidly developed themselves, and the history of the Church becomes largely the history of their rival relations. We can only in the most general way glance at these relations and the leaders on either side.

What is known as Moderatism may be said to divide itself into two epochs, during the first of which, extending to 1751, Dr Patrick Cuming, who was Professor of Church History in the University of Edinburgh, was 'the chief ostensible leader of the Church.' Had space sufficed, it would have been interesting to sketch not only Cuming, but the two Wisharts, along with Professor Leechman of Glasgow, who may be said to be representative of this earlier period, although Leechman survived long into a later time. He and Principal Wishart[1] are not only remarkable figures in themselves, but, as both having been subjects of prosecution for heresy, their names gather around them the events in the history of the Church then most deserving of notice. It is with reluctance that we must omit sketches of these men, with the exception of Leechman, whose position as an accused heretic is significant in the decade following the secession of the Erskines. The accusation against Leechman was founded on a sermon on Prayer, which he had preached while minister of Beith. The sermon deals with the general idea of prayer as a natural impulse of the human heart, rather than with prayer as an act of Christian devotion. On his appointment as Professor of Divinity in Glasgow, in 1744, it was objected to him that he had failed in his exposition to recognise the relation which all prayer ought to have to Jesus Christ, and an inquiry was instituted as to his orthodoxy by the Presbytery of Glasgow. There was plainly something invidious in the movement from the first, as Leechman had no sooner an opportunity of explaining his true object in the sermon, than the charge against him fell to the ground. Before the case was fully considered by the Presbytery, he carried it by complaint to the Synod, which almost unanimously found that the answers he had given to his accusers were satisfactory.

[1] He was Principal of Edinburgh University, as Leechman was ultimately Principal of Glasgow.

The General Assembly confirmed the decision of the Synod without hesitation, and the Moderator in his closing address signalised the felicity with which the Church had met a case of more than ordinary delicacy. 'Have we not seen,' he said, 'the beauty of Christian charity in condescension on the one hand to remove offence, and readiness on the other to embrace satisfaction?' There is no doubt that the Church exercised a wise discretion in this case, as well as that of Principal Wishart, which had been decided six years before, and that while due explanations were demanded, there was no disposition to bear hard upon the accused.

Dr Leechman was evidently a man of very high, if somewhat abstract and philosophical turn of mind, of the most devout religious feeling, and earnestness of purpose. Lord Woodhouselee says that his style, 'with equal purity, had more elegance than Hutcheson's,' and that his theological lectures were 'the fruit of great knowledge, and of a liberal and candid spirit.' 'He was a distinguished preacher,' according to Dr Carlyle. 'His appearance was that of an ascetic, reduced by fasting and prayer; but in aid of fine composition he delivered his sermons with such fervent spirit, and in so persuasive a manner, as captivated every audience.' And to crown these other testimonies, Sir Henry Moncrieff Wellwood says of him, that he was 'a man of primitive and Apostolic manners, equally distinguished by his love of literature and his liberal opinions.' He was a warm friend and ally of Hutcheson, the first and not the least distinguished of our race of eighteenth-century philosophers. Hutcheson took a zealous interest in his appointment to the Chair of Divinity in Glasgow, and at this time made use of the expression which has been often quoted, that Leechman would 'put a new face upon theology in Scotland.' He represented, undoubtedly, a new type of theological thought to that which had been conspicuous in the seventeenth century and was still exhibited by many in the Church. But this is merely to say that he was the product of his own century. No one can read the account of his life, and especially of the touching close of it, given by Dr James Wodrow, who edited his sermons after his death, without recognising at once his Christian sincerity and his large-mindedness. It is told that a young Oxford student was brought to see him in his last illness. He was only able to speak in a feeble voice, and had not many days to live, he said. 'But you see how I am. It is not tranquillity or confidence alone—it is joy and triumph that inspires me.' His features kindled, his voice rose. 'And whence,' he continued, 'does all this spring from?—from that book;' pointing to the Bible that lay on a little table by the bedside. Then he added to his young listener: 'You have chosen the Church for your profession. You are of the Church of England; I am a Presbyterian. The difference between us is not great. If you are faithful in the discharge of your duties, you will find your work a source of the highest enjoyment. Your father was my friend. I have been always interested in your welfare, and I am happy on my death-bed to give you an old man's blessing.'

The epoch itself during which the Church obeyed the leadership of Cuming, was distinguished by a clear acknowledgment of the evil of Patronage. The consciousness that the Act of Queen Anne had been unjustly imposed upon the Church was, if no longer universal, still general. Cuming himself made no attempt to defend it, while feeling it to be his duty to accept it, and so far to work it, as the law of the Church. In one of his addresses to the General Assembly as Moderator in 1749—he was three times Moderator—he says expressly, 'the law of Patronage is a hard law;' and according to Sir Henry Moncrieff Wellwood, 'the party under his management did not pretend to attempt the abolition of calls in the settlement of ministers; and always professed to require the call of heritors and elders before they gave effect to a presentation."[1]

[1] Appendix to *Life of Erskine*, p. 457.

It was part of his system also to appoint committees of the Assembly—'riding committees,' as they were called—to carry out the decisions of the Supreme Court when the local Presbyteries were disinclined to do so. The cessation of these committees, which were plainly 'neither sanctioned by constitutional law, nor justified by any expression of expediency,' marks the close of the earlier Moderatism.

With the turn of the century we emerge upon a new era. Moderatism takes a new and decisive shape in the hands of Robertson, Carlyle, and others. Literature finds a familiar home in the Church. It is, as Dean Stanley has said, the era of literary Churchmen. There had been in the previous part of the century some Churchmen of intellectual distinction like John Maclaurin—author of the famous sermon *Glorying in the Cross of Christ*—and Leechman and Wishart, of whom we have spoken. But it is only from about the middle of the century that literature can be said to have become a feature of the Church of Scotland. Every one is familiar with Dr Carlyle's somewhat glowing description: 'We have men who have successfully enlightened the world on almost every branch of knowledge and of Christian doctrine and morals. Who have written the best histories, ancient and modern? It has been clergymen of this Church. Who has written the clearest delineation of the human understanding and all its powers? A clergyman of this Church. Who wrote a tragedy that has been deemed perfect? A clergyman of this Church? Who was the most profound mathematician of the age he lived in? A clergyman of this Church. Let us not complain of poverty. It is a splendid poverty indeed. It is *paupertas fecunda virorum.*'[1]

This is very high-sounding; but it is not without warrant.

---

[1] This speech of Carlyle is found in the supplementary chapter to his *Autobiography*, and was made near the close of the century—in 1789—when the proposal for augmenting the livings of the ministers of the Church was under discussion.

Beginning with Dr Robert Wallace, author of a *Dissertation on the Numbers of Mankind in Ancient and Modern Times*, which anticipated Hume's essay on the same subject, and led the way to later Malthusian speculations, there is a perfect galaxy of distinguished authors to be found in the Scottish Church during the next forty years. 'Robert Watson, the historian of Philip II.; Adam Ferguson, the historian of Rome;[1] John Home, the author of the tragedy of *Douglas;* Hugh Blair, the author of the celebrated *Sermons* and of the *Lectures on Rhetoric;* Robert Henry, the philosophic author of the *History of Great Britain;* and lastly and chiefly, William Robertson, the historian of Scotland, of America, and of Charles V.—were all ministers of the Church of Scotland.'[2] Add to these Dr Thomas Reid, the well-known head of the Scottish philosophy; and Dr George Campbell, author of the *Treatise on Miracles,* in reply to Hume, and the *Elements of Rhetoric,* and the intellectual picture is still more striking. It is only, as Dean Stanley says, within 'our own generation that poetry, philosophy, and history have found so natural a home in the clergy of England, as they then did in the clergy of Scotland.' Nor should it be forgotten that there were many clergy of remarkable powers, although they do not stand out prominently in the general field of literature—men like Dr Alexander Webster; Dr Witherspoon, author of the *Ecclesiastical Characteristics,* and finally President of the New College, Jersey; and Dr Robertson's well-known colleague, Dr Erskine, whose life has been amply described to us by Sir Henry Moncrieff Wellwood. Dr Webster was a man of great mental and social vigour, to whom the Church is especially indebted for the institution of the Widows' Fund. Whatever may be true as to his failings,

---

[1] Adam Ferguson never occupied a parish; but he was licensed as preacher by the General Assembly in special circumstances, and authorised to act as an army chaplain, in which capacity he officiated for many years—from 1744 to 1757.

[2] Dean Stanley's Lectures, p. 124.

Webster was evidently a man of organising and ruling brain, as well as of unusual popular and administrative gifts. Witherspoon's literary power, as displayed in the *Characteristics*, is considerable. His irony is forcible and dramatic, if not very varied or delicate. He was evidently a man of great mental keenness and activity—a force in the General Assembly, as well as in controversial literature, on the popular side. A story is told of Robertson saying to him on one occasion: 'I think you have your men better disciplined than formerly;' to which Witherspoon replied: 'Yes, by urging your politics too far, you have compelled us to beat you with your own weapons.'[1] Erskine is a stainless and noble name, in no respect more so than in the honest and manly tribute of worth which he paid to the character of Robertson after his death—a eulogy without stint and yet without flattery[2]—alike happily conceived and expressed. There were still others, such as Principal Tullidelph of St Andrews, of whose eloquence as a speaker Dr Carlyle gives the most flattering account, comparing it to that of Lord Chatham in all his glory; and Carlyle, who has made himself so familiarly—some are inclined to think too familiarly—known to us in his *Autobiography*.

Much might be said of the deficiencies of Christian character in men like Carlyle and his associates. No one can say that the pictures he has given us of social life and personal manners are in some respects elevating, or in any respects saint-like. They are of the 'earth, earthy;' and we shall not attempt to vindicate for them a character that they do not bear. Carlyle must be judged by his self-drawn portrait; and Home and Webster—whom he has drawn with a specially unfriendly pencil—and others must be estimated in some degree by his statements. The effect is all the more telling that it is off-hand, like the touches which occur in rapid conversation, rather than like any attempt at elaborate or formal description.

---

[1] Account of Witherspoon's Life, introductory to his Works, 1815.
[2] Stewart's *Life of Robertson*, p. 123.

But just as rapid conversation lends itself easily to exaggeration, and points are thrown in for effect which were never intended to bear all the meaning that may be attributed to them, so Carlyle's sketches must be taken with reserve; and when allowance is made for the comparative coarseness of manners, it may be found that the level of Christian principle and character is not really so low as it sometimes appears. There was possibly much even in a man like Carlyle—strong and free a child of Nature as he was—allied to the higher life of which he says so little. And in men like Dr Robertson, Dr Blair, Dr George Campbell, and others, the religious vision must be very distorted which can see anything but good. Dr Johnson spoke of the former two as both 'wise and good men,' and surely his verdict, in all the circumstances, may be allowed to stand. Lives spent in laborious and fruitful application to higher studies—in the cultivation of literature, the amenities of social intercourse, and the diffusion of a spirit of courtesy, charity, and mutual understanding in the midst of deep-seated intellectual differences—are lives which claim not only honour but Christian respect. Of their special labours as Christian divines, Blair's sermons remain a monument which it is the fashion now to depreciate, but which many would find it hard to emulate; while Campbell's philosophical and theological writings have by no means yet lost their value and significance. A higher specimen of the Christian minister can hardly be conceived than Principal Campbell; or a more noble example of a luminous, thoughtful, and candid intellect, consecrated to the highest objects, without any idea of reward beyond the consciousness of devotion to truth and duty.

But while we desire, upon the whole, to vindicate the character of our Moderate clergy in the latter half of the eighteenth century, we hold no brief for the vindication of their policy. It was a high-handed policy, conceived by Robertson in a statesman-like but eminently arbitrary spirit,

That Robertson possessed many of the powers of a real statesman, it is impossible to deny. All the attributes by which his colleague describes him are more or less of a political order. There can be no doubt also of Robertson's honest intentions to serve the Church and the country. The authority of the supreme judicatory of the Church appeared to him to be in real danger. If the voice of the Assembly was to be disobeyed at will by Presbyteries, and temporary substitutes formed for carrying out its decisions, the whole government of the Church tended to lapse into a chaos fatal to any order or efficiency. And so the idea of a bold and authoritative policy seemed to a mind like his—sagacious yet cold, commanding and firm yet unsympathetic—to be the only means of rescuing the Church from perilous confusion. Younger men, like Carlyle and Home and others, entered into his ideas from a sheer wish to shew their power, and put down what they considered as disorder and fanaticism. The policy was so far successful; but the success was of that nature which is almost worse than defeat. It introduced order within the Church. It crushed the revolt of Presbyteries. It silenced in many cases popular clamour. But it quietly and gradually alienated masses of people from the Establishment.

The deposition of Gillespie in 1752 initiated the new policy, and began a second secession known as the Relief.[1] The Act which led to this disastrous result was far less justifiable than the ultimate deposition of the Erskines and their associates; for Gillespie was chosen as the victim of the General Assembly —when it determined to exercise its authority against the Presbytery of Dunfermline—in a purely arbitrary manner. Out of six recalcitrant presbyters, it was agreed that one should be deposed, and the lot, so to speak, fell upon the minister at Carnock—a sincerely pious and meek-minded man, who would gladly have lived and died a minister of the Church, and who

---

[1] *Relief* from the burden of Patronage.

advised his people to return to it after his death, and when the secession, which his deposition originated, had fairly taken root and grown into definite shape. But there was no relenting on the part of the Church, notwithstanding Gillespie's conciliatory attitude, and his almost touching willingness to return to its communion. The Assembly took no steps to undo what it had done. The day had gone by for mild expostulations and deference to conscientious scruples; and the new schism, strengthened by the adhesion of Thomas Boston at Jedburgh, a son of Boston at Ettrick, grew and multiplied as the earlier one had done. In the course of a short time, dissent had increased with such rapidity as to attract the notice of the General Assembly. An overture brought before it in the year 1765, states that 'there are now one hundred and twenty meeting-houses erected, to which more than a hundred thousand persons resort, who were formerly of our communion, but have separated themselves from the Church of Scotland;' and that this progress of dissent is most evident 'in the greatest and most populous towns.'

What has grown into the large mass of Presbyterian dissent, was in short now fairly in progress; and it is unnecessary, as it would indeed be impossible, to say how far this unhappy result is to be traced to inevitable causes, such as the love of religious independence and restlessness, so essentially characteristic of the Scottish people; and how far it is to be directly attributed to the Moderate policy which henceforth for about eighty years held the Church within its grip. The historian may indicate lines of influence which have led to great results, but not even the most acute and comprehensive capacity can disentangle all the causes which have produced these results, and assign to each their definite share.

After the triumph of Robertson's policy in the Church, its annals become comparatively unexciting. The weight of Moderate authority lay upon its councils, and the spirit of

Moderation extended throughout its borders. And yet the old spirit of Puritan earnestness was for a long time powerful and active. This is strikingly shewn by the proceedings in connection with the famous performance of the tragedy of *Douglas* in 1756. This tragedy, now so much forgotten, made a great excitement in Edinburgh in the winter of that year. The fact that a minister of the Church should write a tragedy at all—especially 'of the first-rate,' as Carlyle says—was a startling novelty to many; but the performance of the piece at the theatre in Carrubber's Close, and the attendance of Home himself and many of his clerical friends to see the performance, was something still more startling. It was not many years since the strength of Puritan feeling had compelled Allan Ramsay to close this very theatre. A great change, therefore, is represented by the fact that this feeling should have so completely vanished in the minds of ministers of the Church; nothing could more shew the advance of new modes of thought. But, on the other hand, the fact that the Presbytery of Edinburgh and other Presbyteries should not only have prosecuted the offenders, but done this successfully, proves that the old feeling survived in strength, and was backed by a vigorous tide of public opinion. Carlyle's description of the affair is enough to shew this. There appears to have been no hesitation on the part of the Church courts in dealing with theatre-going as an ecclesiastical offence. One of the ministers of the Edinburgh Presbytery was compelled to acknowledge his fault and submit to discipline; Home was eventually driven from his parish; and Carlyle was charged with a libel which, however, only ended in a rebuke. In the face of such facts as these, it cannot be said that the Church had lost its Puritan earnestness in the beginning of the second half of the eighteenth century.

And so throughout the century it is to be borne in mind that much of this earnestness, or at least of the Evangelical enthusiasm associated with it, survived. A great deal no doubt passed away, or passed into the ranks of dissent, and helped to swell its growing mass; but Evangelicalism continued living here and there in the Church also. The old and the new were both active; while there were those like Principal Hill, who were strong supporters of a Moderate policy, and yet Evangelical in the substance of their theology. Hill, it is well known, became the chief exponent of this policy and leader of the party after Robertson's retirement in 1780; but his *Theological Lectures* remain a monument of candid orthodoxy, which has commended them to many who have no sympathy with Moderatism. Even at the very end of the century, the old Evangelical life had not died out of the Church, darkened as is the picture drawn by Rowland Hill in the *Journal* of his tour in Scotland in 1798, of the state of religion from an Evangelical point of view. The mere fact that the pulpits of the Establishment were not shut against him or Simeon of Cambridge, any more than they had been against Whitefield at an earlier date, shewed that there were still those within its pale who sympathised with their views. The Church itself certainly gave these Evangelical teachers no countenance; and an Act passed by the General Assembly in the year of Rowland Hill's first visit, effectually closed its pulpits for many a year to ministers of other Churches, whether Evangelically-minded or otherwise. But the very necessity for passing such an act proves that there was still a certain activity in the Evangelical party within the Church.

Nor are we to suppose that this party, while beaten by Robertson and his coadjutors in their attempts to regulate the policy of the Church, was at all powerless as a force within the General Assemby. On the contrary, they rallied their strength with great effect repeatedly, especially in the great debate on Schism in 1766; and again in the exciting discussions which followed Robertson's retirement, when the whole question of Patronage, and its unhappy influence upon the Church, was raised anew. The evils of the system are recognised as forcibly as ever in these discussions by some who accepted it as the law of the Church, no less than by its impugners. It was a matter of course that men like Henry Erskine should denounce the so-called ancient rights of patrons—'as old,' he said, 'as the Tory ministry of Queen Anne!' But it was significant that Dr Hardy, who was afterwards associated with Dr Hill in the leadership of the Moderate party, should in a pamphlet published during the controversy in 1782 have proposed the repeal of the Act of 1712. It seemed impossible to him that both 'this Act and the Church of Scotland should stand together.' Nothing could well indicate more strongly what an element of disturbance Patronage had been, or how little a vigorous administration of twenty years had really done to settle the disturbance. And yet it was only two years later that the General Assembly instructed its Commission to drop its remonstrance on the subject, and that the difficulty should have gone to comparative rest for nearly fifty years, destined, however, to a more terrible awakening than ever!

But no further space is left to us for even such imperfect notes as these on the later history of the Church of Scotland in the eighteenth century; and we must bring this lecture to a close. Looking back upon the facts presented to us, there is much to criticise, a good deal to deplore, but also a great deal to admire and be proud of.

No shortcomings of the Moderate clergy can ever obscure the literary lustre which they have shed around the Church, nor have we any right to allow the one to dim the other. But the higher clergy of the Church of Scotland in the eighteenth century were not merely distinguished intellectually. They developed in their social life and public career many qualities of admirable manliness, directness, and vigour. What they lacked was depth of Christian sensibility and width of Christian intelligence. It may seem to many absurd to charge them with want of the latter. But the narrowness not only of their sympathy, but of their spiritual knowledge, had much to do with their mistakes. If they had been more conversant with the movements of Christian thought, they would never have tried to guide the Church by hard and fast rules as they did. If they had known more of the motives of spiritual action, they would never have supposed it possible to restrain enthusiasm by oppression, or ecclesiastical zeal by simply turning a deaf ear to its remonstrances. There can hardly be any doubt, I think, that Robertson was disappointed by the fruits of his twenty years' administration, and retired in some degree disgusted, both with the progress of dissent and the restlessness of many of the younger clergy on his own side.[1]

It is sad, but it is true, that the chief difficulty of Scottish Presbyterianism all through its history has been to combine a cultured and catholic intelligence with enthusiasm, zeal with toleration and Christian appreciation of the motives of others. The Evangelical and rational elements in its corporate life have failed to fuse themselves together so as to brighten into a warm and earnest and yet sweet-tempered piety. The popular and the Moderate clergy of the eighteenth century stand apart. They may know each other well, and even be cordial friends, as Erskine and Robertson were; but their principles never come into union. The fire of the Evangel

---

[1] Dugald Stewart's *Life of Robertson*, Appendix, p. 195. The passage to which reference is here made has been often quoted. It is a statement made to Robertson's biographer by Sir Henry Moncrieff Wellwood of the probable reasons which suggested Robertson's retirement from the General Assembly after 1780. We cannot quote the passage in full, but it explicitly bears that Robertson was dissatisfied with the restlessness of 'the more violent men of his party, especially in regard to a scheme, into which many of them had entered zealously, for abolishing subscription to the Confession of Faith and Formula'—a scheme which, it is added, 'he declared his resolution to resist in every form.' We have not been able even to allude to the great controversy which occurred on this subject in the years preceding Robertson's retirement. The controversy was not *within* the Church courts, probably owing to the influence of the great Moderate leader; and this fact, with the demands upon our space, has precluded our touching upon it.

does not mingle with the reasonableness of philosophy. They remain apart, suspicious of each other, and judging each other with asperity. This of course is true, more or less, of parties in all Churches; but it is especially true of the two parties known as Evangelical and Moderate in the Scottish Church.

If we turn from the administrative and theological aspect of the Church to its internal character—its worship and discipline—it cannot be said that the spectacle is a pleasing one. What may be called Church life—the feeling which binds the clergy and the Christian people together in bonds of mutual action and sympathy—was very low throughout the whole century. There was not only no missionary enthusiasm, but no comprehension of missionary duty. Even so late as 1796, an overture in favour of Foreign Missions was rejected in the General Assembly. The well-known story of Dr Erskine saying to the Moderator, at the close of a speech against Missions by Mr Hamilton of Gladsmuir: 'Moderator, rax me that Bible,' belongs to this debate. It was a striking commentary on the character of the discussion. But there was not only no intelligence of the duty of Foreign Missions, but no thought of making any provision for the growing spiritual wants of the masses at home. This non-appreciation of what we now call Church extension was one of the worst 'notes' of the Moderate party, and indeed of the Church generally in the eighteenth century. Churches were not only not extended, but they were disgracefully neglected or abused. It is usual to blame the niggardliness of the Scottish proprietors and heritors for all that is abominable in the Scottish architecture of the eighteenth century; and the blame no doubt largely lay with them. But they merely reflected the general feeling. They refused money to build beautiful churches, and they allowed many old churches to be hopelessly ruined because there was no compulsion upon them in the prevalent opinion of the time to do better. The Scottish people had unhappily lost the sense, from the Reformation downwards, not only of ecclesiastical beauty, but even of ecclesiastical fitness. They had no thought of making the House of God in itself a house of holy solemnity. This was part of the reaction still unspent against the externalism of Rome, and it may have been associated with so-called spiritual feelings in the minds of some. But to a large extent it was nothing else than coarseness of taste and a want of culture; and its effects were in many ways unfavourable upon the popular habits. The attitude of the worshippers failed in reverence and even respectfulness. Devotion was conducted with a careless indifference of manner, if not of heart. The Scriptures ceased to be read as an integral part of divine service, and the singing was such as it is unnecessary to describe. Discipline for certain offences continued to be publicly administered; and although we cannot be sure that this open severity of a simpler time may not have had deterrent effects that we can now hardly estimate, we know enough to know that the general effect was not good. While little, however, can be said in favour of the devotional life or interest of the service of the Scottish Church during the eighteenth century, there can be no doubt that there was much devout feeling and earnest thoughtfulness surviving among the Scottish peasantry. The *Cottar's Saturday Night* is the touching picture of an imagination which was easily kindled alike by the humour, the pathos, and the solemnity of Scottish life. But it is no mere picture; it was a reality in many a home, no less than in that of Burns's own father, a man of singular clearness and manliness of religious thought, as is shewn by the catechism he prepared for his children. It is to this period also—it deserves to be remembered—that we are indebted for those Paraphrases from Scripture which have continued to be sung in the Scottish Presbyterian service. Much may be forgiven an age which gave us the Paraphrases, the plaintive and measured beauty of many of which, such as the second and thirtieth, and the spiritual felicity and completeness of thought of others, like the sixtieth, have always appeared to me of rare excellence in sacred verse.

The first movement to prepare metrical versions of certain portions of Holy Writ began as early as 1742; but it was not till many years afterwards—in fact, not till 1781—that the Paraphrases were first used in public worship, after having been revised and added to especially by Logan, the well-known minister of South Leith; and Cameron, minister of Kirknewton. The existing collection bears traces everywhere of the tasteful genius of Logan, which admits of no question, whatever may be the truth as to the charges of plagiarism with which his name is unhappily associated.

There was a lack of open vision in the Church of Scotland during the eighteenth century. She failed to realise the greatness of her mission as a National Church. She failed to witness as she ought to have done to the living love of a Divine Saviour. But her spiritual coldness was a feature of the age to which she belonged; no Church was quite exempt from it. And with all her deficiencies, she has claims upon our gratitude and respect. If wanting in zeal, she grew in toleration. If disliking enthusiasms, she cultivated literature. If she had little Church life, she prized freedom and good sense, and wrought no new bonds for the Christian conscience. If her clergy were not adequately inspired by self-denying devotion in dealing with the human soul and reclaiming spiritual wastes, they presented examples of moderation and thoughtfulness and Christian charity. And Scotland would have been a poorer country in many ways, if many of the Moderate clergy had not lived to advance its fame and illustrate the Church to which they belonged.

ST GILES' LECTURES.

FIRST SERIES—THE SCOTTISH CHURCH.

LECTURE X.

THE CHURCH OF THE NINETEENTH CENTURY
TO 1843.

By the Rev. A. H. CHARTERIS, D.D., Professor of Biblical Criticism in the University of Edinburgh; one of Her Majesty's Chaplains.

IT is not too much to say that no previous period in the eventful annals of the Church of Scotland is more memorable than the three-and-forty years with which this lecture has to do.

It is not a period rendered remarkable by a literary galaxy, such as that of which the previous lecture took note. When we look to the Church from 1800 to 1825, we can see among its leaders only one name associated with the highest success in any department of general literature. That one exception is Principal Hill, who, as a leader of the Church, was strangely deaf to the voice of the people, and strangely flexible in the hands of some of the silent leaders of his party; but, as a lecturer on theology, has left a treatise which is a noble monument of fairness, clearness, and learning. Dr John Erskine, who ended his honoured life in 1803, and Sir Harry Moncreiff, who followed Erskine as the head of what was known as the Evangelical party, were ministers and ecclesiastics of the highest stamp, upright, wise, and consistent; but—unlike Carstares or Robertson—they draw more repute from the Church than they give to it. Its annals must record their names with honour, but they do not lend it a lustre from their fame won in other fields. So, too, it was in the later years. The historical works of Dr George Cook, who succeeded Hill in the leadership of the Moderate party, are candid and clear, but they are chiefly remembered because, as we shall see, their author was a prominent actor in memorable scenes. I do not know that any one of even Dr Chalmers' books is likely to have permanent value, although a select few of his greatest sermons will probably always be known and quoted. Other names will occur as we proceed; but this much we may say at the outset, that our period is not remarkable from a literary point of view.

It is the changes which were effected in the years 1800-1843 that make them memorable. Within and without, the Church was revolutionised. In her separate parishes, and as a corporate body, she did and she suffered much. We have to shew what good work she did, and also how her calamities came from her own doings. No former lecture tells of a time when she was so much left to herself. And therefore, when we treat of the events of this period, we cannot ascribe Scottish errors to foreign influence; for they were Scotland's very own. I hope to be judged with consideration for the exceeding difficulty of my task.

(1) The first subject which rises into view is the change in the school system of Scotland. After a century of neglect, the Church set herself to make the existing schools efficient. Hence began—during our period—the annual Presbyterial examination of schools, and after a little while (1819), the Annual Report upon them, which continued with excellent results until the Act of 1872 abolished the ancient connection between church and school. Next (1803), the school salary of eleven

pounds, which had been the figure since the Revolution, was raised to twenty-two pounds (subject to revision, according to the price of grain, every twenty-five years); and it was made imperative on the heritors of every parish to provide a dwelling-house for the teacher, 'consisting of not more than two apartments, including the kitchen!' This statutory provision was happily supplemented in many parishes. It was during our period that the Church of Scotland began to see that taxes are not all, and to realise what a mine of wealth there is in the heart of a willing people; and one of the first shafts driven down into the latent riches of that mine concerned education. The voluntary efforts of the Church were guided for sixteen years by two men whose names may well be enrolled in the list of her worthies. The first was Principal Baird of Edinburgh University, who stirred the whole country by proving that in the Highlands and Islands alone, out of a total population of between three and four hundred thousand, there were twenty-eight thousand between the ages of six and twenty who could not read, and eighty-four thousand of the same age who could not write. For many a day the learned Principal toiled in behalf of the long-neglected Highlanders; and he gradually succeeded in evoking so great liberality that not only in the Highlands, but everywhere, the country was covered with a network of schools. Normal schools were in operation; school-libraries (why so much neglected in later times?) were founded in many places; returns of Presbyterial examination of between two and three thousand schools were called in every year; and about 1842 the Church was nearer to John Knox's scheme, as regards her ordinary schools, than she had ever been before. Principal Baird was efficiently aided by Dr Norman Macleod, whose fervid appeals, like those of his illustrious son and namesake, were a blending of common-sense and Christian charity and infectious zeal, such as stirred all hearts. With the Gaelic Bible—itself a product of this century—and the 'Celtic Collection' of suitable pieces for school-reading, the schoolmasters sent forth by the learned Principal and the eloquent minister enabled for the first time the children of one-third of Scotland to read in their own tongue the wonderful works of God. It was not till after the Rebellion of 1745 that the Protestant Reformation was carried into many districts of the Highlands; and even at the beginning of our century men printed their congratulations of themselves on journeying without molestation among the hamlets and scattered cottages of Celtic Scotland! I do not know that in any country or district there was so great a progress as took place between 1743 and 1843 in those parts of our own land; and it was mainly due to the minister, the catechist, and the school.

(2) In regard to Sunday-schools also, the Church passed through nothing less than a revolution. There were some Sunday-schools in Scotland before Robert Raikes—just a hundred years ago—began his noble work. But the Church had never taken up the subject; and in the very end of last century, when she found that the work which belonged to her was being done without her, she was stung into a most unbecoming passion. It is far from edifying to be told that Dr Hugh Blair lent his gifts of style to the composition of the extraordinary harangue called a 'Pastoral Admonition' (in 1799), which was meant to sweep from the kingdom all preachers unauthorised by the Church, and all Sunday-school teachers who had no commission from the Presbytery of the bounds. The Assembly intended to crush the Haldanes; to keep Rowland Hill from the pulpits; and to scare the people from countenancing those adventurers who wanted to teach the Bible to their children. The Haldanes were two gentlemen of property and of old family, who had given up an honourable career on the sea in order to promote religion in Scotland. Ready to spend and to be spent—Robert Haldane alone gave £70,000 in ten years to the cause of religion—men of zeal, energy, fortitude, and faith, they did more to bring

Scotland into living sympathy with missions in heathendom, and with the reviving faith in the Churches of the Reformation, than any court of any Church in the beginning of this century. Though they were not always right, nor always gentle in expression, they were always upright and self-regulating men whom no party could claim. As at the beginning of their life they defied the careless parish ministers and the angry Assembly, so at the end of it they publicly denounced the Voluntaries who courted martyrdom by refusing to pay the Annuity Tax which supported the National Church in Edinburgh. When they went over the land preaching love and good works, and with such power that Sunday-schools and prayer-meetings started up behind them as they went, they were only doing what the Church herself ought to have done.

The Sabbath-school movement was not paralysed by the Pastoral. Schools grew and multiplied; they became recognised as an adjunct of the Christian Church; but it was not till 1850 that the Church of Scotland had the courage to undo her mistake of 1799, and take cognisance of the Sunday-schools under the superintendence of her ministers throughout the land. It is easier to do wrong than to undo it; and when one sees the youngest and least experienced members of congregations intrusted with the responsible task of teaching those not much younger than themselves, it is impossible not to feel that the Church grievously erred in allowing the system to grow to its present dimensions without her control. Is it not possible for the Assembly to go back to one part of the bad Act which closed last century, and to offer the supervision and examination of her Presbyteries to both teachers and taught; not to check or choke, but to develop the efforts made in the Sunday-school to discharge the Church's duty to the young?

(3) Though the Church was not formally concerned in the Apocrypha controversy—for the British and Foreign Bible Society, which caused it, was not connected with any Church—

the dispute was so keen, and sent its roots so deep, that no sketch of the Church life of the time would be complete without some notice of it. The British and Foreign Bible Society was founded for the circulation of the Holy Scriptures alone; but with the view of securing a readier entrance for the Bible into some countries, the Society, from about the year 1813, had given money grants to aid foreign associations in circulating the Scriptures with the Apocrypha, and had itself issued Bibles, with the Apocrypha sometimes interspersed, sometimes appended. A still more serious fact, which in the end led to greater bitterness, was that the practice was concealed. Contributors were not made aware of the tactics of the directorate; and for this the permanent officials were to blame. Robert Haldane had arranged for a French Bible with canonical Scriptures only, and as usual had contributed generously to it; but even into it the Apocrypha was thrust without his knowledge. When this became known in Scotland, the Scottish contributors were indignant, and after fruitless private remonstrance (continued for three or four years), they stopped their contributions as the shortest way of bringing the Society to a right mind. There was of course a stormy controversy; and pamphlets were strewn thick as leaves in autumn. The Scottish eventually won the day—won it step by step; and the Bible Society at last agreed to promulgate a resolution that 'the fundamental law of the Society which limits its operations to the circulation of the Holy Scriptures, is distinctly recognised as excluding the circulation of the Apocrypha;' and that 'no pecuniary aid be given henceforth to any Society circulating the Apocrypha.' The leader of Scotland in this matter was Andrew Thomson—one of those men whose power is quite inadequately represented by the printed works they leave behind them. His treatment of 'Infidelity' and of 'Universal Pardon' is lacking in mellowness and self-repression, and his 'Catechism for Young Communicants' wants simplicity, tenderness, and fervour. To appreciate him, we of this generation must go back to the generation which it was his highest ambition and his undoubted attainment to 'serve by the will of God.' When we stand anywhere on Scottish ground from 1820 to 1830, there can be no doubt that the greatest personal power in the pulpit, on the platform, and in the press, was wielded by that generous, fearless, wise, and unselfish man.

The chief result of the Apocrypha controversy upon the Church of Scotland, whose fortunes we are following, was that it publicly severed the ministers and members of the Church from their Dissenting brethren. Up till that time, the missionary and philanthropic societies had been national, not ecclesiastical; but when the Scottish branch of the Bible Society was broken up, the Churchmen, with scarcely an exception, were found in the new Scottish Bible societies; almost all the Dissenters, save the Haldanes, clung to their London connection.

(4) From home-work let us now turn to foreign missions. It is a Church's primary duty to fulfil the Redeemer's last command by preaching the Gospel to all nations. But the Confessions of the Churches of the Reformation are all singularly deficient, usually dumb, on this matter; and the Westminster Confession is no exception. Except that the General Assembly, in 1699, 'missioned' four ministers to accompany the ill-fated Darien expedition, not only to labour among the Scotch settlers, but also for the conversion of the natives, and in 1700 touchingly encouraged them, I do not remember that the Church of Scotland had ever specially addressed itself to foreign missions. The Society for Propagating Christian Knowledge (1709) was indeed specially authorised and encouraged by the Church from the first, but it did little for foreign missions, though (in terms of a special bequest) it had usually a single missionary—David Brainerd was one—labouring among the American Indians. At the end of last century, missionary societies not connected with any particular Church sprang up everywhere; the London

Missionary Society (of which a Scottish minister was the originating spirit), in 1795; the Church Missionary Society, in 1799; the Scottish Missionary Society, in 1796, and in the same year, the Glasgow Missionary Society. The Edinburgh Tract Society, the first in the kingdom, was founded in 1794. In the early part of this century, the work of those societies, and of some others for Jewish Missions and for special objects (such as one for the importation and education of Africans and Asiatics), was keenly taken up by many people in Scotland. Deputies from England came to plead the cause of the English societies, and their Scottish rivals or friends also appealed to public favour. The Serampore missionaries, and many others who laboured in the foreign field, had some of their first and warmest friends in Scotland. The efforts made in Scotland for foreign missions before the General Assembly moved in their behalf, were by no means contemptible. For example, in 1817 —I take a specimen, to which many might be added—there was raised in Leith, for Foreign and Jewish Missions and for the Bible Society, upwards of £250.

But there was great significance in the Assembly's action in sending Dr Duff to India. It meant that henceforth the Church of Scotland was to be organised as a missionary association; and that its own courts were to be the directors of the operations carried on abroad.

It marks a new position in the General Assembly, when we find its admirable Pastoral Letter from the pen of Dr Inglis, the founder of the mission, thus undoing, in 1824, the rude rebuke of Missions in 1796: 'Having our own hope in Christ and His salvation, it would be altogether unnatural that we should not have a desire to communicate this blessed hope to those who, with ourselves, have one common Father—whom one God hath created. Is it possible that we can rely on the merits of Christ as a Saviour, for the exercise of that mercy and grace, by which alone we can be delivered from everlasting misery, and made partakers of everlasting happiness, without an earnest desire to make known the way of salvation through Him to others who partake of our common nature? .... Or is it possible that the assurance, which is given us, of the ultimate and universal prevalence of the Redeemer's kingdom, should not establish our minds in the use of all wise and righteous means for hastening that happy time when the knowledge of the Lord shall cover the earth?'

There are few things in the history of the Scottish Church more delightful than the conjunction of men who founded her Foreign Mission. It was no party movement; no Moderate denounced missions, even on the plea that education must go before the Gospel; no Evangelical needed to bid the Moderator 'rax him the Bible.' The mind of Dr Inglis, from which the scheme started, like the goddess of wisdom in ancient story fully armed, was the mind of the greatest of the Moderates of his generation; the missionary, Dr Duff, who threw up the certainty of a distinguished career at home, and went away through perils by sea and perils by land, to a career in which his ardour was only paralleled by his industry, and his great aims by his great success, was an Evangelical who owed his conversion to an echo of the teaching of Simeon.

The principle on which the India Mission was organised was new in itself, and had a completeness which new ideas only acquire when they arise in a master-mind. The principle was that, while the Gospel is to be preached to all who will hear, education, with the definite aim of raising up a native pastorate, is to be an integral part of the work of the mission. Education was therefore not to be elementary only, but catholic and complete. Other Churches have since that time more or less adopted the principle; and even those which did not adopt it are ready to testify to its being an invaluable part of the work the Christian Church has to do in India. The five who entered the Institution the first day Dr Duff opened the doors, had swelled before 1839 into eight hundred; and in our own time a far greater attendance on classes conducted on the same principles, shews how well the programme has stood the test of time and trial.

(5) Let us now turn from these general subjects to try to picture the position of the parish minister in the beginning of this century. That not many ministers were as little concerned about their duties, and as easily induced to find their chief interest outside of their own parishes, as was Dr Alexander Carlyle, the keen-witted incumbent of Inveresk, may be taken for granted. That good men of another stamp lived, and laboured, and died in the charge to which they were first appointed, we know from the Memorials of Dr Somerville, whose life in Jedburgh was of this sort until he completed ninety honoured years. Up till 1810, many of them had incomes as small as Goldsmith's Village Pastor, but a government grant of £10,000 a year sufficed to raise the minimum to £150. Some of them were professors as well as parish ministers; but after many years of dispute on the subject of 'Pluralities,' the not very logical result was reached, that a professor might not hold a quiet country parish, however near the college, though he might occupy a city charge, however laborious, as well as his chair.

The country owed much of its progress in literature and agriculture and comfort to the parish minister in those old days. Perhaps the greatest stimulus to social progress was the institution of savings-banks by Henry Duncan, minister of Ruthwell. He is one of the best possible specimens of the older type of country minister; a preacher who began with no high idea of his mission, but whose conviction and fervour deepened through the honest work of forty years; a man of science; a writer of readable books; founder of one of the most influential of country newspapers; and above all, originator of those noble institutions for the nursing of the poor man's savings, with which his name will be always associated while industry strives for independence.

When we turn to more directly ministerial work, we find one of its chief departments in the practice of catechising, which was usual at the beginning of the century. Every group of houses or district was the scene of a day of visitation, when the minister personally invited each household to meet him in an appointed central place—a barn or farm-kitchen—where not only the children but all adults who were willing to undergo the ordeal, were examined on the words and meaning of the Shorter Catechism. In some cases, the minister spent the night at the successive centres of visitation, so as to make a regular missionary tour of his parish. The minister's visit made an anxious time for many a man and woman as well as for every child; but in faithful hands it was an occasion of useful teaching, both doctrinal and practical. Catechising still lingers in some districts, especially in the North. In two country parishes in the South I found it one of the most interesting and profitable things which it fell to me to do; but over the country, as a whole, it is extinct; and the minister's annual visit brings only a short service of reading and prayer. The Sunday-school is not so robust an ordinance as the domestic and district catechising which it has superseded; and it is scarcely doubtful that it does less to bring the public opinion of the parish to bear on the success or failure of the home-training of the children.

We turn from pastoral work to preaching. There is not much doubt that, in the beginning of the century, the ordinary preaching was of a cold and semi-philosophical kind; a teaching of ethics, with Scripture used as an illustration rather than relied upon as an authority. But the century was not many years old when a change began, and with wonderful rapidity spread over the land. The work of Simeon and Hill and the Haldanes was no doubt in many cases effectual; but it would have done little had not causes of more general power been in operation. The French Revolution, which stirred society to its very depths, and made all thoughtful men consider their ways, brought the mass of the people to a new study of the Bible and a new appreciation of the Gospel of Jesus Christ. In many men unknown to fame, that change which all the world can read in the life of Chalmers was undergone; and he who began to teach in sermons easily written, and heard, and forgotten, was striving ere middle life was reached to utter the thoughts that struggled within him, and to declare the message of the living God. The brilliant career of Chalmers, and the herculean, unselfish labours of Andrew Thomson, were beyond all comparison powerful in guiding this new-born zeal. But the change was not confined to such as they. The party which by tradition bore the name of Evangelical was not distinct, either in doctrine or in practice, from that which inherited the other name of Moderate. While Chalmers was toiling in the wynds of Glasgow, and Thomson was smiting hip and thigh the advocates of the Apocrypha or of gradual abolition of slavery, the chief of the Moderate party was maturing the great project of a mission from the Church of Scotland to the heathen. We all find it easier to give by sight than to give by faith; but the greater work of directing the sympathy of the Scottish Church to realms unseen was distinctively the work of the Moderates. It was a Moderate of the Moderates, Dr Bryce, who laboured so hard in India to bring a mission to Calcutta; and not only was it the wise head of the Moderates at home who planned the mission; but of those to whom, in 1839, Dr Duff dedicated his book on India, two-thirds were of the same party. The great missionary records upon his page of dedication the names of the committee: Brunton (convener from the time when Dr Inglis died), Gordon, Chalmers, Ritchie, William Muir, James Grant, John Hunter, John Paul, and John Bruce, 'under whose wise, paternal, and prayerful counsels the missionary enterprise of the Church has hitherto been conducted with such unbroken harmony of design, and such multiplied tokens and pledges of the divine approbation.' And of those nine men, only three left the Church in 1843. When I know those things, and know how the eloquent pleading of another Moderate, Robertson of Ellon, was widely circulated and of great power in behalf of the India Mission, I must express my deep regret that even in our own day some writers upon missions charge all manner of public and private misdeeds upon the Moderates. There could be no better authority than Dr Inglis, of whom Duff well said that 'his thoughts were never expressed till weighed and re-weighed in the balance of a penetrating judgment;' and he says: 'What I maintain is, that the crime of either contradicting or culpably neglecting the peculiar doctrines of the Gospel, is not imputable to any such number of the established clergy of Scotland as to give the slightest ground for supposing that ecclesiastical establishments have a tendency to discourage Evangelical ministrations. My observation during what has now been rather a long life, entitles me to say that, in the course of the last forty years, there has been a gradual approximation, on the part of the clergy, of what are called the two sides of our Church, to a closer resemblance of one another in all the great features of their public teaching—and it must not be forgotten that any opposite testimony which seems to be borne by our Dissenting brethren refers to a case respecting which their means of knowledge must be comparatively small.'[1] If proof of the truth of those wise words were wanted, I should point any inquirer to the fact that all the missionary, and almost all the active committees of the Assembly, had Moderate conveners, in the very year of the Veto, 1834. Dr Brunton presided over Church Accommodation, as well as over Missions to India. Principal Macfarlan was convener of the Colonial Scheme; and Principal Baird, of the Education Scheme.

(6) All parties in the Church combined in some depositions for false doctrine. Let me speak of one. Edward

---

[1] Inglis, *Vindication of Ecclesiastical Establishments*, p. 232.

Irving seems to me, as I look back over those years with such light as I can cast upon them, to have been the man of greatest genius that played his part while they passed over the world. I have heard from the lips of one who knew him well, that he said, as he paced the college quadrangle in his student days: 'There seems to me to be a new style of preaching possible;' and of that new style his sermons remain the first, last, and only specimen. It is a strange blending of exposition, exhortation, poetry, pathos, and scorn; now, in lofty speculation, speeding like a meteor high overhead; now, as though it were the forked lightning, cleaving at our very side some hoary erection of human fraud or folly; and now melting in the softest tears of human sympathy. Nothing that Chalmers ever wrote rises to the height of passionate meditation which is sustained through Irving's *Discourse on the Book of Psalms;* there is not in all that has ever been spoken from a Presbyterian pulpit since Maclaurin's *Glorying in the Cross of Christ*, anything to compare with Irving's *Ordination Charge* in the little chapel at London Wall; and in some of his *Discourses on the Incarnation* there is a grandeur of thought which seems to me to lift even the reader into a purer air. What it must have been to hear him, there still live those to tell who stood on the hillside for many hours, caring not how the sun crossed the sky while the spell of the great preacher was upon them; but even those who never heard him can say that the old prophetic fire has not come so near us as when Irving lived and spoke. His oldest friend, who has been so lately laid to rest in their native Annandale, and who also brought from the banks of the Solway some such scorn and pathos as one had believed to be impossible save on the banks of the Jordan, never ceased to say of him: 'He strove with all the force that was in him to be a Christian minister. He might have been so many things; not a speaker only, but a doer—the leader of hosts of men. . . . His was the freest, brotherliest, bravest human soul mine ever came in contact with. I call him, on the whole, the best man I have ever, after trial enough, found in this world, or hope to find.' It was this man that the Church he loved with so romantic affection exiled from her bounds. It was really because his enthusiasm had carried him away, so that the decent order of worship in his church was destroyed by a Babel of many voices, which his simple heart believed to be the primitive gift of tongues restored to a long self-impoverished Church; but the avowed ground of deposition was that he believed, and in undoubtedly harsh words declared, our Lord's humanity to have been preserved in sinlessness by the abundant gift of the Holy Spirit, and not by the Incarnate Deity of the Divine Son in His Person. Surely never was there better ground for toleration than in this heresy, which was only the struggle of a loving believer to find that his Redeemer was 'in all points tempted like as we are, yet without sin.'

(7) A question which came into prominence in the very end of last century, was one which has had more momentous results in the Church than any of those already mentioned. It was the question as to the way of enlarging the old parochial system of the Church, so as to keep pace with the growth of the population. There were tens of thousands growing up for whom no church accommodation was provided, and who could not be invited to come to churches that would not contain them if they came. But they were not actually invited. Home heathenism was the consequence. The enormous population made it impossible for the old ideal of the parish minister, as the friend and pastor of all his parishioners, to be realised. Another evil result was found in Pauperism. In the old time, the funds of the kirk-session—drawn from the weekly collections in church—were sufficient to maintain the poor of the parish; and the eighteenth century was more than half done before the power of the heritors and kirk-session to assess the parish for the poor was called into exercise. But as Dissent attracted the population, the collections in the parish church

became too weak for the burden on them, and in large populations, especially in the south of Scotland, assessments crept in. As Chalmers brooded upon this fact, there grew up in his mind an enthusiastic admiration of the old parochial system, and an exceeding bitterness against all and sundry who could be charged with destroying or mutilating it. The masses who belonged to no church—many of them lying low and besotted on the ground, crying for food from legal funds—became a nightmare and a daily torture to him. When he went to Glasgow and found himself in the Tron parish of 11,200 inhabitants, with only 3500 of them connected with any church, he declared war against every system and every practice which made it impossible for him to carry the Gospel to all for whom, as minister of the parish, he was nominally responsible. He stigmatised the Town Councils, which exacted such rents for sittings, that the poor man could not take his rightful place in the pew; he denounced Dissenters, who were fostering the idea that it was enough to open churches for those who might choose to come; he rolled out his sonorous anathemas against the unpatriotic Scots who would not see that legal relief of the poor was destroying the independence and the provident habits of the people. And what he preached, he practised. There was a new church—St John's—opened for him in Glasgow, in which the great orator was allowed to have his own way; with the result of shewing that the parochial ministry drew the home heathen to the Church of Christ, and that in his large and poor parish of ten thousand inhabitants, the sum spent on the poor was never more than ninepence per head of the population.

In whatever light we view Chalmers as a parish minister, he is the greatest man who has ever borne that official name. As Dr Inglis adapted Knox's principles of church and school to India, Dr Chalmers applied them to Scotland with a generous devotedness which swept away every obstacle, and a prayerful patience which never doubted of the final triumph. He was not so unapproachably great when crowds were hanging on his lips, as when by the power of a great conviction, and the example of heroic personal toil, he moved the hearts of his people, as one man, to rally round him, to act for him, to subdivide the parish into districts, to make a record of the state of every family, to make the parish-church and the district-school centres of living personal influence upon young and old, so as to verify his own happy phrases, by 'sweetening the breath of society' through 'the omnipotence of loving-kindness.' It is well to know what men thought and said of him: it does us good to remember that Jeffrey said Chalmers' power made him understand that of Demosthenes; and that the keen and critical Lockhart for a time forgot to analyse, and could only say: 'In presence of such a spirit, subjection is a triumph; I was proud to feel my hardened nerves creep and vibrate, and my blood freeze and boil while he spake, as they were wont to do in the early innocent years.' But these things might become mere traditions, as in the case of Kemble or of Edmund Kean, whereas the principles he revived, expounded, expanded, and verified can never cease to guide men, while churches toil to bring the wanderers to the fold of Christ.

When, therefore, the General Assembly, in 1834, appointed him to direct Church Extension, it was well known that the illustrious Home Missionary was about to move the kingdom to imitate his own example, and to provide not only churches but ministrations for all the people, poor and rich, within the shores of Scotland. The results were immediate and amazing; chapels sprang up on every side (187 in four years); while the parishes which had been united in raising the needed funds had learned their strength, their separate and their united strength, and were filled with the glow of a common enthusiasm. No longer units in action, they were now fused in one living organism, as the members of one body.

It was a fair and goodly scene; but in its advancement to

perfection, the Church was raising up enemies and difficulties that strewed it with wreck and ruin.

First of all, the Dissenters took alarm, and hence came the 'Voluntary Controversy.' The Seceders had done good work in many a parish where they had 'seceded' from the corruptions of the Church in the hope of seeing it amended, or where they had afforded 'Relief' from the evils of Patronage. But they were changed since the first days. There had grown up in the minds of Dissenters an idea that they had some sort of vested interest in the corruptions and weaknesses of the Established Church; an idea that if these were swept away, there would be an unfair blow inflicted on those denominations which were founded as a remedy for them. Thus the still living historian of the Secession Church says: '*The Church Extension Scheme, which was aimed alike at the prosperity of both denominations (Secession and Relief), had led the two bodies to combined deliberation and concerted action, and increased their mutual esteem.*' It is curious that an attempt to benefit the nation through the Church should be regarded as an attack upon Dissent. Yet so it was. It was impossible but that some collision should occur when Dr Chalmers tried to increase the Establishment, because many were ready to say that Dissenting Churches were doing all that is needed. To dispose of that objection, Dr Chalmers proclaimed the fact that men were falling away from all Churches; and at the same time he shewed that the very principle of Dissent, as only meeting a demand, incapacitates it to supply the deepest needs of a nation. In oft-repeated and now well-known arguments, and with unnecessarily stinging epithets applied to his opponents, Chalmers shewed that an endowment is equivalent to the poor man's seat-rent: and that its existence enables a minister within the definite territory of his parish, for which the endowment is provided, to go from house to house offering the Gospel without money and without price. He called this an 'aggressive ministry,' which seeks out and 'excavates' the home-heathen; and he stigmatised Dissent as the means of providing only an 'attractive ministry.'

Thus came the actual collision between the Church and Dissent, which in its deepest meaning was largely political. Scottish Voluntaryism is mainly a political result of the fermentation among the masses during this century; its dogma of the severance of the ruler from religion originated with the French Revolution, and is a part of the democratic upheaving which led to revolution on the Continent. Perhaps it may be well on this hazardous subject to quote the words of an admitted authority. In his life of Dr John Brown, Dr Cairns says: 'It was not till the close of the eighteenth century that the impulse given by the American and French Revolutions, and the impressions made by the constant discussion of the claims of the Roman Catholics in the British Parliament, began to produce a wide and conscious divergence amongst the Seceders from the ground practically occupied by their fathers.'[1] That ground, as is well known, was the support of the Establishment principle.

There had been a solitary voice raised for this political Voluntaryism so early as 1806 by a seceding minister in Newcastle, and there had been much unseen preparation of Dissenters for the coming struggle; but the blast which roused the conflict was a sermon by the Rev. Andrew Marshall, Kirkintilloch, in 1829. He sounded an assault upon National Establishments of religion as unnecessary, improper, unjust, impolitic, a secularising of the Church of Christ, and a setting aside of the positive ordinance of the Saviour by which the Church is to be self-supporting. In his most highly wrought passage there is an elaborate contrast between the Church portrayed in the New Testament and the Church in the condition which he describes as 'incorporated with the State.' It closes thus: 'The one is the bride, the Lamb's wife; the other is more

---

[1] Cairns' *Life of Brown*, p. 169.

nearly allied to her whose name is "Mystery"—the woman who is arrayed in purple and scarlet colour, decked with gold and precious stones and pearls, and who has in her hand a golden cup full of filthiness and abominations.'

It was not likely that words like these would be forgiven; and the defenders of the Church rushed to the rescue. Orators on each side went to and fro as with a fiery cross over the land; and courses of lectures in defence of the Church were delivered everywhere. Those which were delivered in the great cities and afterwards published, are remarkable for ability, and also for strength of sweeping statement. They are fair specimens of the intellectual power and intellectual ferocity which have so often characterised ecclesiastical polemics in our country. The immediate politics of the struggle centred in the Church's claim of state-endowment for her new chapels, and in the Dissenting opposition to that claim. The Dissenters gained the day. Exceeding bitterness was the natural result. And when the Non-Intrusion party tried, about 1839, to secure the help of the Dissenters in curtailing Patronage and asserting Spiritual Independence, those Dissenters, headed by Dr John Brown—one of the most honoured of ministers, but the fiercest of Voluntaries—declared that they could not as citizens consent to liberate an Established Church from national supervision and control. This curious position meant, that being Christian Voluntaries, they wanted to play the part of an oppressing 'Cæsar'! And thus the majority of the Church, thwarted in their claim of Endowment, and unaided in their struggle for Non-Intrusion, were driven to assert their views of Spiritual Independence more loudly. In this way, as Dr Cairns puts it: 'The Dissenters suspended their own exertions to diffuse Voluntary principles, believing that the reforming party in the Establishment were doing their work' (p. 196).

(8) We have seen that politics gave a great part of its force to

the Voluntary Controversy; but we must now say that secular politics originated and shaped the Veto Act, from which the cry of Spiritual Independence and eventually the Free Church arose. Politics came in necessarily at that stage. The Reform Bill of 1832 gave the people new power in the State; and they naturally expected greater power in the Church which had always been the people's Church. The Reform Bill did more; it inspired the Voluntaries to denounce the Church with fresh vigour as a remnant of feudalism that should not be allowed to survive in the glorious days of the people's liberty. The friends of the Church were compelled to think how they could vindicate and popularise the Establishment so as to increase its power for good. The Moderate party, led by Dr George Cook, proposed to call into practical use the long disused but never abolished right of the congregations to present *objections of whatever nature* against the minister who had received a presentation from the patron; of those objections, the Church courts to be the judges. This was a significant though insufficient tribute to the change of the times, and a confession that the rule of Robertson and Hill had unduly repressed the people's rights.

But the popular party in the Church felt that more than this was needed. The policy on which they decided was the Veto Act of the General Assembly, proposed by Dr Chalmers in 1833, and carried on the motion of Lord Moncreiff in 1834. The Veto Act provided that, when the majority of the male heads of families, being communicants, dissented without reasons from the nomination of a minister presented by the patron, the nomination was null and void. Its key-note was that *dissent without reasons* prevented any further proceedings in the settlement; so that the presentee was rejected without any trial of his qualifications by the courts of the Church. I am far from suggesting that the wish to popularise the Church was wholly political. True sympathy with all that is best in her history led naturally to it. But in the particular form of action which was adopted, we see the power of secular politics. The natural course would have been to stand on the old lines of the Church of Scotland; to object to Patronage as a grievance and a burden, and thus to constrain the Reformed Parliament to extend the ecclesiastical suffrage. But this would have been inconvenient for the new ministry. 'There is nothing,' says Dr M'Crie, 'that the Voluntaries dread so much as the abolition of Patronage.' And the Voluntaries were a large and resolute part of the new ministry's following. It was the object of the members of the ministry, therefore, to keep the matter out of Parliament. Brougham, it is said, was eager to get the Church to try her own powers; and certainly his irrelevant start to the floor of the House of Lords to eulogise the Veto as soon as it was passed, and to declare it 'safe and beneficial and in every way desirable,' looks very like this. There can be no doubt that Jeffrey (Lord Advocate) and Cockburn (Solicitor-General) threw all their weight into the scale. 'I am for the Veto,' said Cockburn, 'and as what we are to stand upon finally.' But they would all have been of little weight had there not been in Scotland a man of the highest character and of undoubted devotion to the Church, who was an unswerving upholder of Patronage and a leading Liberal. It was, unquestionably, Lord Moncreiff's attachment to the Church and to Patronage, rather than his Liberalism, which chiefly swayed him. But the result, in his advocacy of the Veto, as the plan which would least injure Patronage, united him with the Liberal politicians. Cockburn says: 'I hear his evidence before the Patronage Committee not only converted the Tory members to the Veto, but the Anti-Patronage men to Patronage.' Upon Lord Moncreiff rests the chief responsibility for the ills that so nearly ruined the Church he loved so well. He pledged his reputation as a great lawyer in behalf of the Church's power to pass the Veto Act; and with ill-fated persuasiveness he urged that if ever the Church went to Parliament at all, the proper time would be when litigation had proved that the Veto Act was wrong, because beyond her own powers. So it came about that, by the lay-politicians, the Veto Act was made a law of the Church.

By the lay-politicians almost alone. There was no living ecclesiastic of sufficient power to hold his own, not to speak of shaping the counsels of the party. Andrew Thomson had always assailed Patronage itself; and had he lived, it is little likely that he would have yielded to this desire to maintain it. When a proposal to abolish slavery by slow stages was all but carried, his famous speech, with its 'Give me the hurricane rather than the pestilence,' took a public meeting by storm, and made the movement for instant abolition, with all its dangers, to be triumphant, in spite of the fears of politicians. One can imagine how he would have spurned the Veto. Chalmers was the only outstanding man, and he was an unwilling convert to the Veto. He wanted anything rather; wanted popular decisions by the Assembly under the old law; wanted to go to Parliament for an Act to make assurance doubly sure. But he was all for Patronage, characteristically saying that congregations are fit to give a 'gregarious consent,' but not to give a gregarious initiative. There was but one minister in Scotland—he was not in the Established Church—who could dare to speak all his mind; and it was no common mind. Dr M'Crie, the biographer of Knox and Melville, and the bosom friend of Andrew Thomson, said: 'A Tory ministry forged our chains; a Whig ministry refuses, when it is in power, to strike them off. Which of them are most criminal? We hold the former as enemies; we denounce the latter as traitors.'

And so, under a mistaken belief that it was in the Church's power, the Veto Act was passed, to gratify the people, to outflank the Dissenters, to preserve Patronage, to save the Whig ministry from trouble. Though Dr Cook argued in 1833 that it was *ultra vires*, and would be overturned in the courts of law, the dissent of the Moderate party in 1834 does not raise that question; but there was left on record by the Dean of Faculty, John Hope, a biting dissent, declaring that any presentee rejected by the people, and not having his qualifications tried by the Church courts, would have a legal right to the stipend and all other rights appertaining thereto.

And so it came about, as we shall see. But meanwhile, we must speak of another rash course to which the sense of the greatness of the Christian people, and of the Church's duty to them, prompted the Church. The taunts of the Voluntaries caused that to be badly done which might have taken another and a better shape. The chief taunt was, that an Established Church is fettered by the State and cannot expand herself—cannot erect new parochial charges as an increasing population requires. To meet this, the Church's ill-advised proceeding was to assume to herself the power of making new parochial charges, so far as to connect an ecclesiastical district with an unendowed chapel, and to give the minister a seat in Church courts. Chalmers was again overruled. He at first denounced the idea of admitting unendowed chapels to 'the high places of the Establishment,' and he knew that all his plea in behalf of Endowment as the poor man's seat-rent was annihilated by this new measure. But it was very tempting. The Church had been established before she was endowed; so that it was a gallant attempt to assert her original power of recognising charges irrespective of Endowment; and as Chalmers believed that Endowment could never be raised by the contributions of the people, and as he was tired waiting for the State, he consented to this impatient enactment. The daring deed was done repeatedly. In 1833, the Assembly admitted ministers of those Highland churches to which a yearly Parliamentary grant was given; in 1834, it admitted at one sweep all ministers of chapels; and in 1839, it received ministers of the Associate Synod of Seceders. On the first occasion (in 1833), Dr Cook was not alive to the importance of the step, and acquiesced, though, it is said, against his better judgment.

One solitary dissent, by the Rev. W. R. Pirie of Dyce, remains as a proof of his sagacity and his courage. He was the first in Church and State to see what all Scotland soon learned in bitter experience. On the subsequent occasions, the Moderate party protested against the admission of chapels as beyond the Church's power.

The storm soon came. Mr Robert Young was presented to the parish of Auchterarder, and was vetoed by the people. He applied to the Court of Session to have it declared illegal for the Presbytery to reject him without trial of his qualifications. His plea was that the Act of 1712 revived the Act of 1592, which provided that the Presbytery be 'bound and astricted to receive whatsomever *qualified* minister presented by his Majesty or other laic patrons.' His claim was to be taken on trial of his qualifications by the Presbytery; and he pleaded that the Church courts had no right to allow the people's dumb dissent to prevent his trials. After five months of pleading and debate, the court by a majority declared the action of the Presbytery to be illegal. After some time, the case was appealed to the House of Lords, and there the judgment of the Court of Session was sustained. Not only so, but Brougham, in a long and rambling speech accompanying the judgment, used many arguments and some phrases which I can see no reason either to forget or to forgive, on the one hand, or to regard as containing good law, on the other.

But meanwhile, the majority of the Church had committed the Assembly to a declaration that they would stand by the Veto. The settlement of a minister was declared to be a matter purely ecclesiastical; and all jurisdiction of the civil courts in regard to it was repudiated. 'What the Assembly was concerned with,' said Dr Robert Buchanan, in proposing the motion, 'was not the wisdom of the Church, but the competency of the Church in making such a law at all.' This unhappy resolution led to all the irreparable evils that followed. Lord Moncreiff's counsel to go to Parliament was forgotten. The majority of the Church made the political interpretation of an Act of Parliament a matter of 'Spiritual Independence.' Meanwhile, another presentee who had been vetoed in the parish of Marnoch, applied to the Court of Session to have it declared that the Presbytery of Strathbogie, within the bounds of which Marnoch lies, was 'bound and astricted' to make trial of his qualifications. And the court accordingly declared that the Presbytery was so bound. Whereupon the Presbytery recorded in its minutes a declaration that it was bound to make trial of his qualifications. For making this minute—they had gone no further—the seven members constituting the majority of the Presbytery were suspended by the Commission of Assembly, and the Commission resolved to send deputies to preach in their parishes. Then they applied to the Court of Session for protection; and the Assembly's deputies were forbidden to use the church, churchyard, or school-house. This was the 'First Strathbogie Interdict.' After a while, the Court granted a 'Second Interdict,' forbidding the deputies of the Commission to preach in any of the parishes, or otherwise to molest the complainers in the functions of the ministry. This last Interdict was passed in absence, without debate; was never enforced, though openly and contumeliously broken by the deputies of the Church; and I suppose that all concerned were glad to let it drop. The Court of Session had no right to prevent the Church from preaching the Gospel in any parish; and it would have been well for the Moderate party if they had openly made common cause with the Non-Intrusionists in publicly denouncing this act of the Court as usurpation. Had they done so, they would have shewn that they maintained Spiritual Independence. By their supine acquiescence, they drove the public sympathy to the mistaken men who believed that every step consequent on the Veto was for Christ's Crown and Covenant.

But the time for wisdom was past and gone on all sides. The Church, by her majority, was defying the statute law, and abiding by an incompetent and impolitic political act of her own. 'Our dearly beloved Venerable proceeds to its annual slaughter of Mother-Church to-morrow,' wrote Cockburn one day. The Court of Session had abandoned its calm serenity; and the judges proceeded in a strange fashion to act as though because 'for every wrong there is a remedy,' therefore, for every wrong done by the Church, the remedy lay with them. The Parliamentary parties had also lost their wisdom. Neither Whig nor Tory leaders could see how great the crisis was, or how imperative some remedial measure. The Duke of Argyll made an attempt to have the Veto legalised. The Earl of Aberdeen brought in a bill to recognise explicitly the Moderate view, that *objections of whatever kind* might be stated by parishioners against the presentee, and that the Church courts must decide upon them. But neither of those proposals came to anything, and the Church hurried to strike the rocks and be rent in twain. The court ordered the Presbytery of Strathbogie (which had previously after trials found him 'qualified') to proceed to receive and admit Mr Edwards, and the Presbytery did induct him in January 1841. The Assembly deposed the seven offenders. The Moderate party, holding that they were wrongly deposed, made common cause with them; and after that time the battle was inconceivably fierce. How Scotland rang with the war-cries; how in every parish the representatives of Non-Intrusion declaimed with earnest eloquence against the doings of the Court of Session, my time does not permit me to tell. At an early stage, Dr Candlish saw that the people would not be moved if the conflict were understood to be merely one of jurisdiction between the courts of the Church and the civil courts of law; and intimated that it must be pleaded as involving the privileges of the people as well as the rights of the Church. And so it was. The Veto which was actually intended to perpetuate Patronage, came to be treated as a kind of Anti-Patronage; and the question of the Church's competency to curtail Patronage by the Veto was described as involving the Crown rights of the Redeemer. It was this which stirred all Scotland as it had not been stirred since the days of the Covenanters. The banner of the Covenant was supposed to be again floating in the breeze, and in the church and in the open air Scotchmen trooped to defend it. And when at last, in 1843, the crash came, many of the best of the ministers and a whole host of willing people left the Church of Scotland. No other result could be expected, one would think; but some who did not know Scotland had a hope of different results. I believe it may now be considered certain that the Scottish advisers, clerical and lay, of the Conservative government, which succeeded to power in 1841, had a deluded hope that only a few of the leaders of the Non-Intrusion party would leave the Church, and that the rank and file would remain in the old citadel. It is inconceivable that any one who had ever gauged the force of religious feeling, or even who had any remembrance of what Scotch Presbyterians dared and did in former times, could believe that the men of 1843 would be detained in the Church by the paltry terrors of the forfeiture of position and stipend. Dr Candlish, in whose speeches were always first and most forcibly announced the principles which afterwards became the rallying-cries of his party, had for years announced the impending secession, the Sustentation Fund for the support of the clergy, and the attitude of necessary antagonism to all Establishments which he and his friends would be obliged to take up. When I read those speeches, so full of nervous force, of passionate logic, and of unparalleled skill in selecting the topics that would longest absorb the attention of the people—and remember how the party took their watchword from the busy brain of that born leader of men—it seems to me unpardonable that any one should have believed it possible for truants in any considerable number to fall out from the Non-Intrusion ranks. The torrent was sweeping all before it; and only a passion like their own could have roused against the Non-Intrusionists the feelings of the Scottish people in behalf of the integrity of the old Church. But the Moderates as a party did not even understand the voices of the storm which was shaking the house of their habitation.

It was here the parties were unequally matched. Dr Inglis had been laid in his grave some months before the Veto was decreed. Dr George Cook, who since the death of Principal Hill had led the Moderate party, was without the qualities needed for a time of commotion. He was learned, upright, wary, sincerely attached to the Church; and one who knew him well, said in after years, 'he was the best business man of a minister I ever saw in the General Assembly.' But he had been identified with the Church's business and not with her action; and he never learned that reason is less powerful than feeling in moving human life. Dr William Muir can never be named without the reverence due to a dignified, generous, unselfish life, devoted with every power of body and soul and spirit to the work of the Christian ministry, and to the manifestation of the Gospel of Jesus Christ; but he attempted to occupy a middle position between those whose views were irreconcilable, and as they drew away from each other, he was left without support and without power. There was one man more powerful than those named, who is said to be as much responsible for misleading the government in 1843, as Lord Moncreiff was for misleading the Church in 1834. The Dean of Faculty, Hope, did his best to verify his dissent from the Veto, and to prove that it was bad law. In many a stormy passage uttered at the bar, or diffused through the press, he repeated this statement; and at last he had as a lawyer the satisfaction of seeing judges who had eulogised the Veto coming judicially to maintain his view. But passion interfered with his intellect, and prevented him during the conflict from understanding that spiritual theory of the Church as possessed of inherent jurisdiction by Divine appointment, which is the doctrine of the Confession of Faith, and as such is recognised by the law of the land; a doctrine which he had indicated in his dissent from the Veto, and which he had in after-days to reiterate, if not to rehabilitate, from the Bench. There was one of the Constitutional leaders of whom I am perhaps debarred from repeating here what I have said elsewhere;[1] but regarding him—Robertson of Ellon—I may quote Hugh Miller's words: 'Dr Johnson threatened on one occasion to raise a mob. . . . The man we describe, if there be truth in natural signs, or if Nature has written her mark with no wilful intention to deceive, could lead and head a mob too. . . . We have before us the redoubtable Mr Robertson of Ellon, the second name and the first man of his party. . . . He has character, courage, momentum, and unyielding firmness.' Though he was never called to lead a mob, he afterwards shewed how he could do a harder thing when he revived a dispirited Church. But he was not in the councils of the Moderates at the last. He was excluded because he would not approve of the second Strathbogie Interdict.

There were others of whom we cannot here take account. The gifted and learned and beloved Principal Lee was never a leader of the party; and some others, as Drs Pirie, Paull, Bisset, and the younger generation, of whom John Cook and James Grant were the best known, were not always members of the Assembly or in the array of the battle. Dr Mearns—clear and cogent—took a less prominent part after his motion was defeated in 1834. It is not wonderful that popular enthusiasm was with the other side. Its nominal head and its great glory was Chalmers; but its real leader, as I have already said, was Dr Candlish. With him in close array were Cunningham, furnishing lore and logic and terse

---

[1] *Life of Professor James Robertson.* I ask leave to refer to the full narrative of the Non-Intrusion Controversy in that volume (1863); and to refer to my pamphlet on *Spiritual Independence* (1875) for an account of the judicial and ecclesiastical principles raised during the controversy.

statement, and sometimes rough personalities, to the service of his party; Buchanan, a born diplomatist, and withal a man of infinite pains in the mastery of details; Dunlop, who dedicated all his powers of legal learning and of lucid statement (not usually giving the opposite side full justice) to the behoof of his party, and afterwards of the Free Church; and Gordon, full of dignity; and Welsh, who seems to have been loved beyond most men; and Patrick Macfarlan, the only considerable ecclesiastic who originally approved of the Veto; and many others whom it is not in my power to name this day.

Behind them, leagued with their leaders in many a hard encounter in Church courts, was a vast majority of successive General Assemblies. There was doubt whether all of them would cohere till the end; and accordingly a Convocation of ministers was called in November 1842, at which, after many days' debate and discussion, the whole of the members were pledged to go on together to the end—out of the Church if need were. This was not what many a man expected when he went. The circular calling the meeting, said Dr Candlish, '*must not seem as if it were intended to commit men who may come as to ulterior steps.*' The circular was open enough; but the Resolutions were very binding. It is only a few months since any report of the proceedings was published; and now that we have it (in the Memorials of Dr Candlish), we see how, in solemn enthusiasm, all the brethren, guided by Candlish's skilful hand—with occasional bursts from Chalmers and others—came closer and more close together, until after ten days they emerged as one mass, molten in the strong heat, ready to take the shape of the Free Church. Of all who were prominent, there is but one survivor; and it is notable that he (Dr Begg), with manly consistency, held his own then, as ever since, denouncing the Act of Queen Anne as the source of all the evils of the Church.

After the Convocation there could be little hope of a peaceful solution of the difficulties of the Church. If there had been any such hope, it was dispelled by the Stewarton case in January 1843. In this case the Court of Session, by a majority (eight to five) declared that the Church courts had no power to make *quoad sacra* parishes. Thus, as the Auchterarder case struck at the root of the Veto Act, so did the Stewarton case take the sanction of law from the other two Acts of the Church in 1833 and 1834—the Parliamentary Churches Act and the Chapel Act. So far as the Court of Session could undo all the work of the Church for ten years, it had undone it.

And on the 18th of May 1843, 451 ministers left the Church of Scotland (289 being ministers of parishes), leaving 752 ministers, of whom 681 were ministers of parishes.

It was not a Disruption of the Church from the State. It was a great secession, and may well be called a Disruption of the Church, one part from the other. It has taught Scotland and all the world how great is the power of an earnest and united membership when it strives to serve Christ. But still it is not on the whole a thing to be regarded with thankfulness. It has weakened the Church of Scotland, which, if it had continued strong, could have evangelised the nation; it has embittered ecclesiastical life, and thereby kept religion at a low level; it has encouraged Church Extension on the principle of supply and demand, so that simple territorial work, not thwarted by visible competition, is impossible; and—mainly in consequence of this competition—while Scottish churches are more than doubled in number, those who are outside of all churches are not fewer but more numerous than before.

ST GILES' LECTURES.

FIRST SERIES—THE SCOTTISH CHURCH.

LECTURE XI.

THE CHURCH FROM 1843 TO 1881 A.D.

By the Rev. ARCHIBALD SCOTT, D.D., Minister of St George's Parish, Edinburgh.

THE story which I have to tell, if less interesting, is not so painful as that of the troubles which culminated in the Secession of 1843. Though differing widely as to the principles which by that event were vindicated or condemned, most people now look back upon the contendings that led to it with surprise and regret. In so fierce a display of the *perfervidum ingenium Scotorum*, candid critics find it very difficult to agree with any party. We are repelled alike by the violence of those who, by persisting in fighting their battle with weapons declared to be illegal, exposed the Church to insult as occupying a false position, and by the doggedness of others who, to maintain a constitutional position, resisted claims which might have been allowed, and more than once evinced a disposition to minimise its rightful independence. We are amazed that the storm should have invaded the calm domain of law, and that judges, allowing themselves to become partisans, could not refrain from accompanying decisions, which in themselves were impugnable, with dicta which were sometimes as indefensible as they were intentionally offensive. And it is especially to be lamented that both Parliament and Government should have proved so unfit to deal with a really national crisis. Misunderstanding, or haply misinformed of its actual gravity, responsible statesmen made almost no endeavour to adjust a movement which manifestly they could not repress, and which issued in a catastrophe which has embittered the national religious life ever since, and threatens still further to rend the unity of the Scottish Church.

The number and quality of the men who composed the Secession, their personal influence, their distribution over the country, made their withdrawal a serious calamity to the Church. All over the land the people in multitudes, many of them unable to comprehend or not troubling themselves to inquire into the question at issue, followed the ministers whom they loved or were taught to revere. The cause may not have been understood, but the war-cry was catching, and the sacrifices which had been made for it could not but raise it in public esteem. It is simply foolish for any one to attempt to underrate the Secession. The applause which greeted its inauguration; the popular support which it received from the first; the streams of wealth which poured into its treasury; the admiration which it excited in the best parts of Christendom, are facts which only a most prejudiced mind can ignore, and which prove the Secession of '43 to be a most memorable event, productive of consequences which not the wisest seer of to-day can venture to predict. It would be worse than foolish so to deal with the Secession; for the fact that, notwithstanding it, the Church continued almost without a pause the course which had been entered upon before those troubles befell it, and that with increasing activity and greatly augmented results, is the most powerful of all proofs that, even tried by Gamaliel's test, not 'of men have been its counsel and work.'

Seceding historians have represented the Secession as virtually the extinction of the Church. So Dr Hetherington declares that 'every man of genius and talent and learning, every man of piety and faithfulness and energy and zeal, followed Dr Welsh from the Assembly.'[1] Dr Buchanan, again, avows that 'the life departed from the Establishment, and those who remained gazed upon the empty space as if they had been looking into an empty grave.'[2] But whence, if such descriptions be true, came the Church of to-day? Time is a slow but sure and impartial dispenser of justice; and now when we look back, after the lapse of nearly forty years, the most prominent feature that arrests us is the manifest continuity of the Church in everything that can express her life. Not a scheme was abandoned, not an enterprise either at home or abroad was demitted. There had swarmed off a new and vigorous colony, but the life and the work of the parent hive went on. A new Church, equipped with Presbyteries and schools and halls of theology, had sprung Minerva-like into being, but the body from which it emerged gave no symptoms of disease or senescence. The river rolled on, for a time in diminished volume, and ever since with less noise than that which had parted from it; but its silence was the token of its depth and power, and its course of beneficence throughout this generation sufficiently attests its origin as one of those streams which make glad the city of God.

The minutes of that memorable Assembly and the pictures that have been preserved of it by eye-witnesses, reveal a very different state of matters, and a very different set of men from what are described by the partisan historians. We can discern in their chivalrous and indomitable determination to maintain the Church the germs of her present prosperity. There was much sorrow in that Assembly, but there was no cowardice; much concern, but no despair. Calmly amid the hissings of

---

[1] *History*, vol. ii., p. 524.   [2] *Ten Years' Conflict*, vol. ii., p. 442.

the mob, as those 'who felt they were suffering for future generations,' they set about undoing one by one the blunders which had caused their troubles. They had maintained the constitutional rights of the people against the encroachment of an ecclesiastical supremacy which would eventually have strangled them, and they now asked the State, with which the Church was in alliance, but to which in spiritual matters it would never be subject, to take such constitutional measures as would conserve the rights of the people and remove difficulties in the way of the Church's progress. So without excommunicating those who had caused this mischief, but deploring their loss; acknowledging the weight of their calamity and taking their own share of the national sin that caused it, evincing neither sign of wavering nor doubt as to the rightness of the course they had pursued, they set themselves at once to grapple with their circumstances and to repair the breaches made in the bulwarks of the National Zion.

Certainly they had need of all their fortitude, for their work had now to be prosecuted in the presence of active and able and vigilant foes. Those who seceded never seemed to feel that they were called to concede to those who remained the same conscientiousness which they claimed for themselves. They went out not as martyrs, but as if they were the hereditary enemies of a Church whose bread they had eaten, representing its ministers as a degraded and hireling order of men, no longer worthy to preach the Gospel. The people were told by responsible leaders of the movement, that the 'idea of the residuary Establishment doing anything valuable for the salvation of souls was simply ridiculous,' and therefore they 'should proceed substantially on the theory that provision for ordinances by it was not to be taken into account at all.'[1] And so while the new Churches were placed as near as possible to the parish church, the parishioners were instructed by

[1] Story's *Life*, p. 302; also Dr Candlish's *Life*, p. 306.

the official newspaper of the party, to 'regard the parish minister as the one excommunicated man of the district, the man with whom no one is to join in prayer, whose church is to be avoided as an impure and unholy place.' Evidently the martyrdoms of '43 were not all on the side of the Seceders. Their sacrifices were ostensible, and were compensated for by great public applause; but the men who remained to maintain what all had solemnly sworn to defend, had to undergo the daily martyrdom of having their best motives misrepresented and systematically outraged. The persecuting spirit of the people was very strongly roused; and wherever the Seceders were numerous, it made fidelity to the Church a painfully trying thing. In the North, the scenes which had occurred after 1690 and in the first twenty years of the eighteenth century, when the Presbyterian polity was being put in force, were almost literally re-enacted after '43, when the Church sought simply to perform its duties. In September of that year, the members of Presbytery who had met to supply the parishes of Rosskeen and Logie, were assailed with stones and sticks. In Resolis, on a similar occasion, a serious riot occurred, in which one man was disabled for life, and another was so wounded that he soon after died. In several other places, men were assaulted and nearly killed for no other reason than that they adhered to the Establishment. It was no uncommon occurrence for parish ministers to find their church-doors battered, and their pulpits defiled. Girls were driven violently away from the wells by elders who would not allow 'false Moderates to pollute the water.' Shopkeepers who would not join the Secession, were treated in many parts of the country as the Irishman is now dealt with who refuses to join the Land League. The very children were banned by their playmates at schools, and even recently might be heard speaking of the Church in which their fathers had worshipped for ages, in terms too opprobrious to quote.

To recall such things is painful; to dwell upon them would

be uncharitable; but they must be taken into account in order to do justice to the men who in those evil times maintained the cause and prosecuted the work of the Church. The very turbulence and intolerance that raged around them was destined to have a good effect both on their councils and action. It not only chastened them, but seemed to crush out that combative zeal which, prior to '43, aimed at domination and conquest of all dissent. If here and there an individual was stung into retaliation, he was speedily rebuked by the better spirit that prevailed among his brethren. It was not by returning railing for railing that the cause of the Church could be advanced, but by a resolute endeavour to remedy all its defects, and to adapt it to the wants of the country and of the times. Consequently, after '43, the Church entered upon a course of steady and continuous reformation in almost every domain of its service. The whole period is one of healthy revival, in which, unvexed by any desire to molest outsiders, it has tried to develop its own resources and improve its own efficiency, and the happy results may now be seen in the vigorous and still reforming Church of to-day.

Certainly there was need for reformation. Arrears of undischarged responsibilities had been accumulating for generations. During the century prior to 1834 the Church had produced some sixty-three chapels, in face of nearly six hundred raised by Dissent, to meet the wants of a rapidly growing population—a fact which at Disestablishment meetings and in Voluntary Town Councils was urged powerfully against the Church. In the city of Edinburgh alone, eleven thousand unlet sittings in the Established Churches—and these generally the cheapest[1]—indicated the indifference that prevailed among the lower orders, and revealed within the Church a state of matters more alarming than any hostility that could be raised against it from without. You have been told of the noble singleness

[1] Cockburn's *Journal*, vol. i., p. 93.

of aim and pure enthusiasm with which Dr Chalmers sought to grapple with these evils, and how his efforts, generously supported, had resulted in the erection of nearly two hundred chapels in large and necessitous parishes. It had even a grander result—that of awakening the conviction that the Gospel is the only power to raise man or masses of men, and that of all the instruments for securing this, none can compare with that of an endowed territorial ministry. Had Chalmers done nothing more than lodge that truth deep in the heart of the Church, he would have made good his title to rank with its Reformers and founders, for out of that seed was to rise a harvest of blessing larger than ever he had dared to dream of.

The difficulties of the Church, confronted with empty pulpits to supply, and empty churches to fill, were for several years increased by the necessity of having to make good its claim to those very chapels. It was not denied that they had been erected by contributions received in its name, and had been inalienably secured in title-deeds to its trust; but the curious demand was made, that the Church should be compelled to cede a property of which as a sacred trust it was not at liberty to divest itself. The reasons alleged were that the chapels were erected by the party composing the Free Church, and that the Church had now no need of them. A comparison of the lists of those who seceded with those who remained will effectually shew that Church Extension was a movement to which the whole Church was committed, and which all parties in the Church supported. The church-door collections for it in the years preceding the Secession, varied from £2445 to £3775; in those immediately succeeding it, they ranged from £2400 to £4000. In the extraordinary emergency of the Secession, it was to be expected that several chapels should be left for a time unprovided for; but it was scarcely fair of the Seceders to plead an embarrassment of which they were the authors as a reason for despoiling the Church of its trust, and it was almost ludicrous to cite individual instances of churches alleged to be locked up and useless, when the parties who made the allegation refused to give up the key. The whole contention seems to have been only designed to damage and discredit the Church. The now disclosed secret history of the Convocation reveals the grim humour with which, even before it was advanced, those who made the claim regarded it. Confessing themselves unable to secure the chapels as the spoils of the contest, it was proposed that 'they should be loaded with debt, which would render them useless, according to the custom of a distressed army to spike the guns which they could not carry off.'[1] As matter of fact, when the protracted litigation ended, and the chapels were declared the property of the Church, they were found burdened with a debt of more than £30,000.

The spirit of the Church Extension movement, far from departing with Chalmers or languishing within the Church, manifested itself in vigorous activity even in the dark days following the Secession. Its operations were of course the more pressing ones of relieving and fostering chapels that had been enfeebled or emptied. Yet year by year witnessed a steady increase over the preceding, both in the number of chapels that were aided and in the number of worshippers attending them. Even before the decision of the House of Lords had been given, a most important step had been taken with regard to the Chapels of Ease. You have been told how these chapels were built in the hope that government would furnish the endowment, and how all endeavours to secure this had failed. The public purse was too empty, and Dissent was too fierce. And if opposition from that quarter was too strong for the Church, when supported by Chalmers, it was hopeless to confront it now, when so much of its strength had gone to animate that hostile power. Yet even then there was one who had faith and courage to assert that the task from which

---

[1] Candlish's *Life*, p. 253.

Chalmers shrank as too gigantic might be accomplished by voluntary effort. Naturally sanguine, the fact that the Church had emerged from the storms of the preceding decade, stimulated in him the hope of great things to come. In the newly formed Lay Association he saw an 'earnest of the new and better spirit with which the whole land would soon be imbued,' and so undaunted by difficulties which were truly enormous, he dared to summon a Church, alleged to be prostrate 'and dying of its own weight of corruption,' to a task of national magnitude.

There can be only one estimate formed of Dr Robertson's character and work. He was of the stuff out of which all true Reformers are made—a man firm and unbending as the granite of his native county, yet burning with unquenchable zeal. It was not as an ecclesiastic but as a patriot that he gave himself to his work; fighting not for the advance of the Church, but for the success of the Gospel. As one of the commission of inquiry into the condition of the poor, he had discovered what social unrest and spiritual indigence stirred beneath the vaunted stability of our national prosperity. His studies in the writings of the Fathers of the Church had furnished him with clear perceptions of its fundamental principles, and experience had grounded him in firm faith in their soundness. He had learned enough of philosophy and history to convince him 'that the welfare of society tends by an irresistible impulse, over which legislation can have little control, to suspend itself in the significance attached to man as man, and that the strength of the empire depends upon the God-fearing and therefore manly and trustworthy self-government of its subjects.' His keen good sense shewed him the value of the instrument which had been placed by Act 7 and 8 Vict. c. 44 in his hand. So we need not wonder that his natural hopefulness, brightened by firm trust in God and faith in the capabilities of a National Church, should have made him even then prophesy of the glory of the latter times for Scotland, 'when those who were a burden to society would be converted into blessings to it.'

The opening of his crusade was encouraging. Even in the sad year of the potato famine, he could report out of a total subscription, £5000 subscribed by the clergy alone, and 'an offering of first-fruits from the enlightened zeal of the nobility.' But he was soon to require all his enthusiasm. We know that it is a fact in nature that 'we cannot raise the temperature of a thawing mass of ice till we have thawed the whole, and that not until the ice has passed into water can we hope to change it into steam.' As in all great Christian movements, a great amount of Robertson's energy was absorbed in this same thawing process. He had to complain, not of the frank opposition of enemies, but of the indifference and dead inertia of friends. But even from the first there went with him 'a band of men whose hearts God had touched.' It would be invidious to mention the living, and though no one can grudge to the dead the tribute of being associated with his name, I prefer rather by silent reference to suggest than recall them. Indeed, no one could come in contact with his strong and noble disinterestedness without feeling that honest resistance could not be prolonged. His speech might be heavy, his manner unattractive, but there was no resisting the man. So one by one at first, but latterly in numbers, there rallied round him the foremost men in the Church, the most influential of the nobility and gentry. Through an unwearied course of fifteen years he lived and toiled for his scheme, and he may be said even to have died for it. His last official action was the penning of an unfinished appeal for it; almost his last words breathed of its burden: 'Not the Convener, not the Committee, but the Spirit of the living God.'

He died in 1860, but as a leader dies in a victorious charge. The very momentum that had been gained made the line sweep on without him. His death, deplored as a grievous loss, turned out to be a real gain to the cause which he served. Its greatness only dawned upon many through the grandeur of the life surrendered for it. Much of the coldness which baffled him in life melted away in his death. The sixty parishes which he had left behind him were, under his successor, in another sixteen years, augmented to two hundred and fifty. At this date, three hundred have been added to the Church, at a cost of nearly two millions of money. But those who have wrought most nobly to produce this result have always alluded to their efforts as the fruit of Robertson's work. The last Convener, a man in every way worthy to succeed him, was on this point the most entitled of our generation to speak; and yet with simplicity, as truthful as it was beautiful, Dr Smith ever spoke of his work as if Robertson himself were directing it—as if, 'having died, he was yet speaking.'

The reforming *afflatus* which in Robertson produced the Endowment Scheme, proved in the life and work of Dr Norman Macleod productive of as beneficent results. Though he was too young to take any prominent part in the contentions preceding the Secession, he was acknowledged to be a power even in the Assembly of '43. In the years immediately succeeding, when the policy of Dissent was to exclude and ignore the Church in every great public movement, his services were simply inestimable. Too energetic to be repressed, he soon proved himself too able and too eloquent to be dispensed with. One whose presence and power were eagerly sought, both in the great May Meetings in Exeter Hall, and afterwards in the Councils of the Evangelical Alliance, could not fail to be recognised as essential to the successful advocacy of any charitable or religious movement in Scotland. And wherever he appeared, he served to raise the credit of the Church that owned him. Translated to the Barony in 1851, he found in Glasgow a sphere worthy of his genius. While multitudes of the most influential classes of society gathered around him, large congregations, composed entirely of working men and of the poor, hung Sabbath after Sabbath on his lips. Those who heard the Word were instructed in the blessedness of doing it. His enormous parish was organised so as to secure a complete visitation of its most destitute districts. Schools were provided, mission stations were projected and equipped, and by-and-by parish after parish was disjoined from it. Things deemed impossibilities to others became under him easily accomplished facts. Success in one of the most trying of spheres helped immensely to inspire courage in others, and ministers all over the Church felt their difficulties become simplicities just in proportion as they allowed themselves to come under the spell of his enthusiasm. When to his already too heavy responsibilities was added the Convenership of the Foreign Mission Committee, he threw himself into its work with all the fervour of an apostle. With a voice like the sound of a trumpet, he summoned the Church 'to the help of the Lord against the mighty.' His labours in this connection cannot be reckoned. I question if even yet we can form anything like an adequate conception of the gigantic tasks which he set himself, and the work which he attempted to do. Equally ready to plead his cause in the obscurest parish in Scotland, and in the stately halls of the Viceroy in India, he may be said to have been consumed by his own ardour. At an age when we were depending on the fulness of his strength and wisdom, he fell the victim of his own enthusiasm—a man mourned alike by his Sovereign and by the poorest of her subjects, whom he felt it his privilege to serve.

No true Churchman—and many have done virtuously during this period—will ever grudge my humble tribute to Macleod and Robertson. They are among the greatest gifts that have been bestowed on the Church of our day. The work which they prosecuted was in every sense of the word a Revival, whose effects may be traced in the immense development of the Church around us. If during this period the revenue and operations of the Home Mission have quadrupled; if the Foreign Mission, deprived by the Secession of all its agents save one, is now strong enough to send its contingent—confessedly still too small—of preachers and teachers, Zenana and medical missionaries, to join at eight centres in India, one in China, one in Africa, that noble army which from all points of the compass aims at the conquest of heathendom for Christ; if the same progress and extension mark the operations of the Jewish Mission; if the Colonial Scheme, now consolidated, exerts its beneficent influence in almost every quarter of the globe in which our army and navy serve, or our countrymen settle; if an ever-deepening sense of responsibility prevails among the congregations and Presbyteries of the Church —this result is due in no small measure to the influence of these two men, who, differing in many things, yet twins in spirit, and united as friends, recalled the Church to the true significance of its position as National, and to its burden and glory of service as a branch of the Church of Christ.

So far the reformation of the Church is indirectly traceable to the legislation of 1844. For though legislation cannot create life, it can remove many obstructions in the way of its growth. The fact that, without taxing any outsider, or burdening a single conscience, a fourth of the whole number has been added to the parochial charges of Scotland; and the additional facts that, in 1878, 129,700 communicants were returned from these *quoad sacra* parishes alone, and that £118,050 was reported in the same year as their contribution to the Christian Liberality Committee, indicate the extent to which the population has availed itself of, and appreciates the benefits secured through, the operation of Sir James Graham's Act. The difficulties which troubled the Church prior to '43 in the way of meeting the religious wants of the people, have so far been removed. Let us now attend to the working of another Act of Parliament, which in August 1843 was passed to meet a difficulty quite as great—namely, the adjustment of popular claims in the settlement of ministers.

By many in the Church, the Scotch Benefices Act was hailed as a highly satisfactory and extremely popular measure. Indeed, both in the Church and in Parliament it was strongly opposed as too liberal. It was said to invest the Church with too ample discretionary powers, and to reduce the right of a patron to all but a shadow. Experience of its working, however, soon revealed that what it gave with the one hand, it took away with the other. Capricious decisions, involving all parties in heavy expense, and producing increasing irritation and secession from the Church, were its inevitable results. So, in spite of all attempts made by the General Assembly to secure by regulation its better working, the conviction only deepened, that, though well intentioned, it could only operate to the disadvantage of the Church and to the damage even of religion.

As early as 1854, Dr Gillan vainly besought the Presbytery of Glasgow to declare that the chief evils under which the Church suffered were inseparable from the system of Patronage which the Act sought to administer. In 1857 he was foiled in a similar attempt in the General Assembly. In 1859, Dr Lee ineffectually argued for a modified veto. But thenceforth overtures brought the unsatisfactory working of the Act before every Assembly, discussion became more frequent and earnest, public feeling was roused, till in 1866 it was plain that a movement was stirring which only required some outward impetus to give it both direction and success. That impetus was speedily supplied by the political events of the time. A vast increase of political power had been conferred by the new Reform Act upon the lower middle and working classes of the country; and even men averse to change had to confess that if the Church was to be in harmony with a greatly enfranchised people, the dead-weight of Patronage must at once be got rid of in some constitutional way.

In the Assembly of 1868, the ranks of the Patronage and Anti-Patronage supporters met in their first earnest grapple;

and after a keen and honourable struggle, it was decided by a very narrow majority to appoint the Committee of Inquiry, which had hitherto been evaded or refused. Its report to next General Assembly was decisive in favour of a modification of the law. A prolonged and severe debate ensued; and when the vote was called, the large majority of 193 to 88 sealed the Church's condemnation of the most fruitful source of all her evils, and committed the Assembly to all lawful attempts to secure its speedy abolition. Petitions brought the decision of the Church before both Houses of Parliament; and a deputation, which had been cordially received by influential men of all parties, on the day on which the second reading of the Irish Church Disestablishment Bill had passed the House of Lords, laid the case before the Premier. His reception was courteous, but his reply, though afterwards interpreted to convey a meaning which perhaps it did not bear, seemed to justify the motion in next General Assembly that the movement should be delayed till the government indicated the course which they meant to follow. The Rubicon had, however, been crossed; the rights of the people could no longer be tampered with. By a larger majority than ever, the decision of the former Assembly was ratified, and from that point onwards substantial unanimity prevailed in the further prosecution of the movement.

The Anti-Patronage movement involved its supporters in no small share of misrepresentation and reproach, as if it originated in, and was governed solely by, hostility to Dissenting communions. Never was reproach more unmerited. If any policy dictated this movement, it was that of conciliating Dissenters. Indeed, there were times when it was felt that conciliation of outsiders was carried on at the risk of alienating many who were within. Its promoters could not hope that union of sundered Presbyterians would immediately follow the abolition of Patronage, but it was plain that until it was taken away, all possible approach to union was barred. As an indication of their hope and intention, at this very stage, upon the call of the late Lord Gordon, a resolution was passed, and a committee was appointed to promote the union of churches that had seceded from the Establishment on account of Patronage, and that still adhered to its Confession and system of worship.

At this period there were probably not fifty men in the whole ranks of the Church who did not most earnestly desire that Dissenting Presbyterians should be embraced in this movement. Never at any time since 1843 had the Church assumed an attitude unfriendly to Dissent. It was remarked, even at that time, that no feeling save that of affectionate regret found expression in regard to those who seceded. In self-defence, it had to rescind and remit to a committee the Act anent 'Ministerial Communion,' repealed only a year before; but no accusation could be more unfair or undeserved than that of Dr Candlish, that by so doing, 'they have virtually cut off all Christendom from their communion.'[1] His party, though dominant for years, made no effort to abolish the obnoxious Act, till in 1842, when affairs were drawing to a crisis, policy suggested its repeal as likely to appease their former enemies. The Church was too leavened by the very spirit against which the foolish Act of 1799 was directed to regard it with favour. Even then, friendly co-operation with other bodies, when practicable, was not only sanctioned but enjoined. Every subsequent enactment has been in the direction of facilitating and promoting co-operation, and at this date the pulpits of the Establishment are practically more open to ministers of other communions, than those of Dissenting denominations can be said to be to ourselves.

It was with no unfriendly eye that the Church regarded the first gathering together of the scattered streams of Scottish Presbyterianism, in the union of the churches of Erskine and Gillespie in 1847. Again, when in 1863, the first proposal for

---

[1] Candlish's *Life*, p. 306.

union between the United denominations and the Free Church was launched, there were very many within the Church who, wearied with the divisions of a family that ought to be united, really hoped that a better day was dawning for all. It seemed to them that if honestly entered upon and honourably carried out, the movement must develop into negotiations for union immensely more comprehensive. The United Presbyterian on one important point was as far removed from the Free, as was that Church from the Establishment on another. It was but reasonable to expect that the Free Church would be as ready to consider with their old friends the principle of Christ's Headship over the Church, as they were prepared to consider with their recent foes the twin principle of Christ's Headship over the State. But alas, the opportunity cannot even be said to have been lost; it was deliberately, by both negotiating parties, thrown away. They could not inaugurate their diplomacy without emitting declarations which, while excluding the Church, were purposely offensive. Her professors were heretics, her ministers were ritualists in disguise. And so by the time that the Anti-Patronage movement had assumed definite form, it was evident that co-operation was simply impossible. Lord Gordon's 'olive branch' was met by resolutions breathing a spirit of determined hostility to the Church. It was the humiliation of the Church, and not union with it, that was desired; and so it was plain that if the Church were to succeed in obtaining the abolition of Patronage, it would be against the combined opposition of those whose fathers found it a yoke too grievous to be borne.

A Conservative government has the credit of undoing the mischievous legislation which an old Tory government had imposed. On 19th May 1874, a Bill to abolish Patronage and repeal the Act of Queen Anne was introduced by the Duke of Richmond into the House of Lords, and through all its subsequent stages it was ably supported by the Duke of Argyll. It was discussed by Peers on both sides of the House with a general desire to produce a measure that would be consonant to the principles of the Church, and the genius of the people of Scotland. The result was that, really amended in some important points, the Bill left the Lords vesting the patronage in the congregation, leaving the Church to define and settle who are its members and who are entitled to be called adherents. Direct opposition to a measure so consistent with the traditions and principles of all Presbyterians in Scotland was impossible in the Commons, so the mode of assault was a plausible motion for delay and inquiry. It became evident, however, that the real objection lay in the new and monstrous doctrine that to do anything favourable to the Church as a national institution is against the interests of those who live by opposing it. It was strange to find this doctrine advocated by men who had just settled, in the interest of the public good and economy, the question of national education in a manner which pressed hard upon many schools and teachers hitherto voluntarily supported. Unprejudiced people could not see that Dissenters had any just vested interest in the abuses of the Church, but they could see that the Bill most highly complimented Dissenters in embodying the very principles for which they had so nobly contended, and in securing, not to the actual ministers and members of the Church, but to the whole Presbyterian polity of the people, a statute which shewed that the old Church of the nation rests still, where, after persecution and martyrdom, their fathers and ours re-established it, on the settlement of 1690. It is too soon to judge of an Act which has so recently come into operation. It has failed, as was foreseen from the first, to conciliate ecclesiastical opponents, but an immense majority of the people of Scotland rejoice in its passing; and yet there is hope that opponents may come to acknowledge that the removal of an ancient grievance was not a sectional triumph, but a truly national gain.

With the Secession of '43, the troubles of the Church as to civil jurisdiction completely ended. In the declamations of that time, and even yet, it is asserted that her peace was only purchased by sinful submission ; but now that in the course of a generation, passion has had time to cool, and prejudice to clear away, men are coming to see that from a contest which, undoubtedly originating in a demand for a popular right, ended in a 'demand for a clerical, which would eventually have scattered popular liberty to the winds,' the Church has emerged with its constitutional liberties intact. Its history since the Secession is a triumphant vindication of its independence. In every case of discipline in which the civil court has been asked to interfere with its decisions, it has declined, on the ground that the proceedings complained of were within the exclusive jurisdiction of the Church. Three times during that period have the Seceders of '43 been before the civil courts in reference to a spiritual sentence complained of as illegally pronounced ; and against their defence that the court could not interfere in sentences pronounced as a matter of Church discipline by an association of Christians tolerated by law, it was held that a voluntary association of Christians has no jurisdiction, in the proper legal sense of the term, and that sentences of suspension and deposition pronounced by them were not such spiritual acts as could not be taken cognisance of by the civil courts.

With such decisions staring us in the face, we might surely expect that spiritual independence should be left by the Free Church as 'open' a question in relation to the Establishment as the great majority of its members are willing to leave the question of Christ's Headship over the State in their relation to the Voluntaries. It is plain that secession can never secure such spiritual independence as is claimed, and that the alliance of Church with State in Scotland is not inimical to it. The Act of 1874, which repealed the Act of Queen Anne restoring Patronage, may be said to have revived all the ancient declarations of Parliament on the subject of the Church's Rights. It can henceforth only serve the purpose of a partisan to describe that Act as Erastian. Mr Gladstone, a most competent judge, in his speech of July 6, 1874, objected to the Bill 'as intended to commit to the Church powers not possessed by any voluntary religious communion in the country.' The Duke of Argyll, again, in a paper reprinted from the *Contemporary Review* in 1878, testifies that the effect of the Act is to 'enable advocates of spiritual independence,' which he thinks 'too wide, too absolute to be theoretically true,' to affirm their view within the Establishment without any practical contradiction from the law.' Surely blindness in part has happened to those who do not see what an enormous advantage is thus secured, not only to the members of the Established Church, but to that Presbyterian polity and creed, which nine-tenths even of Scottish Dissenters profess alike to revere and to believe.

During this last period, the Church has favoured no political party, and if wisely guided, it will not attach itself to any. Its ministers and congregations represent all shades of political opinion in very much the same proportions as they exist in the country. Consequently, in regard to party influence, the Church is virtually powerless; and if political influence be an advantage to a professedly spiritual society, Dissenting communions in this respect excel it. As a national institution, however, the Church has been affected by the political changes of the last generation, and no sketch of this period would be complete which did not notice some of those which have modified and even altered its relation to the country at large.

A Commission of Inquiry into the working of the Poor-law system, appointed long before the Secession, reported in 1844; and in 1845, an Act, based upon the report, was passed, superseding the old system of relief of the poor by voluntary assessment of heritors and offerings of congregations. It is a fashion with some people to decry this statute as one of the most revolutionary of the century, as communistic in its principles, and demoralising in its effects. But such people evidently forget that no human agency for the amelioration of the condition of the poor is perfect, and that the best will contain in themselves, or develop in their working, tendencies of a more or less deteriorating kind, against which we must guard as best we can. They also labour under the common fallacy that the Act created the evils which it only brought to light. It was rendered necessary by the utter break-down of a system, which, though excellent in theory, and successful in certain given circumstances, had proved palpably inadequate to the wants of the age. The chief lesson to be gained from it is the illustration which it affords of the utter failure of the voluntary principle to provide for a want of national magnitude. If ever there was a sphere in which that principle was likely to succeed, it was furnished by the care of the poor. And yet, just as Chalmers predicted, its own keenest advocates were the loudest in demanding that the poor should be rescued from dependence upon its caprice.

The abolition of University Tests was another measure affecting the Church. To secure Presbyterianism against Episcopalian conspiracies, it was enacted in 1690, and again in 1707, that no professor should be admitted to a Scottish chair without first subscribing the Confession of Faith, and promising to adhere to the worship and discipline of the Church. Legislation demanded solely by the exigencies of the time very properly fell into abeyance as the danger ceased. In Edinburgh, during the most of the last century, tests were not applied, and since the Leslie controversy, had only been applied in the case of the theological chairs. At the time when the agitation was culminating, it was discovered that more than a fourth of the professors of Scotland were serving without having signed, and that many of the most distinguished among them were members of the very Episcopalian Church which the tests were meant to exclude. It was not to be wondered at, therefore, that after the failure of several Bills in Parliament, the election of a Free Church Professor to the Chair of Moral Philosophy by the Edinburgh Town Council should have brought matters to a crisis. In the litigation which ensued, it was decided that it was the duty of the Senatus to comply with the terms of the statute; but it was not clear how that should be a duty which had been religiously disregarded for more than a hundred years. Moreover, none but the most extreme men could defend a test which admitted those whom it was meant to exclude, and which could be used to exclude those whom its framers would have admitted. It was now an agitation not without, but within the Church. Prominent Churchmen had been in the movement for years. In the interests both of the Church and of education, it was imperative that reasonable concessions should be made; and even ardent defenders of the Church were glad when the Act of 1853 swept away a 'crumbling bulwark, which had become more a danger than a defence.'

By far the most important change in the Church's relation to the institutions of the country was effected in the matter of education. During the stormy years of 1842-43, negotiations with the Privy Council issued in the promise of aid for Normal schools, and in the establishment of that co-operation of the government and the Church, which has so materially influenced the common school instruction of the people. The Secession, which followed shortly after, proved in regard to education a gain to the country. For once at least division was stronger than union. The efforts made by the Free Church to establish an educational system, produced in a very few years close upon six hundred schools, and stimulated the Church to a rivalry which was eventually to lose much of its bitterness in a field which was large enough for all.

The policy of the government followed closely that of the Church previous to this period. It was to ascertain and make known throughout the country the state of education, in the hope that voluntary effort for its improvement would follow. The ecclesiastical divisions of Scotland presented conditions very favourable to the prosecution of such a policy, and, accordingly, the system of government grants in aid of denominational schools was inaugurated in 1847. It was a bold, and manifest, and eminently successful attempt at concurrent religious endowment. It was eagerly accepted by the Roman Catholics and Episcopalians, and though a considerable number of ministers and others demurred for a time, both Established and Free Churches, by large majorities, accepted a system which, recognising the necessity for religious instruction, dispensed its grants indiscriminately to schools, whatever might be the religion taught in them.

By-and-by this mode of assistance gave way to capitation grants, grounded in and measured by the ascertained progress of the pupils. The minute promulgating the change earnestly engaged the attention of all the churches. Our own General Assembly, led by Dr Cook, while approving of its object, was opposed to nearly all its details. Some two years after, however, he was able to report that most of the defects in the Code originally proposed had been removed. The results of its first trial in 1863 amply proved the necessity for some more stringent test of educational work than had hitherto been applied, and whatever dispute may continue as to the merits or demerits of the system, its leading principle has been thoroughly vindicated by the logic of events.

The interest evoked in education by the working of the Privy Council system tended to further an agitation for proper legislation on the subject. The Act of 1861, making better provision for teachers of parochial schools, and freeing them from the test of connection with the Church, helped greatly to foster this movement. During the ten years that followed, several measures were tried; a Royal Commission had been instituted and had reported, but even a Bill framed according to its suggestions proved abortive. Some of these measures, condemned at the time as revolutionary, may be found to be much more moderate in their provisions than what is now universally accepted; but though they failed to become law, they served in maturing public opinion and preparing the way for the Act of 1872. The agitation connected with the passing of this measure is too recent to permit of detailed account. The action of the Church, however, in reference to it, is easily stated. Recognising many excellent provisions in it, it objected to the entire absence of recognition of the importance and necessity of religious instruction. The author of the Bill maintained that it would neither prescribe nor proscribe religious instruction, but leave the people free to have religious instruction if they desired it. As originally drawn, however, this freedom was very materially proscribed. Nevertheless, it was welcomed by the Voluntaries, and by a majority of the Free Church. The latter were prepared to surrender the obligation of the State to provide religious instruction; the former, by strange inconsistency, were willing to allow Local Boards to infringe their principle of religious equality. The minority of the Free Church, however, were not prepared to abandon their principles, just to make matters smooth with the promoters of the measure. Cordially joining the Church in an endeavour to remedy so grave a defect, they succeeded in carrying amendments recognising the value of religious instruction, and giving liberty to the people of Scotland to provide in all their schools the invariable custom of ages.

The effect of the Act has severed the direct connection of the Church with national education. In 1872, 2400 schools were reported to be connected with the Church. Of these, 1150 were parochial and parliamentary schools, and 1250 owed their connection to the voluntary exertions of its Committee, its kirk-sessions, its members. So, though here again the voluntary principle failed completely to supply a national want —the exertions of all other denominations put together having originated fewer than 900 schools—the Church has no reason to be ashamed of its contribution to the cause of national education. The Normal schools still flourish, but of common schools very few remain, and what remain will eventually be absorbed. But, as there is 'that scattereth and yet increaseth,' so if the Church be wise and tolerant, and keep clear of outside sectarian complications, it will find that its influence in the education of the people, because recognised to be unselfish, is more powerful and beneficent than ever.

The watchword which has most influenced its action during this period has been not the rights, but the efficiency of the Church. The schemes recently developed for augmenting the smaller livings, and for providing for aged and infirm ministers, are notable indications of this. The first, though pressed upon its attention by the great reduction in the stipends caused by the repeal of the Corn Laws, and by the general advance in social expenditure, is pleaded for solely on the ground that congregations must suffer if served by a pauperised clergy. The other, again, proceeds on the idea that congregations must be vigorously served. Presbyterial supervision of ministers is not indeed what it should be, yet public opinion is so maturing, that indolence or inefficiency in the ministry will soon be as little tolerated as open immorality. Even already it has put an end to the times when it could be said that 'ministers only find their office tolerable when they acquire facility in ignoring its responsibilities,' or that Presbyteries are simply tradesunions for protecting the interests of their members. The increasing popularity of the Committee on Life and Work, ostensibly instituted to stimulate activity, betokens a deepening regard to the great interests intrusted to us, and speaks volumes for the hold which the conviction has now gained, that the only right worth fighting for is simply freedom to discharge all our duty.

Prominent among our modern activities is the care of the young. Up till 1843, very little progress was made within the Church in the development of Sabbath-schools. It was only in 1841 that a return in regard to them was asked for. In 1850, the General Assembly formally assumed their oversight, and since then annual reports record, that while in 1850, there were only 76,232 children on our rolls, in 1880, 230,353 of the youth of the country availed themselves of the religious instruction provided in the Sabbath-schools of the Church. The proper accommodation and organisation of those schools, now yearly engaging greater attention, shew plainly that the system is rapidly passing into another and higher phase, which will erelong shew marked results.

The Prayer and Fellowship Meetings, the Mutual Improvement, Temperance, and Total Abstinence Societies, the Associations for providing popular lectures and suitable recreation for the people, which are now considered essential to the economy of a well-served parish, manifest that the pastors of 1880 bear a much heavier burden than was borne by their predecessors of former generations. Indeed there is a danger that the many and severe demands upon the 'modern minister' may operate injuriously against his mental culture. The 'learned leisure' of former times would be difficult now to find. Leisure certainly there is not; and though in the parishes of Scotland there is abundance of men of scholarly sympathies, there is a danger of learning diminishing. Yet learning is simply essential, now that literature is immensely more diffused. It is to be feared the modern Church is not sufficiently alive to the danger. The institution of the Croall and the Baird lectures, and the lectures delivered annually in the four universities by men appointed by the General Assembly, are no doubt steps in the right direction. Even a course of lectures like the present may serve to stimulate study, but a far more extensive and systematic and sustained effort is necessary in order to secure that the clergy of the present and future may be worthy successors of those who in earlier times adorned the venerable brows of the Church with laurels won in every department of literature and science and art.

A fiercer light is beating upon the Church of to-day, and stronger forces than influenced preceding generations have to be dealt with and adjusted. The age of Queen Victoria is very unlike that of the Georges. Railways and telegraphs drawing together the very ends of the earth, facilitating rapid exchange of thought, have produced a silent but most mighty revolution. It is an age marked by intense movement in every domain of human activity; by exploration and colonisation of whole continents; by startling discoveries in science; by great inventions in the arts. If the effect produced by the revival of letters and the rise of industry in Europe centuries ago was to close the middle ages, and bring about the Reformation, then unquestionably this fusion of east and west, and north and south in the great seething present, must result in even a grander renaissance, which must powerfully influence the Church. There have been ages in which the clergy were the sole teachers of the world. In the present age, the gifts of the Church, whether of science, or prophecy, or healing, appear more in the membership than in the ministry. The reputed teachers of the people have in many things to assume the attitude of learners toward those who look to them for spiritual counsel. The modern pulpit is not so much marked by originality as by appreciation. If not radiating forth new light, it is quick to catch and reflect it. The religious thought and feeling of the people are not ahead of the pulpit; yea, it is through its ministration that the people in most instances receive what is good in the spirit of the age. The sermon of to-day undoubtedly lacks the polished diction and classic grace of the best specimens of Moderatism, just as the average preacher will not compare in scholarship and culture with the best of those stately and courtly fathers, who, lingering far into our period, have now all fallen asleep. But the pulpit of to-day, with all its defects, is more in accordance with the wants of the people. Were they offered again the clearly reasoned theological or moral essays of a former age, they would unquestionably turn from them, to the living and often rudely expressed *sermo* which stammers under the weight of its responsibilities, as it grapples with the sins, and sorrows, and trials of a most complex daily life.

An age, characterised by a science and literature and art which are all its own, will, as a consequence, be marked by a theology peculiar to it. When the forces are more analytic than synthetic, candid minds will never dogmatise. The ablest judges hesitate to decide how far the progress of scientific research, the revival of grammatical learning, the vast discoveries of the scriptures of long-buried religions, have modified, or are likely to modify, our thinking in the grandest of all themes. Most of us, however, will gladly own that while theology is no less divine than it was, it is now immensely more human. It is no longer prosecuted in order to find defences for an existing system, but scientifically, out of reverence to God and devotion to truth alone. A research which is reverent may well be inexorable, for whatever havoc it may make of opinion, it can never damage, but only confirm, the Faith. It is to the credit of the Church that in such an age it has maintained an attitude wisely tolerant toward those religious difficulties which must exercise all living minds. It has never owned the necessity of producing from its armoury the terrible instrument of libel for heresy, and it has been rewarded, on the whole, by a very general loyalty to its standards. Here and there, indeed, its tolerance has been strained and even abused. Yet, as no one would think of bringing down the whole weight and majesty of law on some foolish boy who, bewitched by the false glory of Jack Sheppard, aspires to play the *rôle* of highwayman, so no one thinks of libelling for heresy persons who plainly are ignorant of the real meaning of the word. Their offences are often only the excrescences of unformed intellects, which we may expect of themselves to yield to fuller knowledge and maturer thought. In any case, the attempt to regulate rather than repress movements whose origin is beyond our control, will prove the truest wisdom in the end.

One of the weak points of the Presbyterian Church is its worship, though the reasons of this have not sufficiently been taken into account. Never at any time very rich in ecclesiastical structures, Scotland, toward the close of the seventeenth century, found her heritage wasted; not so much by the fanaticism of reformers as by the ravages of Southern armies and the evil fortune of several generations of civil war and confusion. The land was too impoverished to repair what the wealth of the old Church reared; and so many a valuable relic was allowed to crumble into decay. For many years after its establishment, the Church was confronted in many parishes by heritors hostile to its polity, and had to be content with such structures as their parsimony permitted them to provide. Then the religious feeling of last century was too weak to be concerned about the matter. Men went about the building of a church as they did about the building of a barn, and did not scruple to use as their quarry the beautiful ecclesiastical relics they possessed. It is a startling fact that the age which produced such structures as still disfigure too many of our towns and parishes, was precisely one that felt no obligation to preach the Gospel to the heathen. The men who could take the stones worn by the devotion of former generations, to build a pen for their oxen or their swine, were just the very men who could condone bribery in a judge, and drunkenness in a minister.

It was not the revival of taste or culture, but the revival of religion, that awoke and fostered that reforming spirit which now strives to undo the ravages of a former time, by replacing the miserable buildings which blot many a landscape with churches worthy of their object, and by restoring in the grand structures that survive, the old sublimity to the arched roof, and the old grace to the traceried window. While we venerate our old cathedrals and parish churches as affecting memorials of our country's past, we do well to prize them even more for their association with our religion; and we are simply doing our duty in dedicating to their restoration something of our wealth, as a thank-offering for the privileges of which they perpetually remind us that we are still the heirs.

Improvement in the services of the house of God went hand in hand with this attempt to improve its structure. One looks back with amazement to the system which generally prevailed scarcely thirty years ago. Worship there could hardly be in a system which lacked its prominent elements. Liturgical it certainly was, but after the worst of types. In some churches, the opening and closing prayers never varied from year to year; psalms and tunes came round with the same unvarying regularity; the Lord's Prayer was seldom heard. In many others there was no reading of Scripture. So thoroughly had the injunction of 1812 fallen into disuse, that in 1856 the Assembly had to ordain the reading of a portion of the Old and New Testament in every diet of worship.

It has been my endeavour, in sketching this picture, to avoid as far as possible all reference to persons; but it is impossible to avoid alluding to one whose name, though recalling keen and bitter controversy, now awakens only kindly memories in all who knew him. What share he had in furthering this reform in our Scottish worship—how far he helped, how far he hindered it—may be questions between parties yet. But no one can question Dr Lee's enthusiastic prosecution of it for the sake and in the interest of the Church. In a matter like this, I chronicle rather than criticise; but the introduction of instrumental music into the service is undoubtedly due to his contendings. Other changes might have come without his advocacy, but it was certainly through his pleadings that the organ, that 'holy Nazarite that will not go to the dance or to the battle,' has been permitted again to enter the house of the Lord.

That the whole Church sympathised in the reform of public worship, even when opposing Dr Lee's method of prosecuting it, is proved by its united action. As early as 1852, it began to consider what was necessary for the improvement of praise.

Though in 1859 the reading of prayers from a book was condemned, a committee appointed before was continued, to prepare forms of worship for the use of soldiers and sailors and colonists. The Aids to Devotion, the Hymnal, the Psalter, and the Psalmody publications; the forms of address respecting baptismal professions and obligations, transmitted in 1871 to every minister of the Church, are the fruits of this action. Further progress in this reform depends upon the moderation of those most anxiously interested in it. There is nothing in its constitution to prevent the Church—free as it is to use for edification the spiritual treasures of Christendom—from yet formulating for the Scottish people their own Book of Common Order. But I am persuaded that if that does appear, it will be permissive rather than compulsory. In poverty and long tribulation, it has learned the value of free prayer. The danger of having no liturgy may be to sever it from the wisdom and piety of the past; but the having one may involve the greater peril of severance from that living fount of inspiration which alone can make it the Church of the Present and the Future.

The enormous increase in the power of the press, which now penetrates for good or evil into every family in the kingdom, is at last coming to be appreciated by the Church. At no time has it encouraged publications professing authoritatively to defend its interests, wisely judging that all such tend only to foster narrowness and excite hostility, and are really unnecessary in a community whose only policy is industry. In 1860, however, *Good Words* may be said to have revolutionised popular religious literature. At first fiercely opposed on account of its very catholicity, it soon came to be earnestly imitated even by those who denounced it; and now among the many periodicals which seek to educate or amuse the world, *Life and Work*, flying the pennon of the Church, holds bravely its way. Here again, however, the aim is neither propagandist nor defensive, but solely to provide a wholesome popular literature at the cheapest possible rate, and to stimulate Christian life in all manifold forms of activity.

In concluding this survey, I would touch very lightly upon the spiritual life of the Church, for the truest and best things of a Church are precisely those which no one can tabulate. The system of results applied to education is said to be injurious, as lowering both its quantity and quality. Applied to the Church, it would simply be ruinous. The life of a Church can never be measured by the amount of its revenues or by the extent and variety of its activities. Where there is life there will be activity; but there may be much showy activity without life. The healthiest Church is the most liberal and tolerant and humble: the severest in its strictures on its own, the readiest to put the best construction on the action of others. That our Church has shared in that baptism of benevolence which stamps the present as one of the most missionary and charitable of Christian centuries no one can deny. The largest individual offering ever made in modern times to the cause of religion is recorded of it. Unsolicited, and solely from a sense of indebtedness, Mr James Baird, one of the shrewdest and kindliest of Scotchmen, crowned many generous gifts by devoting in his lifetime half a million of money to be spent in furthering its usefulness. The very amount of his gift is significant of his faith in the Church. That the people, are everywhere turning to it in increasing numbers, proves that it accords with their national sentiment, and satisfies their spiritual wants. Whatever may be charged against it, it cannot be said to bear itself oppressively or offensively toward any outsider. Its members have no advantages which they are not prepared to share with others on the same terms on which they enjoy them. So if the people are wise, they will not permit the ark of God to be dragged into the dust of party warfare, but will maintain it as a common national shrine to which, after their keenest conflicts, all parties can alike repair.

ST GILES' LECTURES.

FIRST SERIES—THE SCOTTISH CHURCH.

LECTURE XII.

THE CHURCH OF THE PRESENT DAY:

HOW FAR AN OUTGROWTH FROM THE PAST, AND AN EXPRESSION OF THE RELIGIOUS THOUGHT AND LIFE OF SCOTLAND.

By the Rev. JAMES MACGREGOR, D.D., Senior Minister of St Cuthbert's Parish, Edinburgh.

IN discharging the duty which has been imposed upon me, I have, in this concluding lecture, to review the ground traversed by my predecessors; to trace the historic links which connect the existing Church of Scotland with the distant past; and to indicate its present position, aims, and prospects.

It is historically certain that a pure Christian faith reached the Scottish shores some time before the close of the fourth century. The same St Ninian who brought us the great gift, and who built his Candida Casa, or White House, within the roar of the racing Solway, seems to have been the first who carried it to Ireland. It was a time when the Bishops of Rome, though powerful, had not as yet attained to supreme jurisdiction, and when the ministers of religion still claimed to derive their authority from Christ alone. It was the faith of the great Councils of Nice and Constantinople; the faith of Jerome and Ambrose and

Augustine. The isolation of the British Churches from communion with those of Western Europe, consequent upon the withdrawal of the Roman power from Britain in 410 A.D., tended to preserve their pristine purity. In the hundred and fifty years that followed, it is faintest twilight, the movements uncertain, the forms shadowy and dim. The twilight broadens into dawn on the arrival of Columba with his twelve disciples at Iona in 563, the greatest character and the greatest event in the history of the Scottish Church next to Knox and the Reformation. Thanks to the industry of his successor and biographer Adamnan, that great figure stands out, in sharp relief against the darkness that preceded and followed, in a light almost modern in its clearness; and we can see distinctly, what kind of man he was, what he thought, believed, and taught, and how he lived and wrought and died. To all time he will be known as the great apostle of Scottish Christianity, and his lonely, beautiful, and soft-aired Iona as its mother-shrine. We have one strong link which binds the early Celtic Church which he founded with the Church of our modern day, in the fact attested by Columbanus, that 'he received nought but the doctrine of the evangelists and apostles;' and in the evidence of Adamnan, that 'the foundation of Columba's preaching, and his great instrument in the conversion of the heathen, was the Word of God.' No fact could be more significant or prophetic. It was the pure and unadulterated religion of Jesus that was first offered to our forefathers, and that first broke in upon the gloom of our ancient forests. The first strong foundations of the Scottish Church were laid broad and deep, where they rest to-day, on the solid rock of Scripture. It was with this book in their hands that Columba fought and won the battle with Paganism; Knox, the battle with Popery; Melville, the first battle of Presbytery with Episcopacy—the three great struggles which shaped the form and determined the fortunes of the Scottish Church. It has been the living contact of the Scottish mind with its life-giving words which more than all other forces put together have made this country what it is. With the exception of the Roman Catholic period, this note runs all through the history of the Scottish Church.

From the coming of Columba there is light for one hundred and fifty years, and we know with considerable certainty what is going on. It radiates from Iona and spreads over the greater part of Scotland north of the Forth and Clyde. Then comes a long, dark, and much-confused period of four hundred years. One fact stands clear out to the student of that misty time, that from the days of Columba to the death of Malcolm Canmore, Scotland had a National Church peculiarly her own, which was neither Roman Catholic nor Episcopalian nor Presbyterian, and whose direct paternity it is folly for any Christian Church of this day to claim. When the light died out with Adamnan in 704, it was monastic, not parochial nor diocesan; when the light came in with Saxon Margaret and her sons, it was monastic still. All through, it was tribal, not territorial; it was Celtic, not Roman. Its rulers were abbots, to whom the bishops were often subject. Its clergy were not always celibate. They owned no subjection to Rome; and they bore no resemblance to either the secular or the regular clergy of the Western Church. We can also see through those dim years that this Celtic Church has been made familiar with suffering; that its clergy have tasted the bitterness of exile; that it has lost its churches and been stripped of its property. We find traces, too, of that independent spirit—that passionate love of freedom, that jealousy of foreign interference and dictation, that capacity of suffering for what they believed to be right— which a little later were to be tried and tempered in the long war with England, and which have come down to us as one of our richest inheritances from those ancient times.

In the eleventh and twelfth centuries, owing to decay from within and to English influence from without, there came a slow and silent, but important revolution. The monastic system was giving place to the diocesan, and over the whole of the Lowlands of Scotland, the Celtic to the Saxon tongue. The year in which King Malcolm, the saintly Margaret, and Fothad, the last native Bishop of Alban, died—1093—may be said to date the passing away of the Celtic Church. With the establishment of the Benedictines in Iona in 1203, the Roman rule became universal in Scotland. In 1286, the stumble of a horse on the crags of Kinghorn completed the process, by bringing to an end the ancient dynasty of our Celtic kings.

Of the great revolution which then took place, two results have lived on to our day, and distinctly connect the living present with the distant past. Few things in this world of change have vitality enough to carry them over a period of seven hundred years. There are at least two parts of the present Church system of Scotland which go back without a break through that long period of time. The one is our elastic territorial and parochial system, capable of readjustment to the varying needs of the population. No better system ever was or ever will be devised for securing the spiritual supervision of a country, and the whole body of its people. The other is the provision for religious ordinances by the principle of tithe or teind, which was originally the voluntary assignment, not by the State, but by the great lords who owned the soil, of the tenth part of the produce of the parish for the supply of its religious wants; and which thus became the property of the Church by an indefeasible title. So ancient is this system of tithe, that Blackstone emphatically declares that no beginning can be found for it. According to Bede, there was as early as the seventh century a 'kirk sest,' which very probably resembled tithes. In Scotland, there belonged to the Church, besides the teinds, extensive property in land, which had also been the voluntary gift of the great landowners, and which continued to belong to the Church, first in its Celtic, and then in its Roman form, down to the Reformation. In 1587, by what can only be described as a great act of spoliation, this property passed to the crown, and through it became the possession, in too many instances, of worthless nobles. The teinds were not seriously touched, and as rearranged by Charles I. in 1633, still continue as a national provision for religious ordinances. The entire yearly income of the rightful property of the Church from the ancient endowments would amount at the present value to an enormous sum. What has escaped spoliation amounts to only £275,000, which is less than the income of many single noblemen. How many properties in this land are held to-day by so long and so strong a tenure, as the fragment that still remains of that ancient provision for the spiritual wants of the people, and especially of the poor of Scotland; and of what properties can it be said that they have been so faithfully and so consistently employed for the public good? Should the nation ever resolve to reconsider the purposes to which this property is applied, it would be an interesting inquiry to try to ascertain what became of those vast landed estates which, unbought by money or by service, passed from public into private hands, what national interests they have subserved, and whether any portion of them might not still be recovered for national purposes.

Beyond the institution of parishes and of parochial endowments; the effect on the national character of the long and bitter war of independence; and the scattered remains of the great ecclesiastical edifices, no existing link connects the four hundred years of papal domination with the Church of the present day. It was a period which, not without promise at its commencement, darkened deeply towards its close. The Romish Church was everywhere growing more degraded and corrupt, at the very time when, through the revival of letters, a new light and a new life were dawning on the world. There are probably two main reasons why, when the work of Reformation came, it was more thoroughly effected in Scotland than in any other country of Europe; because nowhere had Romanism attained to a condition of more unmitigated vileness, and because nowhere was the work of cleansing more thoroughly the work of the people, and a people, too, whose habit has ever been to do with their might what their hand findeth to do.

The form which the Scottish Church took amid the throes of the Reformation, and which it will probably always maintain, was due to the two greatest and most fruitful facts to be found in the whole range of its history—that the battle of Protestantism was fought by the people, and that the principal weapon used in the conflict was, as we have seen, the Word of God. The result was a Church essentially popular and Scriptural, which recognised in the education and intelligence of the people the best ally of religion, which was built in the main upon a Presbyterian basis, and which (17th August 1560) was established by law.

From the Reformation till the Revolution, a period of one hundred and thirty years, the spectacle which our country presents is that of a people at war with their rulers for their religious rights. During five successive reigns, from Mary to James VII., every ruler who sat upon the throne did his very utmost to thrust his religious views upon the people, with the invariable result of leaving the victory with them. The war of Protestantism with Popery had scarcely ended when the war of Presbytery with Prelacy began (at the Concordat of Leith on Feb. 1, 1572), and raged with ever-varying fortunes through one hundred and eighteen troubled and turbulent years, till in June 1690 it ended in the victory of Presbytery as the permanent and legal form of Church government. Since the war of independence, no struggle so protracted, so fierce, so bloody, has been waged by the Scottish people. The war of independence began with the passing away of the Celtic Dynasty and the establishment of the House of Stuart. The religious war ended in their expulsion from the throne. The inborn love of freedom was the motive cause of both, and both have left their ineffaceable marks on the character of the Scottish people.

So far as the legal establishment of the opposing systems went, the attitude of affairs was this:

PRESBYTERY.	EPISCOPACY.
Aug. 17, 1560—Feb. 1, 1572.	Feb. 1, 1572—June 1592.
June 1592—Oct. 1612.	Oct. 1612—June 1640.
June 1640—May 1661.	May 1661—June 1690.

Of these one hundred and thirty years, Presbytery was the legal system at three different periods, covering, in round numbers, fifty-two years; Episcopacy was the legal system at three different periods, covering in round numbers seventy-eight years. But the periods of possession are no indication of the relative hold of the systems upon the minds of the people generally. In every instance, Episcopacy was violently imposed by the sovereign, and was overthrown by the people. It thus became in their minds the symbol of despotism. There can be no doubt that all through, the feelings and convictions of the mass of the people, except in the North, were on the side of Presbytery. In not one of the many ups and downs of that period of strife was Presbytery overthrown and Episcopacy imposed by the people's will. 'The rational inference' which Macaulay draws from the facts of the case is this, that at the Revolution 'more than nineteen-twentieths of those Scotchmen whose consciences were interested in the matter were Presbyterians, and that not one Scotchman in twenty was decidedly and on conviction an Episcopalian.'

It was not Episcopacy in itself which they resisted, so much as the royal and priestly despotism of which it was the symbol. It was the gross Erastianism, servility, and tyranny with which it was associated, which made it an abomination to the Scottish people. Such is the calm verdict of impartial history.

Another fact must be borne in mind. At none of the periods during which the system was established was it Episcopacy pure and simple. It was Episcopacy overlying a Presbyterian ground-work. The Kirk-session and the Presbytery lived on through the whole period of strife. In matters of creed, worship, and discipline, there was very little difference between the rival systems. Of the two collegiate ministers of the Tron Kirk, Edinburgh, in 1692, one was Episcopalian and the other Presbyterian. There were rival kirk-sessions as well as rival ministers, and the service was conducted at the different diets according to the different forms. Beyond the institution of Bishops, the present Anglicanised Episcopal Church in Scotland bears little resemblance to that which fought so hard a battle with Presbytery in the seventeenth century, and lost.

At the Revolution Settlement in 1690, it was finally determined that Presbytery was to be the future and permanent form of the Scottish Reformed Church, and that there was not to be a union of the two National Churches, even with the union of the two kingdoms; and the first chapter of its history came to an end.

Was it a gain or was it a loss that the struggle ended as it did? That question has been asked before. Of the influence which the issue had, not merely upon Scotland, but upon the United Kingdom, the verdict of one who, though himself a Scotchman, and a grandson of the manse, had certainly no prejudice in favour of his native Church or land, may be taken as probably not very far from the truth. 'There can be no doubt,' says Macaulay, 'that a religious union (between Scotland and England in 1689) would have been one of the greatest calamities that could have befallen either kingdom. The union accomplished in 1707 has indeed been a great blessing to both England and Scotland. But it has been a blessing, because, in constituting one State, it left two Churches. . . . . Had there been an amalgamation of the hierarchies, there never would have been an amalgamation of the nations. . . . Those marvellous improvements which have changed the face of Scotland would never have been effected. Plains now rich with harvests would have remained barren moors. . . . New Lanark would still have been a sheep-walk, and Greenock a fishing-village. What little strength Scotland could, under such a system, have possessed must, in an estimate of the resources of Great Britain, have not been added, but deducted. So encumbered, our country never could have held, either in peace or in war, a place in the first rank of nations.'[1]

Can as high an estimate be formed of the value of the Presbyterian victory as regards the Church? In answer to that question, we must see what that form of Church government was which then became the permanent polity.

'Three elements exist in the Presbyterian system—the authority of presbyters, more especially as subordinate to no office-bearer of higher rank in the Church; the representation of the Laity in its government; and the provision made for its external unity in courts of review.' The reason why not the Church of Scotland merely, but all the Churches of the Reformation, had naturally the tendency to assume the Presbyterian form, and did so wherever they were not thwarted, as in England, by external circumstances, was simply this—that while breaking with the immediate, the Reformers went back to the remoter and purer past, and drew their system from the fountain-head of Holy Scripture. Like the primitive Apostolic Church on which it was modelled, the Presbyterian Church recognises but two permanent offices, that of presbyters or elders, and that of deacons—the one for things spiritual, the other for things temporal; its basis, unit, and type being the congregation, with its court of associated elders called the kirk-session. Like it, it regards the Christian people as the only Christian Church and the only Christian priests. Like it, it unites the congregations of a locality for purposes of government into a higher court called the Presbytery, which consists of a clerical and

---

[1] *History of England*, vol. iii., p. 257.

lay representative from each kirk-session. Each member of the Presbytery is also a member of a higher court representing a province, and known as the Provincial Synod. The highest court of all is the General Assembly, which is composed of representatives or commissioners, both lay and clerical, appointed by the various Presbyteries, and also of representatives from the royal burghs and universities. Each of these courts in the National Church has its jurisdiction, status, and functions secured by the law of the land. From the decisions of the Supreme Court on matters within its own province, there is no appeal. The Church is thus a perfect organic whole; its every separate congregation being not only an integral part, but a fully equipped type or model of the whole Church. There is thus also a simple and orderly gradation in the system of government, one court rising above another, from that which represents a single congregation to that which represents the whole Church, and each and all of them containing that large infusion of the lay element which prevents the governing power from being wielded by a class; and by its practical wisdom, its knowledge of affairs, its variety of status, intellect, and character, constitutes the beauty, the stability, and the freedom of the National Church of Scotland—a Church which is thus in perfect harmony at once with Apostolic practice and with the representative institutions of modern times. What has been declared to be the great want of the Church of England is admirably supplied by the General Assembly—namely, 'a continuously acting organ by which to adjust itself to the needs which changing times must bring upon every living and working society of men.' For capacity of self-extension, self-adjustment, and self-government, for adaptation to widely different circumstances and conditions, for elasticity and catholicity, no system could be more admirable. As a consequence, it is found in somewhat different forms among many different peoples and in widely distant lands. If we leave out the Lutherans of Germany and elsewhere, who are not Prelatical nor even Episcopal, in the sense attached to that word by the Anglican Church, the Presbyterians of the world outnumber the Protestant Episcopalians. 'Of all organisations in the Christian Church,' says Dr Hill Burton, 'Presbytery is, next to the Romish Hierarchy, the most powerful. In places entirely isolated from external aid and countenance, it is far more accomplished in organisation than any other Church.'

There are two eminent advantages which flow from its essentially popular character, and from the large lay element in its government. It requires, and therefore fosters as an essential element in its success, an all-pervading intelligence in the community. In this respect, as in many others, it was admirably suited to a country which could boast that it was not only the best, but the only educated nation in the world. Above all, it renders practically impossible the growth of that sacerdotalism and superstition, whose only logical resting-place is Rome, and which events have proved to be the incurable taint and defect of Episcopacy, wherever it has been held to be divinely authoritative to the exclusion of all other systems of church government. When a Scotchman, from whatever cause, breaks off from Presbyterianism in his own land, he breaks off from the Church of Scottish history, the Church to which we owe so much both of our civil and religious light and freedom, and with whose fortunes and misfortunes the brightest pages of the national annals have been identified.

The system, so theoretically perfect, is not without grave practical defects. There is a want of central control; a want of the unity, concentration, and cohesiveness which diocesan Episcopacy gives. The principle of equality errs by excess. There is no natural initiative; there is no firm and responsible executive; there is no permanent authority. While the system is free from prelatic despotism, it is by no means free from the danger of clerical and popular oppression. When democracy becomes tyrannical, its tyranny is often of the worst kind.

With the Revolution Settlement and the Treaty of Union, a new chapter in the history of the Scottish Church began which is not yet completed; new questions emerged which are not yet answered. The fruitful and far-reaching influence of a great national wrong was never more strikingly illustrated than in the long train of miserable and not yet exhausted consequences which followed the ill-omened Act of Queen Anne, whereby, in 1712, against the unanimous will of the Church, Patronage was restored. A strong consensus of opinion points to this Act, against which the Church continued to protest for more than seventy years, as the principal root of the troubles which followed. It would be difficult to find an Act of Parliament against which so heavy a bill of indictment can be brought. It directly led to the first secession in 1733, which within fourteen years was itself split into two by the Burghers' oath. It had a principal share in the formation of the two great parties known as the Moderates and the Populars, and their long and bitter contentions regarding the presentation and the call. The harsh deposition of the gentle Gillespie in 1752, and the consequent founding of the first Relief Presbytery in 1761, were due to it. A wise voice in 1782 declared that this Act and the Church of Scotland could not stand together. But for it, the Church would never have been induced to go beyond her province, and to exceed the rights secured to her by statute, by passing the Chapel Act and the Veto Act of 1834, and thus to embark upon the most unwise and fatal conflict to be found in the whole range of her history. In spite of the great and honoured men who took part in it, and of the splendid act of self-sacrifice to which it led, no conflict better shews to how large an extent human frailty, passion, and prejudice are factors in ecclesiastical history. No good man can wish that his country should pass through such a time again.

Had the bitter leaven which wrought so much mischief, and which was purged out in 1874, been removed in 1834, the story of the Disruption would never have been written. But what was right in 1834 could not be wrong in 1874. When the Church embraced a favourable opportunity presented to it, and sought for its people the restoration of an ancient and much-prized privilege, which had been violently wrested from it; when it obtained from Parliament the removal of an incubus which Parliament had itself imposed, and which had weighed it down for a hundred and sixty years; when it sought to get nearer the hearts of its alienated children by the removal of the one great cause of their alienation—was that, in the eye of everlasting righteousness, right or wrong? Even granting that the motive was the desire to lessen Dissent, to bring the Churches closer together, and to hasten the day when our broken Presbyterianism shall again be one, and when they who now stand far apart shall see each other eye to eye—was that a mean and ignoble motive? Is schism in itself a blessing? Is Dissent divine? Is the desire to remove the cause of schism in itself a wrong? True! it might have been well for all parties had the boon come earlier. But it is surely true of blessings that they are better late than never. True, too, that the evils which an Act of Parliament can do, another Act may not wholly undo. The stream of tendency which has been set aflowing can never perhaps be wholly dried up or rolled back to its fountain-head. It is easy to divide; it is not easy to unite. But surely an unjust Act, pregnant with mischief, is better off than on the statute-book. It is hard, no doubt, for the Free Church to feel, 'If Patronage had been done away with in time, there would have been no occasion to suffer as we have done.' But it is not a high or noble or justifiable ground for even a suffering Church to take with regard to another—' because we did not get a loaf of bread when we were hungry, we shall take care that you do not get it either.' On no intelligible ground can the abolition of Patronage be made, as it has openly been, the occasion of an attack upon the National Church, save on the principle that Dissenters have a vested interest in the defects and abuses of the Establishment. A more disingenuous or a more repulsive doctrine was never fashioned in the brain of Christian men.

On no part of its long and chequered history may the Church of Scotland look back with more unfeigned thankfulness to Almighty God than on the period that has elapsed since 1843, and during no period have there rested on its labours more manifest tokens of the Divine blessing. 'In quietness and confidence has been its strength.' Because 'peace has been within its walls,' there has been 'prosperity within its palaces.' Itself habitually maligned and traduced, its bitterest enemy cannot charge it with having ever, even in the heat of the strife, uttered a harsh word or done a harsh deed to those who left its communion, and whose very nearness of relationship, as so often happens, seems to have intensified their enmity. A common danger past, drew its members closer together. A meeker and more patient, a more temperate, tolerant, and united spirit, was born of the sorrows of a troubled time. Clearly recognising that its faithfulness to its great principle and mission as a national Church is its one permanent title to the nation's respect and confidence, it has done its very best, through its Endowment and Home Mission Schemes, to provide the ministrations of religion to every destitute locality of the land. To this quiet and steadfast devotion to its national duty, and to freedom from the curse of internal strife, is mainly owing that astonishing success which has marked the Church during recent years, and which unhappily, in the eyes of some, is its most obnoxious feature and its worst offence.

By far the best evidence with regard to the numerical strength of the different Churches would have been that ecclesiastical column in the census returns which the two Established

Churches have repeatedly sought, but which the Nonconformists have steadily and successfully resisted. We find, however, from their own returns that the communicants of the Free Church are about 230,000, and those of the United Presbyterian Church about 172,000; while from her own and parliamentary returns, those of the Church of Scotland are about 500,000, or more than the other two put together. This would give it 1,750,000 adherents at the ordinary reckoning, or close upon a half of the entire population. It has been shewn, too, that the increase of membership of the Established Church is 8000 a year, or in eight years, 64,000; while in the Report of the Secretary of the Sustentation Fund of the Free Church in December 1875 there are these words: 'It may be assumed that our membership should have shewn an increase over 1867 of 22,100. But it is shewn above, on the basis of Presbyterial returns, that the increase was only 7062. There is, therefore, a deficit of 15,000, or $7\frac{1}{2}$ per cent.' The Report of the United Presbyterian Church presented to their Synod in 1877, declares: 'On the whole, the United Presbyterian Church may have maintained, but has not improved or strengthened, its position in relation to the total population of the country.' In fifteen of the Established churches in Edinburgh and Leith, the membership in 1874 was 17,064, and in 1879 it was 19,485, an increase of 2421; whereas in fifteen Free churches in Edinburgh and Leith, occupying the same localities, and bearing the same names, the numbers were 7430 in 1874, and 7761 in 1879, an increase of only 331. The proportion in these churches is therefore two and a half to one in favour of the Established Church; and her increase in five years is more than seven times greater—and this in a city supposed to be the stronghold of the Free Church. In the same way, the increase in Sunday scholars in the Established Church during twenty-six years ending 1877, exceeded by 20,681 the increase of both the other denominations put together. During the six years ending 1877, the free-will offerings of the Established Church, including £500,000 from the late James Baird, amounted to £2,431,779. All this is a sufficient answer to the common platform assertion that the Established Church is 'moribund,' and confirms the statement that 'it is yearly gaining in numbers, in influence for good, and in the recognition of its merits by the general body of the people.' There can be no doubt that where other things are equal, the drift of the Scottish people is towards the Church of their fathers.

But there are facts far more important than any figures, and whose value no figures can estimate, underlying and explaining these external marks of success. These facts are mainly these —the Church's evangelical doctrine, spiritual earnestness, and tolerant and comprehensive spirit. Such experience as has been given me by a ministry of five-and-twenty years in important centres of influence, is the ground and warrant of my belief that through all these years there has been a gradual deepening of the Church's spiritual life, and that it was never more healthy than at the present day. Never was there more of genuine piety, never more of personal love and loyalty to the Lord Jesus, than there is now among its ministers and people. Never was there a more faithful preaching in its pulpits of the love of God in the redemption of the world through Jesus Christ; never a more faithful ministration of the doctrines of grace throughout the length and the breadth of the land. Never was its worship more comely and reverent, nor its parochial system better manned and wrought, than it is at the present day. Never were its clergy more alive to their duty, more pure in life and doctrine, more abounding in zeal and good works based upon a personal devotion to their great Master. If there are exceptions, they are exceedingly rare; and at what period and in what Church have there not been such?

Another marked and growing feature of the National Church is its breadth and comprehensiveness. All through, it has sought to maintain a friendly relation with other churches.

It is actuated by no narrow aims, and by no sectarian jealousies; its pulpits are open to ministers of all evangelical denominations, and it welcomes to its communion and to a share of its endowments any Presbyterian minister and congregation who may care to take them. It embraces within its membership a wider range of society, a more equal balance of political parties, a richer intellectual life, and a greater variety of religious type than any other Church. It is a striking fact that no considerable secession ever took place from its ranks on the ground of doctrine. With a folly of which it has long since repented, it expelled two of the best men it ever had, Edward Irving and John Macleod Campbell. With an enviable nobility of soul, they both loved it to the last; and Campbell died in its communion. It is of the very nature of a national Church that it be politically, socially, religiously, as broad and comprehensive as the national life which it represents; not bound to one hard and fast line of Christian thought and sentiment, but tolerating and comprehending all shades and types of thought that are consistent with the great root doctrines of Christianity; recognising, respecting, and fostering whatever agencies and forces are at work for the general good, whether within or without itself. A national Church is fulfilling one of its very highest functions when it seeks to utilise and to consecrate all the forces which are at work in the nation—its wealth, its æsthetic taste, its literature, its changing currents of opinion, its political movements, its thought, its culture—to imbue them, as far as it may, with a Christian spirit, and to guide them to high and noble ends. A national Church is, or ought to be, and none but a national Church can be, the spiritual leaven of the nation.

In the Church's contributions to literature, and in the general intelligence and culture of the clergy, the period under review will contrast not unfavourably with any past time.

Such changes as have taken place in the current of opinion and teaching have been in the direction of a gentler theology, more in keeping with the softened manners of a milder time. Far more than in former times is the love of God in Christ the great theme of the pulpit, and far less the terrors of the law; far more the Fatherhood, and far less the Magistracy of God. It is a question whether this milder form of teaching is not carried to excess. A freer but not less reverential handling of the Word of God; a wider latitude of opinion, not as to the fact, but as to the *modus operandi* of the Atonement; a less stern and rigid view of Sabbath obligation and observance; a more merciful and hopeful view of the future destiny, not only of the millions outside the Christian Church, but of mankind in general—these are changes which have come more or less over all churches alike. There are two main directions in which the tide seems strongly running; one is towards a relaxed subscription of the Confession of Faith, the creed of Presbyterians throughout the world, and, all in all, perhaps the noblest creed of Christendom. The consensus of opinion is clearly towards the maintenance of the Confession intact, as too valuable and too venerable to be safely tampered with. That some latitude of interpretation is allowable seems evident from the very nature of the document itself, and from the circumstance that when it was approved by the Assembly of 1647, it was expressly on the ground that it was 'in nothing contrary to the received doctrine, &c., of this Kirk'—that received doctrine being the old Scots Confession of 1560, 'which has never been repealed, modified, or departed from.' If it was expressly allowable to the men of 1647 to treat the new Confession in the light of the old, the same liberty seems allowable to the men of 1881. All that the statute of 1693 requires in the matter of subscription is, that the subscriber accept it as 'the confession of his faith.' Whatever additional stringency has been added to these terms, has been the work of the Assembly; and what the Assembly has done, it can also undo.[1]

---

[1] See this whole subject powerfully handled in the paper on Disestablishment, by the Duke of Argyll. Strahan & Co., London.

In looking back over these five-and-twenty years, nothing strikes me more than the marked change which has taken place for the better in public worship, and especially in the matter and manner of public prayer. Few things more nearly affect the welfare of a Church than that form of worship by which it gives expression to its faith in, its dependence on, and its communion with God; and few things have done our own Church more harm than its long and slovenly neglect of this important department of its work, and its departure in this respect from its earlier and better ways. Among the historical facts which it is neither to our credit nor to our welfare to forget, one is, that for the first hundred years of its existence the Reformed Church of Scotland had a richer and more varied service than it has ever had since. It had its Prayer-book, its order for the administration of the sacraments, its service of praise with Hymns as well as Psalms and appropriate tunes. The loss of all this was due not to Scottish, but to English influence. As time advances and taste improves, there is a growing tendency to return to the moderate and enlightened views of Knox and the early Reformers. The Assembly has sanctioned the use of the Prose Psalter, a Hymnal, and an Anthem book. Instrumental music is being widely introduced as a help to psalmody. Church architecture has been immensely improved throughout Scotland. Fast-days are going; and it is not unlikely that in the course of time their place will be taken by the days commemorative of those great facts and events which secured the redemption of the world. While the privilege of extempore prayer will never be abandoned in Scotland, there are good men in all the churches, and these the very men who have the highest conception of what public prayer is, who would be thankful for the use of a modified and permissive Liturgy, as a blessing to themselves, and some security for a more reverent and decorous worship over the length and breadth of the land.

The story which has now been brought to a close is one of

which every Scotchman may well be proud. If we leave out Palestine and Greece, no country of equal size has played a more prominent and beneficial part in human affairs than our own. In theology, in philosophy, in literature, in science, in jurisprudence, in government, in art, in mechanical invention, in war, in every element that tends to human progress, her children have taken and are taking a foremost place. Though her skies are cold, her soil poor, her advantages in comparison with other countries very small, history will never forget what Scotland has done. In the measure in which we are proud of our country we must be proud of our Church, for until a recent period the country and the Church were one.

One question remains: What is to be the future of the Church whose present condition and past fortunes have now been traced? Is she to be preserved and strengthened with a view to continued and increasing usefulness, or is she to be uprooted as the National Church? We have seen that the three main inheritances which the past has handed down to the present, and of which the National Church is the sacred depositary and guardian, are evangelical doctrine, Presbyterian polity, and legal establishment and endowment. The first of these was restored at and secured by the Reformation; the second was permanently secured by the Revolution Settlement; the third has been the unbroken possession of the Church from the beginning. There was a time when her doctrine was not evangelical. There was a time when her polity was not Presbyterian. There never was a time when she was severed from the State. Wars have raged around her doctrine; wars have raged around her polity; but until recent times there has been no war about that State connection, which is the strong security for both. No account of the Church of Scotland would be historically just which left out of view the most remarkable feature of modern ecclesiastical life.

Seriously viewed in all its lights and bearings, there is

perhaps no more melancholy chapter in the long and chequered history of the Scottish Church than that which is now in the process of being written. In none of all the struggles which have been under review would it be so difficult to detect any trace of moral grandeur, of genuine nobility, of far-sighted patriotism, as in that agitation for the destruction of the National Church which has already begun. This ancient and stately edifice, whose history has been traced in these lectures, which was built by the pious wisdom and hallowed by the blood of our forefathers, within whose friendly shelter was reared and fostered all that has made Scotland great and free, the Scottish people of to-day are asked to destroy. Before they lend themselves to this unhallowed work, there are several questions which they would do well to consider.

1. What is the work which they are asked to do? It is simply the destruction of the Church of Scotland, the oldest, the greatest, and the best of all our national institutions, which, once swept away, can never be restored. No cloud of soft words should be allowed to obscure the real issue. Her connection with the State, as the expression of national religion, is the very thing which, next to her doctrine and her polity, and to her allegiance to her spiritual Head and King, is her glory, her strength, and her joy. It is one of the three strong links which bind the Church of to-day to the Church of the remotest past. To sever that long-continued connection, so fruitful in blessing to Church and State alike, is to lay her in ruins. She would still be a Church of Christ, but she would no longer be the Church of Scotland. Our country would have one sect more, but no longer a national religion nor a national Church; and as nowhere has the relation between Church and State—those two divine ordinances for human good—been closer than in Scotland, so nowhere has the influence of their interaction told more upon the habits of the people and the history of the land. The continuity of our national life would be broken by their

severance, and a religious, social, and political revolution accomplished—the greatest that has taken place since the Reformation. Lord Moncreiff, whose family holds a high place in Scottish ecclesiastical history, and who is himself the most eminent of living Free Churchmen, has said that this would be to 'undo the work of three hundred years.' It would be the greatest possible impulse which could be given to the revolutionary tendencies of the times, to the levelling and communistic spirit which is in the air. There are not a few who think that if the oldest and best of our institutions goes, there will not be much left that is worth the keeping. 'For it must not be forgotten,' he further says, 'that changes of this nature are seldom confined in their operation to the object for which they were effected, but frequently find their main development in results the most unexpected, and sometimes in those which are least desired. It is impossible to root out an old tree without disturbing the soil round it; and the abolition of the Established Church would bring with it many results, religious, public, and social, extending far beyond our subjects of controversy.' The Confession of Faith would no longer be the law of the land. One of the most solemn and binding articles in the Treaty of Union would be erased from the statute-book. The first oath of the sovereign on accession to the throne would no longer be to uphold the Church of Scotland. With the solitary exception of our law-courts, not one vestige of our ancient institutions would be left to remind our children of the day when we were a separate people. When these law-courts shall have been transferred to Westminster, Edinburgh will be a second-rate provincial city, and Scotland a mere appanage of England. As England was a party to the Treaty of Union as well as Scotland, England must be a party as well as Scotland to any interference or tampering with it. It is a question on which more than a few Scotchmen, and more than a political party, are entitled to be heard; it is one in which the whole nation is concerned. The aims of the Liberationists are well known. To them the humble and inoffensive Church of Scotland is a matter of little concern. But they know that as the principle which underlies the Establishment north of the Tweed is the principle which underlies the Establishment south of the Tweed, the destruction of the one would greatly hasten the destruction of the other. And what would then follow? There would follow of logical necessity the repeal of the laws fencing the Protestant succession to the throne; the repeal of the laws for Sabbath observance; the repeal of the laws against blasphemy; the repeal of every law on our statute-book which has been the outcome of a national recognition of God and of His laws. For the nation having disestablished its churches, and thereby ceased as a nation to recognise religion, every law founded on religious considerations would be a tyrannical oppression and persecution of those who do not believe in God and who refuse to recognise His laws. To all this, every one in either country to whom national religion is dear will have a word to say.

In Scotland, too, along with State connection, the ancient parochial system would come to an end, and with it the spiritual provision of the Scottish people, and especially of the poor. Every parish throughout the land would be deprived of a property that has belonged to it since parishes were made; a property held by the very oldest and most sacred of tenures, and designed to secure to it for ever the free administration of the ordinances of religion. The tens of thousands of our Scottish poor who can raise no voice loud enough to be heard amid the din of ecclesiastical and political war, would see in silent sorrow their religious patrimony wrested from them. With such facts before us as this, that, out of the 1032 charges of the Free Church in 1878, only 320 are self-supporting—'that is, yield £157 each to the common stipend fund'—it is idle to suppose that any system at all approaching the parochial system will ever be devised and successfully carried out for securing the ministry of educated Christian gentlemen, and the free and faithful preaching of the Gospel over the length and the breadth of the land. If the mass of the Scottish people should ever consent to such a work of revolution and spoliation, they will belie their whole history. One thing is certain: no such upheaval of the social fabric as this can be accomplished without fierce and bitter ecclesiastical war, and the heart-burning, the dissension, the misery, and the serious injury to spiritual life which such wars always entail. A whole generation would bear upon its breast the scars of the strife.

2. What, I ask, is the time which has been chosen for this unholy war—for this destruction of the Church, this alienation of religious property? In spite of the Church's great success, in spite of the good work that is being done by other denominations, look at what still remains to do. Is there not work and room and need for all? There are 500,000 Scotchmen outside all Church influence. Our intemperance and impurity as a people are scandalously high. Over-churching in some districts, and under-churching in others, prevail to a lamentable extent. The Romish Church is making progress. It has restored its Hierarchy. Since 1851 it has increased its priesthood in England and Scotland from 958 to 2282; its churches, from 683 to 1461; its monasteries, from 17 to 160. In 1851 there was not one monastery in Scotland; there are 15 now. It has already accomplished that supposed impossible feat of directly, and through no intermediate steps, drawing to its bosom members of our Presbyterian Church, both high and humble born. There is an Irish Roman Catholic population seething in the centres of our large towns, as much cut off from all elevating wholesome Christian influence as if they were in the wilds of Connemara, and by God's law of influence dragging our people down to their level because we have not lifted them up to ours. There are much worse things than Romanism making progress among us. Rationalism of the worst kind is poisoning to an inconceivable extent large masses of our intelligent artisans. The last five-

and-twenty years have been in some respects the most fateful which the Church of Christ has yet seen. Never since Christianity began has there been a period of equal extent equally prolific in free speculations on religious subjects and in questionings of those fundamental truths on which religion rests. The remarkable thing is the vast area of intelligence which, through means of the periodical press, these speculations reach and influence. It is a time of general upheaval, doubt, and drift. The Bible is subjected to a rationalistic treatment which leaves it an empty and worthless shell, whose ultimate and not very distant destiny is declared to be the shelves of some antiquarian museum. All creeds and all churches are on their trial. In a day like this, when some of the most powerful forces at work in society are not only hostile, but fiercely hostile to all churches alike, and to those dear and blessed interests which they represent; when men of high culture and learning are calling upon those like-minded with themselves to apply the axe to the very roots of Christianity, and to tear it up as a pestilent and accursed thing; when some of the leaders of public opinion, whose words are heard to the ends of the world, live and die acknowledged atheists; when the highest science of the time is growing more avowedly materialistic; when the authority of Scripture, the Divinity of Christ, the immortality of the soul, are day by day more widely denied; when between the aggressive efforts of Romanism on the one hand, and Rationalism on the other, it would almost seem as if the Reformation-force had spent itself, and the tide were on the turn; when some of the ablest and most pious minds in Christendom are seeing in all this 'that downward sweep into religious doubt which is only the long-predicted and mystic harbinger of the beginning of the end'—in a day like this, it is treachery to their Master and suicidal faithlessness to themselves for the churches in Scotland, so closely akin to one another, to enter on a war that might easily be avoided, and to waste in fighting about Church arrangements those energies which are more than needed to repel the common enemy—the enemy of God and of the best interests of men—who is thundering at all their doors.

3. Who are they who at such a time are summoning the people to such a work, and seeking to spread over a peaceful land the horrors of a fierce and unnatural war?

The agitation is more of English than of Scottish origin. It is stirred and sustained by the Liberation Society, who supply the sinews of war, and who seek to strike through the Scottish, a blow at the English Establishment. Measured by that delicate and accurate gauge of a Scotchman's feelings and convictions—the amount of his contributions—the agitation has a very slender hold on him indeed. So far as Scotland is concerned, it is mainly clerical. As the Free Church General Assembly is largely clerical in tone, its sweeping majorities in favour of Disestablishment are very far indeed from being a certain indication of the convictions of the great body of her people, who do not forget that the principle of Establishment is ineradicably rooted in her own constitution, and that, in 1843, she went forth with the banner flying over her, 'We are no Voluntaries.' With regard to the state of matters at the parliamentary polls, it is enough to say that the question has not yet been generally regarded as coming within the range of practical politics, and that Liberal Churchmen have not abandoned their party on account of a danger which they do not seriously apprehend. Disestablishment meetings have not been remarkable either for number, or influence, or enthusiasm. To the mass of the intelligent laity in all our churches, the agitation is simply distasteful and distressing. They see that the points which divide are trifles in comparison with the points which unite, and they are weary and sick of ecclesiastical strife. On 31st March last, it was said by Lord Provost Ure of Glasgow, himself a United Presbyterian: 'There is no one who can look back on the history of the country for three hundred years, who would think for a moment of blotting out the Established Church of Scotland ; without it, our country would be in nothing better than a state of barbarism. There cannot be the slightest doubt, that without the Church of Scotland, we would not be the people that we are. I, for one, feel the greatest gratitude to that Church, that it has done what it has for the country to which we belong.'

4. Why to such a work, at such a time, and by such men, are the people summoned?

It may well be asked of the Institution which it is sought to destroy—why, what evil hath it done? It occupies to-day no other position than it has always occupied ; it holds no other principles than it has always held. Does it bear upon its forehead the manifest tokens of a Church doomed to, because deserving destruction? What are the reasons on which rests the enormous conclusion that this ancient historic Church should cease to be? It has been asserted that the connection between Church and State is unscriptural, and sinful, and injurious to religion and morality. It must be a poor cause which could use such weapons. One remark may suffice. Whatever is unscriptural and sinful *now*, must *always* have been so : therefore, the Church of Scotland and the Church of England, back to the Reformation, have been unscriptural and sinful ; and Knox, and Melville, and Chalmers, all alike fall under this dreadful appellative.

There is one argument against the National Church as being established and endowed, which is worth looking at. It is this, that it gives the Church an unfair advantage over Nonconformists, and is therefore so far unjust. It contradicts, it is said, the principle of religious equality. This is an argument which is capable of being presented in a very plausible form, and which would not be without some force if the case stood thus—that out of a number of widely different sects competing for the popular favour, the State chose *at the present day, and for the first time*, not to endow—for that it does not—but to select one, and to recognise it as the National Church. That might, with some show of reason, be called a violation of religious equality. But the case is not so. The Church is not a sect now entering into competition with other sects. The root idea of it is, that it is a national institution as old as the State itself, and therefore going back to a time long before sects had any existence, employing its own resources to the best of its ability for the very highest national purposes, and offering its benefits equally to all. It is the friend and the ally, not the creature nor the pensioner of the State. It would be as true to say that it made the State as to say that the State made it. It costs the State nothing. The small portion of its endowments which the State pays in grants from the Exchequer, is only part of what it receives from Church property in the form of Bishops' rents. So far as there are pecuniary transactions between them, it is the State, not the Church, which is the gainer. The Church is simply the owner, or if you will, the trustee of a fragment of a much larger property conferred upon it by private voluntary gift in times far remote, and since then faithfully employed for the maintenance of religion throughout the land. To say anything else, is to say what is not true. Unlike the Irish Church—of whose destruction this at least can be said, that it has not made Ireland any better—it is no mark of conquest, no symbol of external force or dictation, no privileged Church of an alien race, no State-paid propagator of an alien faith. In its doctrine, in its discipline, in its government, it represents the religious convictions of eighty-two per cent. of the Scottish people. Unlike the Church of England, it does not overwhelm by its bulk those who differ from it. Its superiority does not amount to an offence. It is not the author of a social ostracism. It creates no social chasm between its own people and Dissenters. They visit freely in each other's houses. They pass with ease from one Church to another. The social strata from which its clergy and those of the Dissenting Churches are drawn, do not lie far apart. They study at the same universities; they preach in each other's pulpits. The Church hurts no one; it tyrannises over no one; it speaks ill of no one; it is willing to associate with all. Its doors and its heart are open to all. Whatever its privileges and its poor endowments, all are welcome to share them who will, and this because it has ever been the Church, not of a sect, but of the nation.

Where is the religious inequality here? Even if there were, it is not the Church that would be responsible, for it stands precisely where it always stood, but those who chose to leave it, and who are welcome to return. It is not fair for those, who of their own free will refuse to take the benefits of an ancient institution, to turn round and say that they are unfairly treated, because others choose to take and enjoy what their fathers handed down to them, but which they choose to decline. Because they have become Voluntaries by choice, is it fair that they should try to make others Voluntary by compulsion?

One other specious argument is used. After the war, it is said, the combatants will embrace. On the ruins of the Establishment a great United Presbyterian Church will rise. It is difficult to believe that there are men who seriously believe that. They little know how dear the Church of Scotland is to her clergy and her people who could dream this foolish dream. Disestablishment would be the greatest blow ever struck not only at Presbyterian Union, but, so far as Scotland is concerned, at Presbyterianism itself. There is no barrier to hearty fellowship between the clergy and the churches *now*; there would be an insuperable obstacle *then*. Among the few things certain in such an event, one at least is this, that the best of her people and the best of her clergy would never unite with those who causelessly inflicted what they would regard as one of the greatest calamities which ever befell the Scottish people. That were a wrong whose memory would live on for many a generation.

5. Who will be the gainers by the strife, end how it may?

Who will be the gainers, especially if it end in the accomplishment of its destructive aims? Not the poor, whose spiritual provision will have gone. Not the two Churches, the principal Scottish agents in the work. There will be no addition to their numbers, nor to the social status of their clergy, nor to their income, their influence, and their prestige; and certainly none to the existing Church of Scotland, which values a national recognition of religion expressed by State connection as a good thing for it, a better thing for the poor, and the best thing of all for the land we live in. To some extent, perhaps to a large extent, Scottish Episcopacy will gain, within whose more peaceful fold many good men are even now seeking shelter from the strife of Presbyterian tongues. Religious intolerance and bigotry will gain. The day was when Scotland was not a pleasant place to live in; that day may come again. Secularism and infidelity will gain, for they have no better recruiting-sergeants than ecclesiastical wars. Revolutionary principles will gain. The disestablishment of the Church will be one long stride towards the rule of democracy, the abolition of Protestant sovereigns, and the disestablishment of the throne.

6. There is one last question: Supposing Disestablishment, what then? What is the programme? What is the new and superior system which is to take the place of the old? Is the new order of things to be shaped by chaos or by chance? Where is the new Knox who is to guide the new Reformation towards far nobler issues than the old? Let Lord Moncreiff reply: 'The adjustment of the new order of things would not be wholly or mainly in Presbyterian hands; and it were difficult to predict what kind of fabric might or might not arise on the ruins of our Revolution Settlement and the Treaty of Union.' If this, or anything like this, is a true representation of the facts of the case, there never was in the whole course of ecclesiastical history a more wanton, reckless, and suicidal work of destruction to which a Christian people were asked to

set themselves, than the proposed abolition of the National Church of our land.

There is one conclusion to be drawn from all that has gone before in this and the preceding lectures—namely, that if ever there was an ancient institution which was worth preserving for what it has done, for what it is doing, for what it has the promise of being yet able to do, it is that institution 'which alone bears on its front, without note or comment, the title of the Church of Scotland.' It is the fullest embodiment of the traditions of the past; it is the fullest expression of the thought and life of the present; it has by far the richest promise of the future. It is the common heritage of Scotchmen.

It is worth preserving, because its friendly compact with the State is, in the conditions of modern society, the only substantial and the only possible security for spiritual independence.[1]

It is worth preserving, because it provides the best security, especially in a Presbyterian Church, for a cultured, free, and independent clergy.

It is worth preserving as a solid guarantee for the continued purity of the national faith, and for the prevalence throughout the land of a religion that will neither be latitudinarian on the one hand, nor narrow, fanatical, or intolerant on the other.

[1] Such a case as that of Jones *v.* Stannard, which was tried in the Chancery Division of the High Court of Justice, and which lasted seven days, as reported in the *Times*, Feb. 2, 1881, puts beyond dispute the following points: (1) That all Dissenting Churches are subject to the jurisdiction of the civil courts. (2) That the creed of any non-established Church may be considered, and its true interpretation decided, by the civil court. (3) That the civil court may decide questions involving the removal of a minister of a Dissenting Church from his pastoral charge on the ground of doctrine. (4) That no human foresight or skill can prevent the recurrence in Dissenting Churches of similar questions with similar issues. (5) That absolute spiritual independence cannot be secured in a Dissenting Church. As the decision of all such cases in the supreme court of the Church of Scotland is final, with no appeal to the civil courts, which are precluded by statute from reviewing its decisions, all who value spiritual independence are logically and morally bound to oppose the abolition of that Church.

It is worth preserving as the only security that the religious wants of the nation shall be provided for in the generations to come.

It is worth preserving as the only visible rallying point of our distracted Presbyterianism.

It is worth preserving as the nation's testimony to its faith in Almighty God, and in His Son Jesus Christ our Lord. The State is not a fortuitous concourse of men and women, but a living and organic whole, with functions, privileges, and obligations. In a sense different from that which applies to the separate individuals who compose it, it is the subject of the providential government; it is accountable to God; it is by Him rewarded and punished. In its organic and corporate life this State is Christian. That is its very highest characteristic. Its people, its structure, its laws, customs, and institutions are Christian. To the prevalence of Christian principles and ways of living, it owes its commanding place among the nations of the world. It is the duty of a State thus organically constituted, 'through the only channels open to it, its legislature and its laws,' to honour Christ, to acknowledge the source whence national blessings flow, and to support and advance to the utmost of its power that divine religion which is the principal factor of its greatness and strength. For hundreds of years the Church of Scotland has been the authoritative expression of the fact, that the State and the Constitution are Christian. Long may it continue so; for no truth stands out with sharper distinctness upon the page of history—no truth is written in deeper lines across the times we live in than this truth: 'The nation and kingdom that will not serve thee, shall perish.' . . . 'Blessed is the nation whose God is the Lord.'

THE END.

www.ingramcontent.com/pod-product-compliance
Lightning Source LLC
Chambersburg PA
CBHW051241300426
44114CB00011B/833